IRREVERENT RELEVANCIES

Margaret D. Lundvall

SELECTED SERMONS 1983-2008

THE REVEREND
CHRISTOPHER MORGAN BROOKFIELD

EDITED BY KATHLEEN MURAT WILLIAMS

First Printing

Publisher and Design
Wayne Dementi
Dementi Milestone Publishing, Inc.
Manakin-Sabot, VA 23103
www.dementimilestonepublishing.com

Library of Congress Control Number:2019912879

ISBN: 978-1-7330268-4-0

The cover illustration is a detail from the portrait of Christopher by award-winning Richmond painter Loryn Brazier (lorynbrazier. com), used with her permission.

Graphic Design: Dianne Dementi

Printed in the United States of America

A full good faith effort has been made to trace copyright holders and to obtain their permission for the use of copyright material. The publisher apologizes for any omissions or errors and would appreciate notification of any corrections that should be incorporated in future reprints or editions of this book.

*To the honor and glory of God
and in loving memory of our Rabboni,
Christopher.*

TABLE OF CONTENTS

WORDS FOR CHRISTOPHER

Remembrances of my colleague,
teacher, and friend

The Rev. John Edward Miller, Ph.D., Retired Rector,
St. Mary's Episcopal Church, Goochland, VA

I was privileged to serve alongside Christopher Brookfield at St. Mary's Church, Goochland, from 1988-2008. He was my trusted colleague and the beloved associate rector of our parish. But his history with St. Mary's began earlier. Christopher had initially arrived there as a parishioner in the late 1970s, when he became the Dean of the Church Schools of the Diocese of Virginia. Coming from Phillips Exeter Academy, where he had taught philosophy and English and chaired the Department of Religion, Christopher and Lynne discovered the small Carpenter Gothic church as they explored Richmond. The quaintness and simplicity of St. Mary's attracted them, and they formed lasting friendships there. That is where my path crossed his. Without knowing it then, we would shortly begin a journey of ministry together.

After his distinguished stint with the diocesan schools, Christopher became chaplain and religion teacher at St. Catherine's School, Richmond. Meanwhile, I became the rector of St. Mary's. When I proposed that Christopher help me part-time, he said yes, and we began an exciting period of collaboration in 1988. Ten years later, he accepted a full-time role at St. Mary's, as his involvement in adult education and preaching continued to develop and the parish continued to grow.

Like most priests, Christopher had a multi-faceted ministry, but his central vocation was to teaching. There his intellectual gifts shone brightly, gathering a loyal following of those who were inspired by his thought-provoking presence. Christopher led small group studies, Lenten and adult forum series, a literary interpretation group, and Bible studies, among other endeavors. Along the way, I noticed that Christopher's style of teaching was remarkably compatible with the role of mentor, as designed by Sewanee's Education for Ministry program. I asked Christopher to attend an EfM training session at Roslyn to investigate. He returned to St. Mary's bursting with enthusiasm and vigor. He realized that he and EfM were made for one another. His legion of EfM graduates would readily attest to that. Even after he retired, by popular demand Christopher returned to St. Mary's for a decade to lead post-graduate EfM studies.

Christopher was a natural mentor. He did not treat participants as passive recipients of information. Instead, he encouraged his fellow learners to think, to discover, to recognize truth. Christopher was never directive; thus he disliked lecturing. However, when he was called to lecture, he was eloquent, erudite, and riveting. Christopher could facilitate a rousing discussion with a modicum of gentle nudging, especially by Socratic questioning, whereby he became the veritable gadfly that evoked learning. In addition, when his EfMers asked him a question, his answers revealed the depth of his knowledge, his preparation, and his firm grasp of the curriculum.

Christopher shared with us his love of words. He was a verbal artist, painting brilliant word pictures with his smooth, clear prose. His plays on words, puns, alliterations, oxymorons, and subtle innuendos were delightful, and often provocative. He was an inveterate etymologist, using his collections of dictionaries and lexicons to trace the origin and evolution of meanings through a variety of languages, cultures, and eras. Christopher was also an exhaustive editor of texts. He pored over syntax, word order, and the logic of his writings. Perfection was his literary goal, and he worked tirelessly to achieve it.

Christopher's approach to teaching was based in philosophical commitment. After graduating from Union Seminary, New York, where his teachers included Paul Tillich, Reinhold Niebuhr, James Muilenburg, and George Buttrick, Christopher studied philosophy at Columbia University, where his graduate work focused on Soren Kierkegaard, who famously said that there is no disciple *at second hand*. Christopher agreed: discipleship can't be taught; it happens in a personal moment of decision. That existentialist emphasis spurred him to seek boldly his own understanding of writings and traditions the world over. His intellectual curiosity was infectious.

For Christopher, the pulpit was also a context for teaching – a place for intellectual honesty and for probing the resources of belief. His sermons were challenging, beautiful, and open-ended. He left the hearer with questions to be answered, thoughts to complete, and musings to contemplate. His preparation for each sermon was painstaking and thorough. And as he brought the texts to life, he challenged us to pay attention to the interplay of ancient revelation and contemporary experience. Christopher used story, poetry, metaphors, and cross-cultural conundrums, to sharpen our concentration. He likewise introduced us to the commentary of other guides, such as his longtime friend, Frederick Buechner, to help us savor and digest the truth. Christopher's voice, his demeanor, his polished style, his understanding of the Christian heritage, and his courage to speak the truth combined to become a unique presence in the pulpit. He was a true "rabbi," a highly educated teaching elder, who led us in the adventure of the Christian faith.

Finally, I want to mention that, in teaching, preaching, and social circles, Christopher had a great sense of humor. Everyone at St. Mary's knew and appreciated that about him. He was no arid intellect; he always loved to laugh and to make us laugh with him. One of our preschool children saw that and wrote him a note that he cherished. It said, "Christopher is our funniest minister." He placed that note on the mantelpiece in his office for all to see. He was tremendously gifted in many things, and humor ranked high among his natural endowments. He was clever, wry, thought-provoking, and ever so slightly irreverent. I will miss his smile, his hearty laughter, and his ability to poke fun at the pretentious. I will also miss his hugs, his depth of feeling, his expressions of friendship, his words of support, his insights into life, his incomparable handwritten notes, his courage and determination to change when change was needed, and his high professional standards and ever-present loyalty. Christopher Brookfield was not only my dear colleague and friend, he was *my* teacher as well. With his mentorship I became a better priest, preacher, teacher, and rector. I will treasure our time together forever.

Delivered at St. Paul's Memorial Episcopal Church,
Charlottesville, VA
October 8, 2018

EDITOR'S NOTE

This volume of sermons is offered as a labor of love by many hands.

A gifted preacher, mentor, and friend, the Rev. Christopher Morgan Brookfield was our Rabboni.* The ancient and appropriate Hebrew title of respect means spiritual master or teacher. As Rabboni, Christopher served as guide to spiritual seekers of every stripe: fierce intellectuals, creative sorts, doctors, lawyers, cradle Episcopalians and those who only attended church "for the music," if at all. With his playful wit, his scholarly (but never dry) learning, his deft mastery of language and his sometimes wrenching honesty, he opened "the ears of our hearts."

Two years before he died, Christopher finally acceded to the pleas of his students to allow publication of his sermons; he was able to see an early rough draft of the collection, for which we are grateful.

This volume, substantial though it may be, contains only some of the hundreds of sermons, articles and talks Christopher gave over the course of his ministry. His wisdom, wit and intelligence shine through, however. Many who heard these sermons spoken the first time will be transported back in time to the pew lit by multicolored morning light streaming in through a stained glass window – or the folding chair, perhaps – in which they sat at the time.

It was my great pleasure and honor to have edited this collection. I missed Christopher every step of the way, and I often spoke aloud with him in the silence of my office, mystified by an obscure reference or delighted at a surprising turn of phrase. I trusted that in some form, from some higher dimension, our Rabboni was responding and looking out for me – and all of us – as we completed this tribute.

Under the working title of The Sermon Project, this effort was led, inspired and sometimes driven by the hands-on efforts of Mary S. D. Crawford without whose hard work, passion and enthusiasm, this would have ended up as just another "great idea" on the dusty heap of great ideas. The team of visionaries, proofreaders, legal advisors and others who provided innumerable hours of assistance and encouragement included Mary Lou Bean, Martin Betts, Nell Cobb, Jane Covington, Betty Johannessen, Sydna Street and Sally Warthen. Special thanks to The Reverend David Hickman May, rector of St. Mary's Episcopal Church, for his support and encouragement. Finally, our heartfelt gratitude to Wayne and Dianne Dementi of Dementi Books, Art and Photography, as our publishers and co-team members, for their invaluable assistance and expert advice.

– Kathleen Murat Williams

See John 20:16

ADVENT

The "scandal" of the advent of the Christ is that we do not come to him, but that he comes to us, if you will – ready or not, like it or not.

Christopher Brookfield

ADVENT: OF PURPLE CHRISTMAS TREES

1ˢᵗ Sunday of Advent
Matt. 24:36-44
Year A – November 30, 1986

Today is the First Sunday of Advent. (I can see *that* really brings you to the edge of your pew!) Every year at this time, it seems, I tell you my only childhood Advent story, about how as a choir boy in the second grade I found alternately hilarious and incredulous the singing of "Come, O Come Emmanuel," referring to the Savior of the world, because the only Immanuel I had ever heard of was my parents' ancient alcoholic gardener, Immanuel Broncati, who could barely manage to bring himself to work in his Model A Ford, let alone bring salvation to the world. But this year I have something new about childhood confusion in the words of hymns we may sing sometime between now and the 12ᵗʰ day of Christmas.

Robert McAfee Brown, a favorite former professor of mine, reports how the repetition of words lodges images in childrens' minds that are not always the same as the ones an adult pictures they are picturing, particularly as we rush headlong into the Christmas season.

"Is there a single child," he asks, who thinking more naturally about food than salvation even in Christmas carols, "has not wondered about the green-tinged holy infant described in hushed tones as one who could 'sleep in heavenly peas'...?" Or, "Brightly shone the moon that night/Though the frost was gruel" (a modern version of manna). Since Aunt Martha always comes for a holiday visit via a 747, the ancient hymn is consistent with our modern vision when we sing, "Angels we have heard on high/Sweetly singing o'er the plane." Similarly, an unscheduled hijacking might account for "Born a king on Bethlehem's plane."

All that aside, I am aware that we are not yet to Christmas, although the thought of it may bring early intimations of anxiety and exhaustion, not to mention yuletide nightmares complete with processions of gifts advancing upon us like the Sorcerer's Apprentice, and the haunting thought that we may one day be asked to make the gift of ourselves whenever that time comes. "But of that day and hour," the Gospel reading for today reminds us ominously, "no one knows, not even the angels of heaven…" "Therefore you must also be ready; for the Son of man is coming at an hour you do not expect."

What is expected of us and has been said before but needs to be said again, is that Advent comes from *adventus* or *advenire*, meaning "to come to," the season which looks forward to the Feast of the Nativity or the coming of Christ. The "scandal" of the advent of the Christ is that we do not come to him, but that he comes to us, if you will – ready or not, like it or not.

To tell the truth, it is this *unto-us-ness* that is the embarrassing part, because we want to be in control, and we don't want HIM showing up when we're not ready for him (like the people who come on time at the hour we asked them to dinner) – because we are a people who need control. That is what Christmas is about for many of us, not what Advent is about. That is why we like Christmas, when we can choose whom we want to give to and why; and why we ignore Advent, when we cannot choose who will give to us when we are vulnerably unexpectant, or what it is we shall be given.

But most of that Advent admonition you've heard before, if not in quite those words, so I'm going to offer you something different today. In the event that Advent sermons are not your bag or that you are not "sore afraid" at the impending holy birth but are sorely tempted just now to let your mind drift off somewhere, perhaps to add up the numbers of the hymns on the hymn boards in the hope that the total will come out to be even, I'm going to give you something to take away with you right now, so that you will not feel your time has been wasted; something that (who knows) might someday save your life.

⟨∘⟩

> *You may not think you'll ever have to jump off a moving train; but you never know when your time may come, and at an hour you do not expect.*

⟨∘⟩

I am going to tell you how to jump off a train that is in motion, and if that has any analogy to our being propelled rapidly toward Christmas during the next four weeks of Advent, it is purely coincidental and so much serendipity. This is Annie Dillard's advice:

> ...If for some extraordinary reason you have to jump off a moving train, look ahead and try to pick a spot that looks soft. Throw your pack and, as you jump, lean way back (this is the hard part) and take huge, leaping steps in the air. If you lean back far enough, and don't trip as you touch the ground, you will experience the rare thrill of running 35 to 40 miles an hour.

There now, don't say no one ever did anything for you in a sermon in Advent. You may not think you'll ever have to jump off a moving train; but you never know when your time may come, and at an hour you do not expect. (Remember, the hard part is to lean way back as you jump.)

Where are we going in Advent, you and I? It might be well to ask, given the fact that we're likely to end up there whether we want to or not. Some say, it will all end in Christmas. Browsing through a Thomas Crowell dictionary, I came upon the word

"Christmas" and found some interesting definitions I hadn't encountered before, like: "any ostentatious display, as of clothing, jewelry, etc." Or this one: "a shower of metallic foil dropped by an airplane or artillery shell to jam enemy radar or communications systems." (In the face of these, I think I prefer the holy pea-green infant or Harold's Angels harking whatever they do o'er the 747.) Surely such a Christmas is not what Advent expects.

Whatever it is we are coming to at the end of Advent, we're almost always going to get a little of "what's coming to us" (if I may borrow an expression) along the way, because that is the way of life and often what separates our Advents from our Nativities. In this season, no matter how fast we are propelled toward what it is that awaits us, a lot of what it is that's coming to us, we don't need. That was a given for the Magi on their journey. Advent aside, even if we think we're entitled to Christmas because we help bring it into being and fancy we are in control of it; even so, as The Tennessee Churchman put it:

> Christmas is [also] for people with back-aches and car payments and inadequate insulation. Christmas is for tight-fisted, overworked, under-loved adults...Christmas is for us who know that life has its winters, its dark spots. It is for us who know how much a good necktie costs and how little Uncle Horatio will appreciate it. It is for us who [might sometimes] find it difficult to name three other people we'd like to spend an evening with.

In another vein, some years ago (and not, I hasten to add, *here,* but in an elementary school in New Hampshire) my daughter, who had been encouraged by her mother to be imaginative in the use of colors, proudly showed her art teacher in class what she had drawn, a daring, bold purple Christmas tree – which the art teacher promptly tore up. "Everybody knows," she said, "that Christmas trees are not purple." Who knows what is coming to us and at what hour?

The truth is, we can't get from Advent to Epiphany and the 12th Day of Christmas without some adversity, and our true love doesn't always bring to us a partridge in a pear tree. If we fancy we're entitled to Christmas, we are not at the same time entitled to the Christ that Advent expects; and the gifts we are prepared to give are not the same as those we are likely to rush forward to receive unexpectedly.

Advent is about affirming the purple Christmas trees in our lives, whether others understand them or not, whether or not they can accept our offerings, because if we cannot be allowed that extravagance of vision, how in God's name can we accept the unexpected, even unwanted, birth in our lives that tells us the unlikely "You are loved, for Christ's sake."

If there is no peas on earth and no one sweetly singing o'er the plane, how will we ever want to make the journey with the Wise Men, whether by camel or the Orient Express? How will we have the vision to search for God who wants to be born in each of us? What Advent expects and hopes for beyond hope is that on our journey when we find Him and are found by Him we will know that the only appropriate response is to lay ourselves at the foot of the manger because the offering of ourselves is the only real gift we have to give. Advent is about vulnerability, the world's and ours. That may be more than you asked for in Advent.

If you have barely had time to catch your breath from Thanksgiving, and I'm rushing ahead too fast, all you have to do is look for a soft spot and throw your pack. (Remember the hard part is to lean way back.) But before you attempt to stop the world and try to get off, remember that the coming of the Christ child is not something that happened a long time ago when you were a child and Christmas trees were green; that coming is not behind you, it lies ahead of us all in the gift of purple Christmas trees and the promise that, if we will only dare to give it away, the offering of ourselves is the only gift we have to give.

"Of that day and hour no one knows. Therefore you must be ready; for the Son of Man is coming at an hour you do not expect." In the unlikely words of W.H. Auden's Christmas Oratorio:

> *He is the Way.*
> *Follow Him through the Land of Unlikeness;*
> *You will see rare beasts, and have unique*
>   *adventures.*
> *He is the Truth.*
> *See Him in the Kingdom of Anxiety;*
> *You will come to a great city that has ex-*
>   *pected your return for years.*
> *He is the Life.*
> *Love him in the World of the Flesh;*
> *And at your marriage all its occasions shall*
>   *dance for joy.*

AVOIDING THE VISION

Bapfirmation – the Pitts?

2nd Sunday of Advent
Isaiah 11:1-10; Matthew 3:1-12
Year A – December 10, 1995

After reading the terrible words of John the Baptist in the gospel text for this morning threatening those who had come for baptism, "You brood of vipers, who warned you to flee from the wrath to come" – even if this Sunday celebrates John the Baptist – the reading seems thoroughly inappropriate for what has taken place here a few minutes ago. No need to leave tiny Margaret Franklin struggling with the scathing words of John ringing subconsciously in her ears over the years. Perhaps the better part of valor would be to move on to what happens to us after baptism.

Still, on second thought, John has something crucial to tell us about the meaning of baptism. He says those who came to him at the river Jordan were trying to use baptism for their own ends, to absolve themselves from judgment – a kind of fire insurance policy, which they could manipulate for their benefit. Baptism, on the other hand, is a gift to us without strings, given not on the basis of our deserving or merit – let alone on our cleverness or industriousness, good or bad. Margaret Franklin Mansfield, you are accepted by God without having to deserve it or earn it. That is yours although you did not seek it out; God came seeking you, aided by your parents and godparents who brought you to this place.

The ceremony itself speaks all that without words. John Miller, who takes to infants like peanut butter to jelly (hmmm, there must be a less sticky spiritual simile to express it), shows forth the grace of God in his obvious love of those he holds and anoints. (Often children cry in their parents' arms until he reaches for them.) We who witness this and repeat our own baptismal covenant with Molly affirm life anew under God. But what happens after that?

I was indeed blessed last Sunday to be here for Bishop Matthews' visitation, which included the service of confirmation when fourteen members of our parish came forward to accept for themselves, to reaffirm the vows that had been undertaken at their baptism – when at least some of these persons had been puling infants and had no memory of what had been promised for them in God's name.

As you can imagine, I have been to countless such ceremonies in various churches, beginning before I was seven, and sang in a boys' choir at Christ Church in Rye, New York. As I remember it, those occasions were usually dull, tedious, boring, repetitive, comic – and always endless. Some ancient artifact (though in reality he was probably ten or twenty years younger than I am now) would appear once a year; throw the clergy into a panic; get pampered, prompted, and puffed up; repeat the same peculiar phrases over and over; baptize some of the people by the wrong name; preach a lifeless sermon – and, mercifully, leave us for another fifty-one Sundays.

The first such bishop I can recall clearly, at somewhere around age twelve, was called Pitt. (You can imagine the kind of jokes we passed back and forth in the choir stalls about his name: his being the pitts, prune pitt, arm-pitt – we were pitt-yless.) He came every year; there was no relief. We always knew what to expect. He would line up the confirmands en masse at the communion rail, press his pasty hands down with great weight upon one head and the next (which drove the girls wild because he mushed their hair). Whereupon he would peer heavenward, close his eyes, crunch up his face, and recite (some said 'moan') as if it were the death scene in some comic opera, the words we came to know by heart down to every idiosyncratic intonation. His annual aria went something like this: "Defend, O Lord this thy child – with thy heavenly grace. That he may continue, thine for EVER – and DAILY increase in thy HOLY spirit, MORE and MORE – until – he came, unto thy everlasting kingdom, AMEN(?)." We wondered why he ended every incantation with a question mark (amen?). What the words meant, we had no clue. Invariably, after the service we would do "the Pitt" in the parking lot and "bust a gut" (as we would say) over it.

That's the most I can remember about these occasions. They were at best to us antic, at worst ludicrous. What the ceremony had to do with what mattered was lost on us, and whatever the meaning of it all was we quickly forgot – all over again each year.

This past Sunday I felt fortunate to be asked to hold Bishop Matthews' pastoral staff at his side while he received each person who came forward. I had a front row view; close enough to see the beads of sweat on several foreheads. He brought them to him one at a time, took both their hands in his as they came forward to kneel on the cushion before his chair. He looked them directly in the eyes, and asked, "Are you O.K.? Can you speak? What is your name? Say it loudly so the people can hear you. Do you want to be confirmed in this church?" He questioned each one.

When he heard, "I do!" he shifted their hands to his knees, took their head in his hands and prayed upon them the words I had known from so long ago, the same old ones Bishop Pitt had pronounced – but they sounded new. Halfway through the prayer, he slapped each person on the head, to remind them "that God is with them in bad times as well as the good." Then he raised them up, shook hands with them, and said, "congratulations!" It was so personal, powerful, prayerful – provoking from each one a clear statement of what it is he or she intended to do and to be in the world. I am willing to wager that was a promise and a presentation they will never forget as long as they live. Each one was, at least at that moment, convicted of being a Christian.

For my part, it was lucky I had his staff to hold onto. It was all I could do to keep the tears from welling over at every kneeling. I was overcome – with happiness at what was happening, and with sadness at the remembrance that I could not recall anything of what I had hoped for and promised on the occasion of my own confirmation some forty-six years ago. Was I excited? nervous? I can't recall. I do know that beforehand I had wanted to give all I could to the God that had somehow called me there. And I believe at least, that underneath all the funny and festive trappings, I wanted to make a life commitment that I wouldn't have joked about, even at Pitt's expense.

What I didn't know then was that the life I would live would turn out to be so complex; that even when I wanted to give the gift of myself to God, I would know neither how to do it nor know how to summon the will to do it; that sometimes I would even seem to be willingly unfaithful.

***...it is often easy to call good evil
and evil good, in the name of all sorts of
noble intentions.***

Part of my sadness was that what I learned was that courage was more difficult to sustain in the midst of ambiguity and uncertainty; that it is often easy to call good evil and evil good, in the name of all sorts of noble intentions; and that when our values get confused and our vision blurry, we are often the last ones to know it. That is exactly what Isaiah is saying to us this morning: We have forgotten our foremost commitments, what it is we intended to give to God; and we have forgotten how to give the gift of ourselves, trapped in a social value system where we are rewarded for getting what we want at the expense of others. We have forgotten the time when we took our baptismal vows and made our confirmation commitments.

I doubt that any of those who were confirmed by Bishop Matthews will have trouble remembering the significance of the occasion or the meaning of that ceremony. To them, Isaiah's words about the advent of the Lord may not sound so far out, or so wide of the mark in the world, as they might to some of us who can't remember our words of confirmation. (You may not at first recognize Isaiah's words, compared to the translation you heard read this morning):

> The day of the Lord is soon upon us
>> when the kingdom we have longed for will be
>> revealed.
> The darkness of the world will give way
>> to the dawning of a day
>> when violence will cease.
> The wolf will live with the lamb,
>> and the leopard will lie down with the kid;
> Our enemies will live in peace,
>> and a little child shall lead them.
> Violence and war will be no more in the world;
>> the children will be safe –
>> even those with nightmares.
> The weakest and most vulnerable among us
>> will no more have to fear.
> They shall not hurt or destroy in all my holy mountain;
>> For the earth shall be filled with the knowledge of
>> God as the waters cover the sea.

Isaiah is asking us to catch hold of the vision we once had of what the world could be. That's what happened to me last Sunday as I watched those fourteen persons come forward and say what it was they wanted to be in and for the world. Their words and the vision that expressed them – like Isaiah's message – once again seemed fresh. I am no longer ten or twelve or twenty. If I am a little wiser than I was then, I know it isn't easy to keep the covenant which asks us to rise above the realities of the world around us and seek a new vision. Bishop Matthews did not lay hands upon me, but he and those he blessed seized me with the spirit and challenged me once again to catch hold of the vision baptism brings us, confirmation calls us to, and advent expects.

NOËL, HOLY MOTHER

December 22, 1985

Those of you who have endured the incontinent antics of Mrs. Hopewell and the Love Brothers' "Love in the Morning" on FM104, will know that when this season rolls around, Mrs. Hopewell takes to singing her old favorite (to the tune of "White Christmas"), "I'm cooking up a big 'possum, just like my grandma used to bake..." And the given is that today, as in ages past, only Mrs. Hopewell could love a 'possum croissant. Which in a manner of speaking is the essential difference between what E-Z 104 anticipates and what Advent expects ('possums notwithstanding) this season.

In the early morning on the days I teach a class, which several members of this congregation have graciously afforded me the opportunity to do, I see the profusion of dry morning glory vines hanging bleached and hapless from the roof of our front porch, lying like heaps of so much spaghetti on the luxurious brown mulch, or resembling some kind of fudge sundae gone awry. Even though there have been several frosts, not everything is dead. Scarcely a week ago, there must have been 50 flies in our bathroom huddled around the light fixture, and we still worry whether to continue giving our three dogs their daily dose of chewable heart 'n hookworm crunchies. The grass looks almost as though I should cut it and our white baby of a German shepherd still eats a toad or two at night every now and then.

But there is something different in the air. The smell of horse manure isn't as pungent; there's more feeding going on in the stalls; the hunters are sneaking about trying to surprise themselves and blow something's head off; and some of us are waiting for that continuous crunching sound on the ground and the start of the season of frozen watering tubs and burst garden hoses somebody forgot to unscrew. There's something unsettling about the onset of December because I can't help thinking something is coming, or ought to be coming, as if nature herself were getting ready for more than a freeze; something that will set the season right and set more than that right in the world.

... the language of Advent goes beyond theology and church terminology to an affirmation about life itself.

That is what I call the Advent intuition or the Advent admonition or the Advent expectation – even if you aren't a pew-sitter or a registered churchgoer or an altar guild enthusiast, because the language of Advent goes beyond theology and church terminology to an affirmation about life itself.

It affirms something about the world's entitlement, what we can look forward to; no thanks to our own efforts of course, but gratis, as though we and nature and even the Christmas season itself were poised and ready to receive it, just as if we were made that way – except for one thing.

Advent (from the Latin ad+venire) does not mean just "to come to"; it means to come to once again, but to come anew. Not so easy when you've been around the mulberry bush a number of times and have endured endless Advent admonitions from the audio excesses of absolutely every shopping mall you've entered each year. The task of Advent, as well as the promise and the proclamation, has something to do with T.S. Eliot's familiar admonition that "the end of our exploring/Will be to arrive where we started/ And know the place for the first time;" that with God we may dare to expect what we dare not hope for and so redeem the time being from insignificance – ready or not.

When I received John's invitation to preach this Sunday, my wife and I had just come back from a trip to visit our daughter in Paris, I hadn't set foot in the office for 10 days, and my first response was, "How will I get through the next two weeks, let alone prepare to preach on the 12th day?" I am simply unprepared for Advent and everything else.

But when I thought about it, I realized that even after four weeks of prayers and sermons and litanies in Advent, the Church is never really prepared for the Christmas message, first of all because it flies in the face of common sense and then it gets hopelessly confused with the midnight ride of Rudolph the Red-Nosed Reindeer and the promise of the newest Mattel doll that actually wets herself. And certainly the world at large, if it is not ready to let loose in its pants at the prospect of nuclear winter, is not at all prepared for the advent of the Baby Jesus either. Besides, we have never much understood that business about not getting into the Kingdom of God unless we become as little children, or the mystery that the Holy One in our midst is a child. So who's prepared? Let's roll it anyway, I heard myself saying.

Then I looked at the texts appointed for this day and realized that the Gospel reading is a celebration of the gift of Mary. "Holy Mother of God," I said to myself, not irreverently, "What do I know about Mary and motherhood?" That seemed to round out the picture nicely. I wasn't simply unprepared; I was completely unprepared. But, said I, I'll be among friends, many of whom I know are prepared for anything. Besides, maybe being unprepared is what Advent is all about. To receive the gift you hadn't counted on is to break out of the conventional cycle of simply exchanging presents. Maybe I could learn something about motherhood yet. Had I not been a father when my wife was just beginning her mothering? Could I come to know that again for the first time?

I turned to my old friend, Phyllis Tickle. I do not know her, of course, but with a name like that I want to turn to her often, and for me she writes as if I had known her for a long time. She tells a story, some of which I would like to tell you, too. It is a familiar story, even if you've never heard it, and it tells about something that Advent expects – not all over again, but only once again.

"In the weak December light the bed sits in front of the double windows, a disheveled wad of blankets and quilts, a sea of wrinkles still warm from our bodies. As always, I begin by setting off the pillows to fluff them and pulling the bottom sheet taught again. I lay back the covers to air, my hands moving in and out of the night's warmth and a life's memories. For 25 years we have slept here, conceived nine children on this bed and brought seven of them to birth. Here I always rested afterward and here they have continued to join us in the mornings, cold feet and knees hammering against our warmth.

"A scuttle of clouds blows over the lemony sun outside, and the gray pattern swims across the exposed sheets, moves up the bedroom wall and disappears on the ceiling. The wind is too cold today, and I draw the drapes shut, blocking both the light and the cold for a while longer.

"So it begins again, the dying of our year. The long nights I yearn toward, the stripped trees and tan grasses, the graying of the sun. I tie a ribbon around the lamp on the dresser. In a little while one of the children will bring a pine cone or a holly branch in from the field and slip it through the ribbon without my asking.

"It is two weeks yet to the Holy Night, and I have much to do. But first I must pull the covers back up and smooth the spread. Always here, in this place of beginnings, is the center, the order of my day. This first must be right. A pillow or two set just so and then on them the special one that says "Noel." "Birth." All over the world this fortnight will wish each other birth; I will do it here.

"These two weeks will be hard for me because they spend my dearest treasure; our decorations and our feasting are paid for with my privacy. I will buy gifts for people I don't care about and think, however briefly, on the wonder of not buying gifts for some whom I love deeply…. The children, too young still to know that distinction, will go through the stores, allowances in hand, and love for itself every gift they buy. Things belong in one's growing up else one never overcomes the need of them somehow. So we will go, and we will spend and we will have great joy – they in the doing and I in the not doing.

"We will bring in the greens and the cones and consider (but not mention to each other) the dreary December….

"He and I will go out an evening or two and spend the money we have saved for this. Even more, we will spend time walking the aisles, handling toys that charmed us 40 years ago, buying gifts for the children we remember being. Then, weary from so much travel, we will spend more time drinking coffee or chocolate in some little shop until it closes and will come home to this bed and the pleasure of sleeping with a stranger whom we each only thought we knew….

"We will go out each day and wish "Noel" to our friends and neighbors. We will attend open houses and drink eggnog from crystal cups. Before it is all over, we will dress a king or two to make his long trek, blue jeans under bathrobe, down an aisle or two. Knowing that he doesn't know why, we will make him do it anyway. In just a little while, he will understand the painted gold and the fake frankincense and weep for the wonder of it when his own son bears the eternal gifts down some other aisle, and Time, that great mirage, pales before the truth of bathrobes and carols.

"And I, as every year at this season, alone somewhere in some church or card shop or in front to some cheap, dime-store nativity, will stop before a plastic Madonna, arrested by the lie of her. Standing there, I will make a brief prayer to the memory of the real one who, like me, was highway to the world. Hers was the rapture of the Magnificat and mine the fullness of pleasure, but it is our only difference. Ours together is the tearing of the flesh and the pushing, forever the pushing out, of the thing from the body into some other life.

"So, Mary, even on Christmas morning, I will make this bed first, knowing there has never really been anything other than this for you and me.

"Noël, Holy Mother, Noël. It is time I went downstairs."

The Episcopalian, December 1984, p. 19.

"Garrison Keillor has reminded us that the names of the three sheep in the Christmas manger scene were Surely, Goodness and Mercy, who as we know will follow us all the days of our lives, an undeniable improvement, says Robert McAfee Brown, "over an alternative rendering of the same verse that goes 'Surely Good Mrs. Murphy will follow me all the days of my life.' Both are on a par," says Dr. Brown, "with the words of a child overheard singing zestfully in Sunday school, 'Christ the Royal Master, leans against the phone.'"

Christian Century, December 14, 1983, p. 1150

Advent, on the other hand, like grace and the gift of motherhood, "prevents and follows us." I remember thinking, how is it possible to be prevented from coming and at the same time be followed? Perhaps a child's view of parenthood. But prevent in that sense means strangely enough, "to meet in advance." Even "to arrive before." So T.S. Eliot's admonition makes strange good sense when he says the end of all our exploring will be to arrive where we started and know the place for the first time.

What Mary knew at the foot of the Cross, was no more than she knew in the throes of giving birth, what mothers have always known, and what parents try to express when they say, if children leave home they break your heart, and if they stay home, they break your heart. But no one would miss the joy of impending birth if we had to do it all over again. So, come all ye faithful, those who are filled with faith and those without faith who long to be filled: Venite adoremus, it is time to go downstairs.

CHRISTMAS

In the midst of our darkness there is always an opportunity to embrace the good, to show that God is present, is Immanuel "God-with-us;" to repeat the sounding joy that we have not been abandoned, that we have been shown a way to live and to love.

Christopher Brookfield

"WAITING FOR TREASURE"

1st Sunday after Christmas Day
John 1:1-18
December 30, 2001

In the beginning was the Word, and the Word was with God, and the Word was God. He was in the beginning with God. All things came into being through him, and without him not one thing came into being. What has come into being in him was life, and the life was the light of all people. The light shines in the darkness, and the darkness did not overcome it.

There was a man sent from God, whose name was John. He came as a witness to testify to the light, so that all might believe through him. He himself was not the light, but he came to testify to the light. The true light, which enlightens everyone, was coming into the world.

He was in the world, and the world came into being through him; yet the world did not know him. He came to what was his own, and his own people did not accept him. But to all who received him, who believed in his name, he gave power to become children of God, who were born, not of blood or of the will of the flesh or of the will of man, but of God.

And the Word became flesh and lived among us, and we have seen his glory, the glory as of a father's only son, full of grace and truth. (John testified to him and cried out, "This was he of whom I said, 'He who comes after me ranks ahead of *me because he was before me.'") From his full-ness we have all received, grace upon grace. The law indeed was given through Moses; grace and truth came through Jesus Christ. No one has ever seen God. It is God the only Son, who is close to the Father's heart, who has made him known.*

John 1:1-18

Fifteen men on a dead man's chest,
Yo-ho-ho and a bottle of rum.
Drink and the devil had done for the rest,
Yo-ho-ho and a bottle of rum.

Some of you, I hope, will recognize that pirate refrain from the gnarled and craggy old sea dog "Captain" Billy Bones of Robert Louis Stevenson's Treasure Island, a book I recently took up once more because my father told me before he died that he had read it over again every year all his life. Searching for treasure is perhaps a propitious theme as we look forward to starting another year. What sort of treasure awaits us? And where will we find it? Epiphany is nearly upon us – or was it gold doubloons rather than frankincense-and-myrrh-kind-of-treasure you were thinking of?

A word to the wise, or a wisecrack for those who are waiting for the sermon to be over. Overheard, the old inquiry: "What if the Three Wise Men had been the Three Wise Women? Well, they would have asked for directions, arrived on time, helped deliver the baby, cleaned the stable, made a casserole and brought practical gifts" (and we would have peace on earth). I feel somewhat left out in that scenario, but the good news is that I, we, are invited in anyway. And so in the absence of discovering doubloons we await the birth of wonder and the magic of the Magi making their way toward us, and Him, all riding in on Epiphany (which only as an adolescent I learned was not the name of the camel they were riding). Meanwhile, while we wait for that new time or that time to be made new for us, what will we do?

In this about-to-be-new year I am looking for a new voice, a new way of seeing old things, new ways of being in the things I see. Not just because a new year is about to be born, but because it is a ceremonial way of saying I accept it as the first day of the rest of my life. That doesn't mean denying the old life but breathing life into the new. "Behold, I make all things new," says the Lord. Let us seize the moment and make it so: "Carpe vitam" (If I have chosen the appropriate accusative ending for an evocative noun).

Why wait for a new way of being? I can speak only for myself.

This past year there have been some sad and significant changes in my life: Like losing my father, and getting fat, and moving away after 26 years. And if I don't learn how to breathe the possibilities of new life into them I will inhale only the obstacles they present for me, and draw in the difficulties and deaths that they declare. No, New life is needed! "I set before you this day life and death," saith the Lord. "Choose life."

Where is this new life found that awaits us? Where else but awaiting us while we wait for it. And the key is, how we wait and for what, and whether we will choose to wait in the dark or in the light?

The Gospel of John gives us a good way to get into it: "There was a man sent from God, whose name was John. He was waiting as a witness to testify to the light." This comes from that famous beginning in scripture where preachers as well as angels fear to tread. Because this so-called Prologue to John's Gospel is not only a hymn to God's creation, unsurpassed in the beauty and imagery of its language, but a witness to the word that was with God in the beginning, and which is with us always — outside time and history and even our speaking of it.

So, you'll be relieved to hear, I'm not going to try to explain or interpret or extol that venerable passage. "In the beginning was the word" is in whatever way you want to receive it or relate to it. Mercifully and un-preacherlike, I'm going to just let it be. For you, to truly hear it is enough to make you, someday, want to ponder it or be a part of it or simply to praise it. And letting alone that sacred scrap of scripture is my last gift to you in the year we are leaving behind. Except (you knew there would always be an "except"), it would do no harm if there were a way for us to hear it newly, in a way we hadn't, just where we thought we'd heard it all before. Let me proffer a preface:

Some of you know that as a student I went to an all-boys boarding school in the northeast, and I taught at another boys school there, also during the time it became coeducational. And then later was chaplain at a girls' church school here, which meant then my having to prepare four different chapel services each week (that's 18 a month) – which called for a very different kind of language, imagery, emotion, and expression, than I was used to. That set me wondering, what would a feminine order of service sound like? So I got myself six or eight books on the sacred dimension of women's experience in ritual, and fancied I would create a feminine liturgy for Morning Prayer and for Holy Communion.

To my surprise I discovered that I was almost the only one interested in it. I was reminded that there is nothing so irrelevant as the answer to a question that hasn't been asked. Still, one of my former students co-authored The Women's Bible Commentary, so there is some inquiry out there, but in her volume, there appears no explanation of the prologue to the Gospel of John from a female point of view, no new vision to voice. However, recently I came across a response to those verses we heard read this morning, written by a woman – in verse. And to hear her expression of John's vision is indeed a different experience, at least for me – a new telling of what we have been told in John 1:1-18:

In the beginning, back before our imagina-
tions can imagine
In the beginning, there was darkness

Deep dazzling darkness
And in the center of this deep dark womb
    was God
A warm wonderful Word
The pulsing Word of Life.

And then out of the dazzling darkness came
    dazzling light
Stars, bursting sun, glowing moon
A holy metamorphosis
Dazzling light out of dazzling darkness.
This was the light of the first creation.

But then there was the light of the second
    creation.
Out of God's warm wonderful wordy womb
    came flesh,
A holy wholeness with skin on
Glowing with light, glaring and glorious
A human God, full of grace and truth
The Grace to heal us. And the Truth to refine
    us.

And so with no effort on our part,
we were, we are, given a second chance.
The dull, desperate, dangerous kind of
    darkness
has never been able to overcome
    the dazzling light of incarnation.

Now briefly back to the John who is the Baptist, the wild-eyed wild-ass of a man, clothed in camel's hair, with his breath reeking of locusts and wild honey, the one set apart to proclaim the coming of the kingdom of God. How hard it must have been for him, who did not know for whom he was waiting, who did not know a name to proclaim, or where to look. "Why are you baptizing if you are a nobody?" they asked. "Lord knows (he said), I know someone is coming after me whom you do not know." Until that one, whose name he did not know, until that one came, John's life was one long Adventing, a waiting in his dark for the light, a waiting for what would change his life and would change everything. He could not name it; he knew only that it was coming, he himself helpless but not hopeless.

Not so dramatic but not so different in this old calendar year is our waiting, not just for a new year but for something new which we may not even be able to name. For what do you wait?

For certainty, for security, for healing, for love? Or maybe for recognition, reconciliation, retirement, a reserve to pay your bills? And how is that going to change your life? Even if we do not know how to name "whatever it is our hearts yearn for, chances are that it has something to do with our vision of what it would mean for us to be made whole, to be turned into people who are not afraid anymore, ... whose wounds are healed and who are more nearly the people God created us to be," as Barbara Brown Taylor tells it.[2]

And that, as you may recognize, sounds in other words like the vision John was waiting for and proclaimed abroad: the light coming into the darkness of our world, and the darkness has not overcome it, he said. John did not know the name of the one for whom he was waiting in his darkness, or when that would come to light, but he gave to us the vision to hope for, to treasure, to share, to live – which may just turn out to be enough for us who do not know how to speak the name.

Finally, an old friend sent me a card at Christmas, which I treasure, with these wonderful words on it:

And I said to the man
  who stood at the gate
  of the year: Give me
  a Light that I may
  tread safely into the unknown!
And he replied: Go
  out into the darkness
  and put thine hand
  into the hand of God
That shall be to thee
  better than light and
  safer than a known way.[3]

———

1. *Lectionary Homiletics*, XIII.I. – p. 29
2. *Gospel Medicine*, Barbara Brown Taylor, p.141
3. "God Knows," by Minnie Louise Haskins

THE GOSPEL OF JOSEPH

2nd Sunday after Christmas Day
Matthew 2:13-15, 19-23
January 10, 1999

> *Now when they had departed, behold, an angel of the Lord appeared to Joseph in a dream and said, "Rise, take the child and his mother, and flee to Egypt, and remain there till I tell you; for Herod is about to search for the child, to destroy him. And he rose and took the child and his mother by night, and departed to Egypt, and remained there until the death of Herod. This was to fulfill what the Lord had spoken by the prophet, "Out of Egypt have I called my son."*
>
> *But when Herod died, behold, an angel of the Lord appeared in a dream to Joseph in Egypt, saying, "Rise, take the child and his mother, and go to the land of Israel for those who sought the child's life are dead." And he rose and took the child and his mother, and went to the land of Israel. But when he heard that Archelaus reigned over Judea in place of his father Herod, he was afraid to go there and being warned in a dream he withdrew to the district of Galilee. And he went and dwelt in a city called Nazareth, that what was spoken by the prophets might be fulfilled, "He shall be called a Nazarene."*
>
> *Matthew 2:13-15, 19-23*

You have just been through what The Washington Post has called "the week that wasn't much." But not to worry, this is only the ninth day of Christmas; there are still three days left to tell the untold story of Christmas. Which I call The Gospel Enacted in Joseph, with the subtitle, "They also serve who stand and wait" – faithfully. This is for those of you who may have felt left out in the Nativity narrative. It deserves to be told perhaps especially in this place which on River Road (true to form) is called St. Mary's Church, not St. Joseph's Villa. You could call this a Joseph-lib story – out of the silence of the celestial closet into the song of the saints in light.

As I recall it, the angel Gabriel "chief of the angelic guards" appeared to Mary already betrothed, saying, "Fear not, for you have found favor with God... And behold, you will conceive in your womb and bear a son...[who] will be great, and will be called Son of the Most High..." While to Joseph, an untitled angel came, cajoling, "Do not fear to take Mary for your wife...for behold, a virgin shall conceive and bear a son...Emmanuel...(God with us)." And again (in this week's Gospel text), "Rise, take the child and his mother, and flee to Egypt..." And when Herod died, "Rise, take the child and his mother and go to the land of Israel..." So Joseph did faithfully all that the angel had commanded him. He took Mary, great with child, to be his wife and he "knew her not" (as the saying goes) until after she had borne a son, whose family tree Matthew's Gospel traces from Abraham to Joseph although the Holy Spirit was supposed to be the father. But Mary got the praise.

Joseph, the yes-Ma'am man, got a bum rap, with the babe wrapped in swaddling cloths while Mary rapped for us the Magnificat. No Benedictuses for Joseph. He says not a word. It is true scripture throws him a bone, acknowledging him to be "a just man," and "unwilling to put Mary to shame" even though, according to Jewish law, she should have been publicly denounced, disgraced and/or put to death for adultery (in the days when such trifles mattered). Mary "pondered all these things in her heart." Joseph was magnanimously "mum," God's obedient servant, standing in the shadows, on the periphery of light and laughter (no doubt a lot of it at his expense) – while we sing "round yon Virgin, mother and child."

This Christmas, in our house the trouble started when it was time to set up the annual crèche in our front foyer, which we assemble on an unlikely artifact acquired in Princeton, New Jersey, when my daughter graduated from college. In Palmer Square a fashionable dress shop was going out of business. As part of the display decor, dresses were draped over an English nineteenth century portable Benedictine altar, which the worms had their way with winsomely. "Everything Must Go," the sign said, so when I inquired about the altar, they said "Sold!" It is made of heart pine, pecan wood, and a smidgen of maple, with a raised I.H.S. on the front panel – which in the lingo of Kings College Cambridge might have meant "In Her Majesty's Service," but that amusement was lost on the designer dress saleswoman.

---

*...Two sheep with a wad of cotton
cloud stuck on a raised wire, a ceramic snake
from Mexico City, an Inuit soapstone seal ...
all look on the manger...*

We have rules for collecting the creatures in our crèche: Nothing commercially Christmas condoned, a preference for hand made figures, however crude – and the charge is to be creative at all costs. In the center panel of a triptych tacked to the top is an antique Our Lady of Guadeloupe from Santa Fe, replete with gold flames surrounding Mary, which dominates the scene. To one side, is an old crucifix of the Mexican Indian Christo Negro, the Black Christ, copied from one in the Chapel/of the Holy Mud, Chimaio (his nimbus shaped like a war bonnet), which I secured on a trip to Taos. On the other side, sits a bright red lacquered Buddha benignly watching over our flock of motley figures in the foreground – peace on earth to all, after all – a present from our son who was in Tibet-abouts. Two sheep with a wad of cotton cloud stuck on a raised wire, a ceramic snake from Mexico City, an Inuit soapstone seal, and others, all look on the manger made from a small Spanish shipping box which enfolds an abandoned tiny baby doll which I think was once our daughter Nora's.

But where was Joseph? For years we could find none and the Babe was fatherless (in a certain sense). Then, unaccountably there appeared a curly-haired gorilla, which, though a quarter the size of the omnipresent Mary, was just the right height to hold on to the manger (with its hairy hands) – and all was well. But this Christmas, the gorilla was not anywhere to be found. "Oh, he must be in the box with the Christmas balls," I was told, but when the tree was all dressed at last, Joseph was (as history also has it) nowhere. An ill omen. Who would look after the family, holy or otherwise, heaven only knows.

So this year in our home it came to pass that "'Twas the night before Christmas and all through the house not a creature was stirring, not even a mouse" – because we were all freezing our buns off. It was a holy time (someone added "wholly" unacceptable) because in good trinitarian fashion we had no heat or light for three days. Eleven were coming for Christmas Eve dinner (including a baby and her four-year-old brother, who with six others were spending the night). All was not well. As the Joseph joke, I was trying to do what I was told, cooling the crab soup (which had been cooked before the power pooped) by putting it out on the porch railing, which was lightly basted with ice. I turned to explain the rationale for why I had placed the pot outside, when I heard the crash. No one would let me scrape up the scattered soup to save from our now freshly festooned darkened deck.

As the dinner hour approached we were in sore need of a stove. To borrow a phrase from the fifties, I'd gladly have "taken gas" for my gaff with the soup, but our street had none. So a make-shift grill had to be constructed in the fireplace, which would serve as a sort of stove insert constructed of loose bricks which lay about the yard, where with to cook the upcoming casserole. That put in place by my swifter son-in-law, my mission was then to go in search of some light. Out into the icy evening I went. "Candles," I had been commanded, but I would go one better – a fusillade of flashlights, I figured. I just made it to three stores before they shut for the night – but to no avail. Some wise men had been there before me and there were no torches left to trade. The last store at the last minute had no cache of candles either, which was unconvincing to the unbelievers at home, who would rather have lit a candle than curse the dark. We had to make do with stubs. And I began to feel in outer darkness myself.

When the one-year-old child awoke in want throughout the night, who would arise to strike the tinder and start the fire to warm the bottle? Alas, like another Joseph, I was lost in dreams of many-colored coats and could not enkindle the coals for the kinder. I realized ruefully how kind, caring, and courageous the real Joseph had acted, all unannounced and uncomplaining, and I was determined to give him his due. He had the heart as well as the will, even if scripture didn't give him voice to say so.

Actually a friend of mine, many years ago, had beat me to it – although his project was more in protest than in praise. When he finally was old enough to move out of his family's house, each year at Christmas he would make his declaration of masculine independence (long before women's issues were an issue). He would set up in the front entrance of his bachelor pad an elaborate Joseph crèche, as he called it, where Mary (in a manner of speaking) was "magnificat-ly" missing – prominently and permanently excluded in protest of all the Christmas cards and carols that extolled the mother of Christ and made no mention of Joseph. That was my friend's way of preserving the promise of Christmas in the face of his exuberant and overbearing mother who overburdened him every year with extravagant gifts and excessive advice. So Joseph alone ministered at the manger, attended only by the animals and the angels and the star-struck shepherds. The Joseph crèche restored him to his rightful place where there was, as scripture said it, "peace on earth, good will to men."

What my friend didn't know was that Joseph knew he couldn't handle this heavy burden by himself; and so, without so much as a sound to speak for himself, he let God be in charge and chose to affirm that the life being borne by Mary was, in fact, of God. Therefore, Joseph called the child to bear his family name and also named him Jesus, meaning "God saves." Was Joseph a "wimp" in modern day terms? If so, I submit he was a holy wimp, a willing wimp in God's name and for Christ's sake. A silent servant willing to suffer ridicule and rejection for the sake of love.

Only one of us could have been Mary, but all of us can choose to be Joseph – if we have the heart, not just the will to say "yes" to God. In the midst of our darkness there is always an opportunity to embrace the good, to show that God is present, is Immanuel "God-with-us;" to repeat the sounding joy that we have not been abandoned, that we have been shown a way to live and to love. That's the word Joseph enfleshed in flesh not his own and why at least I want him with us always as our witness.

MAY A MULTITUDE OF CAMELS COVER YOU

2nd Sunday after Christmas Day
Isaiah 60:1-6,9
Year C – January 4, 2004

Arise, shine; for your light has come,
        and the glory of the LORD has risen upon
        you.
For darkness shall cover the earth,
        and thick darkness the peoples;
but the LORD will arise upon you,
        and his glory will appear over you.
Nations shall come to your light,
        and kings to the brightness of your dawn.
Lift up your eyes and look around;
        they all gather together, they come to you;
your sons shall come from far away,
        and your daughters shall be carried on their
        nurses' arms.
Then you shall see and be radiant;
        your heart shall thrill and rejoice,
because the abundance of the sea shall be brought
        to you,
        the wealth of the nations shall come to you.
A multitude of camels shall cover you,
        the young camels of Midian and Ephah;
        all those from Sheba shall come.
They shall bring gold and frankincense,
        and shall proclaim the praise of the LORD.

For the coastlands shall wait for me,
  the ships of Tarshish first,
to bring your children from far away,
  their silver and gold with them,
for the name of the LORD your God,
  and for the Holy One of Israel,
  because he has glorified you.

Isaiah 60:1-6,9

"Kings shall come to the brightness of your dawn" Isaiah writes, and "a multitude of camels shall cover you" – I love that expression, which I'll leave you with before we're done.

You have heard another saying from me before, and I hope you will hear it many times more: "I said to the man who stood at the gate of the year, 'Give me a light that I may tread safely into the unknown!' And he replied, 'Go out into the darkness and put thine hand into the hand of God. That shall be to thee better than light and safer than a known way.'" [1]

To understand the light of that saying in whatever the dark of the year holds for you is not just to be enlightened, but to have an epiphany. The same might be said of the saying, "You are the light of the world, but the switch must be turned on."[2]

I have chosen the lectionary propers for Epiphany this morning because the 2nd Sunday after Christmas is followed fast by the feast of the Epiphany (just two days from now), when most of you won't be liturgically present since this year we don't celebrate it on a Sunday. We all know a little something about that time because we may remember that was the day when the Magi, the Three Kings, as scripture says it "all rode in on Epiphany" (which in my youngster years I naively assumed was the name of a camel). But the word epiphany comes from the Greek, meaning "showing forth" – in this context, the manifestation of Christ to the Gentiles. Tradition tells us this was the time when the first Gentiles, guided by a mysterious star, came from the East to Bethlehem to bow down before the newborn King – offering him costly gifts of gold, frankincense, and myrrh. Hence Jesus was called "the king of kings." But what does his epiphany mean for us today? What will we come to see this new year that will make a difference in the way we perceive our lives? "Arise, shine," the prophet Isaiah beckons us. "Your light has come." The problem for most of us is we don't see the light. "The glory of the Lord," as Isaiah calls it, is not like the light we're used to. Or is it – only we are blind to the sight it sends us? Do we have any way of comprehending it? "Take infrared light. We cannot see it, but in that case our blindness is a blessing. Since any heat-emitting object glows with infrared light, we would be constantly distracted by the wavelengths if we could see them."[3] We would not know how to process that light. The light that Isaiah calls "the glory of the Lord" also requires a different kind of receptor than what we normally see through. It needs more than our processing information from the visual world around us that we can see and measure. What we need to perceive it are eyes of faith. To paraphrase the gospel of John from last week, only when we perceive that the Word of God becomes flesh and lives among us do we see "the glory as of a father's only son, full of grace and truth"[4]

A question we might ask ourselves at the beginning of 2004 is: What do we seek to guide us in this New Year? What kind of vision will shape what we see? Our old way of seeing may not be sufficient for us. The eyes of cynicism tell us that we can't live lives of compassion and selflessness. And the eyes of rationalism don't get us much further. If the only world that is real to us is what we can understand through what we can see, touch, taste, hear, smell and reason from, then it is not likely we will believe there is an unseen God who cares about us. As far as we can see, all we are left with is "a bunch of promises made by a make-believe deity for the popular consumption of the gullible and naive."[5] We may not be able to become the light of the world for others, but if we can learn to perceive and cherish the world through the eyes of faith, some of that light may help others make their way in the world with a different perspective. A story which demonstrates that we do have a choice about the way we see things and deal with our world is also a true story, one that was reported in the newspapers you may have read and shown on TV you may have watched. Some call it "The 6th Man Story" (I suppose that title appeals to me because I remember the name of a very popular movie that moved me many years ago, called The Third Man, a thriller that was also about the darkness of the world and how strong is our yearning for the light.) You may recall that nearly two years ago, an Air Florida jetliner crashed into the Potomac River in Washington, D.C. "There were 79 people on board, but only five of them survived the crash into the icy river water. David Van Arsdale reminds us that the five who survived owed their lives to an unknown person referred to by rescuers as the 'sixth man.' The rescuers reported that the rope from the helicopter came to this man over and over again, but he passed it on to the other five as they hung on for life, floating on debris in the frozen water. By the time the helicopter returned for the sixth man, he had slipped beneath the ice and drowned.

"Reflecting on the event, the pilot in the rescue helicopter said, 'Imagine! He had just survived that horrible crash. The river was ice-cold, and each minute brought him closer to death ... He could have gone on the first trip but he put everyone else ahead of himself.' The sixth man was a brave and good man, a person who had not asked the others about their religion, job, political preferences or even family status. No, he simply did what he could to save them ... "[6]

I remember thinking to myself at the time, that guy must have been crazy – either that or a saint. But that's a facile way to see it. In a world of so much darkness, that was a flicker of light. Did it somehow signal the presence of God, or only the unusual goodness of a man – or both? It takes eyes of faith to see them together, regardless what the man who gave his life may have believed. We are not given eyes of faith at birth; they are developed in us over a lifetime of looking, searching for the light of God in times of deep darkness.

In our own dark days, how do we keep our focus on the light? We know almost nothing about the Wise Men from the East who came looking for Jesus and had to find a way to get around the dark of Herod. They came seeking a light in the middle of the night, searching in the dark for a sign of the presence of God which the darkness could not overcome. In our time, wisely or outrageously, we take Isaiah's words as a celebration of that vision for us: "Kings shall come to the brightness of your dawn" and "a multitude of camels shall cover you." The traditional Three Camels cannot do justice to the occasion – there must be a "multitude." Not only "the young camels of Midian and Ephah," but "all those from Sheba" are invited too. What a vision! Is it an epiphany or only Isaiah out of his mind?

As Herbert O'Driscoll sees it, "The Magi represent forever and for all of us the wisdom that recognizes human life to be a journey [toward the light] taken in search of One who calls us beyond ourselves into faithful service..." The Magi could discern the light hidden in the darkness of their days. "And so we too, daily engaged in our all too human journey, searching for that which would have us be so much more than we are, and bearing [what gifts we have to offer], kneel on the stable floor beside those royal ones," there in the dark which is light enough to see by through the eyes of faith.[7]

My best wish, my hope, for you and for all of us as this new year begins, is that one way or another in the brightness of that dawning, you too may be covered by a multitude of camels to come.

---

1. "God Knows," by Minnie Louise Haskins
2. Austin Alexander Lewis
3. *Homiletics* 16, 6 – p.11
4. John 1:14
5. *Op. cit.*, p. 12
6. *Op. cit.*, p. 13
7. *Christian Century*, December 27, 2003, p. 18

EPIPHANY

Today being Epiphany, which word comes from the Greek *epiphaneia*, meaning to show forth or make manifest, a sudden realization or revelation of the essential meaning of something, I'm going to begin this morning by giving you the ending of my sermon first, so you don't have to worry about whether you can stay awake long enough to hear the end of what I am going to say.

Christopher Brookfield

THE JOURNEY

The Epiphany
Matthew 2:1-12
Year A – January 6, 2008

In the time of King Herod, after Jesus was born in Bethlehem of Judea, wise men from the East came to Jerusalem, asking, "Where is the child who has been born king of the Jews? For we observed his star at its rising, and have come to pay him homage." When King Herod heard this, he was frightened, and all Jerusalem with him; and calling together all the chief priests and scribes of the people, he inquired of them where the Messiah was to be born. They told him, "In Bethlehem of Judea; for so it has been written by the prophet:

> *'And you, Bethlehem, in the land of Judah,*
> *are by no means least among the rulers*
>   *of Judah;*
> *for from you shall come a ruler*
> *who is to shepherd my people Israel.'"*

Then Herod secretly called for the wise men and learned from them the exact time when the star had appeared. Then he sent them to Bethlehem, saying, "Go and search diligently for the child; and when you have found him, bring me word so that I may also go and pay him homage." When they had heard the king, they set out; and there, ahead of them, went the star that they had seen at its rising, until it stopped over the place where the child was. When they saw that the star had stopped, they were over-whelmed with joy. On entering the house, they saw the child with Mary, his mother; and they knelt down and paid him homage. Then, opening their treasure chests, they offered him gifts of gold, frankincense, and myrrh. And having been warned in a dream not to return to Herod, they left for their own country by another road.

Matthew 2:1-12

Today being Epiphany, which word comes from the Greek epiphaneia, meaning to show forth or make manifest, a sudden realization or revelation of the essential meaning of something, I'm going to begin this morning by giving you the ending of my sermon first, so you don't have to worry about whether you can stay awake long enough to hear the end of what I am going to say. In fact, once you've heard the ending, you may want to go to sleep so you won't have to endure what has to be said in order to get there. That's my first point.

And my second is that at the writing of this sermon I didn't really know for sure where it was going or how I was going to get to the end of it, so that you and I may both be surprised before I finish, or you wake up, whichever comes first.

Now to the ending, which epiphany has haunted me for many years and continues to trouble me because deep inside I have not made my peace with it, and my vocation keeps whisper-ing in my ear or shouting in my heart: "By now you ought to know for certain the answer to the question." Unhappily for my peace of mind, the ending is not a conclusion, but a question; and my com-passionate duty is to pass it on to you so that you may have the opportunity to struggle with it too and I can feel some measure of comfort in knowing that mine is not a solitary journey.

These are the words of one of the three Wise Men who journeyed from the east, following a star, to find the Christ child and to kneel down before him, offering him their gifts, and having been warned in a dream not to go back the way they came, had to return home by another way. Now are you ready for the ending, the hearing of which, who knows, may make a beginning possible? The wise man – does it matter which one? – reflects on what they found at their journey's end, after traveling so far from the East, over 500 miles in the desert, and staying, as he puts it, "only a few minutes as the clock goes, ten thousand, thousand years," just to "set our foolish gifts down on the straw and leave":

"I will tell you two terrible things, he continues. "What we saw on the face of the newborn child was his death. A fool could have seen it as well. It sat on his head like a crown or a bat, this death he would die. And we saw, as sure as the earth beneath our feet, that to stay with him would be to share that death, and that is why we left – giving only our gifts, withholding the rest." And then the troubling question:

"Now brothers, I will ask you a terrible question, and God knows I ask it also of myself. Is the truth beyond all truths, beyond the stars, just this: that to live without him is the real death, that to die with him is the life?"[1]

It's a good thing that was only a dramatic presentation, a fiction I just read from, and not something we would have to take seriously or personally. The setting for that story when I first heard it was one cold weekday morning on the second floor of the Academy Building at Exeter Academy in New Hampshire, in a large room which was the assembly place for the whole school, and that meeting was called, strangely enough, morning chapel. The few of us faculty stragglers who actually managed to get there at eight in the morning were, clown-like, arrayed before the students, seated up on the stage raised in front, looking down upon and facing some 700 or 800 boarding boys who were there in various forms of waking and incomplete dress, many without socks, because they were required to be there. Not an ideal situation for a serious address which, with scripture reading, a hymn, and a prayer, could take not more than ten or fifteen minutes at most, because first period classes followed which were serious.

The speaker that morning was my boss and colleague, Frederick Buechner, the School Minister, whose arbitrary turn it was to take weekday chapel, determined by the Dean who assigned various faculty members this onerous task throughout the year in a sequence determined by whim or by fate. The students were for the most part polite, yet generally out of hearing. But Fred decided not to try being a friend, rather simply to be himself in front of the horde that stretched before him on long creaking wooden spindle benches. His main assets, as far as the students were concerned, were that he had a sense of humor and irony as well as a golden speaking voice. And he had a theory about why it was important to attempt to speak faithfully to that mass of cultured despisers, most of whom couldn't have been dragged to Sunday services unless the Dean or his minions were there to check them present each week.

Although most of the students that morning "sat sloughed in their seats, staring up at the ceiling, every once in a while you could tell they were listening in spite of themselves...." He said, "I don't think it was so much my words that held them as it was the haunting power of the biblical narrative itself" (– whether it was the fearful struggle of Jacob at the river Jabbok, who wrestled all night with God, or the strange story of the Wise Men who came from afar to Bethlehem, guided by a star whose meaning they did not understand).

"I had a strong suspicion that once [the students] left Exeter, most of my captive listeners would never be caught dead in church again, and that gave me a strong sense of urgency. It might be the last time anyone would try to persuade them that religious faith was not as boring, banal, irrelevant, and outmoded as they thought it was.... I tried to be suggestive, elusive, and unpredictable... I never took for granted that they believed even the most basic affirmations of the Christian faith... but always tried to speak to their skepticism and to honor their doubts.... I was candid about what, like them, I was puzzled by and uncertain of.... I tried to be honest."[2]

What particularly prompted Buechner to speak about the Wise Men in such a foolish setting of morning assembly, I can't remember. Probably it was the week before the students got out for Christmas vacation and they would miss the coming of the Christ child in Exeter or wherever they went and surely take no thought about the journey of the Magi on Epiphany and the significance of the birth they came to celebrate, which manifested to the world the message that that gift was for everyone, not just for the Jews.

What in heaven's name could the students care that the Wise Men anointed the head of the child with the oil of myrrh as Israel had done for their kings, or lit the frankincense as the people had done in the temple for their God, or offered to him their precious treasure of gold which most of us keep for ourselves? But the way the Wise Men told the story must have caught the students' imagination or at least their attention for a few minutes. For all I know they may have recognized in the ruthless King Herod their picture of the Dean and felt that the 500 miles journey across the desert was what it would be like to make their way back to the home they longed to return to or dreaded with whatever awaited them there.

That morning I could see the change come over their faces as they listened, at first unwillingly, and then heard the odd quiet without coughing that crept across the room. Even the scarecrow faculty seemed to sit straighter in their seats, feeling not laughable sitting on the lordly stage, but included. Somehow there came to be there something like a little epiphany of each one's making, maybe not exactly Christ-like so to speak, but a deeply religious longing or questioning that took them, just for an instant, by surprise. So much so that at the end there was a storm of loud unaccustomed spontaneous applause which left everyone wondering and slightly foolish.

I doubt that anyone there could tell you today what went on in Fred's story, but that was not the end of it then for some students who took a part of it with them, not the narrative necessarily, but the questioning in the heart of the Wise Men in their search for the secret they longed to behold and be beholden to. That was the gift. I realize that now, uneasily and unnervingly. Because I still remember the Wise man's question, whether I would rather forget it or make it into a different asking for my journey. Lord knows, I wish it had been asked in a different way, one which wouldn't have disturbed me so over the years:

"Is the truth beyond all truths ... just this: that to live without him is the real death, that to die with him is the only life?"

------

1. Frederick Buechner, Secrets in the Darkness, pp. 12-13.
2. *Op. cit.* pp. xiii-xiv.

EPIPHANY – A TIME TO PONDER

1st Sunday after the Epiphany: Baptism of Our Lord
Isaiah 43:1-7; Psalm 29; Acts 8:14-17;
Luke 3:15-17, 21-22
Year C – January 12, 1992

What we are doing this week, in a manner of speaking, is getting back to reality. It takes about a week and a half for reality to really set in. Because we've spent a good month or more in the unreality of merry making, preparing for Christmas and parties and football games and producing predictions about the new year and resolutions about how we're going to change it and us. And, suddenly, we've got to go back to work, or get down to work.

Christmas has come and gone; however it was – good, bad, or indifferent – it's over, as Robert Fulghum puts it. "The relatives have gone home. New Year's Eve and New Year's Day are finished, and whether you whooped it up or just pooped out and went to bed, that's done. The holiday mess is cleaned up, the tree and the leftovers have gone out with the garbage," when here come the Three Wise Men, bearing more gifts – to celebrate a new life and a new year, even a new reality – for us all. They do not bring us a partridge in a pear tree, but light into a darkened world. That is the meaning and gift of Epiphany.

One of the gifts (which the Bible does not name) that Epiphany brings to us at this time of year – since it's too early to plan a spring fling or to work on taxes, and we know we'll have to get out in the snow before we can work in the garden – one of the gifts we are given at this time is the privilege of pondering. Pondering about what we are going to do about it.

It all started with what happened when the Angel Gabriel was sent to Mary and told her that she had found favor with God and would conceive a son whose name would be Jesus, the one who shall be called Emmanuel – meaning "God with us." And when this happened, Mary (as well she might) "pondered all these things in her heart," as scripture says it.

And we, as we wait for reality to settle in upon us, have the same privilege, to ponder: What will happen to us and to our world, say, as early as January 15th? It is true that whatever happens in Westhampton will not be the same as what happens on the West Bank or in Croatia or Russia – but that too will happen to us, and our world. What will we do about it? We will be changed by it: We need to ponder that, along with what it is we can change.

To ponder, it has been said, is not to brood or grieve. It is to wonder at a very deep level – which invites the pun that at this time of year we can afford to wonder around for an afternoon or two as Mary must have.

<hr />

To top it off, the animals who are jammed in there with her talk. Not many cows speak Hebrew, but that seems to be what was going on.

<hr />

Robert Fulghum wonders what the scriptures meant by saying, "Mary pondered all these things in her heart." When you think about what the phrase "all these things" refers to, it's no wonder she pondered, he writes. Here's a teenage kid who has just had a baby in the back stall of a barn, with some confusion about just who the father is. Her husband is muttering about taxes and the fact that the head honcho in these parts, Herod, has opted for infanticide. (That's killing babies.) And if that's not enough to think about, there's all this traffic of visiting astrologers (Wise Men), sheep ranchers, and angels, who keep dropping by with questions and proclamations and chorales. To top it off, the animals who are jammed in there with her talk. Not many cows speak Hebrew, but that seems to be what was going on. It certainly would give a person something to do some heavy thinking about. I'd say "ponder" is the perfect word for what Mary was doing.

We too, ponder, even if we don't wonder about. At least we have the opportunity to do it in these first days before reality has fully descended upon us. Before we are changed by it, for good or for ill, we need to ponder what it is we can change. Fulghum ponders: Perhaps you returned to your job or your homemaking or to school "swearing secretly to yourself that you are going to do better this year. And for a few days at least you really are doing better. You may not always keep doing better; but in spite of such a dreadful lot of distractions – for a few days at least – a few days of hopeful possibility – you may have proof that you really could do better. If you wanted to." That, too, is Epiphany, when our personal gifts are affirmed and our outward journeys – wherever it is we are headed this year – reflect our inner light, which shows us the way.

This gift of pondering allows us to ask once again not only where we are going and how we can get there – but who it is that matters most to us among all those things that really matter: a precious time, a fleeting time, a foolish time some might say because some people think that wondering is a waste of time. If it is, it is a holy waste that I, for one, hope is not wasted on us. For it gives us the opportunity to believe not only that I can make a difference, that I can make things happen, but it frees us to believe that almost anything can happen.

Fulghum tells a story he heard about a man who found the horse of the king and he didn't know it was the king's horse and he kept it, but the king found out and arrested him and was going to kill him for stealing the horse. The man tried to explain and said he would willingly take his punishment, but did the king know that he could teach the horse to talk and if so the king would be a pretty impressive king, what with a talking horse and all? So the king thinks what does he have to lose and says sure. He'll give him a year. Well, the man's friends think he is nuts. But the man says – well, who knows? – the king may die, I may die, the world may come to an end, the king may forget. But just maybe, the horse may talk. One must believe that anything can happen.

That, at its very deepest level, is the gift of Epiphany. And it is ours to ponder.

Prayer is a form of pondering – and we have much that needs praying about at this time.

"Hear the anxious, unspoken fears
of those who are productive
successful
comfortable
finding satisfaction in their work
pleasure in life
love at home
You in your heaven and all right with their world.
They never step on the sidewalk cracks
they say their prayers
they see their children beautifully, peaceful asleep in bed
and want so much to stop time
that
this innocence, security, and safety may be preserved
       forever.
Speak to them the saving word
the strange good news
that persons will not stay the way they are.
The word of faith is the same for us all:
we are always unfinished;
You are not through with us yet
In the painful and pleasant changes of life
we meet You
and the Christ.

We call Him the Way and mean only the destination;
He is also and especially the journey
the process
the getting there within amid through
the heart attack, the conversion, the birth, the death
the growing up and growing old and becoming like a child.
Good news to her who is not as lost as she thinks.
Good news to him who is not as saved as he imagines.
Good news to us all.
Way to go
amen.[1]

———

1. Frederick Ohler, *Better Than Nice and Other Unconventional Prayers*

(YOU ARE) AGENTS OF UNANTICIPATED EPIPHANY AND BEARERS OF BAPTISMAL BLESSINGS

1st Sunday after the Epiphany: Baptism of Our Lord
Genesis 1:1-5; Psalm 29;
Acts 19:1-7; Mark 1:4-11
Year B – January 9, 2000

Today, in liturgical terms, is called "First Sunday after the Epiphany" and "The Baptism of Our Lord," even "Second Sunday in Ordinary Time." That's a mouthful (or an earful), and without seeming to be cynical I would say most people don't give a fig for the finer points of theological theory behind those divine designer labels. So I'm going to try to say something about all of that in a way which is confessional without being "churchy" and relevant without being "religious." Beginning with the observation that regardless whether you enjoy entering into our services of baptism, I suspect you would probably choose cooperating with or conniving in the corporate christening of Grace Stryker Davis at eleven o'clock rather than enduring my esoteric explanation about the importance of Christ's immersion in the river Jordan by John.

Suffice it to say "Baptism," according to the Young People's Bible Dictionary, says simply: washing with water to symbolize repentance and forgiveness of sins." Epiphany" isn't in it at all. And "Ordinary" is omitted as well. At least it isn't listed under time or experience, let alone what you would ordinarily call a bishop exercising his ecclesiastical jurisdiction (nor even explained as a tavern or eating house where regular meals are served). So I'm going to give you instead a snapshot explanation of what you would see when you first step into my office adjacent to the old parish hall in Little Saint Mary's – set alongside the sign that says "Thou Shalt Not Park Here" (Ennion Williams ingenious invention) – as a surrogate sermon.

Actually, it isn't an office as much as an entrance into the quasi kingdom of Christopher, the unlikely Christ-bearer (to be faithful to the meaning of my name). I say "kingdom" because even when a while back I was a prominent Pooh-Bah in the portals of the Diocese of Virginia and was called "Very Reverend" (which Bishop Lee always said didn't signify it was true, anymore than his title testified that he was "Right"). Anyway, even then, when I was named a "Special" or a "Peculiar" (which meant I wasn't subject to the Ordinary, meaning ordinarily not under the control of the Bishop – now there's trouble.) Even then I didn't have a fireplace, a full-length mirror, a swinging black recliner-with-hassock, and a bathroom all to myself. Sounds like a kingdom to me – except that it is chiefly a kind of classroom where unaccountably extraordinary insights emerge everyday if not all the time from most of the stalwarts who sit there.

The focal point, in the center of the room, in full view of Vishnu the Sustainer, is a long dining-room table, a gift to St. Mary's from Sandy Lind – appropriately, because as he said he always hungered and thirsted after righteousness and his curiosity and questions were often food for thought rather than hot tamales. The table seats twelve, which is the sacred number Sewanee says we may not exceed in any Education for Ministry class that has gathered there these past three years. So we are Kosher in configuration as well as comradeship, in and out of EfM.

I doubt you would not notice that the regal red tablecloth which attends us continually is unselectively stained: the grease from butter, brownies, and homemade pound cake; the marks of jostled coffee cups and carafes of Cran-Raspberry; the dribbles of merlot, not to mention milk and honey, and crumbs of oven fresh bread – all of which adorn the cloth of inquiring minds, needy souls, and compassionate companions testifying to our fond feeding of one another. The only potential pariah at the party is the person who volunteered to bring food but forgot, God forbid. Since Gina Taylor says it costs $35.00 to get the tablecloth cleaned, we accept the stains and slops upon the shroud as secret sharing and sacred scars of our steadfast food for one another – up to a year at a time. Even the irrepressible Bible study brothers and sisters turn a benignly blind eye to the inadvertent excrescences of the EfMers. In the middle of said tablecloth are four artifacts that observe our ongoing adventures: a box of Kleenex, a laughing Buddha, a stately saucer of St. Peter's Church in St. George's Bermuda, and an old Indian grinding stone, each an agent of unanticipated epiphany and bearers of baptismal blessings, if you can believe it.

Beginning with the benevolent Buddha that I trekked back as a teenager from my first trip to the temptations of Europe. He is missing one eye and a set of upper teeth, and one of the Sunday School groups accidentally amputated a forefinger last year (they also made him a green brassiere and a silver toupee, now confiscated). He is no stranger to the stains and scars of life, but looking upon his infectiously beneficent and joyful countenance can't help but restore your faith in the forgiveability of life and the power of love to uphold you in the pits. His call for compassion and kindness to all sentient being makes him a companion with Christ and opens our eyes to the oneness of truth and the unexpected forms it can take. One imaginative Sunday School class seated him atop a copy of the Koran, not in triumph but as testimony to his being a fellow traveler – an enduring epiphany for those who hadn't expected to understand that.

The Kleenex box used to be at a safe distance, secure in the sedate bookcase on the wall, now suddenly at hand to all. But it betokens not sorrow or sickness, only the unexpected significance of the stories we somehow manage to share there with each other in our ventures in EfM. One student said she had signed up specifically to explore the academic instruction of EfM, which excited her. But now she willingly assures us that the self-revelation and spiritual growth that goes on is what she has learned to treasure – the testimony of tears notwithstanding.

The saucer of St. Peter's is special to me because it was a surprise souvenir secreted back from Bermuda for me by my wife. It reminds me not only of a sacred peace that such a place secures; it is a symbol of connectedness beyond the life of our little parish of St. Mary's. St. Peter's too is small in space, distinctive with its highly polished cedar beams and pews, elegant 18th century silver and manners; and it "occupies the oldest Anglican Church site in the Western Hemisphere." A modest, magnificent, and remarkably pleasant unpretentious house of prayer, which has the feel of home in a foreign place – with permission to be a human being not a human doing.

Lastly, the old Indian grinding stone, unlooked for implement of Hope Springs, which sits awaiting to be seized in the scramble to say something in the sessions of Monday evening EfM. Enthusiasm often overpowers a person's patience and the only way to ensure being heard is to grab the stone – only the person who has it has the right to speak. The ensuing silence is surprising, but the spirit isn't stifled. It seems to say, Savor this moment; it may not last but the truth in it will endure always. Who "rocks it" is no Sisyphus but an unsuspecting saint in the making.

Which brings me back to this place and time where we have witnessed once again in Word and deed the life of Christ in us and celebrated Grace upon Grace (Stryker to be specific). No ordinary occasion except that it is offered in the ordinary course of our worship. Epiphany and Christmas are intertwined in Mark's gospel reading because no matter how the story he tells is told – "as a birthing narrative, as a baptismal narrative, as poetry [or epiphany] – the facts of faith remain the same: Jesus has come among us, bid us follow him into the water, die to our old ways; and 'Behold, new things spring forth'" (as Isaiah enunciated it). "God has created a new day and a new way," and calls us to walk out of whatever darkness we have dwelled in in the past into the light of this day – in cahoots with the Holy Spirit, God love us.[1] What does that mean?

Maybe we have to look at our own baptism, not Christ's, to explain it. Whether you were sure what you were about at your baptism or all unknowing, whether you knew what it meant or had no knowledge of it, like many of us in the intervening years you may have drifted away, even acted as if it never happened. That's not the problem; it is a common occurrence. The issue is not the ineffectiveness of a bungled baptism; that beginning was just fine – in fact, all you need. The task is for us to live out or live into what was begun in us. It takes a whole lifetime to finish our baptisms. We don't need a new start, only the intention to live up to the promises we made or our sponsors professed for us.

What did it mean when you were baptized? Can you remember what you thought and felt and did that day? (Mark wasn't around to record that for your family scripture.) But the main meaning emerges in what you think and feel and do this day, and in the days to come. In what ways are we grateful for the Grace we have been given (not just for Grace Stryker Davis)? Or, what are we willing to do today that we wouldn't have done if we had not been baptized?[2] That's the baptismal question that "The Baptism of Our Lord" leaves us with today – and tomorrow and tomorrow.

––––––

1. *Christian Century*. 116, 36-p 1249
2. *Lectionary Homiletics*. XII, 2-p.15

WHY WATER INTO WINE?

2nd Sunday after the Epiphany
John 2:1-11
Year C – January 14, 2001

On the third day there was a wedding in Cana of Galilee, and the mother of Jesus was there. Jesus and his disciples had also been invited to the wedding. When the wine gave out, the mother of Jesus said to him, "They have no wine." And Jesus said to her, "Woman, what concern is that to you and to me? My hour has not yet come." His mother said to the servants, "Do whatever he tells you." Now standing there were six stone water jars for the Jewish rites of purification, each holding twenty or thirty gallons. Jesus said to them, "Fill the jars with water." And they filled them up to the brim. He said to them, "Now draw some out, and take it to the chief steward." So they took it. When the steward tasted the water that had become wine, and did not know where it came from (though the servants who had drawn the water knew), the steward called the bridegroom and said to him, "Everyone serves the good wine first, and then the inferior wine after the guests have become drunk. But you have kept the good wine until now. "Jesus did this, the first of his signs, in Cana of Galilee, and revealed his glory; and his disciples believed in him.

John 2:1-11

Somewhere among the arcane artifacts in my archives is a picture presented to me a while ago showing Jesus smoking a fat cigar, a smile on his face and a good-natured gleam in his eye. Later I learned it is a Xerox copy from a page out of Playboy Magazine — which may be something of an anomaly since some of us would be hard pressed to picture Jesus with just his sandals on, posing as the playboy of the Greco-Roman world (even though in some epithets assigned to him by his enemies he was called "a glutton and a wine bibber"). Symbolically at least, this snapshot must have seemed to the person who presented it to me as apt for my efforts to portray Jesus after I had preached a sermon on some aspect of his life (which now conveniently escapes me) for which the picture was apparently appropriate.

Whatever the reality, we don't hear a lot about the joy of Jesus; his earthiness, appetites, or inappropriate associations. We want him upright, ethical, inerrant, inspiring if not austere — so that he ends up being unapproachable, untouchable. Yet here in this morning's scriptural passages assigned to us at the onset of Epiphany is the unique portrayal in John's gospel of Jesus' first miracle at a wedding in Cana of Galilee, also always referred to in the opening exhortation of our marriage ceremony signifying to us "the mystery of the union between Christ and his Church."

Some scholars, unsettled by its inclusion in the beginning of John's account at the start of Jesus' ministry, have suggested that there might be "strong pagan influence behind this odd story of Jesus turning water into wine," commenting that there may be more than coincidence in its connection with the feast of Dionysus celebrated each year in the ancient world on January 6th, now our Epiphany.[1] Was this a bacchanalian bash blessed by the early Epiphany liturgy? Or is this account underlying the miracle a significant expression of the exuberant joy that permeated the understanding of the early church?

To answer that we first need to address a number of questions John's account raises. What is remarkable about his gospel story is what it doesn't say; it is narrated leanly, to say the least, and we are left to fill in the holes or gaps in the tale as it is told. Unfortunately, for many of us the story is so familiar that we have lost the benefit of our fresh critical faculties and the questions we might have thought to ask when we first heard it. John's account includes assumptions we have to express for ourselves if we are to interpret what is essential in it.

For example, John tells us that while Jesus and his disciples are attending the wedding festivities "the wine gave out." But when? How long had the wedding been going on? How much longer was it expected to last? How big a crisis is it that there is no more wine? Marriage festivals in that culture often went for a whole week. Did the wine run out on the first day of the feast or on the sixth? Although guests might be expected to bring some provisions, it was assumed the groom would see that food and drink were available throughout the festival. And often the water was not safe to drink; wine was the only way to go. How would this serious social faux pas or flagrant shortfall of responsibility affect the groom's reputation and the family's respect? Why would Jesus be inclined to become involved with the wine in the first place, and why would his mother ask him to?

And what was it she expected him to do anyway, engineer a miracle or offer his and his disciples' denarii so as to send the servants out to buy more wine? Regardless, the results were staggering, literally as well as figuratively, because filling the six stone jars used for the Jewish rites of purification would have yielded as much as 180 gallons of wine, which with my unreliable math, amounts to more than 23,000 ounces or 966 bottles of wine – more than enough for some major merriment. Moreover, this wasn't mediocre merlot. Surprised, the wine steward said to the bridegroom, "Everyone serves the good wine at the start, and saves the second-rate spirits for when the guests have become drunk, but you have kept the good wine until now."

Apart from the appalling amount of it, why did Jesus change his mind after he announced to his mother when she had spoken to him of the shortage, "What concern is that to you and me?" And why did he decide to involve himself in the situation as though he was concerned with the shortfall when, as he put it, his "hour had not yet come?" Another issue: John does not say that the servants said anything to anyone about the wine having come out of the vats filled with water. "Neither the steward nor even the groom (in the narrative) seems aware of the miraculous origin of the wine, or that Jesus was in anyway connected with it."[2] And yet, in spite of these omissions and all those who were oblivious of what Jesus had done, John insists that the significance of the story speaks of Jesus' glory being revealed – so much so, you may remember, that because of it "his disciples believed in him," something that otherwise often seemed to elude them.

I promise not to prolong the probing of impertinent questions, but one could wonder why John would bother to speak of the story at all, let alone proclaim it was "the first of Jesus' signs" at the start of his ministry. "Is providing wine to stave off social embarrassment really worthy" of being remembered as the mainstay of Jesus' mission? "Conjuring wine at weddings seems more like ... magician's [magic] than a miracle revealing [God's] glory."[3] But maybe it is a means of saying to us that uncommon truths can come to us in the common places where we are often oblivious to the outcome – a wake up call.

And maybe since I have made this morass for you I might need to find a means of making sense of the situation so as to avoid our assigning this story to an arbitrary obscurity. What kind of "sign" would be significant for our understanding? Here are some suggestions. Timothy Cargal says, "For some, the key is to recognize in the water and the wine symbols of the sacraments of baptism and communion. For others, the defining feature of the story is the quality and abundance of the wine ..., which reveal the glory and the abundance of God's care for even seemingly trivial aspects of our lives. Still others find in the setting of a wedding ... the language of lovers and marriage partners used to express God's love and relationship with the people of God."[4]

Marcus Borg elaborates on that. This is John's way of saying to us that "the story of Jesus is about a wedding feast at which the wine never runs out.... It presents us with a Jesus and a God who are concerned about people's joy and who participate in it.

Jesus does not appear here as an ascetic [in contrast to John the Baptist], shunning celebration, feasting and sociability.... Wedding feasts were one of the happiest kinds of occasions people in Jesus' culture ever knew.... For the wine to run out would have been very sad. What Jesus did saved the party from being a disaster. People who are accustomed to seeking God's presence only ... when they are sad and need comfort, or those whose idea of God is that he is a cosmic killjoy, need to look carefully at this story.... The coming of the LORD is the time of gladness, rejoicing, exultation, and joy.... God 'delights' and 'rejoices' in this relationship." [5]

Finally, returning to the significance of the staggering amount of wine, what we might imagine an over-abundance, because "the wedding guests went from having no wine at all to having almost enough to swim in." According to the Old Testament Prophets, the new age of Messiah was to be characterized by an abundance of wine. So for those "who have eyes to see," this miracle as a sign of Jesus' Messiahship, the one who would purify all people, not just Israel.

The purification Jesus brings with the wine of the new age replaces the water of the stone jars, which was for the Jewish rites of purification. "The good news is that every moment and every place Christ is transforming the world.... The wedding is a sign that we are all included. The feast is for everyone.... We need not fear that there will not be enough for me."[6]

"I have come that you may have life," Jesus said, "and have it *abundantly*."

_____

1. *Lectionary Homiletics XII, 2* p.11
2. *Op. cit. p.9*
3. *Ibid.*
4. *Ibid.*
5. *Op. cit. p.10*
6. *Op. cit. p.14*

SAVING WINE

2nd Sunday after the Epiphany
John 2:1-11
Year C – January 14, 2007

Those of you who know me well will have guessed that I would choose Jesus' first miracle in Cana of Galilee, where he turns water into an abundance of wine, as my text for today. Not only because there was a time when I would have chosen an abundance of wine – the more the merrier – but because the story confounds our conventional expectations of Jesus in that happening.

True, the gospel story refers to Jesus elsewhere as "a glutton and a winebibber," but that is not John's point in telling this story, and it is not Jesus who is intended to imbibe here, but us – we are to drink in both the experience and whatever we can make out that it means for our faith and understanding.

However Jesus' ministry, or his disciples' response to it, may have been characterized as being "drunk with the spirit," Jesus was no lush. And when he asked his disciples later "Are you able to drink of the cup that I drink?" he was not referring to the idea that he had saved the best wine for last. The vintage he spoke of was bitter as well as all consuming. But not on this occasion in Cana, which was a wedding feast.

What are we to make of this story, other than "It's a good story," unforgettable even. What does it mean? I can only address what it means to me since I can't drink your wine for you. The first thing I like about it is that it is unexplainable. We could play with the notion that if the wine had run out early in the wedding feast it would have been a disaster, both embarrassing and humiliating to the host. Hospitality was paramount, and to send guests away prematurely would have been a social catastrophe for the ceremony; so that could explain Jesus' decision to save it.

But in this story, or sign, or parable, or imponderable, Jesus does not merely provide some wine to last for the ceremony, he floods the party with it. He transforms 6 very large stone water jars used for Jewish rites of purification, each holding 20 to 30 gallons, into an abundance of rich wine – for no reason, pure grace – so much that the steward is astounded at the taste and goodness of it. And he calls the bridegroom, saying with pleasure and perplexity, "Everyone serves the good wine first, and then the inferior wine after the guests have become drunk. But you have kept the good wine until now." (He did not know that Jesus was the one who provided it.) Whatever else you want to call the miracle, extravagance was at the heart of it. It reminds me of the parable of the sower and the seeds and the feeding of the 5,000.

Theologians are forever fond of trying to explain the miracles of Jesus so as to make them more acceptable to our understanding – such as saying when Jesus seemed to be walking on water, in that section of the lake there was a series of stones seated just under the surface for him to step on. But this passage in John precludes our provisional acceptance; it does not invite an acceptable explanation. It simply celebrates the event, leaving us to struggle with what this miracle says about Jesus and about the status of our faith. It does not say why or how. No rationale is offered, only that it happened.

The essence of miracle, of course, is that it shatters conventional explanations and expectations, and I do not intend to diminish the extraordinariness of this story in any way. We contemporary hearers of it must be allowed to struggle with whatever it might have meant then and may mean for us now. Maybe it tells us as much about ourselves in our reaction to it as it does about what Jesus intended in it. Living in a rational and scientific age, this story is astounding and inexplicable at best, and embarrassing and offensive in its extravagance at worst.[1] No explanation of the event is presented to us any more than there is an attempt to explain the resurrection on Easter. It is simply asserted.

Of course we are tempted to say that apart from the event itself, there is symbolic significance to it. Some have said that since the new wine was created in the "old" vessels of the Jewish purification rites, that means Jesus thereby rejected the waters of purification and the claims of Judaism. But an equal time observation says simply that the old forms are now given a new content for the possibilities of the future and that in Jesus' actions there is neither a rejection nor a replacement of the old, only the experience of a wondrous new gift – such that his stolid and stultified disciples are now not coerced but convinced to believe in him. As John puts it, this is the inaugural event of Jesus' forthcoming ministry already beginning.[2]

If we can manage to remember that Jesus was a Jew, not a Christian, we might find it useful to recall that "in the Old Testament, an abundance of good wine is an eschatological symbol, a sign of the joyous arrival of God's new age." So that Jesus' act would portray him as the fulfillment of that hope and the sign that the salvation which God had promised has started.[3] Maybe that's not too much to read into this event.

A word about the odd exchange between Jesus and his mother. His response to her telling him that the wine had run out sounds to us something like "Cry me a river" or "Why don't you tell that to someone who cares?" He speaks to her impersonally and distantly: "Woman, what concern is that to you and me?" And then he adds, almost as an everyday explanation, "My hour has not yet come." While the word 'hour' in Greek can be used to indicate the passing of clock time, *chronos*, it can also refer to the awaited time of eschatological fulfillment, *kairos*, or time that is pregnant with meaning – as in "It's now time for you to tell the truth."[4]

At such a time, no one, not even his mother, has a privileged claim upon him; he must be governed not by anyone else, by our time or will, but by the hour set by God. Curious that his mother thinks she can tell him what to do; the Jewish mother, for whatever reason, decides to take on the wine problem. I can hear her saying, "Don't worry about it, I'll talk to my son – he can fix anything." Then she bustles up to Jesus and says to him out of nowhere, "They're out of wine." And Jesus tries to blow her off.[5] But ever the dutiful son, never known for his sweetness in speaking about or to his family, as the gospel accounts record it, nevertheless ventures this sign – whether for her sake, the bridegroom's, or ours.

What sin is, is not being full of joy.

What I like about it is not the theological import but his puzzling and playful concern about the wedding feast in progress. It may be that in this event Jesus revealed his glory, but he also made the occasion memorable and joyful. Many weddings are forgettable (except our own, of course), unless something horrendous happens: the bride's dress is lost, the groom doesn't show up, the mother passes out in the service, the minister repeatedly calls the bride and groom by their wrong names, or some such – including a member of the congregation who in the service challenges the legality of the marriage for the couple about to take their vows. But no one will forget the wedding in Cana – not because of some mishap, but for the joy, the exuberance and extravagance of it. No grim theological warning, no dour moralistic expectation, no tiresome and troubling message – only a joyful, grateful, and gracious gathering. I think of that unusual definition: What sin is, is not being full of joy.

We Episcopalians are not noted for joy in our gatherings for worship – nor even in our coming together for cocktails, beyond the teen and college travesties. We've lost that Hebrew sense of holy chutzpah in our singing and psalms, prayers and personal petitions. How can we reawaken ourselves to the realization that what we are here to celebrate is Grace, the life and love we have been given gratis, not the entitlements we have earned by the skin of our teeth or the seat of our pants, but the glimpse of glory we are given by the grace of God? That may be more than what we can expect 120-180 gallons of wine will give us, but our longing for joy is somewhere for us all to start seeing life differently.

John's story says that the wedding in Cana is where Jesus "revealed his glory" and when his disciples first "believed in him," but what does it mean for us? That's the question you and I have to answer for ourselves. But what we have in common to begin with is the wonder of Jesus turning water into an overabundance of wine – a sign that says if he can make that kind of change, he can change us also. Maybe not a transfiguration of us but a transformation for us. Maybe a marvel, but more likely a miracle of a new beginning made possible for us – if only we will drink it in, metaphorically or more personally. My parting word for you is therefore, *Prosit!* -or if you prefer, Here's mud in your eye!

------

1. *New Interpreter's Bible Commentary* Volume IX, p.539
2. *Op. cit. p.538*
3. *Ibid.*
4. *Op. cit. p.537*
5. *Homiletics 16, 1-p.22*

"GOOD LUCK, MR. GORSKY"

2nd Sunday after the Epiphany
1 Corinthians 6:12-20
Year B — January 19, 2003

You were washed, you were sanctified, you were justified in the name of the Lord Jesus Christ and in the Spirit of our God.

"All things are lawful for me," but not all things are beneficial. "All things are lawful for me," but I will not be dominated by anything. "Food is meant for the stomach and the stomach for food," and God will destroy both one and the other. The body is meant not for fornication but for the Lord, and the Lord for the body. And God raised the Lord and will also raise us by his power. Do you not know that your bodies are members of Christ? Should I therefore take the members of Christ and make them members of a prostitute? Never! Do you not know that whoever is united to a prostitute becomes one body with her? For it is said, "The two shall be one flesh." But anyone united to the Lord becomes one spirit with him. Shun fornication! Every sin that a person commits is outside the body; but the fornicator sins against the body itself. Or do you not know that your body is a temple of the Holy Spirit within you, which you have from God, and that you are not your own? For you were bought with a price; therefore glorify God in your body.

I Corinthians 6:12-20

History buffs will recall that when Neil Armstrong, the first astronaut, walked on the moon, he said, "One small step for man, one giant leap for mankind." What few people don't know is that as he re-entered the lunar module, he made the comment "Good luck, Mr. Gorsky."

Many people at NASA thought it was a casual remark concerning Russia. That perhaps some cosmonaut named Gorsky was Armstrong's rival and that it was some blow below the belt at Russia's failed attempt at a moon landing. However, upon checking, there was no Gorsky in either the Russian or American space programs. Who was Gorsky? People always confronted Armstrong and asked about Gorsky, and Neil would turn red and smile, but never talked about it.

Recently at a press conference in Florida, a reporter brought up the enigmatic Gorsky to Armstrong. He asked the question that many reporters had attempted to ask and never got an answer. "Who is this Gorsky guy you talked about while on the moon?" For 26 years he avoided the question because he didn't want to embarrass Mr. Gorsky. But this time it was the reporter's lucky day. Armstrong finally responded. Mr. Gorsky had died so Neil felt that answering the question wouldn't harm anyone.

Armstrong related the story that when he was a kid, he played baseball with a friend of his. Armstrong threw a pitch and his friend hit a pop fly ball, which landed in front of his neighbor's bedroom window. Mr. and Mrs. Gorsky were his neighbors. Neil ran to get the ball. As he leaned down to pick it up, he couldn't help but overhear Mrs. Gorsky yelling at Mr. Gorsky. There she was, screaming at the top of her lungs "Sex?! You want sex?! You'll get sex when the kid next door walks on the moon!"[1]

True story? Not quite. It is total "urban legend." But it does bring us to an explicit appeal from Paul this morning about the place of sex in our lives.

One member of our congregation said to me not long ago, what I'm really waiting for in this church is for someone to preach a sermon some Sunday on the subject of sex and the gospel. Well, I'm not going that far. I'm only going to offer some observations on the epistle. Our reading is from Paul's letter to the Corinthians, where he is concerned about their sexual conduct within the Christian community.

The key words here are Paul's insistence that "All things are lawful for me, but not all things are beneficial" and "Do you not know that your body is a temple of the Holy Spirit within you and that you are not your own?" The conflict between Corinthian attitudes toward sexuality and appropriate attitudes according to Paul arose out of what was commonplace in Greco-Roman culture where the free person was permitted to do whatever he wished. "All things are permitted" was a popular upper-class Roman proverb. It is perhaps important for me to point out at the start that Paul is no more preoccupied with sexual sins than with any other sin that causes separation from one another and from God.

The assumptions of our contemporary culture concerning sexuality and the relation of male and female are no less controversial or conflicted in our time than in Paul's. The contention between Christian sexual ethics and culture did not begin with us. But today, for many in the Western world, sex is simply a form of play, if not a particularly profound form; it is a pleasurable way to spend some time. The problem is, what about people who prefer to see sex as a means of adding meaning and significance to their lives? Is there a place for that in a society that perceives sexual activity as something like purchasing a sun roof on a new car: You can take it or leave it, an optional extra but nothing profound or personal? Joanna Adams points out that these days when we consider the question of fidelity, few people want someone else opposing our personal opinion of what constitutes sin and what doesn't. In a recent book, Moral Freedom, Alan Wolfe presents the findings of a study about where Americans stand on sexual matters. Overwhelmingly, he reports, respondents' conceptions of right and wrong are guided by subjective feelings rather than faithful aspirations. He calls those persons "moral moderates." Americans may "honor their marriage vows, but most no longer consider their vows as binding under all circumstances. They are likely to act on the basis of practicality rather than on religious principle."[2] The human question there, even apart from the religious issue, is do we have any longer "an ability to ask, when faced with a crisis or decision, not simply whether it will satisfy my needs, but whether it will be good for the person to whom I am married and ... for the marriage itself'?[3] Not to mention the "moderates" who do not see the sanctity of marriage as socially significant.

How did we get there? When I was growing up, more often than not sex was a taboo subject. If we were tempted to go "too far" (the accepted euphemism), guilt was expected to keep us in line. Some will remember being told as boys that our bodies were intended for us to engage in "manual labor, sports, and war." Then in the sexual revolution of the 60's "Modesty was abandoned, guilt [became] obsolete, responsibility mitigated, and profligacy admired," while many of us were misplaced Rip Van Winkles in the midst of it. When we woke up, two decades later, sexual behavior seemed strangely dangerous because of AIDS, which might lead to death. We missed the pleasures of permissiveness both coming and going, with or without the ease of enjoyment and the avoidance of meaning.

Today in Washington "people talk about sex much more readily than religion ... a hundred years ago, sex was private, religion was public."[4] I am told if you "plug the word 'sex' into an internet search engine, you'll get over 72 million hits.... Search for the word 'God' and you get about 36 million websites. So sex beats God by a 2-1 margin." Some would say sex has become our ultimate concern. Ironically then, to borrow a definition from Paul Tillich, sex has become our surrogate religion. "The global offerings made to the little blue deity called Viagra soared to more than $1.3 billion in the year 2000."[6]

The Apostle Paul is prudent, but he is not a prude. He minces no words – shun fornication, adultery, prostitution, he says. He challenges us "to take sex seriously but to take our re-lationship to God even more seriously ... to have a close and intimate connection [with God] ...that rivals sexual intimacy in its closeness and intensity."[7] It is perhaps not accidental that the He-brew word to "know" God is the same verb that is used for sexual intercourse, meaning the most intimate and profound knowledge of another person possible.

Paul is not calling for censorship or the cessation of sex or insisting temptations should not be tolerated. He is simply say-ing that sensuality should not control us and that sex should not be self-destructive. Our body is not to be "shared with anyone who wants it, as though it were a snack to be passed around and enjoyed by all."[8] Sex is not for sport, for conquest or control of another, for self-gratification at the expense of someone else. Sex is not a substitute for love.

In this morning's newspaper I spied an ad for a medical group. The headline shouted "Sex for Life!" but it misspoke itself because the group of doctors was only promising "immediate re-sults" for men with various sexual dysfunctions, not for reenergiz-ing their love relationships.[9] It might have said what people need is not more sex in their lives, but more life in their sex. What does it mean to practice sex for life?[10]

I would argue that if we are honest, intuitively we often know what sex is not. What then does Paul propose we practice to affirm what it is? If our bodies are nothing less than "a temple of the Holy Spirit," as he says, then it is an organism wonderfully designed for wonderful purposes – and worthy of being protected from diseases and thoughtless self-destruction of all sorts. Sex is first of all unitive, capable of creating a loving union between partners which mirrors the loving union between Christ and his people, which breaks down barriers and draws different persons to become one in spirit. It can be the source of reconciliation that restores the broken relationships between people, something like God's seeking to heal our broken relations with him.

Second, of course sex is creative, allowing us to become cocreators with God, joining ourselves in marriage as "one flesh" to begin a new life together and to create a brand-new life out of that union. Few experiences can move us closer to the wonder, mystery, and awesomeness of life than participating in the conception and birth of a child.

Finally, Paul would not oppose the perception of sex as fun and funny, although he might substitute for that the term ecstatic. It keeps us from taking ourselves too seriously. Our awkward and antic behavior is accepted and affirmed in a loving and committed marriage of two persons – devotedly, delightfully, and deeply moving.

Whatever hang-ups we may impute to Paul, he presents us with a unity, creativity, and ecstasy that we won't find in the movies or the internet. And it is not rated NC (Non Committal) 17 or PG (Protected Generation) 13, but a grateful G, for Glorious — as God intended it.[11]

———

1. *Homiletics* 15, 1, p.30.
2. *Lectionary Homiletics* XIV, 1, p.58.
3. *Ibid.*
4. *Homiletics Ibid.*
5. *Homiletics.* pp.26-27.
6. *Ibid.*
7. *Ibid.*
8. *Homiletics* p.28.
9. *Homiletics* p.26.
10. *Homiletics* p.28
11. For Paul's "three points" I have adapted parts of the exposition in *Homiletics* from the commentary *Sex for Life*, p.28

SEX AND THE HOLY

2nd Sunday after the Epiphany
1 Cor. 6:12-20
Year B – January 15, 2006

I'm sure you are all dying to know that three years ago, apparently, I was the preacher on the second Sunday after Epiphany (this Sunday). And my sermon then was about sex and the gospel. I remember after the service someone challenged me, saying: "Well that was all right, but I wanted you to preach just about sex for our time." And I said, "you want me to get ridden out of the church on a pole?" Besides, I'm not qualified. As a teenager I wasn't a model for much of anything, sex included. On the contrary, at least in my fantasy, I was committed to the wayward path of excess in all things – it seemed my duty if I were to become a full human being (or at least that was my rationale at the time, full of blarney or something else).

Lord knows what must have saved me from my "full" self. And I had it easy then: sex was not socially acceptable the way it is now, and it wasn't wafted under my nose like a Snickers bar. Skirts were mid-calf length and you almost had to pay money to see a belly button. The church still spoke about the sin of self-gratification, and the raciest game I got to play then was called "Under the Blanket" (played in the dark), where when we got to be 11 or 12 and spin the bottle, you had to crawl under the ratty comforter in the boathouse and kiss whomever had been secretly

Brookfield turns on the charm.

chosen to sit and wait there for the winner (or loser) to find him or her. Frustrating, it was, filled with anticipation, trepidation, and little consummation.

I have been thinking back over the years since then, about all I missed and what I might have to say about it, if mostly to myself. When, lo and behold, I discovered that apparently the apostle Paul had been saving up his thoughts too, which he wanted to communicate to the wayward Corinthians, beginning with the byword "All things are lawful for me" — which made me sit up and take notice because that's right where I was (or wanted to be) as a teenager. I was also intrigued by his injunction "Shun fornication!" which if I had known what the word meant then, would have said "Why"?

So I am going to accept our parishioner's challenge and speak about sex without directly referring to the gospel — because that's where you come in. You've got to read the gospel into what I'm saying or you won't find it there this morning. I'm reluctant to remind you that it's there anyway even if, like Samuel, you don't at first choose to hear it, because the gospel is the good news we are all dying to hear — and it is in, with, and under all our undertakings whether we recognize it or not. Whether I succeed in that endeavor or not you can tell me later or ride me out on a pole. But I do have to begin by reminding you that sex is not a fourletter word; it is, in case we've forgotten, not the be and end of all things, but it is the beginning. You remember God told us in Genesis, when the world was new and all and we didn't yet get the full meaning of what it meant to be connected to all things: "Be fruitful and multiply and fill the earth and have dominion over it." We were hard of hearing even then, because we thought to "have dominion" (from the Latin dominus) must mean to dominate, to lord it over all things — forgetting that to be lord of someone or something meant to be responsible for it, to tend and keep it, to look after it.

That might have gotten us off on the wrong feet (biblically speaking), but that doesn't let us off the hook (to mangle the metaphor). Research tells us that when a television or print ad uses sex to promote its product, people remember the sex, but forget the product. "We use sex today ... [as] a way of expressing power. It is a vehicle for getting what we want. And just as we use sex, we use people to give us sex. We are turning into a nation of users... and our most intimate physical experiences have lost their beauty, their romance, their intimacy and their holiness."[1] Holiness. More about that later.

Philip Turner asks this question: "What is it that Christians ought to say and do about the issue of sexual relations between single people [or even among marrieds]? This question currently presses most painfully upon the life of the churches. The real issue is not whether the churches ought to adopt a new sexual ethic, but whether the new sexual ethic they are adopting is one that is 'worthy of (their) calling.'"[2]

Now, apart from specifically Christian concerns, a few definitions to consider: Holiness, to start with — except that I'm going to get to that in the end. Fornication, Paul's particular prohibition, which I as a teenager would have promptly managed to forget if I had ever known what it meant — not because it was forgettable but because I was so seldom faced with the opportunity for it. The word comes from the Greek porneia, which most often meant the practice of prostitution, exchanging sex for money, but which in the early church was also used to mean "unchastity." "The Hebrew term closest to the Greek porneia is zonah, which also includes general unfaithfulness as well as idolatrous worship"[3] (You see, it's difficult to get away from religion even if you're only endeavoring to talk about sex.) But in Paul's use of porneia in his letter to the Corinthians this morning, he is not poetically protesting the worship of other gods; he is speaking specifically about the practice of actual, not metaphorical, sexual wantonness.

Why? Was Paul a prude? By no means — at least not in this passage anyway. What he is pointing us to are the verses in Genesis, chapter 2, where the Hebrew speaks about a man and a woman becoming "one flesh" with each other. That term has a double meaning, which refers to the union between family groups as well as the physical union of two persons. He says "the one with whom you engage in sexual activity should by rights become a member of your family with all the attendant rights to shelter, support and protection that family relationships imply. To have casual sex, ... [results in] a great social injustice. [Because] It denies the women affected, and the [possible] children [of it] to a legal place within society... and the community, whose standard of love does not allow for disposable relationships between its members."[4]

Now we can pooh-pooh that of course, saying it smacks of an uptight, moralistic, defensive Jewish society deprived of sexual freedom and the morning after pill, which would have changed its point of view about the role and function of sex. But would it?

That would only have de-Pauled the prevailing positive perspective that "sexuality is essential to being human, the life force that creates passion.... Sexuality is the energy that fosters joy and openness and communication, the power to give and receive, the reaching out and the inviting in. In sexual expression is an image of and path to the holy."[5]

There's that word again: "holy," which does not imply "holier than thou" — quite the opposite. It comes from the same root as the words for whole(ness) and heal(ing). Holy(ness) is the expression that "to be in touch with our sexuality is to [affirm] our wholeness. Whether you are in a physical relationship or not, sexuality is that part of us through which we reach out to other persons and to God, [by] expressing the need for relationship, for the sharing of self and of meaning with another."[6]

... we like definitions to be uncomplicated, straightforward, and self-defining.

That may be too messy an explanation for us (or sound too theological) for some of us simple thinkers; we like definitions to be uncomplicated, straightforward, and self-defining. But the truth of it is, that's the way we were made if we want to be fully human and not at the expense of our fellow human beings in the process. In becoming "one flesh" with another person we have become part of one another – physically part of one another's bodies, but also a part of the human family which understands that "the gift of your body is not something to be given away recklessly ... not to be shared with anyone who wants it, as though it were a snack to be passed around and enjoyed by all"[7] – that's holy unacceptable.

It may be that some of us (maybe a lot of us) still like to think "All things are lawful for me," especially if we have decided we are at the moment safely God-less or religion-less. But there is a law innate in the creation of human relationships that trumps our attempts to use them for our own satisfaction, to be a law only unto ourselves. Some would say it's not a law at all, but a lure. I'll not say who said it (except to say that it's not Hugh Heffner), but you can probably figure it out for yourself: "Love, then do what you will" is the way it is usually quoted. But the Latin can also be translated: "Love, then what you will, do." That may not be gospel, wholly or otherwise – but of course you could complain it certainly smacks of it.

_____

1. *Homiletics.* 15, 1, p.29
2. *Ibid.*
3. *Op. cit., p.28.*
4. *Op. cit., p.29*
5. *Ibid.*
6. *Ibid.*
7. *Op. cit., p.28*

"BORN AGAIN" IN CARITAS

5th Sunday after the Epiphany
Matthew 5:13-20
Year A – February 7, 1999

> *Jesus said, "You are the light of the world. A city set upon a hill cannot be hid. No one after lighting a lamp puts it under a bushel basket, but on a lampstand, and it gives light to all in the house. In like manner, let your light so shine before others, that they may see your good works and give glory to your Father in heaven.*
>
> *Matthew 5:14-16*

There is a story in me that wants out – a sermon of sorts, which I am going to call "Born Again" in Caritas, as unlikely as those words may sound coming from me.

I haven't forgotten what I have said to you before, that in the Episcopal Church at least, giving a title to your sermon is gauche, tacky, even theologically a no-no – and for good reason. To title a sermon is to say this is a speech or dramatic presentation or a literary piece, not a proclamation of the gospel – which is unfinished and ongoing and a living witness. But since exceptions are sometimes made in order to preserve the rule, I am going to risk reaping a reputation for being tacky or theologically inept – I hope, for good reason, and partly out of being partial to puns which are potentially powerful.

Caritas, as you may know, is an acronym for Congregations Around Richmond Involved To Assure Shelter. St. Mary's is one of the churches in this area that helps provide a place to sleep, food, and clothing for some of the homeless people, and our turn came the second week in January. Caritas is, of course, also the Latin word for love, so that Born Again in Caritas need not be a special name for a particular type of Christian involved in a mission to the homeless – but simply the reality of being born again in love in a way that may be special but which touches a universal experience we all could name. I'll let you be the judge in this case.

I'd never been in Caritas at St. Mary's before this year, and I asked Nancy Ritter the naive question, "Could I be of any help on the Thursday evening which is a free night for me?" By then of course, most everything was planned and taken care of, but Nancy said, "If you want to show up and help with the evening meal, we might be able to use an extra pair of hands." So I asked, "Should I wear my collar or come incognito?" Nancy smiled, "If you come, someone might want you just for your collar."

I showed up in my clericals, except that I wore my brand new Donegal Irish tweed greenish sport jacket; I didn't want to be in black for the occasion. As I suspected, the evening's events were superbly organized, and I watched with my hands in my pockets while the grace was given by the guests and the dinner deftly served by dozens of people. Finally, when folks gathered at the piano to sing old gospel hymns, I found I could do something, add an enthusiastic bass.

I was just getting into the singing when I was tapped on the arm: "Someone wants you to pray with him." I was led down the hall toward the transept door where a person was awaiting me – striking, a black man in a black wool hat, with black jacket and pants, leaning heavily on a black cane. "Come with me," he said.

"Wait, what is your name?" I asked. "Nathanael," he said.

"What a name!" I replied. "It means 'God has given' – why were you named that?"

"I don't know," he smiled. "What's your name?" "Christopher," I said, "which means 'Christ bearer'."

"Father Christopher," he declared.

"Whatever you say," I replied. "I've been called a lot of things."

"You the right man," he said decisively, grabbing hold of my hand and literally pulling me into the church.

I thought to myself as I was being pulled along, that's what a lot of my younger years had been like, being dragged into the church, God always wanting me to be somewhere I wasn't.

When we reached the prayer desk beside the lectern, he pulled me down next to him on my knees on the cushion where only one person was intended to kneel, grunting as he released his cane, letting it fall to the floor, "There," he said. I had to put my arm around him because there was room for only one of my knees on the cushion; I was holding on to him to keep from falling over. It was then I noticed how pervasively bad he smelled, but it was clear we were wedged together kneeling to stay.

"What shall we pray?" I asked. He looked at me quizzically, "You the preacher," he said. "Pray for my leg, it pains bad." So I prayed, thanksgiving for warmth and food, for friends and shelter from the dark and cold, for help and healing – for him and for me.

And then we kept silence together.

"Why am I shaking?" he asked after a bit.

"Maybe it's because you hurt. Or because God is in you," I ventured, "It might be a good sign." He pointed to a Hymnal: "Read me some scripture," he said, "I can't read."

"Well, we sing out of that one," I said, but the Eucharist Lectionary readings book was on the shelf below; so I lifted it up, flipped it open, and began to read from the page that lay before us. The text happened to be Jesus' parable about sowing wheat and the unwanted tares. Don't try to pull out the tares while the grain is ripening, but let both grow together; and when it is time for the harvest, the tares can be weeded out and burned in the fire.

When I stopped reading, he started shaking again: "That's me, I'm the tares that's going to be burned!" "But how do you know you're the tares, Nathanael?" I asked. "I'm a terrible sinner," he said. "Baptize me."

"Have you ever been baptized?" I asked. "I think so, when I was little," he said. "Then I can't baptize you" I replied.

"Why not?" he asked.

"Because being baptized is indelible, once for all, Nathanael; you only do it one time," I answered.

"You the third preacher says I can't be baptized," he said, "but I'm a terrible sinner."

"You don't have to be baptized to be forgiven, Nathanael," I assured him.

"But I'm not sure I really was baptized, my mother only told me, I need to feel baptized. Why won't you baptize me?" he pleaded. He was in anguish, and the silence that followed implored me.

I remembered the part of the Prayer Book that provides for provisional baptism, called "Conditional," so I said, "O.K., Nathanael. I have to go get some water and a Prayer Book." He smiled broadly and started out of the transept toward the kitchen. After I had moved the baptismal font and filled a pitcher with water and secured a Prayer Book and all was ready, Nathanael was not there. So I went to see whether he really intended to go through with it. He had gone back to his cot in the parish hall, changed into his best shirt (a flaming red turtle neck), smoothed back his matted hair, and was coming down the hall toward me – followed by a small band of some other homeless companions he had asked to come and be with him.

When we reentered the church, the choir was in process of practice in the loft, loudly; the music melodious and haunting, but also halting and distracting. I wondered whether we would be able to hear the words of the service; but here was an unplanned, unvarnished, and unpretentious accompaniment which seemed appropriate for the occasion. Besides, I can shout.

Our parishioners Mary Moore and Virginia Patterson had come from the kitchen to join the little group. I was thankful because they could help people find the right pages and follow the service in the Prayer Book. I hoped some in the gathering could read, and I assumed I could exclude what was inessential for this impromptu immersion.

After offering the opening sentences of the service, I suddenly realized I couldn't remember where to find the collect for Baptism, so I made one up. I didn't think God would mind. And since some scripture had already been spoken, I went straight to the baptismal questions. I said to Nathanael, "I'm going to ask you six questions in this service and never mind what's in this book, just answer them as best you can with your own words. He nodded. All of you are probably familiar with those questions – you've heard them spoken in so many services here.[1] But as I addressed them to Nathanael, it seemed as though they were new; this was for real and he was ready for them. To each one he answered simply, "Yes," with his own conviction. "Do you renounce the evil powers of this world which corrupt and destroy the creatures of God?" and "Do you turn to Jesus Christ and accept him as your Saviour?" and so on. They did not sound ancient and arcane; it seemed as though they were made for this moment.

When it came time for the water, I asked Nathanael to pour it high up and with a joyful splash, which he delighted in doing. Then he leaned over the font, trying to put his head in it. "Just stand tall," I said, "the water will come to you." And it did, as I said to him, "If you have not already been baptized Nathanael, I baptize you in the name of the Father, and of the Son, and of the Holy Spirit." So he was sealed by the Holy Spirit and marked as Christ's own forever – and you should have seen how he beamed while some of his friends wept. And when we passed the peace, everybody hugged everybody. (My description may sound a little hokey, but I at least was very moved by what went on there.)

"I need a new haircut. Who will cut my hair?" He looked back at me. "I don't do scissors," I said, but that didn't slow him down.

When all the hugging was finally finished, Nathanael marched boldly toward the kitchen. "I'm born again, I've got a new life," he said, "I need a new haircut. Who will cut my hair?" He looked back at me. "I don't do scissors," I said, but that didn't slow him down.

I followed after him, carrying the cane and hat he had left behind on the floor by the font. And we all rejoiced, the tears glad and full of gratitude; surely something had happened that was more than the words we had spoken in his service, and more than one life had been changed.

That night I thought I needed to have my new coat thoroughly cleaned, but I've decided against it. I want the smell of Nathanael with me to remind me of that time and of so much of the world that I have missed. Nathanael would have said of that Thursday evening, he was born again in Caritas, in love – and even I can understand that, and I have no problem with those words. In fact, they seem just right.

*　　*　　*

There is an epilogue to this story. Some will say it's the sermon part, but I would say that's already been spoken. Later, in the book at St. Mary's where we keep track of the services we hold and how many people come to them (so we can report them accurately to the Diocese), I had to squeeze in Nathanael's between two others already recorded. I wrote down the number "fifteen" for those who were there; there had to have been twelve, the holy number of God's people.

Only the name Nathanael is written in the book; no one knew his last name. But I'm sure that's good enough for him – it's his Christian name – and it was more than good enough for me to do what was important to be done, and no doubt good enough for God: after all, Nathanael is what God has given – to him and to us.

———

1. *Book of Common Prayer*, pp.302-3

WHAT IS WORTH FRYING YOURSELF FOR?

5th Sunday after the Epiphany
Mark 1:29-39
Year B – February 6, 2000

And immediately Jesus left the synagogue, and entered the house of Simon and Andrew, with James and John. Now Simon's mother-in-law lay sick with a fever, and immediately they told him of her. And he came and took her by the hand and lifted her up, and the fever left her; and she served them.

That evening, at sundown, they brought to him all who were sick or possessed with demons. And the whole city was gathered together about the door. And he healed many who were sick with various diseases, and cast out many demons; and he would not permit the demons to speak, because they knew him.

And in the morning, a great while before day, he rose and went out to a lonely place, and there he prayed. And Simon and those who were with him followed him, and they found him and said to him, "Everyone is searching for you." And he said to them, "Let us go on to the next towns, that I may preach there also; for that is why I came out." And he went throughout all Galilee, preaching in their synagogues and casting out demons.

Mark 1:29-39, RSV

At first glance today's gospel reading does not appear well suited to this occasion in the Church Year, which has been designated Theological Education Sunday. Jesus' casting out the unclean spirits of "all who were sick or possessed with demons," as Mark describes it, doesn't seem like the most propitious passage to persuade us of the power of divine wisdom. However, on second thought, it does tell us about what matters, what is life-giving, and thereby perhaps what is worth knowing – and that may be worth more than reminding us of all the knowledge we have yet to learn, sacred or profane.

Our proposal to start a new school here at St. Mary's, which we are busily trying to bring about, may be the most appropriate response to Theological Education Sunday we have thought up yet. A fitting motto might be the venerable Ea discamus in terris quorum scientia perseveret in coelis: Teach us those things on earth, the knowledge of which endures in heaven. But that may be too high-falutin' for us who are looking for an education leading to a more immediate outcome, such as how we can prepare our children for kindergarten. So I'll try to explore the question "What is worth knowing?" in nonacademic language with a little help from Don Marquis and Robert Penn Warren.

Don Marquis, in his charming stories about the unusual friendship between a cockroach and a cat, includes this poignant passage in the conversation between archy and mehitabel, where archy the imaginative insect is asking what even to a cockroach is a question of ultimate concern (to invoke Paul Tillich's term for the religious quest) – namely (in archy's language), "What is worth frying yourself for?" This little piece is called "the lesson of the moth":

> *i was talking to a moth*
> *the other evening*
> *he was trying to break into*
> *an electric light bulb*
> *and fry himself on the wires*
> *why do you fellows*
> *pull this stunt i asked him*
> *because it is the conventional*

thing for moths or why
if that had been an uncovered candle
instead of an electric
light bulb you would
now be a small unsightly cinder
have you no sense
plenty of it he answered
but at times we get tired
of using it
we get bored with the routine
and crave beauty
and excitement
fire is beautiful
and we know that if we get
too close it will kill us
but what does that matter
it is better to be happy
for a moment
and be burned up with beauty
than to live a long time
and be bored all the while
so we wad all our life up
into one little roll
and then we shoot the roll
that is what life is for
it is better to be a part of beauty
for one instant and then cease to
exist than to exist forever
and never be a part of beauty
our attitude toward life
is come easy go easy
we are like human beings
used to be before they became
too civilized to enjoy themselves
and before i could argue
him out of his philosophy
he went and immolated himself
on a patent cigar lighter
i do not agree with him
myself i would rather have
half the happiness and twice
the longevity
but at the same time i wish
there was something i wanted
as badly as he wanted to fry himself

"What is worth frying yourself for?" may not sound to you like a theological question, but in educational terms it is the ultimate question. Or rather, it questions the ultimate end of education: Is there any thing worth risking your life to know?

In another vein, in his novel All the King's Men, author Robert Penn Warren explores an answer tailor-made for Theological Education Sunday, which he expresses this way:

> "...when you come home late at night and see the yellow envelope of the telegram sticking out from under your door and you lean and pick it up, but, don't open it yet, not for a second...the clammy, sad little foetus which is you way down in the dark which is you too...shivers cold inside you for it doesn't want to know what is in that envelope. It wants to lie in the dark and not know, and be warm in its not-knowing. The end of man is knowledge, but there is one thing he can't know. He can't know whether knowledge will save him or kill him. He will be killed, all right, but he can't know whether he is killed because of the knowledge which he has got or because of the knowledge which he hasn't got and which if he had it, would save him. There's the cold in your stomach, but you open the envelope, you have to open the envelope, for the end of man is to know."

Something about that explanation uplifts me, but at the same time it spooks me. The knowledge Robert Penn Warren is talking about is not the garden variety rational cognitive we usually settle for in our schools (public or private) it is saving knowledge, so to speak – something that could make a difference between life and death.

"The end of man is to know," he writes, "but there is one thing he can't know. He can't know whether knowledge will save him or kill him." Then, of all the terrible things, he adds, "He will be killed all right, but he can't know whether he is killed because of the knowledge which he has got or because of the knowledge which he hasn't got and which if he had it, would save him."

We are used to the idea in education that the increase of knowledge is a good thing, but theological education asks, "What kind of knowledge is worth knowing?" We presume that what we call higher education is necessary as well as beneficial for our survival in life. But some years ago Professor Grant at Michigan State University published his research on the question "What are the advantages of going to college?" And he reported that college students have fifty per cent more mental and emotional problems than the general public, that there are twice as many suicides among college students as among the general population, and that there is little or no correlation between grades in college and success in later life.

Which returns us to the question: What is it that is really worth knowing (let alone the cost of tuition)? Getting back to Robert Penn Warren's passage, I would like to add to the end of it: if the end of man is to know; it is also to be known – which just might be the difference between being killed and being saved.

Persons who are new to educational institutions, including our church, are not the only ones who need to be known. Each of us hungers to be known truly for what and who we are. We long to break the uncomfortable silence that surrounds the lives of people with whom we may be all too familiar but whom we really do not know – the strangers we sit next to in church, or work with on committees, or maybe even eat with from time to time because occasions put us together. Lives who ought otherwise to know each other but are hidden behind our faces, wrapped round with silence – or noise – unless one of us breaks in upon another with some word or wordless cry of pain that means "Know me." Then darkness no longer broods upon the face of my face; a word has been spoken that calls someone into being, into life – a person has been created.

"...Chit-chat games in which 'How are you?' means 'Don't tell me who you are!' and 'I'm alone and scared' becomes 'fine thanks'."

Maybe the knowledge we all hunger for, what we really want to know (even when we don't know it), is how to make ourselves known and to know one another. For without that mutual knowledge, we cannot be healed and forgiven by each other. Otherwise, as my friend has put it, "With words as valueless as poker chips, we play games whose object is to keep us from seeing each other's cards. Chit-chat games in which 'How are you?' means 'Don't tell me who you are!' and 'I'm alone and scared' becomes 'fine thanks'." (Buechner, Alphabet: p.58)

We often forget that in the beginning of all things created was the word that God lent us; that most holy and ancient miracle that gives life, that summons me to be, of all things, myself; that healing word which is sometimes only spoken by listening to someone else; that word which becomes inexplicably the means whereby our hearts are opened, our desires known, and in whose presence no secrets are hid, as the Prayer Book puts it.

To say it in the language of worship, we come together as pilgrims from many places, from afar. We come with a variety of names and in various disguises to a center of life, which is us here and now. We have come to be together in a place where we can confess that we do not always search out and embrace the need and shadow in one another's lives; that in this we find we are not alone; that sometimes the words we have spoken to each other are exactly the words we would not want to have spoken to us, or that the words we have neglected to speak to one another are precisely the ones we most need to hear spoken to us.

Maybe the deeper knowledge we are all searching for, often by another name, is finally the presence of God, which we know through one another. So in seeking that being within ourselves and others, we approach the mystery of all being, which is where religion and education find their common being. Where if the end of man is to know, it is also to be known; where to speak the healing word is also to be healed; where the knowledge we seek may someday, when the chips are down, turn out to be the knowledge of someone or something we would be willing to live and die for, which would be in a word, *what is worth frying yourself for.*

I would like to leave you with a piece that was written for us in one of the Education for Ministry sessions during the time for worship. Mary Alice Beck wanted to say what was important, what was in her heart, in hard times:

Holes in the Heart
A Prayer

Father, sometimes it feels like we have holes in our hearts.
Someone dies, or moves away,
And we are left with a hole.
Other people disappoint us.
Life disappoints us.
More holes.
We disappoint ourselves with our own failures.
It's too hard to be the people we want to be,
And that causes the biggest hole of all.
Let us remember that the holes are there for all of us who love.
The loving is not wrong,
And the holes are part of living. Please fill these holes with Your love.
Show us the joy that comes where we least expect it
When Your love flows through us.
Give us full hearts,
In spite of the holes.
Amen.

ON THE SENSIBILITY OF KEEPING SILENT

(A practice practically impossible for preachers)

The Last Sunday after the Epiphany
Luke 9:28-36
Year C – February 25, 2001

About eight days after Peter had acknowledged Jesus as the Christ of God, Jesus took with him Peter and John and James, and went up on the mountain to pray. And while he was praying, the appearance of his face changed, and his clothes became dazzling white. Suddenly they saw two men, Moses and Elijah, talking to him. They appeared in glory and were speaking of his departure, which he was about to accomplish at Jerusalem. Now Peter and his companions were weighed down with sleep; but since they had stayed awake, they saw his glory and the two men who stood with him. Just as they were leaving him, Peter said to Jesus, "Master, it is good for us to be here; let us make three dwellings, one for you, one for Moses, and one for Elijah" – not knowing what he said. While he was saying this, a cloud came and overshadowed them; and they were terrified as they entered the cloud. Then from the cloud came a voice that said, "This is my Son, my Chosen; listen to him!" When the voice had spoken, Jesus was found alone. And they kept silent and in those days told no one any of the things they had seen.

Luke 9:28-36

It is only appropriate after all, that on this the last Sunday of Epiphany our lectionary lays upon us one last lulu of an epiphany to expand our expectations even as we are led reluctantly toward Lent. As you may know, the word epiphany is formed from epi, meaning forth or upon, and phany, meaning to show or manifest: To show forth the phany of Theos or God. A mouthful; and in this case, a sight for sore eyes – so much so that even Moses is afforded only a glimpse of the backside of God's glory, for it was well known in Hebrew wisdom that no one may come face-to-face with God and live. Human beings can tolerate only so much of divine communication. Constant communion is overwhelming; we cannot bear it.

Luke expounds the experience (as we express it) of Jesus' "Transfiguration," a term testifying to an occasion or act of being changed in form or appearance, an exultation defying our explanation, where scripture says his face shone like the sun and his clothes were dazzling white. This incident occurred, as our text tells us, "after about eight days, when Jesus took with him Peter, James, and John and went up on a high mountain apart to pray." What mountain, we do not know (it is unnamed), where the appearance of his countenance was altered and his garments glistened. There, appeared to them Moses and Elijah; and as Luke says, although the disciples' eyes were heavy with sleep, "they saw his glory." What a story! And what are we to do with it? This is one of the most remarkable and least remarked upon events in the life of Jesus, an experience attested to by all three synoptic gospels, and yet the Transfiguration appears to play almost no role in the rest of Jesus' ministry or in the unfolding understanding of his disciples. In fact, it is almost as if the church seems more uncomfortable claiming the occasion of this miracle than it does all the other significant events we speak about but are at a loss to explain. If not causing an embarrassment for the early church, the Transfiguration continues an enigma, for them and for us. No one knows what really happened there; only that Jesus and three of his close disciples climbed a mountain and entered the presence of God. So wondrous and radiant was that mystical moment that years later Peter could not escape the afterglow of it (cf. 2

Peter 1:15). Whatever else, it was for those present a personal and private spiritual experience, such that for us words fail or even increase our inability to understand it. Simply said, "they saw his glory." What more could we say, what more would we want?

Maybe at this moment it would be fair for me to confess before going further, that I find the Transfiguration difficult and frustrating, almost impossible to understand in any familiar fashion. It flies in the face of belief – at least in any literal sense of believing. It sounds to me similar to the story of Jesus walking on the water. One writer presents the problem this way: "I know, and you know, that people don't all of a sudden start glowing like a light bulb with voices booming from heaven while the ghosts of [heroes] appear [out of the ether]." My rational response is to reject this story – which may well be the point. Because it is not a story of fact but of faith. "It introduces us to a God who cannot be explained, a God who only can be experienced."[1]

If one can say it this way, the story is "in fact a myth – not in terms of make believe, but a symbolic story that leads us beyond the confines of our rational knowing into the world of spiritual knowing... a world we do not create or control, a world which, instead, creates us."[2] And one which asks us interesting, even intimate questions, leading us to consider candidly not whether we would want to have a mountain top experience, but asking when do we take time to get away from whatever claims our regular commitments to consider intentionally seeking out God? "Do we even believe that God is there to be found?"

Talking about the Transfiguration in temporal or tangible terms can be tricky.

Do we, like the disciples, dodge the discipline of personal prayer – unable or unwilling to dig deeply into the mystery unless it is manifest to us directly? Do we do what they do when something unthinkable happens? – in the midst of the mysterious try to make sense of, to make it fit what we know, to categorize and quantify it, to reason it to death? How do we handle the possibility that the holy can inhabit the human, that the extraordinary can enter the ordinary? Not easily, I expect.

Talking about the Transfiguration in temporal or tangible terms can be tricky. But while words may fail us in explaining a profound event, maybe that might be the start of a spiritual experience which can survive our insistence on understanding it. We do not have to talk the life out of an experience to recognize the reality of it. Maybe when we know we don't know, the mystery itself will endure. "Sometimes the most significant, substantive and spiritual thing we can do is to say nothing." Nowhere I know of is it written that even in faith we will suddenly see all, know all, and be able to expound our spiritual experience. No doubt there are times when God does not speak, "when God has nothing to say, when God is silent – either waiting for us to ask or waiting for us to grow in wisdom" in our silence."[3]

What the Transfiguration story asks us to accept is that it was not something the disciples conjured out of their imaginations, not something they did; it happened to them. They simply saw the glory of God (if one can say such a thing simply). Barbara Brown Taylor tells us: "What we are asked to believe is that at certain moments in time, the glory of God is visible.... But we are also asked to believe in the glory even when we cannot and do not see it.... We live in the hope that glory may [yet] happen to us, or at least ... so we can [come close enough to] see it. We may also have to live in a world where all we have is the story of glory happening to [someone else]. Such is the struggle and challenge of faith."[4]

Time for Silence. Christopher Brookfield walks with Bishop Robert Bruce Hall (left) on the day of John's ordination as deacon. The Rev. Holt Souder rings the bell of Little St. Mary's at the appointed hour.

Before the mystery of it all we are left only with our blasted or our blessed silence. The same silence we sometimes keep when we come for communion – to commune and companion God's presence – where our summons is not to make sense of it but simply to receive the bread and the wine, to take Christ into us, so that in his absence he literally lives on in us. Something so sacredly inexplicable that silence is the only sound that makes sense of the mystery. Maybe that explains why, as Luke tells it, the disciples did not do what we might have expected of them after their mountain-top epiphany. For as they descended to the destiny that awaited them down below, at the foot of their peak experience, scripture says they "kept silent" and "told no one any of the things they had seen." How could they communicate what they were caught up in to those who weren't there? How to communicate cognitively our communion with God? It isn't sufficient to say, "You should have been there."

Our task is not to speak, but to respond as though God is still with us, to respond to people that cross our path with the presence of God we are empowered to share. Sometimes that means offering a kindness to someone whose life has been shattered, or responding to an inner urge to change the direction of our lives, or transfiguring our understanding of what is valuable to pass on to our children and so worth trying to change the world – with the wisdom and wonder of one small silence at a time.

———

1. *Lectionary Homiletics XII*, 3-p.30)
2. *Ibid.*
3. *Homiletics 7, 1-p.36*
4. *Lectionary Homiletics XII, 3-p.29*

WHERE THERE'S A WILL, THERE'S A WAY

I Corinthians 15:35-38, 42-50; Luke 6:27-38
February 23, 1992

Two tough texts this morning. Try as I would, I could not will them away!

In 1st Corinthians, Paul says: "I tell you this ... flesh and blood cannot inherit the kingdom of God; the perishable does not inherit the imperishable."

In Luke's Gospel, Jesus says to his disciples, "I say to you ... Love your enemies, do good to those who hate you, bless those who curse you, pray for those who abuse you..." And so on.

It may take will power to listen to the lessons appointed for today.

If our task in the first half of life is devoted to building up our ego, the last half is dedicated to letting it go. If the first half of life is consumed with learning how to live, the last half is concerned with learning how to die. In our youth we would say, "where there's a will, there's a way."

In our old age, when there may no longer be a way, we can say there is at least a legal will. It may be difficult to die without a written will; it is almost impossible to live without a willing heart.

Set side by side, in scripture and in life, are the material and the spiritual – the financial need of having a will to save what we cannot preserve, and the spiritual need of having a willing heart to preserve the quality of life which we cannot save. OR, to say it more succinctly: the ungraspable Gospel set alongside the grip of "Grits, Grats, and Gruts."[1]

I want to make it clear that I have not pestered an estate planner in preparing this pitch. Neither have I been needled into this annunciation by John Miller or Wally Stettinius. If this turns out to be a misguided ministry to mediate money and meaning, I alone am the miscreant.

I begin with the assumption that "We should not disparage wealth and possessions. There are many things money cannot buy, but there are some things money can buy. Church treasurers know this better than anyone. A story tells of a wealthy parishioner who was dying. His pastor had spent many hours working on the parishioner to give his life to God – to no avail. Now the time had come for the affluent parishioner to meet his maker. 'Do you think if I left my entire estate to the church' he asked the pastor, 'it would guarantee me entrance to heaven?' The pastor thought for a long while, struggled with himself, and then said, 'It's worth a try.'"

When Paul says "The perishable does not inherit the imperishable," he means "You can't take it with you." Estate planning may not be the sole means of building up God's kingdom, but it can put whatever is left of our kingdom to work in God's service and at the same time, survive the grim reaper of taxes.

"Grits (Grantor retained Income Trusts), Grats (Grantor retained Annuity Trusts), and Gruts (Grantor retained Unitrusts) allow you to write your will so that charities and churches can receive generous contributions at the same time you leave your assets to heirs, keep control of your resources, and drastically reduce gift and estate taxes." Which is another way of saying, "It is more deductible to give than to receive."

I am told there is a "new PC software called 'Willmaker' which allows anyone to prepare a will without a lawyer in less than 30 minutes." That may not be thrifty; and I would not want to suggest it is wise to will your wherewithal to anyone without benefit of a lawyer, but I am suggesting that worthwhile work to consider is including the church in your will. After all, it is said that God loves a willing giver.

To those of us who can't rely on having a great deal left over at life's end, Grits, Grats and Gruts may seem an illicit use, or abuse, by individuals whose bank accounts are more developed than their sense of responsibility and benevolence. But they do open a way for mammon and meaning to commingle. How could we have the St. Mary's which is before us (that is to say, in front of us) if we had not been given that St. Mary's which is behind us (the St. Mary's which is here)? Given to the glory of God, Grits, Grats and Gruts become gifts of grace that enable us to serve others as well as give to God.

Now, to the other interpretation of the word "will": "I say to you: Love your enemies and do good to those who hate you." Jesus commands us to love, to will the good of another, even if it may be to our own immediate disadvantage. What sense is there in that? To will our love, even to those who are unworthy of it? Jesus holds up to us a willing heart as an asset to life, this one or the next – a love we may not want, a love which we can only will.

I don't know about you, but I am more likely to act out of my physical being than my spiritual being because my physical needs are more present to me. Material and financial needs for survival and status often come first. Jesus' injunction to servanthood, to love those who hate us, to pray for those who persecute us, somehow seem last on the list, if not ludicrous. It requires will power to reverse our priorities. If that is what Jesus meant by a willing heart, it is a lot harder to offer up than a generous bequest.

Only intentional acts of the will enable us to give without expecting anything in return. And these are learned only through patience and practice – whether in weeding the garden, memorizing the periodic table of chemical elements, or learning to play the piano or some other musical instrument. The task, a friend told me last Thursday, is not to learn to work at what you love to do, but to learn to love what you have to work at. Each of us may be given a spiritual self, but it will not develop until we have a heart to will it in the midst of hard choices:

> A seeker after truth came to a saint for guidance.
>
> *"Tell me please, wise one, how did you become holy?"*
> *"Two words."*
> *"And what are they, please?"*
> *"Right choices."*
> *"And how does one learn to choose correctly?"*
> *"One word."*
> *"May I know it, please?"*
> *"Growth."*
> *"How does one grow?"*
> *"Two words."*
> *"What are those words, pray tell me?"*
> *"Wrong choices."*

(As cited by William Boggs, *Sin Boldly: But Trust God More Boldly Still*)

Where a willing heart intersects with a winsome will is where both require a willful act, one that reflects the condition of the heart. My former Bishop, Bob Hall, said "What people don't even understand until they do it, is that giving of their money (just as in giving of themselves) is fun! But giving is a learned habit – one that we have to will, over against our willful habits to the contrary." Giving gives us the greatest freedom, more than over what we most fear to give up. But that freedom is not something we just find; we have to will it.

The way to will it may well not be through will power – but through will prayer. How else could we be willing to give up what it is we really think we have control over?

Will you join me in a prayer attributed to St. Francis:

Lord make us instruments of your peace.
Where there is hatred, let us sow love;
where there is injury, pardon;
where there is discord, union;
where there is doubt, faith;
where there is despair, hope;
where there is darkness, light;
where there is sadness, joy.
Grant that we may not so much seek to be consoled as to
        console;
to be understood as to understand;
to be loved as to love.
For it is in giving that we receive;
it is in pardoning that we are pardoned;
and it is in dying that we are born to eternal life.

Amen.

––––––

1. This device and several other quotations shamelessly stolen from Help and Hints in *Homeletics*.

RAT THIS DOWN

The Last Sunday after the Epiphany
Mark 9:2-9
Year B – March 2, 2003

> *Six days later, Jesus took with him Peter and James and John, and led them up a high mountain apart, by themselves. And he was transfigured before them, and his clothes became dazzling white, such as no one on earth could bleach them. And there appeared to them Elijah with Moses, who were talking with Jesus. Then Peter said to Jesus, "Rabbi, it is good for us to be here; let us make three booths, one for you, one for Moses, and one for Elijah." He did not know what to say, for they were terrified. Then a cloud overshadowed them, and from the cloud there came a voice, "This is my Son, the Beloved; listen to him!" Suddenly when they looked around, they saw no one with them any more, but only Jesus.*

> *Mark 9:2-8*

Long a New Englander, when I first heard the country hit "Rat" This Down I didn't immediately understand what the words meant. I soon came to realize that song is one Southern way of a guy's trying to tell his wife what's important. If she writes (rats) it down, he thinks, she won't forget it. Not a bad suggestion for Bible Study, if you can get with the quaint way of saying it.

I listen to Country 99.7 on the radio when I drive from Charlottesville to St. Mary's in the morning, and although I lived in New York and New Hampshire for my first 39 years, 99.7 can sometimes change the way I think and even the way I speak. Take for instance the scene described in this morning's reading from Mark. I want to tell you, that passage is Wahld – this Transfiguration thaing. You got to get "into it" in order to get it.

Mark's story is not quite what you'd call a Jewish Western – there's no shoot-out. But there sure is a shoot down: Jesus gives it to Peter rat between the eyes: Can't "build three booths" here Pedro, he says in effect, you got to walk with me back down the mountain into the valley, the shadow of death not withstanding – and there's plenty of that waiting for us. There's also more to the story of course, that's just for starters – and that's the first thing you've got to rat down.

Today is Transfiguration Sunday, and I wonder how many of us came here this morning expecting – or willing – to be transformed. That's what transfiguration means, after all: an act, process or instance of changing or being changed, of undergoing spiritual transformation. I would guess that's not on many persons' agenda today – but that's what the gospel reading is all about, whether we like it or not.

In plain speaking, of what use to us is this strange tale told on top of an unnamed mountain that doesn't even fit the location where the text tells us Jesus and his disciples were geographically? And just how literally are we to take this passage? And does it matter? – or to put it more bluntly, Do we care? Maybe we can make more sense of it if we think back over our own adventures. When was the last time you had a mountain-top encounter with ... whatever? A "peak experience," as Maslow expressed it? And what happened to you after it was over? Was your life left the same? Or was it somehow changed?

Joseph Campbell, the celebrated comparative mythologist, said the greatest peak experiences he had were when he was a star runner for Columbia University. On a couple of occasions, as anchor in a relay, running far behind in the track meet, he was suddenly overcome with the conviction that he knew he was going to win; he became "fearless" in the face of what seemed insurmountable odds and dazzled everyone, ran a "perfect" race – inspired, unbeatable.

Now in Mark's narrative, the Greek word we translate as "transfigured" does not mean merely changed, it is more of a metamorphosis; not a mere "flood of glory" from without, but an inner effulgence, a change of heart from within. Pretty poetic picture. Of course, we could say that Mark's story is simply all symbolic; it was only intended to call our attention to an inward awakening among the disciples, and the voice from the cloud was just a way of announcing the urgency of the intense visionary state they shared. Strange speculations and crazy biblical commentaries abound about it, trying to explain it. But does it really matter? It's doubtful that the author could have clearly articulated what really happened anyway – it was that exciting! We are left to conjure, if not construct the situation for ourselves.

The Transfiguration takes us up a "high mountain" and shows us Jesus shining in unearthly white; words fail to convey the brilliance of the light from his garments. Some translations say "as snow," or "as no fuller could have bleached them," a garment of glory – the disciples dazzled, left dumbfounded. Except for Peter, of course, who utters his clumsy and ineffable, if memorable, "Let us make three booths." But all that in Mark, to mangle the metaphor, is no more than a smoke screen. It conceals from us the first consequence of transfiguration: The transformation of our understanding of God's way apart from our expectations of authority and power, giving them up on the mountain for the insistence of the valley below that summons Jesus to suffer in the service of those he loves.

No wonder Peter didn't want to leave the safety of the summit.

Peter, who was to embody the church, wanted to preserve the experience, enshrine the elation, freeze it forever. But, as

Raymond Anderson explains it, "When the church focuses on institutionalizing and memorializing its bases and buildings, [booths] 'tabernacles' [or temples] to the past, it is not [willing] to follow Christ"[1] who consciously chose to swap the safety of the ethereal heights for life among us ordinary people in our struggles and sufferings in the world beneath.

Imagine the disappointment of the disciples who, after this astounding epiphany, find themselves alone with Jesus, the meeting with Moses and Elijah over, the voice from the cloud concluded, eyeing one another anxiously, eager to avoid the aftermath and escape his invitation to accompany him back down the mountain into the ordinariness of the everyday.

Not to pick on Peter particularly, or only abjure James and John, like most of Jesus' disciples, we are masters at seeing and hearing only what we want, at screening out events and other people when they are at odds with our expectations, at creating our own reality regardless of what has been revealed to us. I know: often I am inclined to make up my own Jesus, gleaned from the gospel of my own generation, picking and choosing what I find compatible and closing off conclusions I cannot accept, steering clear of what I do not want to hear, veiling from myself what I don't want to value – because it's safer. But the Transfiguration is not about safety. Whatever else it was, it describes an attempt by God to pierce the pretense of the disciples, to unveil them, to reveal to them the radiance that would release them from the fear of consequences to their lives.

Even if I can acknowledge all that; still, as a friend once said, "I'm no hero." I guard against the glare of glory – let God keep it to himself and let me alone. Yet what the Transfiguration is trying to tell us, even though we hide from it, is that glory is not something God keeps to himself; it shines forth in those who are willing to share it with others. Rat that down.

I see that radiance whenever I see the outpouring of time, talent, gifts and service of one person to another. Trust and caring give rise to faith and action in those who receive them. I find the touch of God in music as well as in the care of persons. A song, a hymn, an anthem or an organ offering can lift us out of ourselves and lend us enthusiasm and even courage for our journey. In the loyalty and devotion given to an aging parent or terminally ill spouse, surely we see the face of God. Maybe we sense the mystery of God's presence in moments even in church, in the prayers or praise we remember and speak – or have forgotten and keep only in our silence.

We need to cherish those moments in which we are willing to receive the radiance that reaches through our business-as-usual and reveals to us a glimpse of the eternal in us and around us. But the harsh reality of life is we cannot stay on that mountain; we must return to where we are here, where we're willing to minister and be ministered to – not out of but in the midst of God's world. We need to take the glory of the mountain top along with us – not leave it there – transfigured here, assured that God is with us in our fears and failures as well as our finest moments.

Now rat this down: Our part in that Transfiguration thaing is in the here and now, not in the there and then – even if, like Peter, sadly we only "get it" when we get it rat between the eyes.

———

1. *Lectionary Homiletics XIV*, 2-p.30

LENT

The Dalai Lama, among other sages, told this story of a life: Chapter 1: I walked down a familiar street in which there appeared a big hole. I didn't know it was there, so I fell in – and I almost didn't make it out. Chapter 2: I walked down the same street in which there was a deep hole. It wasn't my fault that the hole was there, but I fell in and had to fight like the devil to get out. Chapter 3: I walked down the street again, knowing that the hole was there, but somehow, I managed to fall in anyway, and after a struggle was able to get out again. Chapter 4: I walked down that street which had the hole in it – but this time I walked around the hole. Chapter 5: The next time, I walked down another street.

Christopher Brookfield

WHAT ARE WE LENT TILL EASTER?

An Ash Wednesday Offering
April 1996

I can remember clearly, as a child captive in a church school, my anger at Ash Wednesday services, which seemed so somber and severe. They upset me. So at the start of such a solemn season in the cycle of the church year perhaps you will permit me a little levity before looking at today's lectionary. Actually, it's a legitimate lead-in to a Lenten lection that over the years has lasted with me long after the other readings passed into oblivion: "Remember that you are dust, and to dust you shall return."

Perhaps you will remember the often-quoted Schultz comic strip where Charlie Brown asks his mother if his Sunday school teacher is telling the truth when she says that we came from dust and we will return to dust. When his mother replies, "That's the truth," Charlie Brown says, ''Well from what I see when I look at the floor under my bed, there must be a whole lot of us either coming or going."

Not long ago Bishop Lee began one of his pastoral letters saying Lent is a time to remember who you are; it begins with a reminder, a realistic if somber statement of who we are: "Remember that you are dust, and to dust you shall return." He recalled the children's game which I remember being forced to play at birthday parties – clasping hands and dancing 'round in a circle, singing "Ring around a rosie, a pocket full of posies; ashes, ashes, we all fall down." It was a stupid game, it seemed to me, and I disliked all of it except the part that followed "all fall down" – when the ring would fly apart and we would hurl ourselves in a heap on the floor, squashing the little girls underneath us. (The mothers berated this boyish brutishness, but that didn't dampen our enthusiasm for the deviant ending.)

At such a tender age no one told us that sing-songy ditty dated from that time of the great bubonic plague which ravaged Europe in 1350, that "ring around a rosie" referred to an angry rash which encircled a bubo or boil on the body brought about by the Black Plague, which meant that death was near. "Ashes, ashes" reminds us that sooner or later we all "fall down" in the grave. Had I known all that gruesome stuff then I might have enjoyed the ritual more, although I doubt it would have affected my efforts to avoid Ash Wednesday services like the plague.

However, the Lenten reminder of our mortality, says Bishop Lee, is not intended as an exercise in morbid self-contempt. Rather it is a call to remember that we have life, *our* life, as a gift – from the God who breathed into us, into the dust of the earth he scooped up from the ground, the breath of life which inspired or inspirited a living being, as the book of Genesis puts it. (Adam, "the man," you may recall, is taken from Adamah, the Hebrew word for dirt, dust, soil, sod, mud, manure). It is a reminder that we live dependent upon God; and as creatures that are frail, finite, and fleeting, we all go down to dust – return to the earth from which we were taken. That is who we are, who must make our song at the grave if we would affirm that life means more than just dust dancing in the wind.

In that same chapter of Genesis we are told, "It is not good that the man should be alone," and yet the one thing we have in common with all human beings, and with Jesus himself, is our knowledge that we are destined to be alone and to be aware of it. Not even God can take this away from us. One theologian has ventured that in the most intimate union between man and woman, we remain alone because even in our nakedness with one another we cannot penetrate each other's innermost being.

Lent is about loneliness and trial and the temptation to flee rather than face them. It reminds us that we do not possess the password to bypass the human predicament, that we pass through it when we are willing to endure until Easter which, we are well aware, is on the far side of what we have come to call "Good" Friday. So we say, "We are dust, and to dust we shall return." Ashes to ashes, dust to dust, Ash Wednesday got its name from an early practice in the Roman Catholic Church of putting ashes on the heads of public penitents – despite the lessons appointed for this day, which enjoin us not to look dismal or disfigure our faces and so make an outward show of our piety and repentance.

"Beware of practicing your piety before others in order to be seen by them," says the gospel of Matthew. "Do not be like the hypocrites... [who] love to stand and pray in the synagogues and at the street corners, so that they may be seen by others... Whenever you fast, do not look dismal, like the hypocrites; for they disfigure their faces so as to show others that they are fasting." Your father who sees in secret knows your need before you ask.

Ash Wednesday invites us to participate in the most solemn penitential season in the church year so that we will have something more substantial to celebrate at the end of it than the Easter Bunny or the parade of hats down Monument Avenue. Lent asks us to take a long, hard look at ourselves. For if we have neither the time nor the courage to assess ourselves honestly, we will be unable to answer ourselves honestly how things are between us and God. Perhaps that is why Jesus needed to be with himself in the wilderness for forty days – to ask the hard questions.

Among the hard questions is our awareness that not only at the start and finish of life we are essentially alone (no one can do the dying for us), but that when the outward gaiety and grace are peeled away from our public faces, we are also lonely. We can be lonely when we are surrounded by people, perhaps even specially then. We can be lonely with our oldest friends and family –

even with the one we most love in the world. That is part of what is meant by the human "predicament."

But from a positive point of view, to be lonely is also to be aware that there is an emptiness in us which takes more than people or possessions to fill, a sense that something essential is missing – even though we cannot name it. Whatever that name-lessness we are lonely for, it may be that we can come to know it only when we are aware of our longing for it, for the person or place wherein we are accepted as we are. Where we will be able at last to become who we were intended to be. Which we can finally call home.

———◦———

So in this season we are lent more than loneliness; we are given the opportunity to name the love we are seeking in our wilderness - on the far side of the hard questions.

———◦———

There are many names for that, not the least of which is the God we can call upon when we ask (or pray) to have our emptiness filled. So in this season we are *lent* more than loneliness; we are given the opportunity to name the love we are seeking in our wilderness – on the far side of the hard questions. Our friend Frederick Buechner offers us some of those questions that can help us name our inmost longings:

"When you look at your face in the mirror, what do you see in it that you most like and what do you see in it that you most deplore?

"If you had only one last message to leave to a handful of people who are most important to you, what would it be in twenty-five word or less?

"Of all the things you have done in your life, which is the one you would most like to undo? Which is the one that makes you happiest to remember?

"Is there any person in the world, or any cause, that, if circumstances called for it, you would be willing to die for?

"If this were the last day of your life, what would you do with it?"

To hear such questions, regardless who speaks them, as if you had asked them for yourself; and to hear what it is you say to yourself as you attempt to answer them – that will tell you who you are, what you are longing to become and what you have failed to become. That can be a lonely undertaking, God knows, which may taste mostly of ashes. But if we are destined to begin in dust and ashes at the start, as my friend says, our longings will lead us to Easter at the end.

"CAN ONE BE BORN AGAIN?"

2nd Sunday in Lent
John 3:1-17
Year A – February 28, 1999

There was a Pharisee named Nicodemus, a leader of the Jews. He came to Jesus by night and said to him, "Rabbi, we know that you are a teacher who has come from God; for no one can do these signs that you do apart from the presence of God." Jesus answered him, "Very truly, I tell you, no one can see the kingdom of God without being born again." Nicodemus said to him, "How can anyone be born after having grown old? Can one enter a second time into the mother's womb and be born?" Jesus answered, "Very truly, I tell you, no one can enter the kingdom of God without being born of water and Spirit. What is born of the flesh is flesh, and what is born of the Spirit is spirit. Do not be astonished that I said to you, 'You must be born from above.' The wind blows where it chooses, and you hear the sound of it, but you do not know where it comes from or where it goes. So it is with everyone who is born of the Spirit." Nicodemus said to him, "How can these things be?" Jesus answered him, "Are you a teacher of Israel, and yet you do not understand these things?

"Very truly, I tell you, we speak of what we know and testify to what we have seen; yet you do not receive our testimony. If I have told you about earthly things and you do not believe, how can you

believe if I tell you about heavenly things? No one has ascended into heaven except the one who descended from heaven, the Son of Man. And just as Moses lifted up the serpent in the wilderness, so must the Son of Man be lifted up, that whoever believes in him may have eternal life.

"For God so loved the world that he gave his only Son, so that everyone who believes in him may not perish but may have eternal life.

"Indeed, God did not send the Son into the world to condemn the world, but in order that the world might be saved through him."

John 3:1-17

After last week's "Episcopal version of fire and brimstone," as one person called my sermon, you can relax this morning because I simply want to tell you a story. I hasten to add that I know you know I have told this one before – it's not that a "senior moment" has overtaken me unawares. In good Jewish or Chinese tradition, telling a familiar story has the advantage that since you already know how it is going to end, you can concentrate along the way on trying to discover what it means – and, perish the thought, how it might possibly relate to problems or possibilities in your own life.

The story I have in mind comes out of a particular art form in Zen Buddhism, called koan, somewhat similar to what we would call parable in Western thought. A koan is a kind of riddle, often invoking a paradox, which is used as an aid to meditation and a means of gaining intuitive knowledge. Let me see if I can say that more simply. A koan is a phrase or sentence that both confounds and transcends logic in an effort to shock the listener into a new level of consciousness and wisdom. To say it more sharply, its intent is to frustrate our usual attempt to intellectualize – and thereby, to bring on an experiential crisis in the learner, which provokes a response. An example you may be familiar with is for the master to demand of his disciple an answer to the question, "What is the sound of one hand clapping?"

Spoken parables of Jesus in the New Testament tend to sound gentler than koans, but their intent is also to set accepted wisdom on its head and to prevent the hearer from taking refuge in the rational or conventional truth he is comfortable with, or takes for granted, as, for instance, in the story of the Prodigal Son or the Laborers in the Vineyard who receive the same wage whether they worked the whole day or only one hour. An example of an acted-out parable is Jesus' feeding of the 5,000.

The story I said I was going to tell you, before I got side-tracked, is an acted-out koan in which the disciple seeking enlightenment asks permission to speak with the learned and illustrious Zen Master. Having at last been granted an audience, the eager disciple bows down, and raising his eyes asks the master, "Most honored and wise one, tell me please how I may come to know the truth?" The master sits silently for a time, the disciple waiting patiently for an answer. After a while, the master takes in hand a stout stick by his side and gives the disciple a clout on his head with it.

Inwardly hurt and cast down, the disciple silently withdraws. But the next day, his courage revived, he once again earnestly seeks an audience, and after bowing humbly ventures his question again with the master – who again sits in silence, and after a time picks up his stick and deals the disciple an even harder blow on the head than before. The disciple, despondent and wounded, withdraws painfully.

But on the third day, the disciple after bowing once more asks the master the same question, and this time he is rewarded for his effort with a beating that barely spares his life.

That's the story. But what does it mean?

I take it that the answer to the disciple's question lies in his realization that the truth cannot be taught; wisdom cannot be pursued, it will seek you out. You cannot reason your way to it and grasp it; it will strike you unawares and grasp you. And finally, you will know the truth only when your life is changed by it.

Jesus, we have been told, was a more tender teacher, a more restrained roshi than the Zen Master, but his message to Nicodemus in this morning's reading is much the same; and as a learner, Nicodemus is just as hard headed. The story in John's gospel is characterized by a play on words, an ironic dialogue, and an awareness of (if not an intentional) misunderstanding. The climax comes in the well-known words of the verse which is cited on billboards at baseball games, on bumper stickers and Christian T-shirts: John 3:16, "For God so loved the world that he gave his only-begotten Son, that all who believe in him should not perish, but have eternal life." The truth of which for Nicodemus could only come at the cost of changing the mind and substance of his former life.

On one level at least the story is straight forward and self-explanatory. Nicodemus is a learned and well-respected Pharisee, a leader of the Jewish ruling council, who is bothered by and curious about Jesus' controversial teachings, and ventures to pay him a personal visit. The problem is, he decides to play it safe, and so his seeking seems half-hearted, hidden under the cover of night, when he thinks no one will see him. That is the first clue as to how John understood it, because in his gospel "night" is used metaphorically to represent separation from the presence of God, which the very last verse of the pericope confirms, where it reads, "But whoever lives by the truth comes into the light, so that it may be clearly seen that his deeds have been done in God." (vs. 21)

Before going further, I have to confess I have some sympathy for poor Nicodemus, not only because he honestly questions what he can believe, but as a lifelong academic he has a hard time accepting the limitation of logic in overcoming his uncertainties. I've been there. And what Jesus is asking of Nicodemus is to let go of all he has known in order to take the risk of being reborn in the realization of what Jesus alone has to offer. Furthermore, the gospel writer is asking us to understand what Nicodemus can only misunderstand. This is done with a play on words which is almost impossible for us to comprehend if we don't know the Greek.

When Nicodemus says to Jesus, "Rabbi, we know you are a teacher who comes from God," Jesus answers him, "Truly, I tell you, no one can see the kingdom of God unless he is born from above" (as our English translation explains). But what the Greek text actually expresses is unavoidable and intentionally ambiguous – namely, "No one can see the kingdom of God unless he is born *anothen* (ανvθεv)." Which means both "born again" and "born from above." The double meaning presents a problem because there is no equivalent word to use for it in our language, even though John intends both meanings to be heard simultaneously – because it challenges Nicodemus and underscores his stubborn misunderstanding.

The highly educated Nicodemus is seemingly oblivious to the obvious two levels of meaning, focusing on only one interpretation, which he protests to Jesus is impossible: "How can anyone be born again after having grown old?" he asks. "Can one enter a second time into his mother's womb and be born?" (Actually, I can imagine myself saying something like that, perhaps in an inappropriate attempt to lend a little levity to an uncomfortably heavy conversation, or even to avoid responding to an observation that calls into question the direction of my life). Whereupon, Jesus lets him have it: "Are you Israel's teacher, and yet you do not understand these things? ... If I have told you about earthly things and you do not believe, how then will you believe if I tell you about heavenly things?"

What he means, I take it, is that eternal life (not meaning unending life as we know it, but rather life lived in the unending presence of God) is available only to those who are willing to be born in the spirit ("from above") – not "born again" in the life we know, as Nicodemus insists on understanding it. And eternal life,

Jesus is saying, is not held out to us like a carrot, for the future, but begins now in the believer's present. "So, Nicodemus, when are you prepared to begin your new life?" is the question Jesus throws out to him.

All the religious beliefs and practices that Nicodemus had been raised in, his devout and faithful keeping of worship, theological doctrine, and observance in the Law had little to do with his relationship to God. They had left him no room for deeper reflection and response to the acts of God that give life in our daily living. He had learned and mastered – been born in – the great intellectual truths of his religion. But on the level of faith, he could not believe in the life of the spirit "from above" that shows itself in all we do. Which is the key to life beyond the one we think we know and understand and control, John tells us. The task is not for me to become a better-educated person, or even a better person, but a new person through what I believe and live. "For God so loved the world ... that all who believe in him might have eternal life." The last dark and uncomprehending words we hear from Nicodemus form his question "How can this be?" How can I come to that life as I am? he might have said, with an ache of regret in the pit of his stomach. John leaves us with his question and challenges you and me to answer for ourselves, squinting as we may in the presence of the light and holding on nostalgically to the old womb of our former life.

OF KEEPERS AND SEEKERS: WATER OR FIRE?

2nd Sunday of Lent
John 3:1-17
Year A – February 24, 2002

The Dalai Lama, among other sages, told this story of a life: *Chapter 1:* I walked down a familiar street in which there appeared a big hole. I didn't know it was there, so I fell in – and I almost didn't make it out. *Chapter 2*: I walked down the same street in which there was a deep hole. It wasn't my fault that the hole was there, but I fell in and had to fight like the devil to get out. *Chapter 3*: I walked down the street again, knowing that the hole was there, but somehow, I managed to fall in anyway, and after a struggle was able to get out again. *Chapter 4:* I walked down that street which had the hole in it – but this time I walked around the hole. *Chapter 5:* The next time, I walked down *another* street.

Something to ponder if we are preparing to pursue a new perspective in our lives.

Or you may say that the subject of the story was anything but a quick study. Why would anyone want to repeat that kind of behavior when he knew the painful consequences? Why indeed? It may not be your story. But for some of us hard heads, it's the same old story. You don't have to worry; if the shoe doesn't fit, you don't have to put it on.

But I want to speak with you for a moment about pain. I'm a big pain avoider; I say to myself, "Who needs it?" Yet some people who have observed me over the years might say I sometimes ask for it. That I spent so many years of my life with competitive rowing in school and college and beyond and was captain of a boxing team might support that notion. But the main reason I would say I'm a pain avoider is that I'm a slow learner. Pain is a swift teacher, but many of us will go to great lengths to avoid learning that way. We hold on for dear life to the ways we have always known.

We prefer the pronouncement of John the Baptist when he said, "I baptize you with water…." We're not so accepting of the last half of his sentence, which says, "The one who comes after me, … will baptize you with the Holy Spirit and with fire." With fire! I don't know about you, but I would prefer to be baptized with water, rather than be transformed by fire. Yet one thing I have learned recently is that unlike the story of the street with the hole in it (or maybe it is the counterpart of that story) sometimes the most effective, the most redeeming way of dealing with pain is not to avoid it or to step around it, but to go right through it – to accept it as a part of life, not as an intrusion into the way we think life ought to be.) That, of course requires us to accept that the gift of God's goodness can come to us through pain, not just through pleasure. I started to learn something about this some time back when I was teaching teenagers in a boarding school where a sign on the boathouse wall (I coached rowing then), a sign which could have been hung on the classroom walls as well, said "Winning isn't everything, it's the *only* thing." In such an atmosphere, which encouraged cut-throat academic competition and a "winner takes all" mentality, I had a terrible time trying to teach the truth that the pain of our failures and weaknesses is what draws us together, what brings us close to one another; whereas, the pleasure of our successes and triumphs separates and divides us, one from another. Have you heard the saying, "We are like angels with broken wings; only when we cling to one another will we be able to fly."? To embrace the pain, to share it, to walk through the fire, forges for us a baptism that endears, enlarges, and endures.

As we approach Easter, that may help us understand why Jesus chose to go to Jerusalem, where they had put to death the prophets before him, rather than to seek the safety of his home-town and avoid the inevitable anguish, ostracism, abandonment, and eventual execution. He prayed, "Father, let this cup (of suffer-ing) pass from my lips." But then he added, "Nevertheless, not my will but thine be done." Those are the words we have trouble with if we are keepers rather than seekers.

<hr>

Jesus tried to teach us, not with words and wisdom, but by the way he lived and what he did, that in order to keep what we have, we have to give it away.

<hr>

Jesus tried to teach us, not with words and wisdom, but by the way he lived and what he did, that in order to keep what we have, we have to give it away. For some of us that may mean ma-terial things, for others that might be a part of ourselves we hold dear. I'm not Jesus, and I probably can't or won't give my life away as he did. But there's an adage: "If you want to be healed, start by trying to help someone else be healed." That's a lesson to listen to if I would hope to be a seeker not a keeper, if I want to be enlight-ened rather than stick to the safety of the darkness that allows me to avoid the light.

Irreverently, but not incidentally, I have been told that the best way to catch cockroaches is to sneak up to them in the black-ness; leave them alone in the dark a while, then suddenly turn on the light and come in for the kill. If you'll pardon the analogy, symbolically, it can be the same for us on our spiritual journey. Many of us unconsciously avoid the light as if our lives depended on keeping it away. I know. The dark is comforting, mysterious, a place to hide; the light shows up our secrets, our hiding places, and the pain of being seen for who we are.

Maybe that's why I'm drawn to the story of Nicodemus, whom scripture shows skulking about under the cover of dark-ness. Somehow, I sense he's given a bad rap, because I suspect that, appearances to the contrary, he is a seeker. At least that's the way I identify myself with him. Of course he is a pain avoider. He didn't want to be seen by his fellow Pharisees consulting with the opposition, with Jesus, as though he were a kindred spirit. So Nicodemus could not come to Jesus in the light. Or maybe he is there in John's gospel simply as a foil – to discredit his own kind, an embarrassment, too dimwitted to comprehend the implications of a controversial word that in Greek means both "born again" and "born from above" – or pretending not to understand that the term has two meanings and so protesting that being born again is impossible; after all, a man cannot get back into his mother's womb.

It is easy for us to deride his stupidity or his duplicity as a seeker, so we are taken by surprise when Jesus decides to accept him as a sincere seeker. Instead of condemning Nicodemus as a klutz or a turncoat, he has compassion for him and offers him not only another opportunity, a second chance, but the possibility of a new life. Why? Perhaps because Jesus is drawn to a spiritual pilgrim who is willing to risk leaving the truth as he has known it and start down an unknown path to explore something new. The journey is precarious, because he is torn between the world where he knows his way and feels safe, where he is recognized and accepted and esteemed, and the new world he is called to – where life in the spirit is unpredictable, akin to the blowing of the wind: "You hear the sound of it, (he says), but you do not know where it comes from or where it goes. So it is with everyone who is "born of the spirit" (that is, "born from above"). To tell the truth, I'm feeling a little precarious here because I sense that I am trying to justify Nicodemus for my own sake because I see so much of myself in him. Perhaps the wind I ought to fear is being a windbag of a preacher.

The Greek word for wind, *pneuma,* also means spirit. And the symbol for spirit is fire. Spirit is not wisdom or knowledge or even truth, it is not something we can keep or possess; it gives us life only when we are willing to let go of it, to let it have its way with us, to let it light a fire in us so that we can warm others by living out of it.

Patricia Farris calls Nicodemus the Patron Saint of Seekers, not the father of Pharisaic keepers. We see no more of him in scripture after he comes to Jesus in the dark, until the very end of the gospel when we spy him "accompanying Joseph of Arimathea to the darkness of Jesus' tomb, offering his teacher gifts of precious ointment, aloes and myrrh."[1] Having been so long in the dark he is at last reborn by the Spirit into the light that leads to eternal life. He can, finally, offer without apology the invocation we ourselves may be reluctant to voice aloud: "Lord, take my lips and speak through them, take my mind and think through it, (but most of all) take my heart and set it on fire with yourself." *Amen.*

———

1. *Christian Century*, Vol. 119, No. 3, p.19

GOING TO JERUSALEM

2nd Sunday in Lent
Luke 13:31-35
Year C – March 8, 2004

Some Pharisees came and said to Jesus, "Get away from here, for Herod wants to kill you." He said to them, "Go and tell that fox for me, 'Listen, I am casting out demons and performing cures today and tomorrow, and on the third day I finish my work. Yet today, tomorrow, and the next day I must be on my way, because it is impossible for a prophet to be killed outside of Jerusalem.' Jerusalem, Jerusalem, the city that kills the prophets and stones those who are sent to it! How often have I desired to gather your children together as a hen gathers her brood under her wings, and you were not willing! See, your house is left to you. And I tell you, you will not see me until the time comes when you say, 'Blessed is the one who comes in the name of the Lord.'"

Luke 13-31-35

You have probably heard that disturbing observation, which a friend sent to my wife, embroidered on a hand towel (the saying, that is – not my wife): "It takes courage to grow up and turn out to be who you really are" (e.e. cummings). But I had not heard it, and I have mulled it a lot in my mind recently, reflecting on what it might mean as a Lenten message and how it might change my life if I took it seriously. Pondering the gospel reading in Luke for this week and the curious and famous statement Jesus makes toward the end of it, about the hen gathering her brood under her wing, I realized the saying on the towel might help me understand what Jesus meant and why he chose to go to Jerusalem where he would take his life in his own hands and offer it up. "It takes courage to grow up and turn out to be who you really are."

Backing up a moment in my thinking, in the Education for Ministry program, we are asked again each year to look at our lives as far back as we can remember in order to understand how, through the experiences of the past we got to be who we are (or aren't) spiritually in the present. So I'm going to revisit some former thoughts about my own life, which have somehow helped me come to terms with where I am and what Jesus might have been saying to me in his time, even though I may have told some of these thoughts to some of you sometime before.

I remember my mother sometimes succumbed to a somewhat uncharitable and strikingly simple way of referring to my father's faults. She called him, alternately, "grim death" or "old blood and guts" – occasionally "the colonel." (Before he became a stockbroker, Father had been in the military – "forever," as my mother put it, "and that's where he should have stayed," she would add.) That was her way of putting him in his place. He was a young man during the Depression, trying to make a living in New York City. He often said, "Life is hard" and "Nothing is safe." (I shall not repeat what he said about Franklin Roosevelt.) My mother, brought up in Brookline in Boston and raised by my loving and indulgent great aunt, admitted she was spoiled and almost always "got what she wanted" and "had her way" in the end.

And so she got what she wanted, a divorce, which my father regretted but finally gave in to. Looking back, my mother once said to me seriously, "I'm convinced the reason I married your father in the first place was just so I could get out of Boston."

There may be some truth in citing simple solutions to the mysteries of life's serious stumpers. For example, asking: How did

I end up being a priest? The short solution? Could it be because when I was a choir boy at age seven and sought asylum from the world, from my family, and from making friends by retreating to my room as many hours of the day as I could manage – I heard the minister of our church speak each Sunday of "the peace which passeth all understanding."? That's what I wanted more than any-thing.

My mother irreverently called the minister "Fat Wendel;" he was the talk of the beach club we belonged to because he dared appear at the pool without wearing the required wool bath-ing suit top for men, without which they were considered "inde-cent." Ladies would follow behind him all the way from the bath-house to the pool, commenting to one another on the cute little handles of flesh that disgorged themselves over the waist of his short tight wool trunks (which were also required). "Disgusting," they would disclaim, and "How sensual." His hair was black and curly- and too shiny. Too much Wild Root. But he had "the peace which passeth all understanding."

I remember he would stretch out his sounds: "God grand you peace-s-s-s," he said.

Based on that simple assessment of why I am standing before you, I shudder to think of what I might have said here that may even now be pointing some poor impressionable youth toward the mystery of ministry, misled by the ill begotten allitera-tions I am fond of forming.

What does all this have to do with our Gospel reading? Patiences-s-s. There are several surprises in the text, what one commentator calls "odd comments on the road to Jerusalem," warning us against the familiar and simplistic solutions we are used to applying to this passage.[1]

First, we are astonished that it is the Pharisees who warn Jesus of Herod's wrath. If we are used to lumping people under one label we may judge them unfairly. Surely there were some Pharisees who were friendly to Jesus, and even some indication in scripture that Jesus may have counted himself as one among them. Still, it seems odd to us that the opposition took the opportunity to warn him. Second, it is odd that Jesus affixes the epithet "fox" to Pilate, because that indicates Jesus understood Pilate's underhanded scheming against him. And yet Jesus decides to continue his journey to Jerusalem where he would undoubtedly be trapped and unjustly put to death, which he could have avoided or put off.

Then there's the odd blessing Jesus expects from the people who would forsake him and who might yet come to him in the name of the Lord. Not to mention the unusual image Jesus invoked of a mother hen to describe God. "Shepherd" we expect – but "hen?" What is odd about all these taken together is that they put forward a gospel that flies in the face of simple solutions – which speaks of a God who for no reason refuses to abandon a faithless world, a gospel that tells of finding life and treasure in the demands of dying and giving away, and a faith that is fulfilled in the certainty of a cross. No simple solutions for us to savor this morning.

Lent may be the last outpost in our modern world to hold out that life's lessons are hard, in spite of the media, which guarantee problem-free living. Like instructions for putting together infant jungle gyms for grandchildren. "Easy to assemble" or "No tools required" are nonsense of course: You can't even open the box without a pair of pliers to pull out the staples just to get started. How about "Three easy steps to a stunning complexion." Or "Four simple steps to lose all the weight you want." "Cut your painting time in half." In other words, take the work out of working, the travail out of traveling, the calories out of cooking – leave the driving to us! That's the gospel of simple solutions.

Such a perspective is not exclusive to the temptations of our time. Remember last week's lection: the classic scene set in the wilderness, where Jesus is bedeviled by the enticements of the Tempter. Just turn these stones into bread; people are starved for miracles. Just jump off the pinnacle of the Temple to prove God will not let you fall on your face. Why do it the hard way, "Just bow down and worship me," declares the devil, "and all the king-doms of the earth are yours." A lot faster and surely more satisfying than the slow and painful steps to Jerusalem.

But Jesus saw that to be faithful to what he believed, there was no simple way, no easy solution. Life is just more complicated than that; it's going to cost us plenty before we're through.

Nevertheless, Jesus said, "I must go on my way today, and tomorrow, and the day following; for it cannot be that a prophet should perish away from Jerusalem. O Jerusalem, Jerusalem... how often I would have desired to gather you as a hen gathers her brood under her wings, and you were not willing!"

Some of you will remember playing the game "Going to Jerusalem" at birthday parties as a child. (Significantly, I must have repressed it because I can't for the life of me remember how you play, only that I loathed it.) But for Jesus and his generation it was not a child's game, played with a pack of Gospel cards ... It was the imperative of journeying to the holy city of God, the heart of the spiritual world, the place where the fate of much of humankind was to be decided. Going to Jerusalem was doing life the hard way, but there was no other place and there was no other way.

Where is Jerusalem for each of us? Jerusalem is the op-portunity for change in our lives: maybe to stop doing something we have always done – or to start doing something we have never done. Not all of which will be life threatening. For instance, giving up dependency on alcohol means learning to live in the pain of the real world from which we have been sheltered or numbed by the comfort of drinking.

———◦◦———

For some of us, going to Jerusalem may mean taking a stand for something we know is right and being willing to pay the cost for it: Speaking out against what is unjust when it is safer to remain silent.

———◦◦———

For some of us, going to Jerusalem may mean taking a stand for something we know is right and being willing to pay the cost for it: Speaking out against what is unjust when it is safer to remain silent. Opposing public or institutional opinion when it is not "smart" or self-serving to do so. Acting on what we believe in faith when others advise us it is idiotic or "out of touch."

Maybe going to Jerusalem means making the difficult acknowledgement of a long-ago offense, when for years we have taken the easy road of silence. Maybe we once spoke a word that hurt a husband or wife or child very deeply. Once the word was out of our mouths we didn't know how to take it back – or didn't want to, or were afraid to. In time perhaps we returned to the routine of our relationship and even laughed together. Still the wound was there in each of us, needing to be confessed and, if possible, forgiven – but it is not an easy step to take. It is going to cost us a lot one way or another.

Going to Jerusalem can be painful, but maybe it is also a step toward "that peace which the world cannot give" – "the peace which passes all understanding," or whatever it is we need to become fully human in our own skin. Our world assumes there is an easy way, a simple way, to get wherever we want to go. And our first response to that is essentially healthy: "Stupid, it's just not that simple." But the next step is not so easy, as Jesus reminds us. As we wipe the sweat off our brow with the hand towel someone sent us, we glance uneasily again at the words embroidered on it: "It takes courage to grow up and turn out to be who you really are."

-----

1. *Homiletics.* VI, 4; pp.14-15.

UNTITLED

4th Sunday in Lent
John 6:4-15; 12:24-33
March 13, 1988

In the first gospel reading: At Passover, Jesus took the loaves (the five barley loaves) and when he had given thanks, he distributed them to those who were seated (the five thousand); so also the (two) fish, as much as they wanted. Which is to say, he fed those who were gathered round him, until they had had their fill, and the bits that were left over also filled twelve baskets.

In the second gospel reading, Jesus said, "Truly, truly, I say to you, unless a grain of wheat falls into the earth and dies, it remains alone; but if it dies, it bears much fruit.... He said this to show by what death he was to die." Which is to say, when his followers' hunger was abated, Jesus talked to them about his own death, though they did not believe him.

There's the drama of Lent to Good Friday in capsule form. Feeding and dying is what those lessons are all about, and they belong together in one story, which is why I cannot separate the gospel readings for this week and next. You can't get much more basic than that in our relationships, with our neighbor or with God. Feeding and dying. What more can a person do with or for you in life? First about dying:

A story — a confession, really — I read recently affected me personally because it woke old feelings and recalled the savage in me I had conveniently forgotten. The writer recalled Easter 1917 in his backyard, which began as a truly lovely morning:

I went out into the yard and saw a robin perched on the clothesline. Without a thought, I rushed into the house to get my brother's slingshot, and rushed back to find to my delight that my prey was still there. I stood directly under it, took aim, and shot. The bird fell at my feet. I instantly felt remorse, though my answer to the question of why I killed the robin was just this: I did it for the hell of it. Nothing else. Even as a child, killing one of God's precious creatures just for the hell of it; how could it be? I've long given up trying to find an answer to that question in philosophy or psychology.

The only thing certain is that something happened to me at the center of my being, unbeknown to me and unwilled by me…. My action was the outward and visible sign of my having inwardly and spiritually joined the fallen human race.

Death at the hands of that writer, or my hands, or yours is something we are no strangers to at age five or fifteen or twenty-five or fifty-five, though it may take other forms among our friends and often in our families, which are the very source of our nourishment. As one of my students parodied a familiar Shakespearean sonnet, "How can I kill thee, let me count the ways." That is why we need to take the Lenten story seriously at least once a year.

We have excuses of course; no one wants to own up to being a death dealer. "Oh, but you were only a child. Lord knows, you didn't know any better." I remember in nursery school, lining up those big orange and black fuzzy caterpillars in a neat row, then running them down all at once with one tire of my blue express wagon, just for the hell of it. I wonder why I don't remember as easily my own secret elation at my friend's misfortune when we were competing for the same girlfriend and a debating prize. Or why I can so easily refuse to deal with my wife's anger and grief when they threaten me or get in the way of "something I need to get done."

Somewhere along the line, something happened to each of us at the center of our being when unwittingly or otherwise we joined the fallen human race. Rather than deal with that, we would like to race ahead to Easter, only after which the worst Friday on record became known as *Good* Friday. But, if I may make a Lenten pun, we cannot "Passover" death. Sooner or later we have to own it.

Look after the needs of the day while you can, because you cannot know when your life may be called into question.

Fortunately, that is only half the story in this morning's readings. The other is feeding, life, nourishment. Feed my flock, Jesus said. Feed one another, even as I have fed you. Look after the needs of the day while you can, because you cannot know when your life may be called into question. Do not ignore the little acts of love and feeding, the "small change" of our daily existence, because sooner or later in your life, an event or decision or act of great price must be affirmed or embraced.

I have been told that Jesus had an uncommon sense of humor about the shepherding and pasturing he spoke of frequently. His commending of the "Good Shepherd" was an oxymoron, a solemn joke, like the term "down escalator" or "military intelligence" or "United Methodism." The quality of shepherding is at best conflicted or ambiguous to those who know about sheep and shepherds of ancient days. "Shepherding was a despised trade. [Imagine] thieves: they had their sheep graze on other people's lands, and they pilfered. Pimps, drug pushers: these are their analogues in status today. Shepherds could not fulfill judicial office or be witnesses in court. You could not buy much from them because it was assumed that what you bought was stolen property." (*Context* 3/15/11 p.1) Likely as not, a shepherd not only carried a crook, he was one. A "good" shepherd was a contradictory term. "Only the oxymoron Good Shepherd gives his life for his sheep." Even that greatest act is not portrayed as perfect in an imperfect world. The other day, my wife showed me another imperfect passage from Thornton Wilder's *The Skin of our Teeth*, which read in part:

"I didn't marry you because you were perfect. I didn't even marry you because I loved you. I married you because you gave me a promise. That promise made up for your faults. And the promise I gave you made up for mine. Two imperfect people got married and it was the promise that made the marriage... And when our children were growing up, it wasn't a house that protected them; and it wasn't our love that protected them – it was that promise.'

Feed my sheep, Jesus said. Feed one another. Even as the Good Shepherd feeds you. Give life to one another now, because we will all face death sooner or later. Jesus speaks to our lives out of his own. Feeding and dying, what more can a person do with and for another.

Feeding. Whether we speak of life-giving milk from a mother's breast, or a door-opening education in a competitive world, or the unlikely nourishment of loaves and fishes among so many on a Galilean hillside, or the unbelievable promise of bread and wine in an upper room to twelve Jews smelling of fish at Passover – that is life, however you name it.

Dying. Whether giving up of hopes and plans that you had counted on, or being thrust into the world as a teenager to make your own decisions and own the consequences, or painful letting go of friends and love ones, or accepting the death of your parents or spouse and fending for yourself, alone – that's death only by another name.

We do not have feeding apart from dying. We have been given our lives at the expense of others. That is what is so disturbing about the Lenten lectionary. That is why we cannot separate the gospel lessons for this week and the next. No doubt we would prefer to become adults without the pain of adolescence, to flour-ish forever on the brink of middle age without having to grow old, to be free from and with our parents without finally having to give them up, to have Easter without Good Friday, to have feeding without dying. But that is not in the cards, so to speak. What we are promised is that if we accept the hand that is dealt us in life, grace shows up as the wild card.

Grace be unto *you* and peace, in the name of the Good Shepherd for whom the crooked will be made straight.

LOOKING FOR A WAY HOME

4th Sunday in Lent
Luke 15:1-3, 11b-32
Year C – March 25, 2001

Jesus said, "There was a man who had two sons. The younger of them said to his father, 'Father, give me the share of the property that will belong to me.' So he divided his property between them. A few days later the younger son gathered all he had and traveled to a distant country, and there he squandered his property in dissolute living. When he had spent everything, a severe famine took place throughout that country, and he began to be in need. So he went and hired himself out to one of the citizens of that country, who sent him to his fields to feed the pigs. He would gladly have filled himself with the pods that the pigs were eating; and no one gave him anything. But when he came to himself he said, 'How many of my father's hired hands have bread enough and to spare, but here I am dying of hunger! I will get up and go to my father, and I will say to him, "Father, I have sinned against heaven and before you; I am no longer worthy to be called your son; treat me like one of your hired hands."' So he set off and went to his father. But while he was still far off, his father saw him and was filled with compassion; he ran and put his arms around him and kissed him. Then the son said to him, 'Father, I have sinned against heaven and before you; I am no longer wor-

thy to be called your son.' But the father said to his slaves, 'Quickly, bring out a robe – the best one – and put it on him; put a ring on his finger and sandals on his feet. And get the fatted calf and kill it, and let us eat and celebrate; for this son of mine was dead and is alive again; he was lost and is found!' And they began to celebrate.

"Now his elder son was in the field; and when he came and approached the house, he heard music and dancing. He called one of the slaves and asked what was going on. He replied, 'Your brother has come, and your father has killed the fatted calf, because he has got him back safe and sound.' Then he became angry and refused to go in. His father came out and began to plead with him. But he answered his father, 'Listen! For all these years I have been working like a slave for you, and I have never disobeyed your command; yet you have never given me even a young goat so that I might celebrate with my friends. But when this son of yours came back, who has devoured your property with prostitutes, you killed the fatted calf for him!' Then the father said to him, 'Son, you are always with me, and all that is mine is yours. But we had to celebrate and rejoice, because this brother of yours was dead and has come to life; he was lost and has been found.'"

Luke 15:11-32

The Parable of the Prodigal Son is probably the most familiar of all the provocative stories Jesus used to instruct us with, unless perhaps you prefer to pick the piece about the proverbial Good Samaritan. On this one, a preacher could protest that there is precious little left to say about Luke's beloved parable of our wayward younger brother, which hasn't been said before and which would wake us out of our apathy in assuming we've heard all there is worth hearing about it. But being ornery, I'm going to assert that the point of the parable is often misrepresented and the story ought to be called the parable of the prodigal father and the impenitent older brother.

I can say that after all these years because I have finally figured out who I am in this upsetting incident where, arguably and unjustly, the one who was lost is found and the other who was found is lost. You may remember Robert Frost said wryly that home is the place where when you go there they have to take you in. But it is to me instructive what he wouldn't or didn't want to add is that home is the place where when you go there they *want* to take you in. Wouldn't it be an unbelievable gift if the rest of life had a built in delete button? With the stroke of a key we could cancel, cross out, erase all our errors, offenses, inexcusables, and execrables. Which is why the father in Luke's story, by our worldly standards, is the wayward one. To me, the most problematic part of the parable for the person who wants to make his peace with it is what I perceived to be the requirement of repentance. I say "requirement" because when I first read it *my* particular response (not the father's requisite) persuaded me *that* is what you must master if you would be made whole and allowed to embrace the ending of your personal parable, which intends a celebration of joy. Alan Culpepper proposes that for the younger son, repentance means learning how to say "father" again; and for the older brother, repentance lies in learning to say "brother" again.[1]

Although in my family I am in fact the younger brother, all my life it seems I have embodied the anger of the older brother. "There was a man who had two sons," the story starts out. And already I am upset because I relate it to my own situation whose stress reflects the sound of that Teutonic theological term for it: *sitz im leben* – which means no more than "the setting in life," but sounds like an outraged objection to it. My older brother was suave, smooth, socially celebrated, coordinated, clever, and con-fident (Did I forget to say universally loved and could do no per-manent wrong?). At 18, he was spotted at the swank Stork Club in New York City dancing with an older airline stewardess. Before he was 20, he had wangled a yellow Triumph to drive out of my great aunt's generosity (and in spite of the apoplexy of my father), which he totaled under a truck. And not even a month after the accident he managed to talk some other member of the family into giving him the money for another car.

Needless to say, he was a great salesman, an engaging extrovert, who made everyone he encountered feel special. His only apparent flaw to onlookers was his adamant refusal to write letters – to anyone, anytime, for anything. Once my father sicced the Red Cross on him to chase him down throughout Korea and after in Japan while brother was serving out the term of his draft in the Army – but to no avail. Not one missive ever emerged from his splendid isolation – not for gifts, favors, or even money – although apparently that omission was infinitely forgivable for our family.

I, on the other hand, was told my unfriendly introversion was an embarrassment to my parents whenever I accompanied them to the stores of local shopkeepers in the village. My brother, four years older, used to pin me down, sit on my chest, and threaten to beat me up if I kept getting good grades in school (which made his look bad). He finally flunked out of college freshman year, refused to wear a tie to get a job, went into the chicken-beak-searing business, while I was wiling my time away after college trying to earn three graduate degrees and teaching chemical, biological, and radiological warfare to wary and recalcitrant recruits at night. Airborne Officer Training, Seminary, and book publishing schools notwithstanding, my father was still suspicious that I had abandoned the last useful direction in my life, and he worried I would never be able to support a wife – which *he* couldn't afford since he was often assisting my brother financially.

So you can see where I (the younger brother) finally found myself in the parable of the Prodigal – plop in the part of the self-righteous older brother and angry at the role reversal as well. For years I rejected and reviled the predictable religious role-playing that preachers put upon us in explaining the parable. But I've since learned to appreciate the power of it in spite of my misplaced personal part in it.

The first step in escaping my opinionated prison was to admit that since I'd spent so much time attempting to color inside the lines, it was hard for me to find compassion for someone who didn't follow the rules. Having successfully struggled against temptation, it was easy for me to be intolerant of anyone who hadn't succumbed to self-discipline. I was addicted to justice, merciless in admonishing anyone who didn't get what he deserved, determined no one would get *more* than he deserved. I was a Pharisaic Jew through and through. Never occurred to me *I* had a problem.

What I couldn't put up with in the parable was the father's indiscriminate compassion – which seemed to me softheaded sentimentality. Hebrew justice would judge the father perverse and profligate; he had no right to dispense the family inheritance while he was alive. Therefore, if the younger son went wrong, the father had condoned if not caused it by giving into the deplorable demand of his second son. But that's not the half of it.

When he sees his dissolute son returning home, the father's reaction is so overwhelmingly joyful and ebullient, so unexpectedly elated, that the reader is rightfully surprised and stunned. Seeing him approach from afar, the father runs to meet him, his royal welcome really ruining the carefully contrived scene of contrition that the younger son had constructed to obtain mercy. The climax comes when the overjoyed father proclaims, "This my son who was dead is alive again, and the one who was lost is finally found." What the son had done is of no further concern to the father; his being found and alive is all that matters.

Meanwhile, the older brother, returning to the house from his labors in the field, hears the reveling and rejoicing of the feast for his squandering sibling and becomes "angry" (surely an understatement). And he wastes no time telling the father secret and salacious details of his brother's shortcomings. He professes to know the sordid and seedy particulars of the prodigal's sins – the money spent on prostitutes (he presumes). The father "pleads" or "entreats" the older son to join in the festivities, but he will have none of it, dwelling on the dissolution of the inheritance instead.

What our Bible translation "calls 'dissolute living' sounds somewhat darker and more insidious than the equally [adequate] translation of '*asotos*' as 'extravagantly' or as 'a spendthrift' or 'recklessly' ... and no particulars are given...." [2] In any case, the father refused to be riled, shocked, or saddened – insisting on celebrating the new life of the long-lost child, and assuring the elder son of the special place he holds in the father's heart, promising that all the father has left will be given to him – whereupon the story stops without further explanation.

What took me so long to understand is that what is really most shocking about this story is how it seems to celebrate the gift of grace over against – indeed, at the expense of – justice and even fairness. Because they are antithetical in our system of justice. All these years, that was the bitter pill too hard for me to swallow. What I (the younger), as the elder brother in this instance, overlooked and refused to understand is that God's love like parental love doesn't follow the rules of logic, nor is it bound by our rigid childlike conceptions of fairness. "The father loved the son who'd flouted him and offended common decency; and he loved the son who'd scrupulously and sometimes smugly kept the rules." [3]

Did you notice in the story that the father first took the initiative to go out and greet each son, both the one who disgraced himself and the family household and the one who was grimly faithful and self-righteously presumed to judge the father as well as the other brother? In the father's house are many mansions – room for anyone who seeks to enter there, a place for all who long for a way home. Remember that Jesus asked compassion for those who may have messed up their own lives and probably other's too, and he also offered mercy to those who would repent their unmerciful keeping of the law. At the end of Luke's story, one could argue, the elder son as well as the younger son is found, the rule-keeper and the rule-breaker – because the father delights in both simply because they are his sons. The good news in this parable, which still may be difficult for some of us to swallow, is that God does not give up searching for us, no matter how many times we may have managed to shut him out. In fact, the father will not give up on us until *every last one* of us has been found and welcomed home.

Thanks be to God.

------

1. *Biblical Preaching Journal* 11, 1 p.32
2. *Homiletics* 7, 1-p.51
3. *Biblical Preaching Journal* 14, 1-p.36

THE COST OF COVENANT

Counting on the "Delete" Key?

5th Sunday in Lent
Jeremiah 31:31-34; John 12:20-33
Year B — April 9, 2000

In our gospel reading John quotes Jesus, saying: *"Very truly, I tell you, unless a grain of wheat falls into the earth and dies, it remains alone; but if it dies, it bears much fruit. Those who love their life (try to save it) will lose it, and those who hate their life in this world (are willing to lose it) will keep it for eternal life. Whoever serves me must follow me, and where I am, there will my servant be also" (John 12:24-26).* If that text weren't intentionally coupled with the reading from Jeremiah, I might pretend I didn't hear what John was saying.

* * *

"I'm all for gun control," vents Jesse Ventura, the big, beefy, boisterous ex-pro wrestler governor of Minnesota," I just define it a little differently. If you can put two rounds into the same hole from 25 meters, that's gun control."

The man is rough, tough, gruff, and ready to rumble; but in the words of his recent autobiography, he "ain't got time to bleed," which is the title of his book, taken from the best-remembered line in a best-forgotten Ventura film debut called *Predator*. He's "a savior to some and a scoundrel to others." Uncomfortably, not unlike the labels laid on Jesus in the first century.[1]

144

I wonder whether one can be saved, let alone be a savior, if he "ain't got the time to bleed," if, to borrow the expression, we won't consider going to a cross for our convictions. Bob Wendel has come up with a ten step *Cross Scale* (to measure our level) of Commitment. At the high end of the scale is Number 10, which is: Go to the cross and rise in three days. Number 9 and 8 reduce the time on the cross to two days, and then one. Slipping to Number 7: Watch someone else go to the cross. 6: Visit Golgotha on vacation. 5: Wear a cross at work. 4: Wear a cross to church. 3: Buy a cross for a friend. 2: Look at the crosses for sale in the Cokesbury Bookstore. 1: Write with a Cross pen. (I'm offended by that last, because I have one.)[2]

Wendel asks, "Do we have time to bleed?" But if Christ has shed all the blood for us, what does he mean when he says, "Whoever serves me must follow me, and where I am, there will my servant be." And what about "Those who love their life will lose it, and those who are willing to lose it will keep it." What's it going to cost us to keep a covenant like that? What will it cost to keep our part of the covenant God makes with those who want to follow his ways?

*　　*　　*

I am sometimes surprised at how beautiful particular passages of the Old Testament can be, even occasionally surpassing anything expressed in the New Testament. One such portion of scripture is found in this morning's sayings of Jeremiah: *"The days are surely coming, says the Lord, when I will make a new covenant with my people, not like the covenant I made with their forefathers, which they broke again and again. This time I will put my law within them, not upon tablets of stone, and I will write it upon their hearts, so that everyone will know me; for I will forgive their transgressions and remember their sin no more"* (Jeremiah 31:31-34).

Numerous times in my life, that has seemed to me too good to be true. I could not accept it. I could not believe it. I allowed myself to be crushed by the weight of my failures and transgressions, even though God has already offered not only to forgive, but to forget them.

—◦—

Wouldn't it be an unbelievable gift if the rest of life had a built-in delete button?

—◦—

I am a newcomer to the computer, to say the least. It's like a miracle to me, as well as a mystery and a misery. The best thing about it is its power to obliterate my mistakes, to forgive my missteps, to delete the undesirable. Maybe you've guessed that I am grateful above all for the "delete" key. I now have the power, with the press of a button, to clean up, cover over, clear out cantankerous letters, incorrigible sermons, lousy lesson plans. Wouldn't it be an unbelievable gift if the rest of life had a built in delete button? With the stroke of a key we could cancel, cross out, erase all our errors, offenses, inexcusables, and execrables. As with a VCR, our past life could be re-wound, reversed, relived (or unlived). Alas, for us, I'm afraid not even God can change the past.[3]

I think not only of those things I ought to have done, but of things I ought not to have done. My guess is, every one of us has actions and events we would like to unlive. How many of us in a marriage, in a moment of weakness or anger, have uttered unfair unmentionables? Told truths better left untold? Chastised a child beyond deserving; hurt, abandoned, or abused a spouse? Even the alcoholic who has already dealt with his/her addiction has to live with the fallout, the failure and falsehoods of the old life. And the husband or wife who regrets being unfaithful cannot erase the betrayal, the adultery, the absence, and the agony. Longing to start life anew is not enough to overcome the pain and distrust that linger in the other.

Not altogether unlike the situation of the Israelites in exile to whom the prophet Jeremiah is speaking in today's reading.

They had been banished to Babylon; they were painfully aware of their past mistakes, their disobedience and disregard of the Law, their unfaithfulness to the covenant and to God. In spite of the prophet's warning and despite God's pleading with them, they had their way, had turned away, had gone astray. But now Jeremiah proclaims to them the promise of a new day, a new life, and new chance for a new covenant.[4]

That's the promise of an impossible possibility, to start all over again – with a new beginning. An offer God alone could make. Even so, it does not erase the past. Although Jeremiah calls it a new covenant, in fact it is a re-newed covenant, not because of what Israel has done or left undone, but because of who God is. God will be God, we say, even in the face of us uncooperative, unresponsive, unfaithful people. God does not depress the delete button; he is willing to work with what's there, with betrayal and brokenness. Unfortunately it is *not* "an offer we can't refuse."

That God is willing to work with what's there might be more mercy than we could bear. But even when *Genesis* says "the wickedness of man was widespread on the earth, and that every imagination of the thoughts of his heart was only evil continually," even then God refuses to blot out man from the face of the earth. God sets his bow in the clouds as a reminder that he will never utterly destroy mankind from the face of the earth by the waters of a flood. A new beginning begins right there where the pain and sinfulness are, where the mistakes of the past can be recognized and repaired. If the past cannot be erased, it can be transformed and redeemed.

But do we really believe that is possible? Can such new be-ginnings become a reality for us? For me? It is after all an offer we *can* refuse. If new beginnings are indeed possible, in my experi-ence at least, they *are* only by the grace of God, because that can-not happen unless we are willing to let go of the past, or (to say it another way) to let go of the sins, the failures, the hurts that have held us prisoner. The alcoholic cannot rebuild his/her life with-out giving up the drinking. The unfaithful husband or wife cannot rebuild the marriage while remaining unfaithful. We cannot enter into a new relationship unless we are willing to give up the past and embrace the future, however scary that may be – and however prone we are to repeat the pasts.

Where do I appear in this picture? Well, I know that without a Promethean push or promise I am reluctant to change the very things that keep me a prisoner, that wrack my life. Even if God offers us the possibility that we can change and begin again, you know, while I want, need, am dying for a new beginning, I act as though I only want to sort of start over. I'm willing to change, but only a little – not enough to make me uncomfortable or different. I want to alter the outside, clean up the image others may have of me, polish the tarnished portions of my life – but I don't really want to become something different, something new. I like the safety, the security, the comfort and company of what I know best – although it's obnoxious and unacceptable even to me.

But God asks not just that we change the way we act on the outside, rather that we be willing to have a change of heart on the inside. Willpower may change the outside, but only the power of love can enable us to change on the inside. Otherwise, in our own striving, we are doomed to have a half-way, half-hearted, half-baked "sort of" faith. (Ever tried to eat a popover that's only half done?) God's love is like the yeast that helps us rise from what we were to what we can become. Can you imagine the freedom and joy of believing that the hurts you have caused and the harm you have done to the ones you love will never be held against you? So that even though you may remember them, the love in which you are held has forgotten. I told you it sounds too good to be true. Yet that is exactly what God proposes and promises: not only the forgiveness of our sins, but that they will be forgotten, as if they had never been, our transgressions slipped from the remembrance of God as a dream slips from our consciousness on waking. In the days that are surely coming, nothing can separate us from the love of God, not even our memory of the past separations, a time when we are no longer driven by fear of the Law of God and our need to obey it – a day when our will is overwhelmed by our heart, and when we are willing to believe it! Thanks be to God.

---

1. Quoted with some paraphrase from *Homiletics* 12, 2-pp.47-8
2. Ibid.
3. This idea and many of the phrases used are shamelessly taken or adapted from "Everything Old Is New Again" by Rene Rodgers Jensen: *Biblical Preaching Journal* 13, 2-pp. 5-6
4. Ibid.
5. As above and in the ending I have subverted Ms. Jensen's direction leading to Romans 7. I am indebted to her insights as well as incorrigible in applying them to my own ends. Apologies.

A LAWLESS COVENANT

5th Sunday in Lent
Jeremiah 31:31-34
Year B – April 6, 2003

*Behold, the days are coming, says the Lord,
when I will make a new covenant with the house of
Israel and the house of Judah, not like the covenant
which I made with their fathers when I took them
by the hand to bring them out of the land of Egypt,
my covenant which they broke, though I was their
husband, says the Lord. But this is the covenant
which I will make with the house of Israel after
those days, says the Lord: I will put my law within
them, and I will write it upon their hearts; and I will
be their God, and they shall be my people. And no
longer shall each man teach his neighbor and each
his brother, saying, "Know the Lord," for they shall
all know me from the least of them to the greatest,
says the Lord; for I will forgive their iniquity, and I
will remember their sin no more.*

Jeremiah 31:31-34

I was looking for something jolting to say about Jeremiah
to start with and I found this:

> The word jeremiad means a doleful and
> thunderous denunciation, and its derivation is no
> mystery. There was nothing in need of denuncia-
> tion that Jeremiah didn't denounce. He denounced
> the king and the clergy. He denounced recreational

sex and extramarital jamborees. He denounced the rich for exploiting the poor, and he denounced the poor for deserving no better. He denounced the way every new god that came sniffing around had them all after him like so many bitches in heat; and right at the very gates of the Temple he told them that if they thought God was impressed by all the mumbo-jumbo that went on in there, they ought to have their heads examined.[1]

The personal struggle of the prophet Jeremiah was mainly an inner one, although his life and limb were outwardly attacked. In relation to the war in Iraq, his battle may seem inconsequential to us. Though Jeremiah's very being was threatened, for him what was most at risk was his spiritual life. He was angry at God because, it seemed to him, there was no justice, only self-seeking and arbitrary violence. Still he was called to prophesy in God's name nonetheless. It went down hard with him, yet strangely enough – and in spite of himself – his message was one of hope and redemption.

One of the greats in my educational experience was a revered professor of Old Testament, James Muilenburg, before whose last class each year, students would take off their shoes and leave them in the hall outside his lecture room, because they knew that this was holy ground. For first year seminary students he unlocked a lot more than the Hebrew Text; he taught us what it was like to be a flawed, fearful, insecure, self-deceptive, secret slob before God who nevertheless was the first to extend the hand, without condition or even our contrition, and offer us a welcome home, warts and all.

Yet James Muilenburg himself never completely conquered his own feeling of unworthiness, his neuroses, his suspicion that he was inwardly a fraud, even though he empowered and emboldened any number of his students, enabling them to accept the seminary mantle and venture out at last, full of fear and trembling into the real world which lay in wait for them all unprepared and ill-equipped as we were. When Fred Buechner (also one of his students) wrote Muilenburg into one of his novels as a major character (albeit under another name), Muilenburg was very upset, thinking that then his scholarly colleagues would surely see him revealed for who he really was, unmasked, unqualified, bogus and a humbug.

What moved me about Muilenburg more that I can say was not his scholarship, although "un-degreed" he brought the text of the Old Testament to life as no one else I have ever encountered. He made it my story – complaints in the wilderness, Golden Calf and all. It was his humanness, his self-doubts, his insecurity and vulnerability that allowed us to become fellow travelers in faith, to trust his theology of trial and travail. He saw in himself and in his own life the seedy, unstable, belligerent and ungodly struggles of Jeremiah. Muilenburg's only prominent published work, on the sufferings of Second Isaiah, did not relieve him of this identification with the idiosyncrasies, ambivalences and blasphemies of Jeremiah who shook his fist in God's face.

At that time an aspiring editor, I had been sent to the seminary with the assignment from *The Seabury Press* to set down the substance of Muilenburg's Old Testament lectures, which somehow no one had then so far succeeded in doing (indeed, no one ever did). I was up for the adventure, I thought, until I realized that the adventure I first had to face and confront was my own. If I couldn't enter in to the journey of Jeremiah, I couldn't complete the first page of my journal.

In contrast to the anxieties and insecurities that Jeremiah awakened in me, this morning's excerpt exposes the heart of what he won through to after the trials of his tormented life. However comforting this part of his prophesy, his was no Pollyanna perspective. This is the triumph of tested love. I know of nothing in the New Testament that can surpass it in insight or significance. If there ever was such a thing, this is the gospel according to the Law and the Prophets.

It was my salvation in seminary, because when I started out, Jesus seemed to me too devout and difficult to follow, a deity distant from my own experience; he didn't draw me in. When Jeremiah all but cursed God to his face, called him a deceiver, and said "I will no more speak again in your name," I knew what he was talking about. What took me longer to discover was that his fight with God was a lover's quarrel, not a grudge match.

***Maybe it was the words of Jeremiah
that emboldened Jesus to proclaim the gospel
to the people of his time.***

The good news of God in Jeremiah may actually be more outrageous than anything Jesus ever said: Maybe it was the words of Jeremiah that emboldened Jesus to proclaim the gospel to the people of his time. If your spiritual life is serene and secure, Jeremiah's words will not seem astonishing. But if faith is something you struggle with and doubt daily, his words carry the curative power of *Imitrex* for the migraine sufferer – almost too good to be true. Hear again the words of Jeremiah:

The days are surely coming, says the Lord, when I will make a new covenant with the house of Israel and the house of Judah, not like the covenant which I made with their fathers when I took them by the hand to bring them out of the land of Egypt, a covenant that they broke.... I will put my law within them, and I will write I upon their hearts [not upon tablets of stone] and I will be their God, and they shall be my people. And no longer shall they teach one another, saying "Know the Lord," for they shall know me ... for I will forgive their wickedness and remember their sin no more.

Imagine what the hearers of Israel, then in exile in Babylonia, must have thought of that. No longer the Ten Commandments of Moses? No need to teach anyone anymore about God and his ways? Sins not only forgiven but actually forgotten? How can you run a religion like that? If it's not anti-American it's surely antiHebrew. The next thing you know, we won't need the temple anymore either, and the priests will be out of a job. "Halleluiah," I would say, if it weren't forbidden to use that word during Lent. That's vintage Jeremiah, not just sour grapes from someone who thought God had deceived him, because every time he spoke the name of God Jeremiah became a laughing stock and a mockery; beaten and derided, lucky to escape with his life.

Imagine that – no churches? We would have to be the church ourselves. No one to teach us? We would have to help each other share and secure what is worth knowing and aspiring toward. No ministers or theologians to make sense of the meaning of our sufferings? We would have to become pastors and priests to one another and decide just what in our gospel is worth saving or speaking about. Who will tell us the sacred stories, the story of Jesus, and that we are a part of that story, that we are children of God and of the promises of God? Who will remind us that in clinging to our lives and grasping for the things of this world we will lose the value of the life we have hoarded so carefully? Who indeed? We would have only God to turn to, to rely on, to fulfill the promises he has made to his people.

And have you ever needed to be forgiven – when you were least forgiving? Needed to be loved when you are most unloving? That's Jeremiah's story, and why I can claim it as my own. He came to that understanding not on the other side of suffering but in the midst of it. He couldn't save himself from the pain, or anyone else from it either. What he told himself first of all, and then anyone who would listen to him, is our greatest problem is not that we lack the knowledge of what we know we need to do, but that we lack the will to do it. Our problem is not one of mind, but of the heart.

We can change the way we live outwardly, but that will not fundamentally change *us*, Jeremiah knew, until we have a change of heart from within. "Give me a break," we might say, "Give me a chance to start over new; wipe the slate clean, so that I can show what kind of person I can and really want to be." That's exactly what God has done, says Jeremiah – and is doing for you and me: "I will make a new covenant with my people, says the Lord, not like the one of old which you broke again and again. I will write it in your hearts and you will all know me, for I will forgive your iniquity and remember your sin no more." That's a gospel good enough for me. I am told that from time to time some of the choir bet when I am going to end my sermon. I'm not beyond ending in mid-sentence, but I'll try to be more delicate. I can't speak for you, but Jeremiah – is more than enough gospel for me. If so, then the natural outcome of what he said is that we will be willing, we will *want* to show forth in the way we live the new heart and the new spirit God has promised us – and which, Lord knows, we don't even have to ask for.

――――

1. Frederick Buechner, *Peculiar Treasures* pp.59-60.

"JESUS SAVES"

Sunday of the Passion: Palm Sunday
Matthew 27:33-44
Year B – March 16, 2008

And when they came to a place called Golgotha (which means Place of a Skull), they offered him wine to drink, mixed with gall; but when he tasted it, he would not drink it. And when they had crucified him, they divided his clothes among themselves by casting lots; then they sat down there and kept watch over him. Over his head they put the charge against him, which read, "This is Jesus, the King of the Jews. "

Then two bandits were crucified with him, one on his right and one on his left. Those who passed by derided him, shaking their heads and saying, "You who would destroy the temple and build it in three days, save yourself! If you are the Son of God, come down from the cross." In the same way the chief priests also, along with the scribes and elders, were mocking him, saying, "He saved others; he cannot save himself. He is the King of Israel; let him come down from the cross now, and we will believe in him. He trusts in God; let God deliver him now, if he wants to; for he said, I am God's Son.'" The bandits who were crucified with him also taunted him in the same way.

Matthew 27:33-44

One part of the several passion narratives that never fails to move me is where one of the two thieves who was crucified with Jesus rails at him: "Are you not the Messiah? Save yourself and us!" And then the second one, the so-called good thief, says, "Jesus, remember me when you come into your kingdom." And Jesus says to him, "Truly I tell you, today you will be with me in paradise."

While I may have a problem identifying myself with Jesus, I have no difficulty identifying myself with the criminal.

*   *   *

I begin my meditation this morning with the conviction of Ebbe Hoff, several times Senior Warden of St. Mary's, who (as some of you will remember) said to the congregation at one Annual Meeting in the early seventies, "The future of the church is in our children" (at that time there were only 13 children in Sunday School classes.). "So," he said, "Gentlemen, go home and do your duty." And look at us now: over 800 children, approaching nearly one half the membership in this parish.

As Easter advances upon us, I think particularly about the young and wonder what the lectionary readings for the difficult days leading up to Easter Sunday might mean for them. At this time of year I find myself moved quite often, and it's not just because retirement is bearing down upon me more rapidly than I care to think about, but because the pain of the world is so much with us, in the media and among the young; and, at least liturgically, Easter invites us to consider seriously the struggle of life and death.

For many years I tried to speak to the children in the Church Schools of the Diocese about the value of life reflected in Holy Week, to make them gently aware (in spite of their impatience with church services) of the inevitability of pain as a part of life, not just as something to deny and get away from. In part because of my certainty that the world or their lives will surely teach that to them before they're done – and not so gently.

The problem is to somehow get young people to see that there is value in pain, and that our task as human beings is not simply to figure out how to turn away from it, but to take seriously the proposition that pain has the possibility of becoming their richest possession if they will allow themselves to be taught what it is like to be fully human through it. Which means being willing to feel the pain that life brings us.

This morning's Gospel reading is all about that, and anyone who can read it without setting up an enormous distance between themselves and the biblical narrative will not fail to be moved by it. Because it is not just the story of some quaint historical character named Jesus, but a picture of the possibilities we will encounter in one form or another before we're through – perhaps by another name and no doubt in different circumstances. The Passion Narrative, as we call it – from the Latin word passio, to suffer – is not just the story of one person's death.

⸻

...the closest I have ever come to my own death...was when I sat in the electric chair in the Trenton State Prison.

⸻

If it does not seem too superficial to say, the closest I have ever come to my own death – that I am aware of at least – was when I sat in the electric chair in the Trenton State Prison. I have also jumped out of airplanes and driven 120 mph on a highway where the speed limit was 40. I once waded out into the warm water in Louisiana at a difficult time, wondering what it would be like if I were to breathe the water in rather than holding my breath to keep it out. When I was a child I was taken to the hospital with suspected spinal meningitis, and more than once I have experienced the kind of back pain that made me want to die.

But I remember, with a palpable feeling of anxiety and dread on that day in Trenton, tying to strap myself into "Ole Sparkie," as the guards called the electric chair. I remember, too, being outraged that it squeaked as if it had a screw loose, and was so rickety – as though with a good jolt or two the wooden contraption would fly apart in the middle of a scheduled execution, and they'd have to pick up the pieces (not to mention the person) and put them together and start over again.

I was a college student at the time, taking a course in criminology – and this was part of my field work, the "practical" part of it, carelessly called in the syllabus the "real life" experience of our course work – so I was quite safe. But it gave me a terrible feeling because precisely because I could get up and walk away, I wondered what it would be like if I were strapped in for good and could not escape, helpless in the face of my own impending death. Or worse still, I pondered, what if I were free to walk away but decided to go through with it anyway. That's what really evoked the chills and the sickening sensation inside me. And that's where we find Jesus in the Gospel reading for today. All that preamble is to say that the cross was the first century's version of the electric chair, and Jesus resolutely refused to avoid facing it.

Which makes all the more ironic the railing of one of the criminals crucified with him, who said, "Are you not the Christ? Save yourself and us!" The name, Jesus, means "he saves," after all, which is, I suppose, where that (for me) uncomfortable evangelical saying "Jesus saves" comes from. During those same college years I used to see that saying "Jesus saves" mostly in improbable places, such as on a tall bridge or overpass – somewhere where seemingly almost no one could get to – high up on a mountain; or, on the other hand, in the men's room in public places. There was something always unlikely, slightly obscene, about where it would show up. It was even embarrassing, because to be caught saying "Jesus Saves" as other than a caustic comment on the naiveté of religious slogans was to risk being called a Christer – which in those days in the northeastern collegiate establishment was the equivalent of being a fool, a simpleton, or a crusader – all of which were viewed as misguided, misinformed, and likely missing a screw somewhere.

In the face of the Passion Narrative, to say "Jesus saves," not only sounds ridiculous but terribly ironic because Jesus does not even save himself from the pain of the world or from his own death. And the words of the two thieves on either side of him one asking to be saved, are spoken when all is lost. "Jesus saves" – indeed! A friend of mine says there is something embarrassing about saying "*Jesus* saves" – just "*Jesus*," with no title to soften the blow.... the words "Christ saves" would not bother us half so much because they have a kind of... theological ring to them, whereas "Jesus" saves seems cringingly, painfully personal – somebody named Jesus, of all names, saving somebody named whatever your or my name happens to be." [1]

To see "Jesus Saves" in a public place makes it cheap on the one hand, slightly out of taste if not indecent. On the other hand, maybe the reason "Jesus Saves" is embarrassing is because it seems to say to us – to me – that *I need* to be saved.

But can such a one as that Jesus save *me* (if, indeed, I want to be "saved" at all)? What a question. Not that we do not deserve saving, but that we are so much hopelessly who we are that we might wonder whether we could be saved from being anything other than who we are, even if we wanted to. So from the place in me that is empty in my darker moments, I ask what can fill the emptiness in me with whatever name we chose to call it – truth, fulfillment, salvation, Jesus?

The problem is the picture we are given of Jesus who saves is on the cross, and it is painted with the words that come from "the pain of the good thief, which" (as one commentary has put it) "is the pain of surrender, the pain of acknowledging finally our utter helplessness to save ourselves. In the depths of his own pain the good thief said, 'Jesus, remember me when you come in your kingdom.' Remember me. Remember me,"[2] he said.

And you may remember what preposterous thing Jesus said to him in reply: "I will" (he said in effect, out of the depths of his inconsolable pain) "Today you will be with me in Paradise." He does not say that we will come to paradise painlessly, or that we can avoid it if we draw near to him, or even that we will not experience the pain of the world if we choose to have nothing whatsoever to do with him (which might be paradise enough for some people). No, the biblical text asserts that in the *midst* of pain *it is true*, "Jesus Saves," that he gives life, he makes whole, and if you choose to be, you will be with him in Paradise."[3] Preposterous? But what if it were true?

If it is *not*, then of course we are safe, not only from having to think about the inevitability of our pain in the face of it, but from having to deal with his. On the other hand, if it is true, then it is we who are preposterous in our attempts to avoid the pain that draws us near to him. How can we know which one is the truth? The only way I know is by being willing to draw near to him, to offer up the pain that matters not only to me but to him who saves, by not drawing back from those difficult moments in my own life when something of his truth, his life calls to mine and draws me close to him.

What, you may ask, does any of this have to do with young people whose main suffering is hating to endure the pain of endless academic classes or the boredom of unplanned weekends? Or to some of us older adolescents who might possibly be embarrassed by the saying "Jesus Saves"? Just this, and I came across it in a book I had read a while ago and put down – but which suddenly made sense to me in the context of the scripture readings for this week. It speaks about – of all things – an improbable meaning of the word adolescent which "has no basis in linguistic fact but... suggests that the word adolescent is made up of the Latin preposition ad, meaning toward, and the Latin noun dolor, meaning pain. Thus adolescent becomes a term which designates human beings who are in above all else a painful process, more specifically those who are in the process of discovering pain itself, of trying somehow to come to terms with pain, to figure out how to deal with pain, not just how to survive pain but how to turn it to some human and creative use in their own encounters with it.

"So adolescents, ... in terms of that spurious etymology, are growing in this one specific area of human experience, ... discovering that in addition to good, there is also evil, that in addition to the joy of being alive, there is also the sadness and hurt of being alive and being themselves. Adolescents are like Gautama the Buddha as he recognized the first of the Four Noble Truths, which is that life is suffering, that at any given moment life can be lots of happy things too, but that suffering is universal and inevitable and that to face that reality and to come to terms with that reality [as he did and as Jesus did] is at the heart of what human growing is all about."[4]

The passion of Jesus following Palm Sunday does not end on the cross but in a prayer that can make our spiritual adolescence whole if only we will draw near enough to him to hear it, the one I began with: "Jesus, remember me when you come into your kingdom, *Remember* me. Remember *me*." If in the pain of the good thief we can say that Jesus saves, without embarrassment, then who can dare to say that paradise holds no promise for us?

———

1. Frederick Buechner, *Secrets in the Dark,* p.28
2. *Op. cit.*, p.33
3. Frederick Buechner, *The Hungering Dark*, p.67
4. Frederick Buechner, *The Clown in the Belfry,* pp.85-86

THE MAUNDY MANDATUM

The Fish Bowl Blessing

Maundy Thursday
John 12:20-36
Year A — March 24, 2005

When Jesus had thus spoken, he was trou-bled in spirit, and testified, "Truly, truly, I say to you, one of you will betray me. "The disciples looked at one another, uncertain of whom he spoke. One of his disciples, whom Jesus loved, was lying close to the breast of Jesus; so Simon Peter beckoned to him and said, "Tell us who it is of whom he speaks." So ly-ing thus, close to the breast of Jesus, he said to him, "Lord, who is it?" Jesus answered, "It is he to whom I shall give this morsel when I have dipped it." So when he had dipped the morsel, he gave it to Judas, the son of Simon Iscariot. Then after the morsel, Sa-tan entered into him. Jesus said to him, "What you are going to do, do quickly." Now no one at the table knew why he said this to him. Some thought that, because Judas had the moneybox, Jesus was telling him, "Buy what we need for the feast;" or, that he should give something to the poor. So, after receiv-ing the morsel, he immediately went out; and it was night.

When he had gone out, Jesus said, "Now is the Son of man glorified, and in him God is glorified; if God is glorified in him, God will also glorify him in himself, and glorify him at once. Little children, yet a little while I am with you. You will seek me; and as I said to the Jews so now I say to you, "Where I am going you cannot come." A new commandment I give to you, that you love one another; even as I have loved you, that you also love one another. By this all men will know that you are my disciples, if you have love for one another. "

John 12:21-35

What I am wearing may be a sermon in itself; it is to me symbolic of these days in the Church year and also of what I shall say of Maundy Thursday. This is an African ceremonial gilet, which, surprisingly, is worn at both funerals and at weddings, for impor-

tant celebrations and religious occasions. Yet its colors express traditional theological themes familiar to us: Brown is the color of earth that overtakes us, as well as the earth that brings forth life. The cones, pointing upward and pointing downward, represent the mountains from which come great power; and the wavy lines are the waters which can cover the mountains but which also quench the thirst of the land and awaken the crops. The diamonds stand for our ancestors, from which we learn wisdom, how to live and how to honor our families. The red-orange delineates the human struggle and the bravery that uplifts us. Pre-

dominant brown reverences the earth that buries us and the life that springs forth from it – a visual expression of Holy Week.

*   *   *

Not everyone knows the meaning of the term Maundy Thursday. Being a coin collector, for many years I assumed that Maundy was a quaint adaptation of an Old English word for money, because I knew about Maundy money, the special coins (one, two, three and four pence) especially minted for distribution to the poor by the British sovereign on Maundy Thursday. And although my labors in the study of Latin were long, they were also languid; I had overlooked that *mandatum* was the term for "command," and in my wisdom I'd forgotten that the traditional English name for the Thursday preceding Easter was derived from the first antiphon of the ceremony of the foot washing, "mandatum novum," a new commandment.

We are, of course, familiar with Jesus' saying to his disciples: "I give you a new commandment, that you love one another even as I have loved you. By this everyone will know that you are my disciples." The "love" there is not invited, suggested, or commended — but commanded. A strange sort of love, I used to think; how can you command love? That goes against our modern western notion that it is not really love unless *you* choose it. We rarely stop to think that if we have made a commitment to the one we love, love is required as our first priority for that person.

I want to say something about the nature of that love embodied in our speaking of it on Maundy Thursday. And I want to begin it with a stone — one I hold here in my hand. It is smooth, rounded, satisfying to hold, one you could grasp fiercely if you had to in the midst of some kind of physical trial or pain. I'm sure you've seen these before in gift shops. They come in various sizes. Some have inscriptions on them. Mine has the word "Wisdom" chiseled into it — a gift to me from a good friend. All's well so far, but that's not the end of the story.

To tell the truth, I was at first flattered by her choice of the word wisdom for me — I fancied she thought it appropriate because I had some. But after my ego trip, the more I thought about it realistically, why would she have given it to me if I already had it — perhaps what she was really saying was what I needed was wisdom and this stone would start me on that way because it would remind me of what I was after. A bit deflating, but I felt relieved that she hadn't given me instead a stone with "love" on it. (More about that later.)

Last week I happened upon a one page commentary by Barbara Brown Taylor on finding some silver "pebbles" (as she called them), some about as big as her thumb, piled in a glass bowl at a gift shop in the High Museum of Art in Atlanta. Even without touching them, she could see through the glass that one said "hope" and another said "love." She thought of her widowed friend who could use some encouragement like that, so she sank her hand in the bowl to see what else she might fish up. "'Tears,' said the next pebble. 'Loss' said the next. Well, (she wrote) I thought my friend already has enough of those, so I put them back and kept fishing... Why pay good money for something that life pelts you with for free?"[1]

At that point I (Christopher) was about to stop reading and flip to find an article more momentous than some cutesy stone sentiments; but as I was turning the page I saw fleetingly the word "forgiveness," something I'm always in need of. Barbara Brown Taylor said she had found only one of those, at the bottom of the bowl – obviously the bestselling stone – and she laid it on the counter along with "hope," "love," and "gratitude." When she looked back at all the tears and loss in the bowl, she realized there were so many of them left because no one wanted to own them; that was the problem. So she chose one of each and added them to the collection she was going to give to her friend.

"I felt almost cruel giving them to [her]," she wrote, "but her sad mouth softened when she saw them. She may not have wanted them, but she knew they were hers, and seeing them in her hand with all the others told her story better than the edited version I first had in mind."[2]

—∘—

"When Christians talk about what the church has to offer the world, one thing we do not mention is an adequate theology of failure...."

—∘—

Then came the part I thought was worth taking your time with on this Thursday evening: "When Christians talk about what the church has to offer the world, one thing we do not mention is an adequate theology of failure .... We live in a culture that adores success, ... Being a successful human being means making straight A's, keeping a well-paid job with good benefits, staying happily married to an attractive person, raising well-adjusted children, and not gaining too much weight. Judging from the commercials on television, being successful also means driving a hot car, carrying a cool cell phone, having young-looking skin and choosing the right medicine to beat depression ... [or sex lag]. [3] Which leaves a lot of room for failure, because who can measure up? "But the same culture that creates these conditions for failure is not equipped to deal with it." Speaking for myself, Barbara Brown Taylor is onto something we need to be reminded of. Our culture may create them, but it doesn't know what to do with losers; it is not equipped to deal lovingly with failure, except in one place – at church.

There "the loser shows up right above the altar. If success was on his list of things to do, then it was not the kind that anyone around him had much use for. Once, in the presence of large crowds, he blessed the poor in spirit, the mournful, the hungry and the reviled. Some of the people ... no doubt wished he had done something to relieve their conditions instead of blessing them." [4] But at least they knew they were not alone. And he did not share simply his wisdom with them; he also offered them his tears and loss.

Pondering that perspective, I decided to name it the fish bowl blessing: If Jesus was right, then we don't have to fish among the stones to find only gratitude and happiness and grace; we don't have to leave our tears and losses in the bowl, we can hold them in our hands along with the others because we have been blessed by a suffering love that didn't hold anything back. His victory was his failure; his love was in his defeat.

The concise commentary says it this way: "I go to church to remember that – not to hear about the victory of the cross but to be reminded that there is no shame in failure at the foot of the cross.... Jesus was not pretending while he was hanging there. He really did lose everything, buying up all the tears and loss [that] no one else wanted. [And] because he did, I know that when I am feeling my most hurt and futile, even most abandoned by God, I can trust that in his love I am not far from him but as close as I can get..."[5]

That's the story of love – told for all of us. But it's not finished. There's a catch. If we believe it, in return we are commanded to offer to one another the love in it. That leads to life, not death; and if we fail at it, we are not alone, supported by the solace of the everlasting arms that seemed to somehow elude us in our success. When I started out this evening with my story about the stone I'd been given, I didn't tell you the whole truth. I made light of my failure in wisdom and joked that the only thing more difficult would have been to accept the burden of being given a stone with "love" written on it. The truth is I have been given a stone that says love, this one that I am holding; only it's in Hebrew. And I want you to know, I' m not hiding it – I'm working on it, mindful of the Maundy mandatum.

———

1. *Christian Century*, February 22, 2005.
2. *Ibid.*
3. *Ibid.*
4. *Ibid.*
5. *Ibid.*

EASTER

If resurrection is to be a reality for us, we are at least in part responsible for it. If we do not witness him in the midst of our own lives, where else are we likely to meet him? That is where we have the best opportunity to seek his presence – not in political speeches, or in Congressional medal-of-honor gestures, or in other heroic acts which most of us don't get the chance to perform. We meet him when we are called upon to have courage in the midst of heartbreak or pain, or by the needs of others, or in our most intimate relationships, or even in the breaking of our daily bread together (which is a symbol for the acts of every day). Either we recognize his presence there, or we will not know him elsewhere.

Christopher Brookfield

RESURRECTION NEVER HAPPENED?

St. Mary's Sunday School
April 14, 1985

Some of you may scarcely have savored the significance of this Sunday; it is the Sunday *after* the celebration of Easter. The glorious proclamations have been promulgated, the trumpets have trumpeted the triumph of our risen Lord, and the old favorite triumphal hymns have been hymned or heard – depending on your gender – for another year. If the truth were known, our appetite for the unexpected is appeased for the time being, celebrated, satiated for another year. What, indeed, is left to say or sing or salute this Sunday?

Were I a paranoid person, being asked to say something (significant or otherwise) on the Sunday after Christmas or Easter, I might be tempted to think there is a message there for me worth noting. At such times, either nothing you can say will make any difference, or precious few will be there to hear it. The point is, that may be the point. But seriously, after Easter, what of importance is worth the utterance?

In preparation for this session, I decided not to ask some theologians but some ordinary people what they thought. One person asked me what I was going to do today. I said quite honestly that I couldn't make up my mind whether to try to teach some theology – and here my mistake was to pause momentarily, whereupon she interjected, "or something useful."

I asked another more or less normal person in a somewhat normal church-going family, "When you use the word resurrection, what do you mean? Her answer was, "I don't use it. I see it as a church word and we don't talk church at home." When I asked, "If a preacher uses the word resurrection, what does he mean?" She said, "It means the Easter event, on that day." When I protested that the meaning was perhaps broader than that, the reply came, "The Church doesn't speak to me much about the resurrection every day, only about Christ rising from the dead." "Too bad," I said.

I next went to the office dictionary to see if I could find anything more relevant, and discovered nothing of any real help, but two things of interest. *Resurrection*, it said, can refer to the state of those risen from the dead," which may shed some light on how we feel in our daily descent from the bedcovers each morning – further defined in the dictionary as a "rising from decay or disease. A *resurrectionist*, I find, can also refer to one "who exhumes bodies, especially for dissection; a body snatcher." Something to think about, if only in passing, in considering the Easter narrative as we find it in the Bible.

At the very least, the Biblical narrative poses – for the believer as well as the unbeliever – two major problems. (I realize that the behavioral positivists of our time regard the word "problem" as inappropriate, "challenge" or "opportunity" is what we should use – even on the first Sunday after Easter.) Perhaps as a cautioning note I should remind you of what Eric Sevareid said, "the chief cause of problems is solutions." Anyway, the challenge today is to share the opportunity to ponder the problems in rescuing the resurrection from the resurrectionists. Forgive me if that sounds flippant, it is intended to be faith-affirming.

In searching out what the New Testament intended in its affirmation of resurrection, I'd have to be honest in saying that the Church lectionary for the forty days between Easter and Ascension is not immediately helpful. The Biblical passages assigned for us to read dwell again and again on the resurrection appearances. When you're asking, "What does resurrection mean? Did it really happen? What are the facts?" to be confronted by a succession of stories of resurrection appearances may be interesting but not necessarily helpful. They are, perhaps, necessary for faith, but are they sufficient?

A sample will suffice: Jesus walks and talks with his disciples on the road to Emmaus; or he breaks bread with them at an evening meal; or he takes a piece of fish and eats it in their presence; or he shows them the wounds in his hands and feet and sides – so that doubting Thomas (which most of us are at least some of the time), whose imagination was not his long suit, was willing to believe what he saw. Here we have in the Biblical text common everyday events, told to us over and over again, instead of a satisfying (or even unsatisfying) explanation of the most extraordinary event that lay behind them and without which they would have little more than illusory significance (in a literal sense).

—◦—

"When Christians talk about what the church has to offer the world, one thing we do not mention is an adequate theology of failure...."

—◦—

But that is not the problem; it is only symptomatic. The odd thing about the story of the resurrection in the Biblical narrative, as you may have discovered for yourself, is not that the Easter occurrence is not described at length or in great detail in scripture, it just isn't described at all. The narrative contains only the barest of information, none of it really substantiated, the sum and substance of which is this: The women went to the tomb, found the stone rolled away; and when they went in they did not find the body. Period. That's it. Some explanation. That's all we have of the story of the most crucial event in the history of the Church. That's the first problem to ponder: In the whole of the Easter message there is no account of the resurrection itself, bodily or otherwise; it is simply proclaimed as fact. (German theologicians have a wonderful word for that kind of situation: *gevorfenheit*, the thrownness of the interpretation upon us: something simply dumped on us to deal with.)

In contrast, the appearances of Jesus to his disciples are described at some length, on various occasions, sometimes in great detail, all the way from Easter to Ascension; the lectionary is relentless. A cynic might say it is almost as though the early church was not quite sure about the proclamation of Easter morning, as though the scripture readings for the forty days of Eastertide were intended for the doubting Thomases for whom the Easter story was not quite convincing enough, as though the Church needed to be assured again and again that Christ was indeed risen.

A word about the second problem. The women. And by that I do not mean that the women's witness at the tomb (the only one we have after all) is problematic. The men, as it turns out, the apostles no less, were the problem, in that they didn't believe what the women said. As scripture puts it, Mary Magdalene, and Joanna, and Mary the mother of James, among other women with them, "told these things unto the apostles." And, as Luke comments, "their words seemed to them [the apostles] as idle tales, and they believed them not." (Their solution, as you may remember, was to send Peter to verify the situation, good old reliable, unstable Peter. But I digress.)

The women's problem (rather than the problem with the women) arose as the New English Bible puts it, when they went to find Jesus on that Sunday morning and discovered the tomb empty and "the body was not to be found." Why? The question of the two men there "in shining robes" is instructive, "Why do you seek the living among the dead?" or in another translation, "Why search among the dead for one who is alive?" Why, indeed?

Had they expected that on the third day he would rise again, why would they have been dismayed to find him gone? Why would they not have expected to find an empty tomb and rejoiced in it? Was that not the good news, "He is not here, but is risen."? Apparently not. In fact, they expected to find him there, for which reason they had brought with them to the tomb the spices and ointments they had prepared with which to anoint his body. Curious, or is it?

Most TV mysteries insist that we can't have a crime without a corpse. Otherwise, it is an insoluble case. It may surprise you to learn that ancient Hebrew psychology and anthropology would have understood that assertion, as did the apostle Paul who accepted human beings as a psychosomatic unity of body and spirit. The Hebrews could no more conceive of a disembodied spirit than they could a disinspirited body. Had the early Church been concerned with the affirmation of a doctrine of bodily resurrection (reflected in the later creeds we are familiar with) apart from the necessity for the proclamation of Christ's resurrection, then the women who went to find Jesus would not have been dismayed to find the tomb empty, his body gone, and him risen, the immortal spirit freed at last from its bodily imprisonment (as the Greeks did). Quite the contrary for those Hebrews, how else could God have revealed to them the triumph of Christ over death except in his bodily presence? That can be the only reason why they were "utterly at a loss" to witness an empty tomb.

One point of clarification, which may be unnecessary for many of you, is to remind ourselves that the Easter message in the New Testament Greek is proclaimed in a tense that we do not use much in our speaking today, the present perfect: "He is risen." Not he *rose*, nor even that he *will* rise, but he *is* risen – and that has made believable the assertion that the worst Friday in Christendom can be called good.

So in the Biblical text, the resurrection is understood as a *present* event, the significance of which lies not in a historical fact nor in a future hope. If what the Church celebrates is the assurance of eternal life, the apostles were clear that it was experienced in the "now" of the lives of those who were able to recognize Jesus' presence among them. Where does that leave us?

Perhaps it leaves us where the Swiss theologian Karl Barth once said it should – at the crossroads of faith, at the entrance to the tomb. He would pound on his podium in Basel punctuating each syllable of his solemn pronouncement to his students: Either you return in faith to the tomb on Easter morning with the stone rolled back, and you affirm with the apostles then and there, "Yes the tomb is empty!" or the rest of it does not matter a damn. You must say "Ja!" in faith or "Nein!" to all the rest.[1]

To sharpen the point further, Paul Tillich, the German theological contemporary of Barth, put resurrection in a perspective that is either a cause for great hope or a cry of despair. He said, either resurrection happens now, today, as a reality in the lives of people in the 20th century, or else the Resurrection never happened at all in the first century.

The message for us is something beyond the Easter proclamation, and it goes something like this: If resurrection is to be a reality for us, we are at least in part responsible for it. If we do not witness him in the midst of our own lives, where else are we likely to meet him? That is where we have the best opportunity to seek his presence – not in political speeches, or in Congressional medal-of-honor gestures, or in other heroic acts which most of us don't get the chance to perform. We meet him when we are called upon to have courage in the midst of heartbreak or pain, or by the needs of others, or in our most intimate relationships, or even in the breaking of our daily bread together (which is a symbol for the acts of every day). Either we recognize his presence there, or we will not know him elsewhere.

----

1. The exact quote is "Resurrection happens *now*, or it does not happen at all." Paul Tillich, *The New Being*, p.24

WHERE THE ALLELUIAS ARE

Sunday of the Resurrection: Easter Day
Mark 16:1-8
Year B – April 23, 2000

When the sabbath was over, Mary Magdalene, and Mary the mother of James, and Salome bought spices, so that they might go and anoint Jesus. And very early on the first day of the week, when the sun had risen, they went to the tomb. They had been saying to one another, "Who will roll away the stone for us from the entrance to the tomb?" When they looked up, they saw that the stone, which was very large, had already been rolled back. As they entered the tomb, they saw a young man, dressed in a white robe, sitting on the right side; and they were alarmed. But he said to them, "Do not be alarmed; you are looking for Jesus of Nazareth, who was crucified. He has been raised; he is not here. Look, there is the place they laid him. But go, tell his disciples and Peter that he is going ahead of you to Galilee; there you will see him, just as he told you." So they went out and fled from the tomb, for terror and amazement had seized them; and they said nothing to anyone, for they were afraid.

Mark 16:1-8

"Listen, my child," [St. Francis] said, "each year at Easter I used to watch Christ's resurrection. All the faithful would gather around His tomb and weep, weep inconsolably, beating on the ground to make it open. And behold! In the midst of our lamenta-

177

tions the tombstone crumbled to pieces and Christ sprang from the earth and ascended to heaven, smiling at us and waving a white banner. There was only one year I did not see Him resurrected. That year a theologian of consequence, a graduate of the University of Bologna, came to us. He mounted the pulpit in church and began to elucidate the Resurrection for hours on end. He explained and explained until our heads began to swim; and that year the tombstone did not crumble, and I swear to you, no one saw the Resurrection."[1]

I hope not to repeat that experience for you here this morning. So although I am ever tempted by the taste of theology the way I am by Hubs peanuts, I've essentially given it up for Easter Sunday so as not to interfere with our rejoicing in the resurrection. I do have to indulge in one little observation, which could be construed as theological, and which explains why the end of Mark's gospel in some of your Bibles (the last 12 verses, cut off in our reading) do not belong to Mark and were simply added on to the original ending. But that won't take long – and besides, it leads to the heart of what I hope to leave you with today.

First, let me say that I am delighted the lectionary insists on our engaging the Gospel of Mark for our Easter enunciation, not because I am perverse, but because, even unfinished, it is the more empowering for us, I believe, and I hope to show you why. Many preachers would prefer to stay clear of Mark and opt for the alternative reading in the Common Lectionary (for Year B), which is John' s Gospel (chapter 20, verses 1-18). Why? Because the conclusion of Mark' s Gospel stops with a conjunction, in the Greek – and, furthermore, it doesn't tell us what we want to hear. As a final statement, it falls flat, the emotional equivalent of the let-down illustrated in this otherwise potentially poignant piece:

The woman's husband had been slipping in and out of a coma for several months, yet she had stayed by his bedside every single day. One day, when he came to, he motioned for her to come nearer.

As she sat by him, he whispered, eyes full of tears, "You know what? You have been with me all through the bad times. When I got fired, you were there to support me. When my business failed, you were there. When I got shot, you were by my side. When we lost the house, you stayed right here. When my health started failing, you were still by my side ... You know what?"

"What dear?" She gently asked, smiling as her heart began to fill with warmth.

"I think you are bad luck."[2]

Emotionally, the last verse, which ends the Gospel of Mark, is a downer. It stops not only in the middle of the story, but in mid-sentence, with the conjunction "because" (translated in English as "for"). Our current translations try to tidy up the syntax, but that won't fix the Greek or finish the story. Where is the appearance of the risen Christ that we expect? Where is the public proclamation of his prevailing presence?

All we have is this: The three women who had been present at Jesus' crucifixion go to the tomb with burial spices in order to complete his entombment, wondering mostly how in heaven's name the large stone will be removed from the entrance. Which turns out to be no problem because it has already been rolled back. But the body is missing, which is a real problem, because if Jesus were to be resurrected – remember, for the Hebrews there could be no such thing as a disembodied spirit or a disinspirited body – the body needed to be there. An empty tomb was therefore no evidence of the resurrection – rather, the reverse. The corpse of Jesus was gone; instead, what the women encounter was what they take to be an angelic appearance who tells them that the Jesus they are looking for "is not here... Go and tell his disciples that he is going ahead of you to Galilee; [where] you will see him." Then follows Mark's last verse: "So they went out and fled from the tomb in terror, and they said nothing to any one, for they were afraid."

There is a great irony in the ending here, in case it escaped you; because throughout Mark's telling of Jesus' story; almost everyone he healed was charged to be silent, since only when the story was complete should the Good News be made known. Of course, rarely ever did anyone keep silent. But now, at last, at the time of the resurrection, when the command is given to the three women at the tomb, "Go and tell..." the Gospel ends by announcing, "They said nothing to anyone."

I can understand why the resurrection account in Mark troubled the faith of the early church, and why by the time of its first circulation other more satisfying endings had been added on to Mark's account. In them, Jesus appears to several of his disciples and he commissions his believers to carry on his ministry (including some accounts about handling snakes and poison, eventually excluded) – but in general, much happier, more comfortable, and uplifting announcements than in the awkward ending of the women fleeing the tomb in fear and saying nothing.

We can concur that Mark's conclusion is odd, abrupt, and perhaps even condone the conduct of the early Christian scribes who felt compelled to "paste a pastiche of proper postscripts upon it" to make it more like the well-loved resurrection accounts in the other three Gospels. Why would Mark, the earliest evangelist, insist on ending his account on such a dismal note? We feel cheated out of a complete and compelling conclusion. We are confounded; the core conviction is unconvincing: saying only that the tomb was unexpectedly empty – barren, bare, blank. Was that God's final statement to an uncertain world? Have you seen a copy of the joke book called *Easy on the Alleluias, Harry?* Is that where we are left, mouthing alleluias to ourselves under our breath, fearful that they are inappropriate or in bad taste?

"Everybody wants assurance about our final destination," write Ross and Kathryn Petras in their book, *The 176 Stupidest Things Ever Done*, to wit: "In 1976 a hijacker got up from his airplane seat. He took out a gun and held up a stewardess, [saying] 'Take me to Detroit.'

"'But we're going to Detroit already,' said the stewardess. 'Oh, good,' said the hijacker and [then] sat back down."[3]

Let's try to take a look at Mark's message from a different perspective. What if he intentionally left the ending uncertain; maybe he intended to confound our most hopeful expectations, to overturn the tame and familiar in order to initiate the kind of change in us that is beyond our wildest imagination.

James F. T. Bugental, in *The Art of the Psychotherapist*, compares and contrasts what he calls the idea of the "zoo god," which we are capable of constructing and controlling, with the "wild god" that is beyond our capacity to conceive or capture.

He writes:

"The zoo god could not take us by surprise; we visited him at our convenience and chiefly as children. The zoo god could not upset the comfortable routines of our lives, and he seemed ... to require little feeding with anything that mattered.

"Not to be so trained is the wild god, who may overturn everything as he comes into our lives. She may demand all we have as it devours our complacency and require us to change violently, totally, frighteningly....

"The wild God is the god of mystery ... Mystery enfolds knowledge, contains knowledge. Mystery is infinite; knowledge finite. As knowledge grows, even more does mystery grow. Mystery is the latent meaning always awaiting our discovery and always more than our knowing.... If we [would] seek the wild god, we must go out into the world, out into the dangers and opportunities, go without a map, without a compass, without enough food, protection, anything. And as we seek the wild god, we may be captured by him. For mystery comprehends us; we do not comprehend it."[4]

So, which one will we have? At Easter do we set out for the tomb to safely embalm the God we have known, or are we willing to expect and encounter the God outside it, who is always elusive and unexpected?

William Willimon tells the story of a pastor "going to visit a church member who had been in a car accident and had lost the feeling and mobility of his legs. At the close of the visit, the pastor prayed and asked God to bring healing. Suddenly the patient said, 'Hey, there's a tingling sensation in my legs. Yes! I can feel my legs. I think I can walk now.' The pastor stammered something about not pushing it, but the patient struggled out of the wheel chair anyway, stood on his feet, and slowly took a few steps. The patient cried out, 'It's a miracle. God has healed me!' When the pastor got to his car, he felt faint. He rested his hands and head on the steering wheel for a moment, then looked heavenward and said, 'God, thank you for healing that man. Now, don't ever do that to me again!'" We don't accept the unexpected easily.

Mark's Gospel leaves us hanging on the promise of resurrection, on a prayer for life out of death. Clearly, the end of his story isn't the end of the gospel; it is in fact only the beginning.

Mark seems to be saying to us that if we look for God in the places we expect to find him, we are likely to miss him altogether because (as the text tells it) Christ "goes on before us." He is always "going ahead of us to Galilee." "God is not apparent to the naked eye but only to the vision of the believer." That's what Mark challenges us to believe – that we can find him with us even in our daily lives, waiting to be recognized in the common places as well as the extraordinary. That's where we should seek to find him – and to be found by him. Resurrection, a story of life coming out of death, is not the gift for a chosen few, but for all. Is there a conclusion in this "unfinished" gospel? For me there is.

Mark leaves us with the antic conviction "Jesus wouldn't be caught dead in that tomb." He wants to be caught alive – seen in the garden, strolling on the road to Emmaus, shining in the faces of people who have recognized resurrection in their own lives – caught alive in us, encountered in our hope and faith.

"Does Mark give us any rock bottom ... certain proof of God's abiding presence? No. Do we ... get to see, with absolute clarity and beyond all doubt, the risen Jesus? No. But faith doesn't need that. The resurrection is not a theory to prove ... [it is] a reality to believe and experience as we go [forward in] faith and hope ... expecting to discover [the presence of] Jesus outside the tomb, [in us], in the Galilees where we live. That's where others have found him. We've heard their stories..."[5]

Go and tell yours – and mine. That's where the Alleluias are easy.

> *The stone in our lives has been rolled away.*
> *The Easter light still shines in our faces.*
> *Go out into the Galilees of this world:*
> *To spread the news that Christ is [on the] loose again,*
> *to join with God in building a new creation,*
> *to live in a way that others will say Christ is risen!*
> *Christ is risen, indeed! Alleluia! Amen.*[6]

———

1. from Nikos Kazantzakis' *Tale of St. Francis*, p. 69.
2. *Homiletics* 12, 2-p.59
3. *Op. cit.*, p.61
4. *Lectionary Homiletics* XI, 5-p.31
5. Larry Paul Jones, *Biblical Preaching Journal* 13, 2-p.11
6. Hope Douglas & J. Harle-Mould, *Homiletics* 12, 2-p.61

WHY ARE YOU WEEPING?

Sunday of the Resurrection: Easter Day
John 20:1-18
Year A – March 31, 2002

Two quotations to take with you today and hide among your jellybeans when you've forgotten all about Easter Bunnies and festive hats:

First from Barbara Brown Taylor, in her book, *Gospel Medicine*: God "is not in the business of granting wishes. God is in the business of raising the dead, not all of whom are willing" [to be resurrected].

The second comes from the magazine *The Door*: "the Devil dressed like a Hollywood agent, with the name 'B. Elzebub' on his desk. Speaking to a black-cloaked figure with a scythe in his hand, he says, 'Death Baby, you need to refocus. Ever since that resurrection thing, your work has lost its sting.'"

I don't suppose that many of you here are from that generation who would greet one another first thing upon waking in bed on Easter morning with the salutation "Christ is risen," to which the expected and more familiarly personal reply was "he is risen, indeed" – and to which a wise guy like me might have added, "How about you?" Assuming you weren't offended, by the suggestion, you could have retorted, "'He is risen' is in the present perfect tense, and I don't do that." But it's a fair question, because however we understand the resurrection, we're supposed to be participants in it, not just observers – at least that was the conviction of those who wrote the Gospel stories. To borrow a phrase, that might be easier said than done, given that the present is so imperfect and a lot of people don't pretend to know what resurrection really is about anyway.

It doesn't help that in the Gospels there is no account given of the resurrection. Did you notice? It is simply stated, assumed; there is no story or explanation of it, and we are left alone to decide about it for ourselves, much as Mary Magdalene was in her weeping at the tomb, where Jesus intensified her sorrow when he said "Do not hold on to me..." or "Don't cling to me." Which doesn't leave us much to hold onto either. How do you grasp the substance of an empty tomb? That's what John's gospel leaves with us, or where we are left on Easter morning – this Easter morning as a matter of fact.

What Mary has left is only the hollow place in her heart Jesus has left her, which is why she is weeping. In place of his living being, she has a "living ache," so much so that when what or whom she has been yearning for at the tomb appears to her at last, Jesus standing there in her sight, she somehow doesn't seem to recognize him. How do you explain that? Over the years, theologians have offered a number of explanations, such as: "it was still too dark to see anything, [or] the tears in Mary's eyes blurred her vision, [or] she was turned away from [Jesus] and couldn't see his face." [1]

Whether or not those reasons make sense to us may not be as important as whether they satisfy us – personally, if not theologically. We might first want to ask ourselves the curious question: Could we accept resurrection if we saw it? More importantly, might we, along with Mary not recognize it because we do not want it? Maybe what we want is things the way they were (or are). How do we deal with what we have lost? How well do we accept emptiness – in our own lives, let alone how we might imagine it in Mary's or in Jesus' disciples' who fled from him? Someone has said that all of life is learning how to let go, suffering to say one series of goodbyes after another. We cannot abide emptiness, or easily accept the loss of all that is good in our lives, any more than

Mary could. Maybe because we can't really imagine what resurrection is like, the empty tomb notwithstanding.

"...for we sense that it's in the empty space where creation happens."

Maybe we first have to look into the emptiness before we can find out. Because the emptiness of God is not just nothingness, but the possibility for creation, which we might be able to understand if we consider "Michelangelo's famous painting of creation for the Sistine Chapel where the hand of God reaches forth to touch Adam's hand. Despite the beauty of the fingers, our eye is drawn to the emptiness between God and Adam, for we sense that it's in the empty space where creation happens. It's in the empty tomb where God ... sees the potential to work new life."[2] In a manner of speaking, Mary cried as though her heart was broken, but it was really simply broken open so that new life could arise – a life not just for Mary, but for the whole community of faith.

Paul Tillich once said that what we call the miracle of resurrection is not something that happened a long time ago. Either it happens in the here and now, as he put it, in and around us as we live out our daily lives, or else the resurrection never happened in any sense that matters to us. Because resurrection is not about the miracle of bodies being flung up to heaven, but the presence of a new reality which transforms our old way of being in despair and death, and brings life and hope out of them – that's the eternal significance of resurrection.

The irrepressible G.K. Chesterton even wrote about our daily experience of resurrection. He said: The greatest act of faith that a [person] can perform is the act we perform every night. [In bed] we abandon our identity, ... We uncreate ourselves as if at the end of the world: for all practical purposes, we become dead men, in the sure and certain hope of a glorious resurrection."[3] We are convinced that we will in fact awake from our sleep to a new day, believing in faith that a new day will dawn for us and that we will arise in it, the pain and problems of yesterday reshaped into the hope that we have a future, at least for this new day we have been given.

In more familiar theological imagery, Barbara Brown Taylor speaks of the power of resurrection to reach us even when in faith or unfaith we are blind to it. Jesus appears after his death to his followers when they least expect him – so much so that, like Mary in her grief, when they encounter him on the road to Emmaus, they fail to recognize him. Yet "the blindness of the ... disciples does not keep their Christ from coming to them. He does not limit his ... resurrection appearances to those with full confidence in him. He comes to the disappointed, the doubtful, the disconsolate. He comes to those who do not know their Bibles, who do not recognize him even when they are walking right beside him. He comes to those who have given up and are headed back home..."[4]

That makes sense to me. Sometimes, in our blindness and deafness, we can only accept and receive the power of Christ when we call it by another name: forgiveness, the gift of a second chance, the grace of those who comfort me in my pain or embrace me in my unlovingness, the acceptance I am offered when I have fallen short. How many times have I received new life that way when I have wanted only to wallow in my own willful unworthiness.

Maybe if the truth be known, what we call the Easter experience is not only the thing we are expecting least but the last thing we want. "That's why it terrifies us," as Craig Barnes puts it, "This day is not about bunnies, springtime and girls in cute dresses. It's about more hope than we can handle."[5] Like Mary, we are summoned to leave the past behind. "Don't hold on to me," Jesus says. The Easter Story draws us into the dark tomb of a place where we have to empty out, leave behind, the "god" whom we have constructed and defined and think we know. So that we, like Mary, may be able to hear ourselves being called from the other side of the resurrection, summoned through the tears to a life beyond them. "Why are you weeping?" Jesus asked. Why indeed, if he is risen and we are invited to be a part of it?

The Gospel of John may focus on the emptiness, but it looks through it toward our fullness, which it does not speak and cannot name for us. Maybe no one can name for us that expression of faith, which we sometimes call resurrection. If only we knew how to pray "Halleluiah" – our language as well as our longing are so limited. Robert Raines made a beginning when he prayed "Let me be like a child surprised to find another Easter egg hidden in a dark place ... "

> *Trigger in me little explosions of*
> > *wonder and delight . . .*
> > *push the buttons, pull out the stops,*
> > *up with the windows, down with the walls,*
> > *over with the fences of exclusion,*
> > > *and the tables of oppression ...*
> > *out with demons of hate*
> > *in with angels of love ...*
> *Kindle in me fires of a strange surmise,*
> > *and stir up wild dreams*
> > > *fantastic and stupendous,*
> > *dreams of nations hugging each other across*
> > > *rivers and deserts and oceans ...*
> > *dreams of a rainbow people holding hands*
> > > *around a city ...*
> > *dreams of friends and enemies leaning over to*
> > > *kiss away the tears . . .*
> *Let me be like a child surprised ...* [6]

In keeping with that metaphor, before we go off in search of our own resurrection refrain to sing, we need to stick around long enough to look into the empty tomb of ourselves until, with Mary, we realize that we do not need to discuss to death the various theories of empty tombs on Easter, because for God, nothing in life is ultimately empty: it is filled with more than we can say. As Jesus might have said to our willing ears, Behold the broken body and the broken bread, and lo I am with you always, even here and now.

———

1. *Lectionary Homiletics XIII*, 4, p.36
2. *Ibid.*
3. *Anglican Digest*, Easter 2002, p.14
4. Barbara Brown Taylor, *Gospel Medicine*, p.22
5. *Christian Century,* Vol. 119, No. 6, p.16
6. Robert A. Raines, *Lord, Could You Make It A Little Better?* 1976. p.87

THEY ALL FORSOOK HIM AND FLED

Sunday of the Resurrection: Easter Day
John 20:1-18
Year C – April 8, 2007

> *But Mary stood weeping outside the tomb. As she wept, she bent over to look into the tomb; and she saw two angels in white, sitting where the body of Jesus had been lying, one at the head and the other at the feet. They said to her, "Woman, why are you weeping?" She said to them, "They have taken away my Lord, and I do not know where they have laid him. "When she had said this, she turned around and saw Jesus standing there, but she did not know that it was Jesus. Jesus said to her, "Woman, why are you weeping? Whom are you looking for?" Supposing him to be the gardener, she said to him, "Sir, if you have carried him away, tell me where you have laid him, and I will take him away." Jesus said to her, "Mary!" She turned and said to him in Hebrew, "Rabboni!" (which means Teacher). Jesus said to her, "Do not hold on to me, because I have not yet ascended to the Father. But go to my brothers and say to them, 'I am ascending to my Father and your Father, to my God and your God.'" Mary Magdalene went and announced to the disciples, "I have seen the Lord;" and she told them that he had said these things to her.*

> *John 20:11-18*

Approaching April 15th, a typical Easter cartoon shows two armed Roman soldiers looking into a tomb hewn out of a rock, with a stone rolled to one side of the entrance, a large gaping hole, obviously empty. One soldier says to the other, "Well I guess this leaves only taxes as being for certain." [1]

I suspect many of you may find that resurrection response less taxing, or more of a fast refund for your faith, than my ensuing sermon.

Years ago, while I was still a student in seminary in New York City, I was appointed managing editor of *The Union Seminary Quarterly Review*, the theological journal of that great graduate school. And so it fell to me from time to time to edit for a publication the writings of some renowned Christian thinkers. Then, I was too young and self-assured to quake before such undertakings, and God knows what problems I may have perpetrated upon the works of such eminent authors as Tillich and Niebuhr, Muilenberg and Bonhoeffer, all of whom were professors at Union. But in the process of preparing papers for print, I did get to know well part of the writings of some foremost Christian thinkers of the 20th century, many of which were in the form of sermons, sometimes spoken right there in the James Chapel at the Seminary.

So it was I happened to notice that Paul Tillich, perhaps the best known Protestant theologian, in the more than sixty sermons I know about, never wrote one using an Easter text from scripture, which is curious because he has some very powerful things to say about the resurrection of Christ (more of that in a moment). It is as though he wanted to speak to the secular experience rather than what we would call the religious, because it is much easier for us to dismiss religious insights than the "common wisdom" of the secular world with which we are quite comfortable. We are willing to wrestle with the common human condition in thought and word more readily than with the rarified realm of the religious (right or left).

Therefore, this rise-up morning I have chosen to reflect not on an expected and faith-*filled* Easter text such as "Why do you seek Jesus among the dead? He is not here, he has risen," but on a more somber passage of scripture that speaks more specifically to our experience of faith*less*ness, in part because that was the situation of Jesus' own disciples. From the gospel of Matthew: "Then all the disciples forsook him and fled."

Why go there at a time when we're all Alleluias? Because if on Easter, all we can repeat about the resurrection is reduced to a familiar religious proposition, which may or may not be interesting to us, then we have missed the meaning of that event in our own experience and for our lives. Maybe we need some convincing secular insights to make us sit up and take the resurrection seriously. Because, as unexalted and inauspicious as it may be, truth for most of us, centers on what concerns you and me.

And the truth is, I can understand why his disciples all fled from him, because I am no stranger to that. For one, it was too dangerous for their well-being. If he was one of them, then they stood to receive the same fate as he; and second, it is easy to understand that in the face of death, their faith fled them also. So it was that "those who were nearest him fled farthest from him." They had died to him and given up the life they had hoped for, returned home in fact to start their old lives over. This passage troubled Tillich, and he asked, "How shall we think about these disciples? – how *could* they forsake him whom they had called Messiah, the Christ, the bringer of new life, for whom they had left everything behind for his sake?"[2]

But later on, after some years of considering the difficulties of his own faith, Tillich came to admire the disciples because they were the ones who left us those troubling words of scripture. They did not hide their flight from us, they stated it in one short sentence that judges them for all time. [They admitted that] "*all* the disciples fled, that none of them witnessed the crucifixion and death of the master" and they were not there to experience the inexplicable event we express as Easter.[3]

Tillich tells us that "From earliest times, the church could not stand this judgment against itself... It has tried to conceal what the disciples openly admitted – that we all forsook him and fled. This is the truth about all [of us], including the followers of Jesus today."[4] So also we flee Good Friday in our efforts to escape to Easter, and even there we stand at a distance, uncertain of what we know and what we believe. We do not want any claims made upon us and our lives; we want things to go on just as they were before.

We flee God even, and maybe even especially, by busying ourselves in the church, the place where we are supposed to be arrested by his presence. And we want to keep God safely *in* the church on Sunday; we don't want to encounter him in our daily life the rest of the week. So we fill our lives with labor and work, with worry and recreation, even with crisis and care giving – where we are free from being found by God, as faithful or unfaithful. We long for the resurrection that lifts our hopes and raises up new life – as long as that's Christ-business, nothing we have a share in.

Yet that is precisely what resurrection is not. As you may know, there is no scriptural account of what happened on that Easter morning. There is no story that explains it, the gospels are silent about it. The resurrection is simply asserted and as-sumed. There isn't even any account of *why* Jesus' disciples who had abandoned him and returned home came back together and individually set about witnessing far and wide to what they had turned away from and denied. However that happened, however they found their life again and were willing to give it away to oth-ers, is a part of what the event of resurrection is and means.

Tillich had an interesting way of putting it, saying both what resurrection *is* and *is not*. It is not about dead bodies leav-ing their graves, flung up from the earth skyward toward heaven, not even Christ's. Resurrection is not about an empty tomb, no body in it. In fact, as Jesus' fellow Jews understood it, there could be no such thing as a disembodied spirit or a disinspirited body, In Hebrew, the self, *nephesh*, is all of a piece, the spirit and body inseparable. For them, the resurrection would not have been about an empty tomb, the body gone, but about Jesus being there in the flesh no body, no resurrection.

But, Easter is not about resuscitated bodies, it is the experience of new life, new being, born out of the death of the old being. In Tillich's words, "Resurrection is not an event that might happen in some remote future, but it is the power of the New Being [in Christ] to create life out of death, here and now, today and tomorrow. Where there is a New Being, *there* is resurrection... Resurrection happens *now* or it does not happen at all. It happens in us and around us" – or *the* resurrection never happened.[5] If that doesn't sound like traditional Easter theology or the religious message you're used to hearing, that can't be all bad; it might even bring new hope for some.

In our gospel reading, we find Mary Magdalene weeping before the tomb, getting up her nerve to look into the gaping hole of it, to see what the blackness held for her. Whereupon she saw two angels in white, who asked her, "Why are you weeping?" and she said to them, "They have taken away my Lord, and I do not know where they have laid him." His body was all that was left in her relationship with him, and now it too was gone.

When she turned around to leave, she bumped into someone she supposed was the gardener, without really seeing him. But when he called her by her name, she cried out in recognition, " Rabboni," my teacher. Whereupon he said to her, "Do not hold on to me" – a saying both troubling and hard to forget. It was curious because there is no evidence that she was trying to hold on to Jesus. But maybe, as Barbara Brown Taylor suggests, "he could hear it in her voice, how she wanted him back the way he was so they could go back to the way they were, back to the old life [the old way of being] where everything was familiar, not new and frightening as it was now."[6]

> *To hunt in the tomb for the past and find instead the future; instead of a corpse, to find the risen Lord, is too much. It's not natural and not what we would expect.*

New life *is* frightening. To hunt in the tomb for the past and find instead the future; instead of a corpse, to find the risen Lord, is too much. It's not natural and not what we would expect. Her life was changed, and she could not go back to the old. For better or for worse, whatever resurrection was, which she couldn't understand, she was now a part of the new life in him – what could she do?

"The only thing [she could not do], *we* cannot do, is hold on to him. He has asked us not to do that, ... [God knows] we would rather keep him with us where we are [the way we knew him] than let him take us [to new life with him], let him take hold of *us* [even] in to the white hot presence of God, [God] who is not behind us, but ahead of us every step of the way"[7]

Does that sound like resurrection to you? I hope so.

───────

1. *Homiletics* 16. 2-p.6l.
2. Paul Tillich, *The Eternal Now*, p.101.
3. Tillich, *Op. cit.*, p.102.
4. Tillich, *Op. cit.*, p.103.
5. Paul Tillich, *The New Being*, p.24.
6. Barbara Brown Taylor, *Home by Another Way*, p.111.
7. Taylor, *Op. cit.*, p.112.

BEYOND BELIEF

Sunday of the Resurrection: Easter Day
Luke 24:1-12
Year C – April 11, 2004

> *On the first day of the week, at early dawn, the women who had come with Jesus from Galilee came to the tomb, taking the spices that they had prepared. They found the stone rolled away from the tomb, but when they went in, they did not find the body. While they were perplexed about this, suddenly two men in dazzling clothes stood beside them. The women were terrified and bowed their faces to the ground, but the men said to them, "Why do you look for the living among the dead? He is not here, but has risen. Remember how he told you, while he was still in Galilee, that the Son of Man must be handed over to sinners, and be crucified, and on the third day rise again." Then they remembered his words, and returning from the tomb, they told all this to the eleven and to all the rest. Now it was Mary Magdalene, Joanna, Mary the mother of James, and the other women with them who told this to the apostles; but these words seemed to them an idle tale, and they did not believe them.*

> *Luke 24:1-11*

A *Rolling Stone* interview, which sounds almost made for Easter morning, contained this quotation: "What a great day," co-median Steve Martin notes as he sits outside at a cafe on Manhattan's Upper West Side, "I wish I were alive."[1]

And from this morning's gospel reading: "Why do you seek the living among the dead?" they asked at the tomb, which is a haunting question anytime but disturbing on this day – even terrifying, because it warns us that to receive new life we have to stop clinging to the old one.

Have you noticed that at Easter in church we focus on the empty tomb, as if it were indisputable evidence of Christ's resurrection? It's odd because "evidence" of the resurrection for Jesus' followers would have been just the opposite. (I'll explain that in a moment.) And we' re also in danger of getting the Easter message mixed up: it's not about swallowing the assertion of being delivered from death, or even announcing the end of death, but affirming that the end is life. Now there's something to chew on!

⟝∘⟞

What really happened, and what does death have to do with it? And what does that have to do with me?

⟝∘⟞

Not as long ago as you might think, it was the custom on Easter at St. Mary's, even in the parking lot, that parishioners would greet one another as he/she arrived with the exclamation "Christ is risen!" and the other would reply "He is risen indeed" (all properly in the present perfect tense). But now, if we remember at all, we mostly mumble it at the opening acclamation of our Eucharist service. As one pastor put it, "We may not greet 'Christ is risen' with disbelief, but we don't quite know what to do with this news."[2] We think we know what life is and what death is about, but resurrection is something else – and what does that say about the time-tested truth, "The only certainties in life are death and taxes"? So on Resurrection Sunday, as some people call it, the age-old questions for us remains: What really happened, and what does death have to do with it? And what does that have to do with me?

Put another way, "Not much has changed in all these centuries of Easter mornings since that first one. It still doesn't make sense to us, at least not the kind of sense we can readily wrap our minds around. We come to church nevertheless, wanting to make sense of this news we have heard, and hoping that perhaps before we are done with it, it will make sense of us."[3]

But back to the tomb for a moment. For the Jews in Jesus' time there could be no such thing as a disembodied spirit or a disinspirited body. The *nephesh*, as they called the self, was a whole package – the spirit inseparable from the body; so if someone were to be resurrected, evidence of that would be in the body being present, not absent. An empty tomb was no proof Jesus had been resurrected, only that someone (the rumor was his disciples) could have stolen the lifeless body so it wouldn't be proven he was dead.

We, on the other hand are Greek-thinking people who tend to believe that the soul or spirit is separate from the body, so the empty tomb for us is: "He is not here. He is risen. Alleluia." We cry for joy; whereas, the women who went to Jesus' tomb were in tears; the body would have been present if he were risen. The empty tomb was not triumphant, but life-less; it signified empty hopes, a hole in the heart, the promise of death. In effect, I argue, we Greeks misread a Jewish narrative and draw from it the opposite conclusion from those who went there to witness it.

What then are we to believe about the resurrection if the empty tomb tradition is not evidence that Jesus had been raised? Plenty, I say now, but I had to get there the long way.

More than 40 years ago, when I was hired as Instructor in English at Exeter Academy in the fall of '62, Fred Buechner was School Minister in charge of Phillips Church which functioned on Sundays as the Academy chapel. I was hired with the understanding that I would have nothing to do with church services. I was not ordained. Besides, that was Fred's department and he was, even then, a renowned preacher and author. I had never given a sermon.

*I told him it wasn't in my contract. He
asked me if I wanted to be employed.*

But by the summer of '63, when Lynne and I arrived at
the Academy, newly married, with all our possessions in a U-Haul
truck, I should have suspected all was not well because some
Exeter employees told us at first that we were to live in "Amen"
Hall. The Principal, Dr. Saltonstall, who had offered me the appointment in English and coaching hockey and crew, had by then
departed to become head of the Peace Corps in Nigeria and the
Acting Principal had other priorities. He said to me I would share
the preaching every other week at Phillips Church. I told him it
wasn't in my contract. He asked me if I wanted to be employed.

Perhaps you can imagine my fear and frustration. Somehow, I managed to find excuses to circumvent the sermon for
the first few weeks till it was high noon for me to be delivered,
which alas turned out to be the very weekend Jack Kennedy was
shot. I felt I might as well be too. Yet because it was a crisis, the
people of the parish and the skeptical students were kind; they
were willing to hear almost anything. But the next time I tried to
preach that same sermon several years later at our sister school,
Andover Academy, as soon as I had finished, the School Minister
there abruptly ascended the pulpit and preached his own sermon
in rebuttal.

Still, looking back, I think my greatest trial was the time I
was at last assigned to preach the Easter sermon. It was not just
that I couldn't bear being compared with Buechner, but that he
had said to me something like: If I were asked to explain what I
believed happened in the miracle of the Resurrection and all I
could speak about was "the 'miracle' of truth that never dies, the
'miracle' of a life so beautiful that two thousand years have left
the memory of it undimmed, the 'miracle' of turning doubt into
faith"[all of which sounded pretty good to me at the time]; then

I would, he said, turn in my certificate of ordination and take up some other profession.[4]

I swallowed several times and thanked Fred for his help. Maybe he would be sick the day I preached my Easter sermon. I recalled Woody Allen's words, "I don't mind dying; I just don't want to be there when it happens."

I was further disheartened when I discovered that the scripture readings assigned for Easter contain no story of the resurrection – it is not described at all – there is only the tale of the empty tomb. So what is there to be said about the resurrection when those who went there to witness it either "said nothing to anyone" about it or told their "idle tale" to the apostles "who did not believe them" (depending on which gospel account you read). What I concluded was that Jesus' disciples were in no better position to discern what happened than we are. But maybe that's just the point. It is an ongoing task for each one of us in our own time.

Resurrection comes from a word meaning to rouse or rise up. Maybe it's something we are a part of too: what rouses you or can raise you up? Most of us know what it is like at some time to feel in the grave, devoid of life, hopeless, life-less. And surely some of us have known times so dark that suffering found us asking, "Is life really worth it?" "My God, my God, why have you forsaken me?" – Jesus did not have to speak these words for us; he knew them for himself, when the end we all await could not come soon enough. Dead, scripture says.

But it is right there (I began to understand what Buechner meant), where words fail us, and I don't know exactly the meaning of what I am speaking, that whatever we can say about the resurrection *happens*. Where death was, somehow (how to say it) he got up without it – roused – with life in him – and glory, whatever that is. Not speaking metaphorically (which may surprise some of you who know me), but life-fillingly. The way when you wake, the dream clings to you and life is unbelievable. Maybe the word resurrection is just not large enough to hold that reality. The scriptural words do not explain what we want to know, but they help us glimpse the glory we can't imagine.

And then he said, so we can hear him, "Don't be afraid," even when I am full of fear and anxious, cowardly, fearful of the life that lies ahead of me. "Fear not," he says – when I am dying to hear it. The gospels contain other words – pick your own.[5] To Peter, who betrayed him, and to me, he asks, "Do you love me?" And before my answer can silence the silence, as he stands there by the charcoal fire, Jesus says, "Come and be fed, be filled." Then to Peter and to all of us after him: "Feed my sheep." Terrible words for us who have abundance and do not see the terrible needs of others, even of the one who sits next to me this morning.

"For I am with you always even to the end of the world," he says. "Shalom," God's peace which the world cannot give, that peace which passes all understanding – as I stand before him, if I will stand before him, with him, in him, with him in me – as the words of Communion promise, Holy or otherwise.

The Easter message is not only for those who know God, but for whoever longs to know God; for us who know what it is like to live separated from God and from what gives us life, a cross upon our hopes. Because in the end, even in spite of us, love will win out; his will, not ours. What we know by faith and by God is that death is not the end. The end is the life we live with him in us and for him; because the life I have now been given, he gives to me – and to you. That's what the Eucharist says and what the Eucharist does. Receive it as though your life depended upon it – because it does. That's what *happens* Easter morning, believe it or not.

———

1. *Homiletics* 12, 2-p.56
2. *Biblical Preaching Journal* 4, 2-p.8
3. *Ibid.*
4. Frederick Buechner, *The Hungering Dark*, pp.78-9. These were not his exact words at the time, but what he wrote later.

5. Some of these quotations are Buechner's scriptural favor-
ites because (I surmise) they are words we want to hear
and are willing to hear even now.

BELIEVING IS SEEING

1st Sunday after Easter Day – Thomas Sunday
John 20:19-31
Year B – April 10, 1994

James Harnish tells of the man who came home one day to find that his wife had hung a plaque on the wall which read, ''Prayer changes things.'' Within twenty-four hours the plaque had been removed. She asked, "What's wrong? Don't you like prayer?" He said, "Sure, I like prayer. I don't like change."

Do we need a change of perspective in the way we see things?

I expect you have heard the expression "Seeing is believing" – which I take to mean, "Unless you can prove to me what you say is true, I won't believe it." Or, in Harry Truman's terms, "I'm from Missouri, *show* me."

Doubtless, named in honor of the great Missouri disciple, this Sunday is called Thomas Sunday or more familiarly, "Doubting Thomas Sunday." Which title, ironically is the exact opposite of the point made in today's reading from the Gospel of John.

''Seeing is believing'' is a saying which at first seems to come directly from John's text: Thomas says, "Unless I see in his hands the print of the nails, and place my finger in the mark of the nails, and put my hand in his side, I will not believe." But the point of the narrative is actually quite the opposite. We are told that we need to believe in order to see. (Now let me see if I can show you how all of that works.)

Last week I happened on a magazine article which began this way:

> We are just suckers if we let the current intellectual fashion decree that the resurrection is unbelievable. What is believable changes from generation to generation.
>
> Seventy years ago, for example, some schol-ars judged Jesus' healing miracles to be impossible because they violated the "iron laws" of nature. Then, with the rise of psychosomatic medicine, the "available believable" changed; now Jesus could have healed psychosomatic disorders but not other diseases. Today, in the light of scientific studies..., we no longer know the limits of what can be healed by faith.[1]

Returning to the reading from John, what has happened just before the narrative begins is that Mary Magdalene has reported to the Disciples her encounter with the risen Jesus. But if the Disciples believed Mary's testimony, they also believed that "lying low" was the way to go. So on the eve of Easter Day, they were gathered in a house with the doors locked, fearing that they would be found out. That is the way Jesus found them, locked together in fear for their lives when he suddenly appeared in their midst – unannounced and apparently undeterred by the defiance of enclosed walls and locked doors.

The words he spoke to them there were words of comfort, the same words he said to them at the Last Supper: "Peace be with you." Peace, of course, was what they had none of – either inwardly or outwardly – and what they longed for. "Peace be with you," he said, and "he showed them his hands and his side. Then the disciples were glad when they saw him," John writes.

But Thomas was not there when Jesus came and stood among them, and Thomas's sullen response was even more negative than our prettied-up translation puts it. What he says is not "put" or "place" my finger, but more accurately "jab" my finger (in the mark of the nails). Thomas is more emphatic: "I will never believe," he says.

Moreover, Jesus's response to Thomas is less gentle than our conventional translation; he is less than genial. The Greek syntax is rough, "Take your finger, here are my hands; take your fist, jam it in my side. Don't be faithless, but be faithful!" Jesus confronts Thomas with his wounds and (by inference) with Thomas's own disbelief. While Jesus was known for his compassion for the weakness of the human heart, here he insists on a new commitment to the Gospel and faithfulness to it.

What Thomas asked for from Jesus is, I suspect, not very different from what you or I might have asked in the same situation: a sign – that would prove our faith in the resurrection was well founded, that it was worth the risk to believe. Thomas had to see in order to believe. I can understand that very well.

If we listen carefully to John's narrative, we will hear some good news and some bad news. The good news is that Jesus does not turn away from Thomas for his doubt, for his need to *see*, which is only human. The bad news is, neither does he bless him. His blessing is reserved for those who do *not* see and yet are willing to believe.

Thomas' saving grace is what is not included in the text – namely, Thomas did not take up Jesus' invitation to finger his wounds. Instead of the proof he asks for, he accepts the presence of the risen Lord. And in so doing, he comes to understand what he could not believe. Thomas's concluding words give us the most unqualified confession of faith possible: "My Lord and my God."

Dorothy Sayers notes: "It is unexpected, but extraordinarily convincing, that the one absolutely unequivocal statement in the whole gospel of the Divinity of Jesus should come from Doubting Thomas. It is the only place where the word "God" is used ... without qualification of any kind, and in the most unambiguous form... And this must be added – not ecstatically, or with a cry of astonishment – but with flat conviction, as of one acknowledging irrefragable evidence: '2 + 2 = 4,' 'That is the sun in the sky,' 'You are my *Lord* and my *God*!'" [2]

It is at that point in John's gospel that *I* become the doubting Thomas. I feel like saying, "Wait a minute! There must be some part of the text missing. How could he say that?" I want the old Thomas to stick by his guns, to test out the "proof." Because I, as a creature of the 20th century, have become seduced by the common wisdom objective scientific methods preach: "seeing is believing."

Instead, what Thomas shows us is that you come to "*see*," to understand, only after you are willing to believe: *believing* is seeing. First you believe, then you come to see; because faith changes the way we believe, which changes the way we see.

I am reminded that neurologists tell us we have to learn to see; we don't simply see when we open our eyes. Just because we have eyes that "work," doesn't mean we can see what is there. When people who have been blind since childhood regain their sight, they cannot immediately "see" what their vision registers, because they haven't the experience or meaning necessary to interpret the sight. All the nerves and impulses are there, but they are *mentally* blind.

Jesus accepted those who had to see first in order to believe; the story of "Doubting Thomas" proves that. But John's Gospel adds that to those who believe without seeing, Jesus gives a new insight and his blessing: For the gospel to continue to have life, it has to be passed on to those who, like us, will only hear about Jesus, who will have to believe without seeing.

Believing is an act of the will before it is the gift of the spirit. To get from the need of seeing to the blessing of believing requires jumping over a big barrier. I am told that in a book about how to get horses to jump over tall fences, one author says that the rider has to learn to overcome his own inclination to hesitate. The only way to get over the barrier, he says, is to "take your heart and throw it over the fence; then jump after it."

The question of faith is not a trivial matter of which doctrine we are willing to believe in – but a crucial decision of what truth is worth affirming for our lives.

Madeline L'Engle tells of being with her grandchildren at bedtime for reading, when her grandchild Lena turned to her and asked, "Is everything all right?"

She said, "Yes, of course, everything is all right."

Lena asked again: "Gram, is everything really all right? I mean really?"

L'Engle says she "looked at that little child in her white nightgown and realized that she was asking the cosmic question, the question that is out beyond the safety of [her] home full of love and warmth."

Every Christmas we come to the manger... and ask the same question: "'Is everything really all right?"

Every Easter we come to the tomb and ask that same question: "Is everything really all right?"[3]

Jesus assures us that it is – for those of us who have *not* seen and yet dared to believe.

"Lord, I believe, help thou my unbelief."

———

1. *The Christian Century*, 3/94, p.309
2. Dorothy L. Sayers, *The Man Born to Be King*, pp.319-20

3. Madeline L'Engle, *The Summer of the Great Grandmother*

   Footnote*:* Some quotation and paraphrase above come from homiletical commentaries *"Come On, Come Out"* and *"No Vacation, the Devil, and Sheetrock..."* Dennis R. Bolton*.*

"PEACE BE WITH YOU" … HE SAID.

1st Sunday after Easter Day – Thomas Sunday
John 20:19-31
Year C – April 23, 1995

A contemporary critic observed: "If you think the tomb was empty on Easter, wait until you see the churches on the first Sunday after Easter." Obviously, you all did not get that message. "Low Sunday," as today is often called (in observance of that just cited) is also known as Doubting Thomas Sunday because the gospel reading about the apostle who refused to believe unless he could see for himself first hand is always assigned for the Sunday following Easter perhaps in hopes that since so few will be there to hear it, most of us won't get that message either.

Ironically, of course, the reading embraces the opposite conclusion. Jesus accepts Thomas' disbelieving because he has seen as well as blessed those who have not seen and yet believed. He gives his "peace" to all the disciples (including Thomas) in the midst of their fear and confusion of faith. The more striking because, unlike the women who were faithful and stood by Jesus at his crucifixion and at the tomb thereafter, his trusted disciples, the Twelve, all fled. Even Peter denied him – three times. What could possibly bring them peace in the midst of their travail and turmoil?

When Jesus says, "Peace be with you," what does he give them? Two things, I think. First, he has come among them in person: he brings them the gift of himself. Second, the peace he brings them assures them, "I am with you always." That is, he promises that however we are to understand the meaning of the resurrection – and even if we do not understand it at all, he will not abandon us any more than he abandoned his disciples who abandoned him. That is God's "peace" and assurance that he offers them – and us.

Nowhere is that radical idea explained more clearly and movingly than in Psalm 139, when the psalmist asks God: "Where can I escape from your presence?" The psalm responds to the question in two syntactically parallel assertions. The first goes, in English, "If I climb up to heaven, behold you are there," a rather obvious reply, for where else would God be? And the second one goes, in English, "If I make my bed in Sheol [the abode of the dead], behold you are there," a reply that is not obvious at all, for the psalmist knows very well that Sheol is, by definition, the place where God is not. And as the writer starts to write in the Hebrew tongue about the presence of God even in Sheol, the vision is so overpowering that in some manuscripts the sentence stops in midstream, "If I make my bed in Sheol, behold thou...!"

"God in Sheol, totally unexpected, is the reality beyond all definition, all logic, all syntax, all expectation – acquainting us with the glorious surprise that there is no place foreign to God's healing love and presence."[1]

That's fine for the scriptures, you may say, but how are we to tell the Easter story in our time? And in terms that will transmit God's peace to others? Since the Easter event is not about bodies ascending heavenward, maybe we will have to do what the disciples were forced to do to preserve its message: tell stories. The kind of stories that witness to his presence, his spirit, in our midst even when we may not immediately recognize his being with us. The post-resurrection stories in scripture often witness to one thing in common that many of the disciples, not just Thomas, fail to recognize him even when he walks among them.

One of the most famous of those stories tells of two disciples who encounter Jesus on the road to Emmaus, who walk and talk with him some way but who do not recognize him until the end of the day when he breaks bread with them at supper. Only then "were their eyes opened to him."

⟨∘⟩

Will we recognize his spirit, his life in us...?

⟨∘⟩

My guess is our own stories are not very different. Will we recognize his spirit, his life in us, when we gather in his name or even when we gather not in his name? Let me offer a couple of examples. And maybe that will prompt you to tell or retell other stories you have heard or told:

The first one comes from a recent recounting in *The Christian Century* by Ralph C. Wood, which he calls "Baptism in a Coffin."[2] Wood was invited by one of his former students to accompany him to the local minimum-security prison for a baptism. Reluctantly he agreed, and together they went to the prison. The baptism turned out to be a real joy. "It was as close to a New Testament experience as perhaps I shall ever have," Wood wrote. A guard escorted the prisoner from behind a fence that was topped with razor wire. There were just the three of them, with the guard looking curiously on.

"The barefoot prisoner stepped into a wooden box that had been lined with a plastic sheet and filled with water. It looked liked a large coffin and rightly so. This was no warmed and tiled First Baptist bath, with its painted River Jordan winding pleasantly into the distance. This was a place of death: watery chaos from which God graciously made the world and to which, in rightful wrath, he almost returned it."

"Pronouncing the Trinitarian formula, the pastor lowered the newly confessed Christian down into the liquid grave to be buried with Christ and then raised him to eternal life. Even though the water was cold, the man was not eager to get out. Instead, he stood there, weeping for joy. When at last he left the baptismal box, I thought he would hurry away to change into something dry. I was mistaken." The prisoner, the newborn Christian, told them, "I want to wear these clothes as long as I can... In fact, I wish I never had to take a shower again." They walked to the nearby tables and sat quietly in the Carolina sun, hearing this new Christian explain why his baptismal burial was too good to dry off. "I'm not impatient to leave prison because this wire can't shackle my soul. I know that I deserve to be here, to pay for what I did. But I also learned here that Someone else has paid for my crimes."

Stories we might tell may be similar – even familiar, like this one, which some of you will have already heard: Philip was an eight-year-old boy who looked out at the world with five-year-old eyes. Philip was retarded. But Philip was blessed because his Sunday School class, a group of eight-year-olds had a very under-standing teacher.

One Sunday in the Spring, Philip's teacher brought some L'eggs panty hose containers to class. As you know, these containers are shaped like eggs. The teacher asked Philip's class to take the egg-shaped containers outdoors and fill them with things from nature that reminded them of life. You can imagine the excited scramble as those eight-year-olds went out to collect their symbols of life from nature! When they returned together with their teacher they began to open their egg containers. The first egg contained a flower. "Yes!" shouted the children, "Flowers remind us of life with their beauty, their color, and their delicate petals." Next, they opened an egg that contained a rock. "No," they shouted, "a rock doesn't remind us of life," but that gave their teacher an opportunity to point out that rocks can remind us of permanence and stability in life. When they opened the next egg container it was empty. "Somebody didn't play the game," they shouted. "That isn't fair." During the shouting, the teacher felt a tug on his trouser leg. Looking down he saw Philip. When he had quieted the class down, the teacher turned to Philip, and Philip said, "That is my egg. It is empty because the tomb was empty. Jesus was alive, he wasn't in the tomb."

Several months later Philip became ill, and in spite of all the efforts his little body could make, in spite of heroic medical measures, Philip grew steadily worse – and he died. On the day Philip was buried, an understanding Sunday School teacher and a class of eight-year-olds laid on the altar of that church a host of empty L'eggs pantyhose containers. For surely, Philip, like his living Lord and all the saints before him – was alive and well with those who believe in the Lord of new life and of empty tombs.

There are, of course, stories in our very midst. This last one tells us that the "peace" we are given is not always either what we desire or deserve:

One young at heart person in our parish, who has been afflicted with severe cancer and has already endured more suffering than many of us will have to bear in a lifetime, said to me not long ago: "I knew that I had to change the way I had been living my life since I was 14 years old – and that it would be difficult. I knew that God would have to do something dramatic to get me to change it. He did. That's the cancer part. Now I have a new life. And even if I do not know how long I have to live it, I have a life I have never known before and I am full of life!"

> O Holy Spirit of God
> come again to my heart and fill me
> with thy peace;
> fill me with thy spirit, with light, and truth,
> of myself I am an empty vessel,
> Fill me that I may live the life of thy Spirit,
> the life of truth and goodness,
> the life of wisdom and strength,
> the life of beauty and love.
> Guide me today in all things:
> guide me to the people I may meet and help,
> to the circumstances in which I may best serve God,
> whether by my actions or by my suffering.
> Bind me to thyself by all thy ways, known and unknown,
> by holy thoughts, and unseen graces, and by

sacramental ties, that Christ may be in me,
and I in Him, this day and for ever.

(Adapted from: Walter Julius Carey,
Bishop of Bloemfontein)

––––––

1. Robert McAfee Brown, *Reclaiming the Bible: Words for the Nineties*. Westminster John Knox Press, 1994.

2. Ralph C. Wood, "Baptism in a Coffin." *Christian Century* 109, 30 (October 21, 1992): 925-6

"DOUBTING" THOMAS

Halitosis of the Holy Spirit?

John 20:19-31
Year A – April 14, 1996

I couldn't tell you how many times it has been my service to preach the Sunday after Easter – Low Sunday, as it is often called, because everyone is Eastered out, and not surprisingly, seeks a respite from enchurchment. People are often low on spiritual energy and, low down, relieved that things are back to normal, or at least back to what we expect. After all, resurrection can wreak havoc with our routine. When we have had a peak experience we retreat to the valley to recover from all that outpouring of energy and enthusiasm and to regain our composure.

There's a danger in that, of course, because composure can easily become complacency. The Church lectionary may actually be a lure to the languid because the Gospel reading assigned for this Sunday is relentlessly the same, year after year – always the story of so-called "Doubting Thomas," which I have read and re-read religiously, so to speak. But I was determined this time to see if there was not something *new* that my eye, accustomed to the usual, had inadvertently ignored. And what I discovered was so obvious I was embarrassed. Two things really:

The first is that "Doubting Thomas," now a proverbial expression in our English of everyday, was not a doubter. A dullard, perhaps – imagination may not have been his long suit – but not a doubter or disbeliever. He may have been from Missouri, like most of us who seek the security of "show me." We want a sign of certainty because we are spiritually insecure. Like Thomas, many of us are locked into a belief system that is safe for us, which we were taught as children and has been tried and tested over the years. If seeing-is-believing has stood us in good stead since we can't remember when, and is our strength against hearsay [heresy?], why try to validate our vision some other way? Why do we need to change? I can only tell you from my own experience.

For years I relied on my physical being to bolster the measure of myself. Through school, college, and even after I depended on sports to preserve my health, stamina, and self-discipline; to keep me fit, trim, free of fat and sickness – energetic, agile, and (almost) always agreeable. Physical expression was a source of power, pride, and preservation. Until the onset of those afflictions that affect "other" people. No doubt it is a truism to say that with advancing years "practice makes perfect" becomes "practice makes pain." I hadn't counted on being attended by tendonitis, arthritis, bursitis; tennis elbow, wrist, and shoulder; torn ligaments and floating cartilage. My previous strength was becoming my present weakness – and eventual undoing if I persisted in doing it. You cannot turn back the clock or reverse the image in the mirror. That's life – even if I refused to accept it.

With reference to the reading this morning, among Jesus' disciples, Thomas was not known for his watered-down commitment or frail faith. Quite the reverse. Earlier in John's gospel it is Thomas who "loyally if bluntly declares his willingness to follow Jesus back to Bethany and Lazarus' tomb, even though [the] people [there] had nearly stoned Jesus a short time before." While the other disciples were cautious and prudent about whether to make the journey, Thomas says, "Let us also go, that we may die with him." Whereupon, Thomas's faith was rewarded by witnessing firsthand the evidence of Lazarus's being raised from the dead. Thomas's commitment to Jesus' actions and affect in his mission and ministry was wholehearted. In fact, that became the problem.

In today's lesson, when the disciples were huddled together in fear behind locked doors, Thomas has for solace only hearsay, mere words, to attest to Jesus' miraculous resurrection from the dead. He had not seen it; how could Thomas integrate the alleged appearance of the risen Lord into his previous first-hand experiences which had been the foundation of his faithfulness? Seeing-is-believing had served him in good stead before; why change his attitudes and expectations in this situation? But life had changed dramatically. All would have been as he had expected had it not been for the Easter event which altered the operation of Jesus' ministry forever. The actions of Jesus' earthly mission were no longer to be the means of his ministry – something inconceivable to Thomas.

But the reading makes clear that Thomas does not cling to his old way of belief which had been his source of strength. When Jesus offers Thomas the opportunity to verify for himself the signs he demanded in order to believe, to thrust his finger into the mark of the nails and his hand in Jesus' side, the text is silent where the reader expects action. When Jesus says, "Do not doubt but believe," Thomas – choosing not to validate the evidence he sought – confesses his faith: "My Lord and my God." Had he insisted on the demonstrable signs and actions of Jesus' earthly ministry, the mainstay of his early belief, he would have failed to accept the new life that was before him, the gift of the spirit. How easy it is to insist on what we have always known – while the world passes us by.

Jesus' gift of the spirit to his followers is the second obvious point I had passed over in my previous readings of this familiar text. When Jesus appears among the disciples, his first words to them are "Peace be with you," which we might take to be a standard form of greeting. But it is far more than that. It is an ancient Hebrew blessing, which offers the Shalom of God (which we exchange with one another at the Eucharist – "Peace be with you."); but our word "peace" does not adequately translate "shalom," which means "wholeness" (whole, holy, and health are all derived from the same root). This wholeness is the gift of life or what we might also call salvation. That explains the accompanying enigmatic saying "… he breathed on them and said … 'Receive the Holy Spirit.'"

I had to laugh when I came across the following commentary which suggested that an appropriate children's sermon would be to say: "Jesus appears among the disciples and says, 'Peace be with you.' Then he does something many children and adults will find repulsive. He breathes on them. Ask the children if they would want to have someone breathe on them. (The strongest breath would certainly be a weakness at this point!) Ask if they would want Jesus to breathe on them. Pass out the breath mints to remind all the children that Jesus breathed on the disciples and they received ... the Holy Spirit." [I'm not making this up.] "A dummy used to teach mouth-to-mouth resuscitation might be an effective way to show the power of breath in giving life." [Surely the message cannot be: "Save us from the halitosis of the Holy Spirit!")

The crude theological reference there is in Genesis, to God's breathing into a clod of earth the breath of life, the breath of God giving us the gift of life. We have life because we are inspired or in*spirit*ed by the breath of God which creates a living being – whole, holy, healthy. Thomas's faith was based not on the "proof" of Jesus' risen-ness or resuscitated body but upon his promise of forgiveness and redeeming love, which he also offered to all of us who come after Thomas: Jesus says to Thomas, "Have you seen me and believed? Blessed are those who have not seen and yet have come to believe" – the Gospel in a new form, empowered by the Holy Spirit, no longer dependent on "signs" but upon the life giving word to all who will dare to bear and share it in Christ's name. "Shalom," he said. "Shalom," we shall shortly say to one another.

Footnote: I am indebted for help, hints, and insights to Homiletics 8, 2 in which many of the quotations above are included.

JOYFUL, JOYFUL, WE ADORE THEE

3rd Sunday of Easter
Luke 24:36b-48
Year B – April 13, 1997

One of the books I taught in Senior English at Exeter Academy, more than 30 years ago, was an unexpected autobiography by C.S. Lewis. Actually, it was a spiritual autobiography that tells of his conversion to Christianity, which was also the story of his rediscovering the faith he had lost in childhood. The one thing I haven't forgotten about that book over the years is its unlikely title (or so it seemed to my hyper-skeptical students): *Surprised by Joy.* Imagine that! Of all places to discover we are surprised by joy – be honest – would the church be the place you would pick for that to happen? I would be surprised if it were.

Which reminds me of a commentary I came across recently that reminds us: Occasionally we may imagine the joy of discovering old friends. Perhaps (if you are lucky) you might hope to find joy at a family reunion. Maybe that's what you would feel if you were caught off guard at a beautiful sunset or moonscape on your vacation. But the ritual rounding up of the household and showing up at church services on Sunday morning probably would not be the picture you would pick to portray potentially joyful moments in your life. But why not? Why shouldn't it be?

How many times have you sung on Sunday the "Jubilate" – which means, "Be joyous"? – except that no one could tell it by the way we sing it. That's our fault, not the church music's. We do not arrive at church expecting to be shaken by the spirit, grabbed by the Good News of the gospel, tickled by the teachings of the

219

church. Episcopalians often unintentionally embody that old un-energetic epithet: "God's frozen people." We need to remember that being joyful is neither awkward nor out of taste and it is not some silly sentiment that devout Christians should disdain. After all, we are reminded "Taking delight in life, living life to the fullest, is what God intends for people of faith."[1]

Some people I know think it is slightly demeaning, even embarrassing, that the first miracle of Jesus was at the wedding in Cana, where he turned water into wine. It's true his mother told him to do something when the wine ran out, but he understood without her saying that a wedding is not just a celebration of life in the flesh, it is also a time for drinking in the spirit. Drunk with the intention of love and service of one another, we can be inspired in spirit and in truth, even unawares and unknowing. There is something unexpectedly uplifting and instructive that Beethoven should have performed his Ninth Symphony (the final movement when he could no longer hear his music or the thunderous applause of his enthusiastic audience).

Today's Gospel reading at first glance is nothing unexpected, only what we have in fact come to expect in the Easter lectionary – another appearance of the risen Christ to his own. Even though this happens week after week in the Easter readings, Jesus appears unrecognizable to his disciples. It is almost as if those endless encounters were included in the gospels to reassure the church itself that Christ was really risen. Actually, I think that it is not what Luke and the other evangelists had in mind. What they hoped to awaken in us is (to borrow a phrase) to "disbelieve for joy."

As someone else has said, the best way to explain that phrase may be to liken the disciples' encounter with Jesus to the unlikely appearance of the Publishers Clearing House Prize Patrol. Think for a moment how you would feel if on Sunday morning you were awakened by the ding-dong of your doorbell. All unprepared, you put on your pants or towel, plod apprehensively to the front door and pull it partly open. What you see is not at all what you expected. There is the gaudy glare of lights and video cameras, someone standing before you with an oversized cardboard check for $ 10,000,000 – and you barely dressed. Against all odds apparently you have won the sweepstakes or the lottery or whatever. How do you suppose you would react?

"The film clips of big winners (I have seen) on TV, shows them with their mouths and eyes wide open, dancing around screaming, 'I don't believe it? I don't believe it!' Two almost opposed emotions compete at the same time: first disbelief ... 'Nobody ever wins these things ... the odds against wining are astronomical' (one in 53 million?), coupled with, second, unbridled joy: 'Yes, yes, yes, it's really happened to me. It's what we've always hoped for ... Our lives are changed forever.'"[2] That reaction is what one commentator has described as our experience when we "disbelieve for joy."

The proof of the resurrection was ...
eating a fish, no less, before their incredulous
eyes.

That seems to capture the situation of Jesus' disciples pictured in Luke's lesson for this morning when Christ appeared before them. They "disbelieved for joy." Like winning the Clearing House Sweepstakes, the chance that Jesus could have been miraculously resurrected after his very final and public death are, what – "one in eternity?" Yet when Jesus came before them, stood in their midst, and spoke to them in familiar words, "Peace be with you," the flicker of faith that had faded out when his disciples all forsook him and fled, suddenly returned to life and burned within them. They were filled with unlooked for and unexpected joy. The proof of the resurrection was preposterous yet all-too-apparently poised in their presence – eating a fish, no less, before their incredulous eyes.

When was the last time you can recall being consumed with joy, unexpected or otherwise? Surely, we don't experience it on a regular basis; our over-scheduled lives don't allow much time to permit unlooked for joy to jar us loose from our familiar routine. Maybe we manage to make time for a little peace and quiet or some infrequent fun in our lives. But joy?

Perhaps part of the problem is that the church has chosen to be safe rather than subversive, respectable rather then risk-taking, calm and cerebral rather then confrontative and celebratory. Wouldn't it be sad for us to say that sermon snoozers among us may not have missed anything significant? Have we proffered the well-worn path to the point that we operate, as one preacher put it, with a "dangerously high delight deficit."[3] We may expect to be jarred by justice and judgment, but what about joy? To put it in a more contemporary vein, Where's the "wow" in our worship? I wonder. I think of Ann Hill Williams who on occasion, when something in the service particularly pleased her, would simply start clapping.

"When Jesus emerged from the waters of his baptism by John in the Jordan, scripture says that God himself speaks, saying, 'This is my beloved Son in whom I am well pleased' (our version), but I am told that a better translation would be 'This is my beloved Son who brings me great pleasure' – another way to say that Jesus delighted the Father who speaks of 'pleasure' at his faithfulness."[4] Were we not also created to express God's pleasure? To rejoice in the joy of the Good News we are entrusted to offer everyone?

"What if one day we are invited to stand before God, wondering whether we will be welcomed to his kingdom? We will hear one or two types of words: The worst would be to bear the brunt of 'Depart from me, I take no pleasure in your person.' The wonderful words we would want to hear, then and now, are 'Well done, good and faithful servant. You have brought me great pleasure. Enter into the joy of your master.'"[3]

If we are, as John Miller assures us, an Easter people, we ought to be able to express in our own individual ways that we rejoice in the presence of the Risen Christ among us. That is why,

I assume, the Evangelists offer us each week in Easter words that witness to the presence of Christ in his disciples. We, like they, don't easily understand and enter into the continuing presence of Christ in the church, even in the invitation of the Eucharist. We sometimes ask "What takes place in the presence of the bread and wine we are offered? We seldom speculate about what is supposed to happen in the person and life of the one who receives that sacrament." Is it too much to say that we are expected to "be what we have received? To become the bearer of the body and blood of Christ for one another? To embody the continuing presence of Christ in the world and rejoice in the community of the church that offers healing and reconciliation to each one of us" – and to take joy in such service? [4]

One critic comments that when Christians cease coming to church, it is not because they no longer believe in God or in Jesus, but because that community has ceased to be the place where, however they understand it, they can encounter the reality of the risen Christ. We need to be reminded that ministry is not the mark of the professional pastor; it is the offering of all who enter into the community of Christ. It is high time each of us celebrated the offering of our own gifts and rejoiced in the right to be of service to others. Who knows, that might effect an Easter every day.

Lord, no Easter ever celebrated a world without death
and this day is no exception.
In the world
in our community
in our souls –
while we live we are always being given up to death...
Nevertheless
Christ's resurrection prevails and therefore we cry out...
To Life! –
that in-credible
in-soluble
un-stoppable mystery which is Yours to give
and ours to live...

Lord, we are grateful
for despair that is in vain and labor that is not
work that is worship and worship that is play
being part of a world that includes April
and even us,
who can rejoice
that the risen Christ
is among us
and in us
this day —
here
and everywhere.[5]

———

1. In spirit and in truth this sermon is specially indebted in paraphrase and perception to "Count Your Wows," *Homiletics*, April-June 1997. This quotation, p.10
2. "Wows," p.9
3. "Wows," p.11
4. *Lectionary Homiletics*, VII, No. 5, p.11. Adapted, emended, and added on to Frederick Ohler's "The Sun Also Rises (A Prayer for Easter)."

BROKEN BREAD AND BREAKING HEART

3rd Sunday of Easter
Luke 24:13-35
Year A – April 14, 2002

That very day, the first day of the week, two of the disciples were going to a village called Emmaus, about seven miles from Jerusalem, and talking with each other about all these things that had happened. While they were talking and discussing, Jesus himself came near and went with them, but their eyes were kept from recognizing him. And he said to them, "What are you discussing with each other while you walk along?" They stood still, looking sad. Then one of them, whose name was Cleopas, answered him, "Are you the only stranger in Jerusalem who does not know the things that have taken place there in these days?" He asked them, "What things?" They replied, "The things about Jesus of Nazareth, who was a prophet mighty in deed and word before God and all the people, and how our chief priests and leaders handed him over to be condemned to death and crucified him. But we had hoped that he was the one to redeem Israel. Yes, and besides all this, it is now the third day since these things took place. Moreover, some women of our group astounded us. They were at the tomb early this morning, and when they did not find his body there, they came back and told us that they had in-deed seen a vision of angels who said that he was alive. Some of those who were with us went to the tomb and found it just as the women had said; but they did not see him." Then he said to them, "Oh, how foolish you are, and how slow of heart to be-lieve all that the prophets have declared! Was it not necessary that the Messiah should suffer these things and then enter into his glory?" Then begin-ning with Moses and all the prophets, he interpreted to them the things about himself in all the scriptures. As they came near the village to which they were going, he walked ahead as if he were going on. But they urged him strongly, saying, "Stay with us, be-cause it is almost evening and the day is now nearly over." So he went in to stay with them. When he was at the table with them, he took bread, blessed and broke it, and gave it to them. Then their eyes were opened, and they recognized him; and he vanished from their sight. They said to each other, "Were not our hearts burning within us while he was talking to us on the road, while he was opening the scriptures to us?" That same hour they got up and returned to Jerusalem; and they found the eleven and their companions gathered together. They were saying, "The Lord has risen indeed, and he has appeared to Simon! "Then they told what had happened on the road, and how he had been made known to them in the breaking of the bread.

Luke 24: 13-35

Have you ever been to Emmaus? That's the question for this morning, for today, maybe even for a lifetime – because it may be worth your life to know the answer to it. Of course, in a way, I already know the answer because even biblical scholars and archeologists haven't been able to locate Emmaus despite Luke's clue that it was 7½ miles (60 stadia) from Jerusalem. But if no one can find it, that means it could be, for Luke or for us, anywhere – that is, wherever it is we might be likely (or, in this case unlikely) to meet Jesus along the way.

For Cleopas and his companion, Emmaus was wherever they were going to to get away from Jerusalem, where Jesus was dead to the world, and where everything they had hoped for was lost and nothing they could do would change that or make any difference. The best thing they could do was try to leave it – and him – all behind. Fred Buechner has a compelling way of interpreting Emmaus: as "where we go, where these two went, to try to forget about Jesus and the great failure of his life.... the place we go in order to escape – a bar, a movie, wherever it is we throw up our hands and say 'let the whole damned thing go hang. It makes no difference anyway.'" [1]

Maybe there comes a time in your life or mine when we end up going there, one way or another. Buechner imagines: "Emmaus may be buying a new suit or a new car or smoking more cigarettes than you really want, or reading a second-rate novel or even writing one. Emmaus may be going to church on Sunday. Emmaus is whatever we do or wherever we go to make ourselves forget that the world holds nothing sacred: that even the wisest and bravest and loveliest decay and die; that even the noblest ideas that men have had – ideas about love and freedom and justice – have always in time been twisted out of shape by selfish men for selfish ends." [2]

The problem with the Emmaus story for us is that it is not just about those two travelers who were trying to get the hell out of Dodge, any more than the story of Easter is over or ends at sundown on that Sunday not all that long ago. They both find a way of continuing on into the rest of our lives, because if we take those stories seriously, catch even a glimpse of ourselves in them; life can never be the same for us again. The presence of God in whatever form we are able to receive it is difficult to dismiss.

Since Cleopas and the other follower are stand-ins for us in the Emmaus experience, maybe we should ask for ourselves why, since they were disciples of Jesus, did they not recognize him? As *The New English Bible* says, "Something kept them from seeing who it was." But what? If Jesus had come upon them in a blaze of glory, in a chariot of fire surrounded by angels and dressed in dazzling white, surely they would have seen him for who he was. That's the problem. Charlton Heston is pretty convincing, but Jesus didn't show up in that kind of dress or in an astounding and stupendous way wherever he went. Where he was mostly present, as the gospels point out, was in the ordinary events of people's lives, among them as any of us might have been. Most of scripture shows us not so much the history of God's mighty acts in nature as the story of his relentless love in the lives of ordinary people. Yet we are likely to go on expecting God to show up in the spectacular – and miss him altogether in the ordinary.

So perhaps it should not surprise us that Cleopas and his companion could not see the risen Christ with them in the weary stranger who had joined them on the road and was walking alongside. The one thing they did right as they approached Emmaus and the stranger appeared to be going further, was to ask him in: "Stay with us, because it is almost evening and the day is now nearly over." They longed to talk more with him, to hear his interesting insights, but it was not until he sat at table with them, in the breaking of the bread, that their eyes were opened to who he was.

Having spent so many years in schools, as student and teacher, that metaphor seems "meet and right" to me at this time of year – for those end-of-year, end-of-school, and sometimes end-of-friends leave-takings, when we are bound to go off for the summer or college or for different lives. Saying goodbye is difficult because for better or worse we have, for a time, been companions along the ways we have taken together (on our journey, so to speak), whether for this one day or for many days – much as Jesus' disciples were when they encountered him on the road to Emmaus.

Hidden among them, and us, and with us, is the face of God which we are often unmindful of, which is why we can be mindless of one another's needs and wants and why we can also be strangers to each other even though we are companions on the way – to class, to lunch, to church, to play, to a farewell or a funeral; or to our families gathering to share our daily bread together, to wish us well, to wish us goodbye. When we gather at table to do that we are companions in more than one sense, because companion comes from the Latin *com + panis* – which means together or *with + bread*. Our companion is the bread bearer, the one with whom we break bread together.

But to be a companion is not simply to break bread with someone; it is to recognize that we are fellow travelers with him or her when we break-fast, (or lunch or dinner) together, even when in a fast-food frenzy we only break bread together fast.

Being a companion, then, is a metaphor for more than gathering to eat; it is for feeding one another. When we pray (when we remember) "Give us this day our daily bread," we are not just asking for a portion of whole grain, diet-sliced, or stone ground wheat; we are asking for what we need to be nourished for this day, "daily bread" meaning the nourishment it takes to get through the day – even when we live in a land where more people die from overeating than from under-nourishment.

I think I told you before that a former friend and faculty colleague, full of wild hair and exuberance and a heart that often invited in more people than she could handle, asked some of her students home on occasion to share a meal. And on one such evening after dinner, when the time together had gone well and those gathered there felt a strong bond with one another around the dining room table, which they hadn't found at school, she said as they sat at that antique family heirloom highly polished table, "What shall we do to remember this time together? How can we mark this evening?" And some one said in fun, we could always carve our initials in this table. "Let's," she said and went to the kitchen to get some steak knives. And they did.

When I first heard about it, I was horrified (not just because it was her husband's table) but because the table in our family came down through a previous generation to us, in trust, to pass on. I couldn't willingly violate it. But she said to me, "Don't we so often violate one another instead of feeding each other? Why can't we mark for once the time we were fed? When we were, for no particular reason, companions to one another?"

That of course, reminds me: Only when Jesus' disciples shared a meal and broke bread together were they finally able to recognize him and remember they had, indeed, been companions on the road, even when they had not understood one another.

These days, we do not always have a table to sit around (let alone the same one from generation to generation) when we break bread together and try to be companions. I think of the companionship I exchanged one time in a hospital, with an old friend who had just had a cancerous kidney removed and whose stomach looked something like a major league baseball with all the stitches in it. I was feeling guilty because I had only been to see him twice during his ordeal, but as I took my leave, he reached out and grabbed my hand. Looking me straight in the eye, he said, "You know, you're a great guy!" I mumbled something embarrassed like "I am?" Then he squeezed my hand and said, "Remember that." And I did – and I do. And I am just a bit more whole today because he was a companion to me in that moment. How many times do we look for God in some far off place but fail to look in the face of the person next to us?

In church we are invited to seek the invisible presence of Christ in the common Eucharistic meals we share. Are we also willing to find there someone to be companion with as we share the bread? Even Luke affirms that the Easter Faith didn't come out of Bible study. Remember, the two companions didn't recognize Christ when he expounded for them the scriptures; it was only in the breaking of bread together that he was made known to them – and maybe it was "not only in the broken bread but in the breaking heart ... [when night came] that Easter finally dawned for [them]"[3] and Christ was risen indeed.

Fortunately for us, it's never too late to be a companion to someone who might otherwise choose to go another way. And who knows, we might not only find there a companion, but get a glimpse of the face of God we hadn't been looking for.

———

1. Frederick Buechner, *Magnificent Defeat*, pp.85-86
2. *Ibid.*
3. *Lectionary Homiletics XII, No. 5, p.13*

THE DARK IS LIGHT ENOUGH

4th Sunday of Easter
Psalm 23
Year A – April 17, 2005

The LORD is my shepherd; I shall not want.

He maketh me to lie down in green pastures: he leadeth me beside the still waters.

He restoreth my soul: he leadeth me in the paths of righteousness for his name's sake.

Yea, though I walk through the valley of the shadow of death, I will fear no evil: for thou art with me; thy rod and thy staff they comfort me.

Thou preparest a table before me in the presence of mine enemies: thou anointest my head with oil; my cup runneth over.

Surely goodness and mercy shall follow me all the days of my life: and I will dwell in the house of the LORD forever.

The 23rd Psalm

As many of you know, I delight in the use (and misuse) of words and in the propagation of puns, which I justify on the basis that the ancient Hebrews used them in scripture as a means of helping us memorialize significant thoughts on sacred occasions. Particularly satisfying is perpetrating the unexpected in reminding people that common usage can contradict the meaning of a word we have taken for granted, such as thanking a person for a fulsome meal or complimenting a young woman on her fulsome figure – forgetting that the term does not mean ripe or replete but rather rotten or repulsive. Or praising the profound *impact* (as they say) that Mother Teresa's loving ministrations have had on the life of the poor of Calcutta; where as "impact" more properly refers to the destructive descent of an object with great force, as in the impact of the atomic bomb on the life of Hiroshima. Or informing unsuspecting people that reference to feet in the Bible is sometimes a euphemism, referring not to the protruding part of the leg on which we stand, but to the sexual organs.

In any case, I am going to suggest in my sermon what some might say is almost a sacrilegious observation about what may be to many people the most sacred saying in all our scripture – verse 4 in the 23rd psalm: "Yea, though I walk through the valley of the shadow of death, I will fear no evil." Arguably the most comforting of assurances we cling to in times of trouble. The problem is we hear the words primarily as poetry, and so may miss the disturbing shadow side of this inspiring and endearing psalm.

There is no word I know of in English to express the exquisite imperfection of its profound insight, so I have stolen an aesthetic expression from the Japanese to explain it: "wabi-sabi," an unexpected and perhaps unwelcome way to speak about the salvation we are assured of in Psalm 23.

Wabi-sabi (this has no relation to kemo sabe) refers to the perfect beauty of things enhanced by the touch of imperfection and incompleteness. The word, made up of two terms, emerged in 15th century Japan as a reaction to lavishness and overstatement, preferring to express the beauty that is reflected only with aging and sadness, in earthiness and impermanence. An example of wabi-sabi for the Jews, would be a suffering messiah – something unthinkable for the Hebrews in their common hope and expectation: messiah is divine, God's anointed, an invincible kingly figure who would restore Israel to its former greatness; no one could bring suffering and defeat upon him. And yet the prophet Isaiah's portrait of the suffering servant of Israel, her redeemer, is an exquisitely beautiful theological expression for God's tender care and compassion – unthinkable, perhaps even outrageous, but profoundly moving.

Two things about the 23rd Psalm are easy to forget when we hear it read in services or speak the words ourselves, which some of us have learned by heart. First, it was written as a Jewish psalm, not a Christian hymn; and although it is heard mostly at funerals, it is not about death, but life – with a catch. It understands death as a part of life, not separate from it or the enemy of it. It is not something to fear but to put our trust in. "I come with joy to meet my Lord" (as a well-known hymn sings it) in death not just in life; it rejoices that no matter how dark the day, God is found in it, even in our suffering and grief; we are not alone. It mirrors Psalm 66 (v.2): "We go through fire and water, yet you bring us to a spacious place." There is no wabi of green pastures without the sabi of sad realities in our life.

"Yea, though I walk through the valley of the shadow of death, I will fear no evil." Our venerable and beloved text, says in Hebrew, simply "deep darkness;" and the similarity between the words for "evil" and "my shepherd" is striking – meaning "the threat is real, but not to be feared ... "[1] God will provide for us in, not in spite of, the darkness. "What the psalm touches may be so deep as to defy articulate speech. It touches the core questions of security and threat; order amid chaos, ... hope amid despair and depression, ... God [found] amid the fleeting nature of life."[2]

What interests me most about the 4th verse of the psalm, the theological heart of the poem or prayer, is that the "valley" it speaks of is also our personal place of "deep darkness," not just in the shadow of death but in our daily lives – "a place of danger and treachery and fear, a place where we find ourselves often, at many different stages in our lives, not just when we are facing death."[3]

Personally, I would prefer that verse to be only about death, so that I wouldn't have to think about the dark side of my life, first of all for fear of what I might have to own there. And then of having to consider that the light of God is found amid the darkness. It is hard to forget the haunting words of the 139th Psalm, addressed to God: "If I say 'Surely the darkness shall cover me, and the light around me become night,' even that darkness is not dark to you; the night is as bright as the day; for the darkness is as light to you" (vv. 11-12). Do we really want to be searched out and known by God in our darkness for who we are? So often I would rather let the darkness cover me. I do not want to walk the valley of myself willingly.

But maybe that is why Psalm 23 has become for so many people one of the most beloved passages of the Bible. Who has not or will not one day find himself walking the dark and difficult valley? What prayer would be more appropriate to speak into that darkness, whether inner or outer? Only then will the truth that God's light shines in the midst of the darkness be of comfort. Entering "the dark night of the soul" that mystics speak about can free us to understand that where God seems to be absent, or the enemy, or not God at all, God is the one who calls to us in the dark places and preserves and upholds us no matter what may befall us, even when we have given up.

We read into the 23rd Psalm, after all, the good shepherd as the one who was crucified, died, and was buried – and descended into hell (one of the sayings a lot of people don't like about the Apostles' Creed). What's Jesus doing there in that God-forsaken place of darkness and despair? What indeed! At this time of year we probably don't have to be reminded who it was that said from the cross, "My God, My God, why have you forsaken me?" (The first verse of the 22nd Psalm). That's the only verse many of us know of that psalm, but to read the psalm all the way through is to realize that Jesus' words as a Jew are not merely a cry of helplessness, but a confession that even in the midst of the experience of darkness and forsakenness, God is present. Jesus has gone before us into the darkness and delivered us from the dark into his light.[4]

In 1928 Ralph Waldo Emerson also preached a sermon on the 4th verse of Psalm 23, and he began by saying the one thing that unites us in all our diversity is the certainty of death. You can be sure that poor and rich, sick and well, young and old, we will one day walk through that fatal valley, the end of all that divides one person from the other. That perspective used to be how preachers brought converts into the church, he said; but maybe today the fear of death no longer fuels peoples' faith. Instead, what may matter more to our spiritual life is the conviction that God is with us even in our dying, a God who stands with us in the face of unimaginable fear and senseless suffering, the faithfulness of the good shepherd that conquers the clouds of fear.

The simple explanation of the 23rd Psalm is that "we can either fear death or we can expect it as an inevitable part of life, [even] welcoming it as one more stage on our journey toward..." what God has promised: "The Lord is our shepherd, we shall not want ... There is nothing we really need that we will not receive."[5] Therefore we can afford to give our life away freely, in our dark or in the light.

———

1. *New Interpreter's Bible IV*, p.768
2. *Lectionary Homiletics, XVI,* 3-p.24
3. *Op. cit.,* p.29
4. *Op. cit.,* p.25
5. *Op. cit.,* p.30

THE COMMANDMENT OF LOVE

5th Sunday of Easter
John 13:31-35
Year C – May 9, 2004

> *At the last supper, when Judas had gone out, Jesus said, "Now the Son of Man has been glorified, and God has been glorified in him. If God has been glorified in him, God will also glorify him in himself and will glorify him at once. Little children, I am with you only a little longer. You will look for me; and as I said to the Jews so now I say to you, 'Where I am going, you cannot come. 'I give you a new commandment, that you love one another. Just as I have loved you, you also should love one another. By this everyone will know that you are my disciples, if you have love for one another."*

> *John 13:31-35*

A police officer with the L.A.P.D. pulls a driver over to the side of I-5, and asks for his license and registration. "What's wrong officer?" the driver asks. "I didn't go through that red light. And I certainly wasn't speeding."

"No you weren't," says the officer, "but I saw you flashing the one-fingered salute as you swerved around the lady driving in the left lane, and I further observed your flushed and angry face as you shouted at the driver of the Hummer who cut you off, and how you pounded your steering wheel when the traffic ground to a stop."

"Is that a crime, officer?"

"No, but when I saw the 'Jesus loves you and so do I' bumper sticker on the car, I figured, 'This car has got to be stolen.'" [1]

You may not be big on bumper stickers and have a hard time remembering what they say. But it's hard to forget what Jesus' words were to his disciples as he was about to leave them: "I give you a new commandment, that you love one another as I have loved you."

As it happens, the 5th Sunday of Easter is also Mother's Day this year, and although mothers are not specifically sainted on the Church calendar, Jesus' task in today's reading is "similar to the lifelong task of mothers: to teach a child to live without you."[2] Jesus' words in John's Gospel are a part of his farewell address to his disciples: "Little children," he says to them "I am with you only a little longer."

What wisdom could he will, what parting gift could he give to his wayward band that would protect them from the way of the world (and mostly from themselves) in the face of their impending loss? Nothing guaranteed, that's certain; but his famous words have come down to us over the intervening 2000 years: "I give you a new commandment, that you love one another. Just as I have loved you, you should also love one another. By this everyone will know that you are my disciples, if you love one another."

Although those words may at first sound comforting as well as appropriate for Mother's Day, they are a two-edged sword, as is our current hallowed Hallmark and fanciful FTD celebration of Mother's Day. "Actually, it's amazing that there is a Mother's Day at all, considering that the woman who worked half of her life to found the holiday spent the other half trying to undo it!"[3]

In 1905 Anna M. Jarvis began to organize a holiday honoring mothers because her own mother had founded the Mother's Day Work Clubs, which had "raised money to improve sanitary conditions in the cities, provided medicines to the poor and, during the Civil War, were one of the only groups authorized to act as neutral agents, serving soldiers on both sides."[4]

Two years after her mother died, Anna set about to gain national recognition for Mother's Day, writing thousands of letters to politicians, businesses and clergy; and finally in 1914, President Woodrow Wilson declared a national holiday. "Now, Mother's Day is the second-busiest day of the year for telephone companies ... the second-busiest day of the year for florists ... the fourth biggest day among greeting card companies" – I have no statistics about the count of chocolate candy purveyors. "Anna Jarvis would have a stroke if she could see it [now]"[5]

As a matter of fact, profit-making ventures began almost immediately after the presidential proclamation, and Anna eventually "admitted to being sorry she ever started the holiday, and spent the rest of her life and all of her inheritance trying to [do away with it]." Not to mention that even for one day a year "Christian community has a struggle being loving and inclusive at the same time"[6] – despite Jesus' parting words to his disciples.

Those words well known as they are, are not as simple to live by as they sound, and they apply to more than Mother's Day. They are a reminder to the rest of us who aren't mothers of what complete and selfless love asks. Jesus' words call upon us to be willing to love in a way many of us have not even thought of loving before. The way Jesus used the word love called for an action rather than a feeling. I don't have to like someone in order to love him, to act lovingly on his or her behalf even if that person may seem to me unlovable. Many mothers *are* love in action, even in the face of childish rebellion and rejection. And that love, I suspect, springs not first of all from justice and fairness but from forgiveness.

—◦—

Jesus was a show-me, not tell-me person.

—◦—

Forgiveness, as well as the love Jesus spoke about, can be expressed in action rather than feeling. I don't first have to forgive a person in my heart in order to act forgivingly toward him. In fact, it maybe the other way around: if I can act forgivingly toward someone who has wronged me, maybe then I can finally come to forgive him. It is a little bit like: *Saying* "I love you" may not be the best evidence of my love, but saying the words may enable an action that will express the love that is in my heart.

Jesus was a show-me, not a tell-me person. And one of the greatest problems we have in understanding what he meant by love comes because he *commanded* us to do it. It wasn't a suggestion or a recommendation. It's in the vocative case, "Love one another." Not if you feel like it, or if the person is loving or even loveable. Maybe that why he called it "a new commandment."

The commandment to love was after all an old one, which lay at the heart of the Torah. Around 550 B.C., the Book of Leviticus (19:18) commanded: "You shall love your neighbor as yourself. I am the Lord." What is new in Jesus' use of that old injunction in the Gospel of John is that to obey it is not a mark of righteousness for us for keeping the law or for doing good deeds; it is simply the distinguishing mark of one who is willing to accept the love of Jesus. It is the only commandment Jesus gives to his disciples — and the only sign that shows we are willing to express our love in the way he loved us.

The key to it for us is not obligation but gratitude, not close-fisted obedience but open handed acceptance. Mother's Day is also about gratitude, not just for what has been but also for the possibilities of what will be. Love does not just look back; it is empowered by the promise of what is to come. A story that says more than it tells expresses that love — which is not just for today:

A little boy's father had died the year before. His mother, in trying to be both mommy and daddy, had planned a picnic. The little guy had never been on a picnic, so they made their plans, fixed the lunch, and packed the car. Then it was time for bed. Ha!

That kid could not sleep to save his life. He kept running into his mother's room to wake her up and talk about the picnic. Finally, she said the inevitable: "If you don't go to back to bed and go to sleep this minute, there won't be a picnic."

> "But Mom," he started.
> "No buts," she said. "Get to bed." "Okay .... but, Mom?"
> (Sigh). "What?"
> "I just want to thank you for tomorrow." [7]
> Love is not just for today.

———

1. *Homiletics* 15, 3-p.26
2. *Biblical Preaching Journal* 14, 2-p.21
3. *Biblical Preaching Journal*, p.20
4. *Ibid.*
5. *Ibid.*
6. *Ibid.*

THE WAY

5th Sunday of Easter
John 14:1-14
Year A – April 20, 2008

"Let not your hearts be troubled; believe in God, believe also in me. In my Father's house are many rooms; if it were not so, would I have told you that I go to prepare a place for you? And when I go and prepare a place for you, I will come again and will take you to myself, that where I am you may be also. And you know the way where I am going." Thomas said to him, "Lord, we do not know where you are going; how can we know the way?" Jesus said to him, "I am the way, and the truth, and the life; no one comes to the Father, but by me. If you had known me, you would have known my Father also; henceforth you know him and have seen him."

Philip said to him, "Lord, show us the Father, and we shall be satisfied." Jesus said to him, "Have I been with you so long, and yet you do not know me, Philip? He who has seen me has seen the Father; how can you say, 'Show us the Father'? Do you not believe that I am in the Father and the Father in me? The words that I say to you I do not speak on my own authority; but the Father who dwells in me does his works. Believe me that I am in the Father and the Father in me; or else believe me for the sake of the works themselves."

"Truly, truly, I say to you, he who believes in me will also do the works that I do; and greater works than these will he do, because I go to the Father."

John 14:1-12

It may be true, as a friend of mine says, that no one normal listens to the scripture lessons being read in church. But in John's gospel reading for today it is very hard to ignore the familiar words of the text we hear read over and over again at funerals. Beginning with the very comfortable saying of Jesus: "In my father's house are many mansions [some traditional translations also say "many rooms"] .... I go to prepare a place for you ... so that where I am, there you may be also."

We imagine that God's house is an endless mansion with a room in it especially prepared for each of the faithful (we might even hope for a room with a view). And we don't much trouble ourselves about whether we have been faithful over many things, or even just a few, because God is, after all, a forgiving God. As one cynic has said, "It's his *job* to forgive."

We take comfort during the Burial Service in the assurance that our loved one who has died will finally be at rest in God's house, the home he or she has longed for throughout life even though we may not have always called it by that name, a room specially prepared for the one we have lost – and by association, also for us. And we hope that God will be, even if we aren't, faithful to his promises.

Also in the same passage in John is the well-used saying addressed to Jesus' disciple Thomas – and all the doubting Thomases among and within us – who asks Jesus, "How can we know the way where you are going?" A fair question, we want to be reassured that the way is evident and available, open to us when we want to follow him into God's loving care in his merciful mansion. That's when Jesus says to Thomas, "I am the way, and the truth, and the life; no one comes to the Father, but by me." A saying that fulfills our unspoken assumption that Christ is the only way to God, and that we are indeed blessed because we know it; and it is not just a blessed thing to be a Christian, but a requirement if we are to be saved from the fate of sin and death. It's good to know that we are on the right team and that all others have missed out, even if they don't yet know it – forgetting that the belt buckle every German soldier wore during World War II had inscribed there "Gott Mitt Uns" – God is with *us* (with them).

So much for the security and comfort that this morning's gospel reading recalls for us. Who would want to challenge such beautiful and sacred thoughts? The biblical scripture says what it says, means what it says, and who are we to question it – it's right there in print, and in some Bibles even in red ink. To suggest that such godly sayings do not mean exactly what they seem to us to mean would be a mean message, the sad spite of a spoiler. I do not intend to be the one who tramples underfoot the texts that express the truth of the gospels, especially in Jesus' so-called farewell address to his disciples. I haven't got the spunk of a Spong this Sunday to send you away sad, outraged, or elated at the exposure of suspect sentences in scripture. But I am convinced that John 14:6, after seeming to assure us of our special place in heaven, has become one of the most divisive and destructive texts in the checkered history of Christianity: "No one comes to the Father except by me." A corollary expression you will recognize is the declaration "There is no salvation outside the church" (the church understood as Roman Catholic). There is not one way, there is the *only* way to God. And if you "don't get it" you don' t get it.

This perspective has justified the exclusion and indeed the persecution of other religions, and even the attack on differing points of view within Christianity itself. Having been a sometime teacher of comparative religions, I am admittedly intolerant of that exclusive and exclusionary position – but, more than that, I do not believe Jesus intended his words to be taken that way, even (and maybe especially) among the faithful.

"This is the only [New Testament] scriptural reference claiming such an exclusive view" for Christians. The gospel writers picture Jesus' "ministry [as] inclusive rather than exclusive,"[1] beginning with the astounding and revolutionary view that Jesus came not to call the righteous but sinners to the kingdom of God – which scandalized the Jewish leaders who insisted that following the Torah, the Jewish law, was the only way to become righteous; that is, to be made right with God. And that outsiders, non-Jews, were not a part of the promises made to Israel and so not to be counted among God's people.

Jesus' threat to the insiders, the religious establishment, was real, symbolized by his overthrowing the tables of the money-changers in the Temple, which in three of the Gospels was what led to his arrest, trial, and execution. And during his recorded ministry, at least three of Jesus' major miracles concerned the healing of persons from foreign and hostile nations.

We have no idea whether Jesus knew of what we might call eastern religions, or of Hinduism or Buddhism, but when he was giving his farewell address to his disciples he was not offering a critique of other authoritative religious claims, implying that Buddhists were bally-hoo, that Hindus were hooters, or that orientals were "out of it" – all other faiths condemned. He was addressing specifically the spiritual condition of his own closest disciples who, as we see, again and again were far from faithful and who never seemed to "get it" whenever he was trying to teach them.

In that context, it seems to me, Jesus' intended meaning is clear: If you would seek to be my followers, within that covenant you need to accept me as the way, the truth, and the life for you; in that way you will have knowledge of God, my Father, through what I tell you and how I live among you.

To put it for us in more modern terms, if we would seek to be his followers, to be Christians rather than (say) Jews or Muslims, then Christ must be at the center of our lives because our faith is formed and determined by our relationship with him. That is the way we have primary access to God. As Thomas á Kempis put it long ago: "Without the Way there is no going; without the Truth there is no knowing; without the Life there is no living."[2] The challenge is not "Is Jesus serious?" but "do I believe it's true" if we [would] walk by faith [and not by] sight."[3]

So, does this new insight rob us of what one commentator called one of "Jesus greatest-hits" passage: In my father's house are many mansions, rooms prepared for us(?). In the process of examining the words in the original language, we risk losing some of the poetry we cherish, but what the passage proposes in the Greek is not There is a room reserved for us; but there is room for all of us if we want to be there. A little like saying to a teenager, "If you want to come home, your room is ready and waiting for you, Why don't you go on in?"[4] As one commentator suggests: On the way "we will recognize Jesus in the hard stretches of that journey, not because he will be wearing a nametag and not because he will be announcing that he is the only way, but because we will have traveled with him enough to know his way can be counted on. We will have sung his name in hymns, heard of his encounters with troubled people, called his name at the Lord's Table, experienced him on the journey and been blessed on the way by his benediction."[5]

———

1. *Lectionary Homiletics XIX.* No. 3-p.23
2. *Op. cit.*, p.20
3. *Op. cit.*, p. 21
4. *Op. cit.*, p.22
5. *Biblical Preaching Journal 21.* 2-p.9

LOVE THRU THE BACK DOOR

5th Sunday of Easter Mother' s Day
John 13:31-35
Year C – May 13, 2001

At the last supper, when Judas had gone out, Jesus said, "Now the Son of Man has been glorified, and God has been glorified in him. If God has been glorified in him, God will also glorify him in himself and will glorify him at once. Little children, I am with you only a little longer. You will look for me; and as I said to the Jews so now I say to you, 'Where I am going, you cannot come.' I give you a new commandment, that you love one another. Just as I have loved you, you also should love one another. By this everyone will know that you are my disciples, if you have love for one another. "

John 13:31-35

"I give you a new commandment, that you love one another even as I have loved you." These famous words from John's gospel (which we usually associate with Maundy Thursday) fall for us on the fifth Sunday of Easter this year – which is also Mother's Day. I received two bits of advice from clergy-types for this occasion. The first is, "Mother's Day is an invention of Hallmark Cards and FTD, not a church festival. Don't pander to the culture; stick to the Lectionary. Preach the Biblical text. If you must mention Mother's Day, leave it for the prayers."[1]

The second sort of counsel may be smarter: "Remember [this] if any of you are tempted to downplay Mother's Day...: "You

247

don't tug on Superman's cape. You don't spit into the wind.... and you certainly don't tell a church it shouldn't celebrate Mother's Day. ... Some causes are worth martyrdom. But purging Mother's Day from the Christian calendar isn't one of them.'"[2]

Oh, and don't forget what Oscar Wilde once wrote: "All women become like their mothers. That's their tragedy. No man does. That's his."[3]

Maybe this morning I can somehow manage to pass through the eye of a needle and (to murder the metaphor) kill two birds with one stone (if I haven't succeeded in shooting myself in the foot by so saying). "In one church, when a Bible is presented to a third-grade child, the child recites a passage of Scripture. On one occasion, everything was going well until the minister came to one little boy who couldn't remember his [own] name, let alone a Bible verse. [At a loss] the boy's eyes frantically [appealed for help from] his mother who fortunately was seated near the front. He was greatly relieved when she whispered, 'I am the light of the world,' to which he bellowed, 'My mother is the light of the world.'"[4]

Before I stray from the sublime to the serious, it might be worth saying for starters that what's special about the "new commandment" is it upsets our assumption that Jesus was speaking about the Golden Rule we are familiar with – namely, "Do unto others as you would have others do unto you." What Jesus is saying precludes that and produces what one person proclaims is the "Platinum Rule," wherein we find at the center of the commandment not the "other" (person) but "ourselves": "Do unto others as I have done unto you."

Wisdom says to me it's safer to stay with the scripture than to seek some way of skewing the passage as a pretext for preaching about the importance of Mother's Day, where there are plenty of pitfalls for the preacher. For instance, some people in our pews will have had a poor experience with their mothers, or among some parishioners perhaps child abuse is a problem, or someone may be struggling with a sense of inadequacy over her improper parenting skills. The Preacher is not protected from becoming *persona non grata* in his own pulpit. And that doesn't touch on another problem, that one way or another Mother's Day is a sad day because it celebrates what she does best – sending us out into the world on our own, strong enough at last to be self-reliant, no longer needing her to lean on.

Which recalls Jesus' words in today's text: "Little children, I am with you only a little longer.... 'where I am going, you cannot come.'" One way or another Mother's Day is about loss. And, coincidentally, "Love one another" are among Jesus' farewell words to those he loved, set not in triumph but in sadness. The first verse of the passage we are pondering is a prelude to sadness. It starts "When Judas had gone out..." (unsaid on his errand of betrayal) – a reminder that we are all vulnerable to straying from our best intentions, as Judas was; committing to a community of love cannot help leave us vulnerable and fragile.

What kind of love do you suppose Jesus was speaking about? Love is surely one of the most overused words in our language, and the fact that we talk about it a lot doesn't mean we know much about it either. But if we are going to consider incorporating the "new commandment" into our lives, we've got to start loving somewhere – maybe with something small, maybe not with abusive husbands and child molesters. Maybe we can manage to act lovingly towards the people with whom we work, and some of those we live with, and maybe even towards the difficult person in the next pew or next to us in our pew.

In John's passage perhaps we could compare Jesus' love for his disciples to the love a mother shows for her children. In fact, as we just heard, our text tells us Jesus addresses his disciples as "little children." Except he doesn't try to explain to them the meaning of love because for him love is not an idea as much as a way of life he lives – for them. That level of love might seem to be beyond most of us, but maybe we could make a start by saying "O.K. Jesus I'll love people. But let me pick the ones I'll try to love." Which is something like what Peter says when Jesus tells his disciples that he's about to leave them. Peter begs him to take him along, saying (in effect) "Jesus, if you take me to heaven with you, I'll do all the loving you want me to do. But don't leave me here with these 11 other schmucks. You can't possibly expect me to love them."[5] Except that is exactly what Jesus was asking.

If you want to know what love is, do something loving.

If we may return to the mother metaphor for a moment, it reminds us that "If her baby comes out kind of squished and funny looking, the mother still loves it. She doesn't wander around the maternity ward seeing if someone wants to trade."[6] Fine, but how is it that we can come to love those whom we are not drawn to, whom we do not find desirable or (if you will) whom we do not find lovable? Unfortunately for us the gospels don't pretend to be a primer on the art of loving; there's no book to look up the answer in. And we may be dismayed to discover that there is almost no place in the New Testament where the love Jesus speaks about has anything to do with our loving *feelings*. What he says is that love depends on what you do rather than what you feel. To borrow (or create) a saying in character with the great philosopher Aristotle: If you want to know what love is, do something loving. A loving action is what defines an act of love. That's why Jesus can *command* love, not merely commend it or encourage it or invite it.

You might be tempted to say, "It's impossible for a person to command me to love someone else; that's something I can't understand, let alone know how to do." But it *is* possible to do if what we are being asked – is to act in our neighbor's interest, to help care for her needs, to act lovingly toward him or her even when we don't find him to be a person we love or like or maybe even if we can't stand him. We may be further astounded or disturbed when we remember that Jesus also said the whole of the law is summed up in the commandment to love your neighbor as yourself (Gal. 5:14). How can I begin to bear the burden of that! The law of love gets heavier and heavier the more I think about it, especially when Jesus put it in the form of this "new commandment."

"Not to worry," says Jesus, "It's a piece of cake" (or maybe to be more ethnically correct, he might have said "a bite of rahat loukoum"). There is no way, locked into our own will and strength; we can embody the love of Christ. But the secret is, we are freed to love others because God has loved us first. That's the way God is made real to us, and through us God becomes real for others. So whether we choose to share God's love with others really matters: God's reputation, not ours, is at stake. "I give you a new commandment," Jesus says, "that as I have loved you, so shall you love one another. That's the way people will know you are my disciples."

Love is not simply a stirring in the loins; it is something we decide to do. Mothers know that, and that expression of love is what we lift up today. If you want a rationale for it or simply a simile to make you smile, let me leave you with this one:

"It's like St. Peter at the pearly gates, who was busy rejecting the undeserving. Once in a while, however, he would turn around and find that those he had rejected were getting into heaven. He complained to Jesus, 'Look, I'm doing my job, but somehow these people go in any way,' and Jesus responded, 'Oh, that's my mother. She's letting them in the back door.'"[7] Amen.

---

1. *Biblical Preaching Journal* 11. 2-p.15
2. Homiletics 1.2-p.29
3. *Ibid.*
4. *Ibid.*
5. *Lectionary Homiletics* XII, 6-p.13
6. *Ibid.*
7. *Christian Century* Vol. 118, No. 1-4 p.13

COMMANDED TO LOVE

A Dogmatic Approach

6th Sunday of Easter
John 14:15-21
Year A – May 5, 2002

If you love me, you will keep my command-ments. And I will pray the Father, and he will give you another Counselor, to be with you forever, even the Spirit of truth, whom the world cannot receive, because it neither sees him nor knows him; you know him for he dwells with you, and will be in you. I will not leave you desolate; I will come to you. Yet a little while, and the world will see me no more, but you will see me; because I live, you will live also. In that day you will know that I am in my Father, and you in me, and I in you. He who has my commandments and keeps them, he it is who loves me; and he who loves me will be loved by my Father, and I will love him and manifest myself to him.

John 14:15-21

Since there's no way I am going to publicly repent of what I am about to say, let me first offer this apology (the word which means a defense of or a justification for what is to be said). Some-where someone wiser than I, specifically Reinhold Niebuhr, said, "Humor is a prelude to faith; and laughter is the beginning of prayer." Not to mention Peter O'Toole's testimony: "In the begin-ning was the word, and the word was ... funny."

Some of you will think my theology has gone to the dogs, but I can't resist tossing you a bone or two to help you savor this sermon more smilingly. In philosophical if not theological doggerel the shaggy sayings I'm going to suggest are "prefatory aphorisms" for what follows. That means they come before we aphor – so to speak. If they do not seem savory at this instant, consider that they could become bone meal for the soul in the course of this sermon.

> *The reason dogs have so many friends is because they wag their tails and not their tongues.*

> *The greatest dog is the hot dog, for it feeds the hand that bites it.*

> *What has four legs and an arm? A happy pit bull.*[1]

There's another story about a pit bull, which I probably shouldn't add; but since it came to me through Carol and Mark Pugh, I know that it is at least pharmaceutically correct:

> *A burglar breaks into a church. He's searching around in the dark when he hears a parrot say, "Jesus is watching you."*

> *The burglar aims his flashlight at it and says, "You're a pretty bird, What's your name?"*

> *The parrot says, "My name is Zorba."*

> *The burglar says, "A parrot named Zorba? That's pretty weird." The parrot says, "Not as weird as a pit bull named Jesus."*

As John said last Sunday, more eloquently than I could articulate on this occasion, saying goodbye is so difficult for us because what we want from a farewell offering, and often can-not promise, is hope and comfort. John, the gospel writer, in our reading this morning gives us Jesus' parting words to his disciples: moving, compassionate – and demanding. "I will not leave you desolate," he says; "I will come to you. Yet a little while, and the world will see me no more, but you will see me; because I live, you will live also." Wonderful, without conditions – except one, which sounds gentle and kind enough: "If you love me, you will keep my commandments." Therein lies the brass knuckles in the velvet glove.

Jesus talked a lot about the commandments of God, but to his disciples he gave only one: "I give you a new commandment," he said, "that you love one another even as I have loved you." That's a command to love, not an invitation, exhortation, or even a strong suggestion. Have you ever been *ordered* to love someone; (like your younger brother or your pushy next door neighbor)? And in this case, the "kicker" is: "as *I*" (the *way* I) have loved you" – the way God has loved us. Is that a comfort or a cross to bear?

Having spent so many years in schools, whenever I approach a subject I become compulsive about doing the homework. So before I preach, I prepare by routinely reading seven commentaries or so, hoping to acquaint myself with what there is to know about the passage – and what others more accomplished than I have had to say about it. The problem is, I am then liable to be left with little or nothing to add on my own – or too undone by the seriousness of the subject to speak at all. Not this week, because one commentator came up with an unexpected and unlikely illustration that got my attention. I must admit, at first it seemed far removed from the problems posed by John's text, let alone for the purpose of helpful theological reflection upon the passage – but it dogged me until at last I invited it in. Here it is, for those who have ears to hear:

The patient, whom we'll call Hazel, entered UCLA Medical Center for quadruple-bypass surgery. Since being moved into the ICU, she had barely moved, or even opened her eyes. It had been days now, and volunteer Betty Walsh was getting concerned. The situation was becoming desperate. She decided to call in a member of the canine candy-striping corps.

The new staffer, a pet-partner, if you will, arrived moments later. Koyla, a 145-pound shaggy white Great Pyrenees, crawled right up on Hazel's hospital bed and snuggled in beside her. There she lay beside her patient, nuzzling her warm and furry body in next to Hazel, who hadn't twitched a muscle for days. Betty and the other nurses gathered around to watch, tense and concerned.

Then, they detected movement.... It wasn't long until Hazel's hand was inching toward the dog. She began to stroke its fur. Within minutes she was smiling and talking, calling the huge dog her friend.

Betty stood close by and monitored her vital signs. The blood pressure monitor began to go down, down, down to normal levels. Koyla is not the only dog in the corps. There's a poodle, a greyhound, a pug, eight golden retrievers, four black Labs, two German shepherds, and several mutts.[2]

You may be wondering what this portrait of the Great Pyrenees could possibly have to do with problems presented by John's pericope or Jesus' farewell commandment to his followers. It's a dog of a passage, even if it is delightful and uplifting. Maybe you have to have a flea-bitten sense of humor to hear it as having any bearing on the gospel reading, but the canine commentator makes this case for it. What Jesus calls for in his followers is not just faith (which, it turns out was in short supply among his disciples), but obedience. Or, if you will, faithful obedience – something that at least some dogs know more about than most of us. It almost seems more in their nature than in our cultured inclinations. Dogs can provide comfort and reassurance that evoke in us a sense of wellbeing, but they also demonstrate a loyalty and obedience that most of the apostles would have died for (in a manner of speaking).

⟿⟾

And then many of you are privy to the peculiar problem of the dyslexic agnostic insomniac...

⟿⟾

And dogs are no strangers to the realm of God talk. A friend of mine, who is a Dominican monk; told me that his order, called the Black Friars, is more familiarly known as the Domini-canes, that is the Dogs of God, whose task is to be "watchdogs of orthodoxy." And then many of you are privy to the peculiar prob-lem of the dyslexic agnostic insomniac: you know, the one who lies awake all night consumed with the question "Is there a Dog?" "Man' s best friend" is hardly adequate to sum up God's action in our lives, but "The Hound of Heaven" might be appropriate. And I hesitate to add the admonition of my mother who insisted that "Dog-gone-it" was infinitely more acceptable than "God-dammit." (But, I doggress.)

I may be a bit more carried away here than befits the substance of a serious sermon, but I am also convinced, along with the homiletical commentary I quoted from, that what we can learn from dogs could help us understand and even act upon the admonition "If you love me, you will keep my commandments." If you suspect that this theology has thrown God to the dogs, as would-be disciples, maybe we ought to at least acknowledge the depth of dogs' devotion, loyalty, obedience, and unconditional love, which offers us an uncommon comfort and reassuring pres-ence. Is that blessing any less godly or more dogly?

A crucial question of the commentary worth considering is: "If we were to have the kind of ministry in our churches, homes, schools and communities that pet partners have in hospitals, what would that look like? What would being faithful, and a willingness to 'come' to the side of others as their Advocate mean in the lives of those around us?"[3]

Our commentary commends what we might call the Ten Dogmandments to nourish our relationship with God. I'll offer you only some of them. Once you get the hang of it you can create your own:

Greet loved ones with a wagging tail. Nothing is more important than feeling loved, ... The wagging tail [says] this is where we belong... where we live, where we're safe... where we're loved. [You have to figure out how to "wag" yours.]

Eat with gusto ... You know how dogs eat: slobber flying everywhere ... eating is a celebration of life. Breaking bread together is holy ... barriers are broken down, friendships ... strengthened. To nourish the body [ought not be] a chore but a sacrament.

Be loyal ... if your dog is nothing else, he is loyal to a fault ... Loyalty is a critical element of discipleship, for it [shapes] our relationship with ... our spouse, our community and our friends.

When you're happy, dance around ... Celebration and Gratitude ... affirm the essential goodness of life ... and carry us through adversity and the low moments.

[Some others that may rub you the right way:]

No matter how harshly you're scolded, don't pout – run back and make friends ... Or, *Avoid biting when a simple growl will do.*[4] And so on.

Think them up yourself. Think of them as trying to get us in the right spirit. Think of this: If our hearts are not in them, we can still decide to do them anyway, to be strong in love, to be faithful to love's commandment. "It is only after we do something, however imperfect and half-hearted ... that we begin to get in the spirit of it and discover [in us] the Spirit that Christ promises us... 'the Spirit of truth', as John says, 'whom the world cannot receive, because it neither sees him nor knows him,'" [But] "you [will] know him, because he abides with you, and he will be in you (John. 14:17)."

If we wait for our hearts to feel like loving, "we will often fail to act just when our action is most needed."[5]

If there is a moral here as well as a message, it could be put like this — forgive me: We could do worse than wake up drunk with the spirit, and take refuge in the hair of the dog. SHALOM.

―――――

1. "All dogs go to heaven," *Christianity Today*, Dec. 3, 2001-15
2. *Homiletics*, May 2002, 14, 3-pp.11-12
3. *Op. cit.*, p.12
4. *Op. cit.*, P.12-13
5. *Lectionary, Homiletics* XIII, 6-p.5

LOVE BROKEN

7th Sunday of Easter
Acts 1:15-17, 21-26; Psalm 1;
1 John 5:9-13; John 17:6-19
Year B – June 4, 2000

Those of you who have been repeaters the last several Sunday services (to invoke the language of my youth when the Daisy BB gun ceased to be a single-shooter) may have noticed that the Bible readings have sounded like repeaters, too – as one commentary quips: "a broken record." They have dwelt upon "the openness, the wideness, the inclusivity of God's unconditional love."[1] And this week's lectionary is not significantly different. So I'm going to set aside those texts and focus on the saying in this service that speaks to us succinctly of God's love in everyday image and metaphor.

It's an easy one to remember, coming from the Last Supper when Jesus was at table with his disciples and he took bread; and when he had blessed it, he broke it, and gave it to them, saying, "Take, eat, this is my body, which is given for you." I want to say something this morning about Eucharist as a communion of blessed brokenness – both his and ours. And if there are moments which sound slightly ribald or irreverent, remember that is unintentional on the one hand and inconsequential in the enormity of God's forgiveness on the other. Don't forget what G.K. Chesterton wrote: "Angels can fly because they take themselves so lightly." Or Reinhold Niebuhr's "Humor is a prelude to faith; and laughter is the beginning of prayer." Or C.S. Lewis's saying that the ability to laugh at oneself is functionally the closest thing we have to repentance. And how about that great fifth Commandment, Humor thy father and thy mother.

Our word eucharist comes from the Greek eucharistia, meaning the giving of thanks or gratitude, from charistos: favor or grace. My first lesson in that came when I was a newly ordained priest and was asked, as Dean of Church Schools in the Diocese of Virginia, to celebrate the opening communion service for St. Margaret's School. After consecrating the bread and wine, rounding the altar headed for the communion rail laden with lovely young ladies, I stumbled and fairly flung the contents of the silver paten on the floor at their feet, the so-called "pennies from heaven" strewn about the sanctuary like so much sacred confetti.

I was mortified – but no one laughed at me or winked or rolled her eyes; and after the service that grand old lady Viola Woolfolk, forever headmistress, mollified me, saying, "That wasn't so bad. Last year when Father Guy raised the chalice and bent down to kiss the altar, he dumped the entire vial of wine down the front of his vestments." Picking up the pieces of my "far-flung" dignity was not so difficult after that. She even added, there was a difference between being a fool for Christ's sake and being a damned fool, and she far preferred the former. So my emersion in eucharist began in gratitude and grace given gratis and in mercy broken.

Eucharist begins when only "two or three are gathered in Christ' s name" because, as the Prayer Book puts the promise, there "thou wilt be in the midst of them." Once during the '60s when I took a group of Exeter Academy (male) student deacons to Concord Academy (when it was all girls), which had asked that we bring a church service to them, at the appointed hour only one young lady showed up. Embarrassingly, there were a dozen of us who had come to "put on" the service. "Wait," she said, "I'll get my roommate." And after about 15 minutes, there were five, I think (plus us iconoclastic religious types), who brought to us what was left of their breakfast, which we all gratefully shared because we were by then famished; we had broken our fast in the wee hours at Exeter before we left. It tasted more like Krispy Kreme than unleavened bread; but when it was done, they actually asked for our service.

One of our students said, "What's the use?" Yet, in the end, we "did our thing," as we called it then. And for the first time we could remember, the face of God was spread upon our faces; and we prayed together, boys and girls (imagine that) — and maybe Concord wasn't moved, but the so-called "scorpions" from Exeter were, in spite of themselves, and eucharist was all in all. The service even included a student sermon, or something like it, although it might have sounded a little like Jonathan Livingston Seagull accompanied by Pachelbel. But the other students had no trouble understanding the word, the flesh, and the devil in them. After that our saying went: "Whenever one or five are gathered, He is there and so are we." Present in His presence.

Speaking of sermons reminds me. Not long ago one of St. Mary's parishioners posed to me a curious question: She said, "What is it that you are whistling during the sermon?" What? I said, wondering how I can whistle when I preach? (Whistling in the dark, I can understand.) "I've been watching you," she said, "when you think of what it is, let me know." I confess this is another of God's mysteries; but if you figure it out, let me know.

When we finally come to the altar in eucharist as separate persons, we also come as com-panions: coming from *cum*, meaning "with;" and *panis*, "bread," to offer "ourselves, our souls and bodies" (as the service says it): a sacrifice acceptable unto God who finds us acceptable as we accept his presence in us — a mouthful, if not a heart filled. This sanctuary in New St. Mary's, in case you haven't seen it up close, is strewn with the signs of sacrifice, bug sacrifice among others, the floor boards stained with the life of luckless lady bugs fallen from the great window. Years ago I vainly tried to prevent the carnage, but some people wanted the "unsightly insects" dead, even though other people purchase bugloads for the life of their gardens. The altar guild is perennially appalled because whenever someone steps on one of the little ladies (the bugs, that is) it is almost impossible to get out the black marks they leave in the wood.

I am mindful of these smudges of brokenness whenever I approach the altar to undress the elements and commence Communion. Because that reminds me of who comes to receive at the rail – not the already redeemed but the often broken, beginning with me. Barbara Brown Taylor states it better than I when she says "A lot of it happens other places, but the breaking of bread at Holy Communion can break you right open. Sometimes you can be right in the middle of it when suddenly the tears start rolling down. It is like the gates to your heart have opened and everything you have ever loved comes tumbling out to be missed and praised and mourned and loved some more."[2]

—◦—

***... when we come to the rail we bring
with us all sorts of life and death.***

—◦—

Ask anyone who has served at the Eucharist; it is moving beyond words (both the words we speak and the ones we don't know how to speak) because when we come to the rail we bring with us all sorts of life and death. You may be one who feels all together when you lift up your hands as well as your heart to receive the bread. (I hope you will lift up your hands, because persons like me with a lower back problem have difficulty bending down to reach you.) But not everyone is together who comes together. Sometimes I receive a silent squeeze of the hand, or a giggle, or a tug on my stole, or a smile. But other times the head is hung down, or the eyes brimmed with tears, the hands shaking or covering the face or shielding the heart. The gift that is given is God's suffering in exchange for ours; so that by taking his body and blood into us, he now lives on in us even though he is gone from us. So that when we leave the altar we live not only in him but also for him. A mouthful indeed! Or have we done it so often we have forgotten how awesome that is, received it without thinking how awful or shocking it is?

262

Jesus said to his disciples when he gave them the cup of wine, "Drink this, all of you; for this is my blood of the new covenant, which is shed for you and for many, for the forgiveness of sins." Do we think about that when we drink it – his blood? We say we know this is Taylor's Tawny Port, not real blood, the black scars of lady bugs and the breaking of bread, not the scourged flesh and body broken. Taylor tells us, "While we tend to keep children away from [this] until they 'understand' what they are doing, most of them understand it better than we do. Try offering a young child her first communion. Hold the silver cup down where she can reach it. Watch her peer inside, sniffing the sweet heavy stuff. 'The blood of Christ,' you say, thinking ... how touching it all is. 'Yuck!' she says, jerking away like she has been stung. 'I don't want any.'

"Would any of us [want *any* of it] if it were the real thing?"[3] "So to eat the flesh of thy dear son, ... and to drink his blood," our service says. Some little one I know was made to sit under the nun's desk because she chewed the bread, "bit the body." That is why we do not pinch the wafer with our fingers as we receive it, but raise it on our palms to our face where, with a little effort and agitation it will dissolve between the tongue and the roof of the mouth. (When I place the bread properly at the parting of the palms, some people look at me as if to say, "Don't you know where to put it, Preach?")

Would we want any of it if it were the real thing (to co-opt the Coke caption)? It is! Real in whatever sense we are willing to receive it. When, for whatever reasons we have for coming here to offer and receive his brokenness and ours, if we also come to receive the love of God poured out for us and to give each other our love – then we no longer have to make-believe it is life for us, not death. We can leave our brokenness there at the altar and take away with us wholeness, health, healing, holiness[4] enough to pray this day: "Lord let our life become your life," Amen.

———

1. *Lectionary Homiletics XI*, 6-p.31

2. Barbara Brown Taylor, *Gospel Medicine*, p.32
3. *Ibid*. p.62
4. All from the same Hebrew word: shalem.

PENTECOST

My friend Fred Buechner reminds me that, all our lip-smacking moralism to the contrary, Jesus never saw the world only in terms of its brokenness and separation from God, but in terms of the ultimate mystery of God's presence buried in it like a treasure buried in a field.

Christopher Brookfield

PENTECOST – ST. MARY'S

May 17, 1986

These are some notes which, God willing or even unwilling, may yet become a sermon – a sermon being something which proclaims the Word of God in spite of the words we use to proclaim it. These are also some reflections on Pentecost, the power and the promise of it, because as the lessons this morning remind us, today in the church year we celebrate Pentecost, the birth of the Church, which, like so many proclamations of promise, had a somewhat unpromising beginning: a small band in a stuffy room in Jerusalem; each one beside himself babbling in a foreign tongue.

The Church, scripture tells us, was born in the midst of terrible fire. Those who were there talked about tongues of flame and the rushing of wind and speaking in strange languages. Were we skeptical, reading the scripture with the insights of today, we might well conclude that the disciples were simply high on something; surely they were full of it, whatever "it" was. Scripture tells us "it" was the Spirit, which like the fever of a lynch mob, was contagious. We don't like to think of spirit in those terms, but we would do well to remember that one can be in-spirited for good or for evil. That is why Jesus spent so much time casting out spirits.

Some witnesses at Pentecost thought they know what kind of spirit had caught up with Peter and his friends in Jerusalem that day. Scripture says, "They are filled with new wine." There must have been some cause for suspicion because Peter, sober old Peter, said, "These men are not drunk as you suppose, since it is only the third hour of the day."

There's logic for you. Had that little band known what future lay in store for them in the early church, some of them might well have been drunk by the third hour. The Church was born in the midst of fire, scripture says. Was that mostly metaphor or the only means of meeting an all-consuming spirit? We know about the power of Pentecost. It produced the most profound cultural and historical movement in western civilization. But what about the promise? Where is the Church today? Did you bring it with you this morning? Propitious that we ask the question on Pentecost.

As with everything else in our health-conscious age, the Church comes in at least two versions: the visible Church and the invisible Church. Which has the greater number of calories depends on which mode is meaningful for most people on a given Sunday, or a Monday for that matter. "The visible Church," says Fred Buechner, "is all the people who get together from time to time in God's name. Anybody can find out who they are by going to look. The invisible Church is all the people God uses for his hands and his feet in this world. Nobody can find out who they are except God."[1] The judgment on whether the two versions ever meet together depends on whether you're an optimist, a pessimist, or a parson paid to celebrate both parties.

"In a fit of high inspiration," says Buechner, "the author of the Book of Revelation states that there is no temple in the New Jerusalem (that is, no church in the new Kingdom), thus squelching once and for all the tedious quip that since Heaven is an endless church service, anybody with two wits to rub together would prefer Hell."[2] Most adolescents I have known prefer the vision of the New Jerusalem (the church-less version) to the reality of regular religion, whether required by proper institutions, promoted by peer pressure, or imposed by family habit. When Church becomes a *place* to be rather than a *way* of being, it no longer seems primarily a matter of the Spirit, faith ceases to be a burning issue, and we no longer perceive tongues of flame among the pews or in the parish house. We need to recapture the power and promise of Pentecost. Perhaps some perspective will help.

In the late 60's, the Church was not born in the midst of a terrible fire, it was nearly consumed by one. The flames of injustice inspired not only the God is Dead theology, but encouraged young people to exit the Church in droves. The Church was in bad odor. When the local Church wasn't being called various names such as "the house on pew corner" or "the God box," and so on, students were protesting that even the drive-in church was no place to refill our spiritual tanks because all we ever got from it was gas.

The drive-out churches responded. Even the Old South Church in Boston, you may remember, was pictured in the newspaper, featuring teenagers doing the frug and the watusi down the main aisle, dancing with the spirit of the times. In New York City, in the cellar of St. Peter's Lutheran Church, downtown office workers were offered a "noon club" review for bag lunchers, featuring sketches on sin, pride, and innocence – in an effort (as they put it) to make a little bologna sound a lot more solemn than it was, and to take a wry look at the original sin sandwich. Uptown, the Moylan Tavern on 124th Street was luring students from my old seminary to abandon themselves to the calling of the newly envisioned bar-fly ministry, and seminarians were majoring in alternate lifestyles. People began to ask what in God's name goes on in church?

While the Church was standing on its head trying to be relevant, churches became the refuge of drug addicts and draft resisters; centers for planning sit-ins, demonstrations, and political protests. When newspaper reporters were hunting up a theological phrase to describe what was going on, "the church turned inside-out" was a phrase fair enough to argue about.

Malcolm Boyd, an Episcopal priest, spelled out the meaning of that concept pretty well in his *Book of Days*: He wrote,

> I can't see you (as a priest) inside a church
> building on Sunday morning at 11:00 am, officiating
> in the tight, formal services, mounting a pulpit to

preach a sermon...I can see you functioning quite easily as an ordained man in the Underground Church.

For that you would need secular employment... This ministry would bring you very, very close to people – people in their natural work and life, not behind the façade of the "hole hour" on Sunday morning.

Have you read some of the "God is Dead" theology? It is one of the few signs of life in Christian theology in a long time. And, of course, God *is* dead, if, indeed, God ever lived; the God of our fantasies, ... establishment and utility...The "tribal" God who loved our nation and hated our enemies in war, won track meets and football games of Christian athletes... and even got a girl into Kappa Kappa Gamma *if* she prayed hard enough.[3]

While Malcolm Boyd saw no Pentecostal flames in church pews, many longtime churchgoers were doing a slow burn. They did not want to go to church to hear that stuff and to be made uncomfortable, and they didn't. Such confusion in our time, some said – playing profane games with sacred things. But we forgot something in those days (or maybe the truth is we have never really understood it for long in any age), namely the radical – that is to say, the root – meaning of the word church.

Originally the Greek word *ecclesia* (from which we get ecclesiastical) meant a meeting or gathering (so also the word *synagogue*, from which we get synagogue). The important point is that the *people* who were gathered and the *purpose* for which they met – not the building itself – constituted the *ecclesia*, the "church." Furthermore, the purpose of that gathering could be secular or religious; emphasis was on the active character of the gatherings rather than a particular liturgy, whether meetings were held regularly or only spontaneously, in a house or in the fields.

The church was committed to operating in the midst of the "profane," the unholy, life, where people live; and it was able to distinguish between that and wallowing in the profanity of life. The Christian church was seen as freeing people from the enslavement of the old legalistic religious law, celebrating and creating life in community in the everyday world, not in a specially consecrated or holy world set apart, on Sunday or Saturday or any other day.

Malcolm Boyd, in his book *Free to Live, Free to Die*, made useful distinctions between a superficial definition of profanity and a more profound understanding of it as obscenity:

> Some people are enraged by four-letter words. These people confuse me... [profanity is useful]

> Obscenity cuts much deeper than this. It involves actions and attitudes. Not to respond to a cry of pain because the words used in anger...disturb the decorum of our righteous self-image – *this* is obscene. Objecting to an earthy vocabulary, but residing by choice in neighborhoods closed against Jews or [Blacks] – *this* is obscene. Remaining silent and smiling while jokes are told which crudely and viciously insult a religion, race or ethnic group...*this* is obscene...

> "Dirty words" are apparently a greater shock that the dirty realities we have been conditioned to ignore, the dirty things we do to each other every day, often in the name of high-sounding words like duty, patriotism, and religion. Why is it that the people who campaign most fervently for "decency" are often reluctant to call so many realities by their names...?[4]

For good or for ill, over the past twenty-five years, in order to regain its voice as a shaper of culture (along with arts, music, literature and drama), the Church has had to become more involved with the secular world. We have had to acknowledge that "religiousness" (at least our definition of it) ought never have been confined to the realm of the sacred any more than the spirit was. Boyd anticipated this, when he wrote:

> Since human life is sacred, what we have traditionally labeled "secular" is sacred. We cannot regard religious services, ecclesiastical persons and forms, church buildings, and a leather-bound copy of the Holy Bible in a hotel desk drawer as *sacred*, and think of race relations, school teachers, a (night) spot, and a copy of a play or a novel as *secular*. All are a part of human life – passionately meaningful, and, therefore, holy.

> The task of the Church is to relate us to the world we inhabit, to our brothers (even those who use a different deodorant, worship in another way, live across town or the world, or have a different background or color), and [thereby to relate us] to the faith or ideology we profess to seek...[5]

Whatever else "worship" in church may mean, it is derived from the term "worth-ship," which means ascribing worth to what we do together in our common life as the Church. Church encompasses those who are inside the church building speaking out, but also those who are outside looking in. The spirit of Pentecost forces us out of the church building into the greater Church. That has always been a burning issue for those who need to preserve the life within. The promise of Pentecost is that we shall have both, but not without a struggle. Do you remember the injunction to us that says if you have a grievance against your brother, do not first come and seek forgiveness; first go out and seek your brother and be reconciled to him, then come and present your gift at the altar.

Whatever we do when we come to worship at St. Mary's, solely or together, whether we struggle well or poorly with that it means to be the Church, we know that when we are invited to come, we are invited to bring the Church with us. If we do not bring it, it won't be here, because the Church (whether with a capital "C" or a small "c") cannot live by itself unto itself. Neither can we. That is both the power and promise of Pentecost.

In touching one another, we touch the spirit. If you cannot pass the peace gracefully, pass on a part of yourself with some-one. It may be crazy to think that when we are able to touch one another we are touched by the spirit, but the point is in leaving every service we always hope we are a little touched.

———

1. Frederick Buechner, *Wishful Thinking: A Seeker's ABC*, 1973
2. *Ibid.*
3. Malcolm Boyd, *Book of Days*, 1968
4. Boyd, *Free to Live, Free to Die,* 1967
   Ibid.

"GO DARK TO KNOW THE LIGHT"

Trinity Sunday
John 3:1-17
Year B – May 25,1997

"In the name of God the Father, God the Son, and God the Holy Spirit. Amen." How else could I begin a sermon on Trinity Sunday, which celebrates what some would say is the doctrine that defines the heart of our catholic faith. But let me not push upon you an answer to a question you haven't yet asked about the Trinity, such as, "What is it?" (if "it" is the proper pronoun to apply to three persons).

If you think I am promoting confusional rather than confessional theology, in this case you are right...

Theology has sometimes been said to be the formulations of someone searching in a dark room for a black cat that isn't there. Nevertheless, I am going to commend to you this morning a theological doctrine some would say fits that definition – namely, the Trinity. But I am recommending you struggle with this idea not so you can be enlightened about it; rather so you will be confused, in the dark, so to speak. If you think I am promoting confusional rather than confessional theology, in this case you are right, but it begins with the confession, "I do not understand."

You might wonder why as a theologian of sorts myself I would be encouraging my own undoing. It is, in a Word, so you'll have a chance to confront God rather than settle for an under-standing of a theological proposition. To begin with, a theological definition of the Trinity proceeds from a problem in the text from which it is taken – specifically, the New Testament nowhere mentions the word "Trinity," let alone commends it as a dogma of the church. From that, one theologian concludes: "Father, Son, and Holy Spirit means the mystery beyond us, the mystery among us, and the mystery within us are all the same mystery. Therefore the Trinity is a way of saying something about us and the way we experience the presence of God" [rather than about God him-self or them-self]. [1]

Lest you think I am purely playing theological trick-or-treat with you, when David Read, the famous Scottish preacher and theologian refers to the venerable Athanasian Creed for a definition, saying: "... we worship one God in Trinity, and Trinity in [one] Unity; neither confounding the persons, nor dividing the substance" you may still be with it. But when the creed continues, speaking of "The Father incomprehensible, the Son incomprehensible, and the Holy Ghost incomprehensible," Read reassures us that the rational mind is "tempted to add 'and the whole thing incomprehensible.' This seems an unnecessarily complicated way of speaking about a God whom we [claim] to know as a living being."[2]

There are, of course other approaches to the problems or the Persons of the Trinity, less orthodox but more user friendly: such as the story that says the great bishop St. Augustine "was walking one day on the seashore trying to figure out how God can be One and yet Three, when he saw a child carrying water in a cup to a small hole dug in the sand. 'What are you doing?' asked the bishop. The child replied, 'I'm trying to pour the ocean in this hole.' The bishop laughed and said, 'That is impossible.' The child looked up at St. Augustine and said, 'It is no more impossible than for you to put Almighty God into your small mind.'"[3]

Undaunted by childish things, I decided to look up the term Trinity in my trusty Episcopalian's Dictionary, and I found this: "To the layman, and for that matter to many clergymen, there is no more baffling, obscure, incomprehensible statement in the whole system of Christian doctrine. There never has been an acceptable definition of the [term] and there probably never will be one."[4] – Which is not all bad, and in fact brings me back to my initial point. Confusion is at least clear about one thing – what it is we do *not* know.

Feminist objection to the Trinity spoken of in predominately male terms for the last 2000 years does not help us with the problem and even oppression that some women feel in the church today, it only contributes to our corporate consternation. I will wager that changing the formulation to read: God the Mother, God the Daughter, and then (in fairness) changing the gender of the Holy Spirit to masculine from the present feminine in Greek will not unconfound us. Somehow I keep thinking what we call the "foolishness of God" is intended to bring our intellect to our knees, in order that our spirit may be set free to experience God without reference to the rime of reason, the guile of gender, or even the throes of theology.

My wife has a wisdom which is frequently fair, feminine, and refreshing. She passed this poem by Wendell Berry on to me – a gift that has given me unexpected illumination:

> To go in the dark with a light
> Is to know the light.
> To know the dark, go dark.
> Go without sight,
> And find that the dark, too,
> Blooms and sings,
> And is travelled by dark feet
> And dark wings.[5]

I recommend this vision with which to visit John's gospel reading this morning in pondering the puzzling picture of Nicodemus and in approaching the idea and invitation of the Trinity. Nicodemus is a Pharisee, a teacher and interpreter of scripture, a religious leader of the Jews, who came to Jesus by night. That he came by night, in the dark, can be interpreted in two almost opposite ways. First, the more traditional interpretation, by visiting Jesus under the cover of darkness, Nicodemus' belief seems false and faithless; he saw to it that his good name and reputation would not be tarnished by being seen with this Galilean wonder-worker – and who knows what Nicodemus might find out in the process.

Or, second, seeing the faith of Nicodemus in an untraditional and more favorable light, he seeks out what he knows he needs; he understands he is in darkness and reaches out for Jesus who is the light, the one who illumines the darkness for those who cannot see. Nicodemus was willing to let his traditional perception of what God is like be opened by new, unfamiliar revelations that would stretch and challenge his faith because he risked encountering in Jesus something that would change everything, not only his understanding of God but his relationship with God. But as a Pharisee, he goes to Jesus for scholarly discussion – and what happens? He doesn't understand a word Jesus says. He is uni-literally "in the dark."

One commentator writes, "Jesus invites [Nicodemus] into the sheltering space God makes for our deepest questions and fears [our dark] ... and tells him he will come out of that space changed, renewed, reborn. Nicodemus, like us, doesn't seem to get it." "[He says, "How can these things be?"] "But his not getting it isn't the point as much as his willingness to venture into the dark with his questions and desires, and into the even darker place of mystery and human-divine encounter ... The point is not finding one answer, believing or not believing, but the transformational welcoming of our questions."[6]

When Nicodemus risks revealing his confusions and questions, he invites us into the dark unknown spaces of the gospel or theological text. He invites us to think about the spiritual and theological spaces we avoid not because we cannot fully understand them but because we are afraid not only of the unknown, where our ignorance might come to light, but of the possibility that we might be changed in the process.

The lesson shows us that our relationship to God and the more-than-trinitarian ways we encounter his spiritual presence in our lives are not a puzzle to be solved, a problem with one right answer, but a different order of experience – which the words do not define. Clear, unambiguous answers are not what we are likely to find there. As someone else has said, we are more likely to "find the Other who waits for us in the night as Jesus waited for Nicodemus." "It raises the question of what 'believing' means. The word, as used by religious people, tends to have some flavor of 'compliance': 'believe' and 'be saved.' But perhaps the believer is one who, like Nicodemus, simply goes out into the dark of his questions looking for God – the teacher letting go the answers and embracing the questions ... listening for the wind of the Spirit."[7]

What does all that mean? Maybe, to come to see the light we first have to know the dark. *"Go dark, go without sight,"* to learn "that *the dark ... blooms and sings, and is travelled by dark feet and dark wings."* To come to the light is to go in the dark of our questions without the light of an answer to guide us. The story of Nicodemus and the explanation of the Trinity have one signifi-cant point in common: to confront God, to encounter Jesus, to know the spirit for ourselves is to have our world transformed, not our questions answered. You might even say in the language of John's gospel, it is like being born again or born anew, discovering the light "by going dark."

Born again? The mere thought of it is at once terrifying and tempting – the chance to rethink my life and to change what is to come? You mean to tell us our lives might be, could be, different?

———

1. Frederick Buechner, *Wishful Thinking*, p.93
2. David Read, *The Christian Faith*, p.114
3. *More Than Words*, p. 190

4. *The Episcopalian's Dictionary*, p. 164
5. Wendell Berry, *Farming, A Handbook*, 1971
6. *Lectionary Homiletics*, VIII, 6, p.33
7. *Ibid*.

LIVING STONES

Cherishing Communion, Compassion, and Commitment

I Peter 2:1-10
May 2, 1999

Rid yourselves, therefore, of all malice, and all guile, insincerity, envy, and all slander. Like new-born infants, long for the pure, spiritual milk, so that by it you may grow into salvation – if indeed you have tasted that the Lord is good. Come to him, a living stone, though rejected by mortals yet chosen and precious in God's sight, and like living stones, let yourselves be built into a spiritual house, to be a holy priesthood, to offer spiritual sacrifices acceptable to God through Jesus Christ. For it stands in scripture: "See, I am laying in Zion a stone, a cornerstone chosen and precious; and whoever believes in him will not be put to shame." To you then who believe he is precious; but for those who do not believe, "The stone that the builders rejected has become the very head of the corner." and "a stone that makes them stumble, and a rock that makes them fall." They stumble because they disobey the word, as they were destined to do. But you are a chosen race, a royal priesthood, a holy nation, God's own people, in order that you may proclaim the mighty acts of him who called you out of darkness into his marvelous light. Once you were not a people, but now you are God's people; once you had not received mercy, but now you have received mercy.

I Peter 2:1-10

At the altar table, the overweight parson is doing something or other with the bread as his assistant stands by with the wine. In the pews, the congregation sits more or less patiently waiting to get into the act. The church is quiet. Outside, a bird starts singing. It's nothing special, only a handful of notes...Then a pause...a trill or two. A chirp. It is just warming up for the business of the day...

The parson and his assistant and the usual scattering of senior citizens, parents, teenagers are not alone in whatever they think they're doing. Maybe that is what the bird is there to remind them. In its own slapdash way the bird has a part in it too. Not to mention "Angels and Archangels and all the company of heaven" if the prayer book is to be believed. Maybe we should believe it. Angels and Archangels. Cherubim and seraphim. They are all in the act together.... And "all the company of heaven" means everybody we ever loved and lost, including the ones we didn't know we loved until we lost them or didn't love at all. It means people we never heard of. It means everybody who ever did – or at some unimaginable time in the future ever will – come together at something like this table in search of something like what is offered at it.

Whatever other reasons we have for coming to such a place, if we come also to give each other our love and to give God our love, then together with Gabriel and Michael, and the fat parson; and Sebastian pierced with arrows, and the old lady whose teeth don't fit, and Teresa in her ecstasy, we are the communion of saints.[1]

That may not sound to you much like the reading for today about the church, from the First Letter of Peter, but it's something like a contemporary approximation of it (in Fred Buechner's words). The communion of saints is one way of talking about the church. Communion means, literally: build together. And saints, originally, were not special people so designated by the church but whoever were gathered to be become "God's own people," as Peter puts it, "living stones" (what a great metaphor), letting themselves "be built into a spiritual house." A "holy" household he adds. But remember that the words whole and holy and health all come from the same root.

If we were to apply those definitions to what we do at St. Mary's Church, that might leave us here this morning with not much more to rub together than you and me, but that's all right if that's all we've got, because all we need is one another to be the church, God calling us to be his saints. Thankfully, as saints, we are not measured by our perfection, only by our willingness to trust in God. We are only the improbable possibilities God is willing to work with. And fortunately, saints are not normally called to be possessed of great courage; they're simply called to be possessed by the gospel. So we can take delight in the description that a church is nothing more than a congregation of great sinners, and nowhere is that more manifest that here at St. Mary's.

Now before I forget, let me give you my main point about the church, appended to Peter's perspective. The church is not the building you are seated in, not the way or the words with which we worship, and clearly not the convening of the clergy. Not even the people we pray with, but what the people we are deem to do with and for one another — and if you think about it, a lot of that is done when the service is ended and we leave the building we have come to call the church. (Let that put an end to the tedious taunt that since heaven is often envisioned as an endless church service, anyone with any sense would feel more at home in hell.)

In the event that being called upon to be the church is not an announcement that impels you to sit on the edge of your pew, maybe it's time to explore some questions we don't often ask. "Once you were not a people, but now you are God's people," Peter proclaims, but what does that mean? If the churches of Christ in which we commune are still in business after 2000 years, an apt question is, what is the business that goes on there and why do people like us continue to come? You could say summarily that I'm paid to come — but that still leaves you.

And when we get here, whose business are we about? Why do people come in the first place? and what do they find – or fail to find – when they get here? Is there any sense in which we could say that God is present in any one of us and in what we do with one another? Maybe at least part of our business in being the church is from time to time to ask what is going on in it? – or, rather, what are we doing in it that makes it the church? If I were to say what we are here for is to become Christs to one another, would that send us fleeing in terror for the first door we could find?

<hr>

"... being the kingdom is what it's all about."

<hr>

As the church, rather than (say) the Rotary Club, we are called to be not just human beings but, of all things, human beings open to the possibility of being transformed by the grace of God, even to the possibility of becoming the hands and feet and heart of Christ to one another, so that the Word we speak as well as receive touches the heart, is at the heart of whatever it is we do here that matters. That, I take it, is in part what Jesus meant we should be about in healing the sick and being healed, in raising the dead and being raised. Doing that is what the church is, and when we don't do that, it doesn't matter much what else we do here. Saying "The kingdom of God is at hand," is a way to start; but being the kingdom is what it's all about. God can use each of us and whatever we bring for the building of his kingdom.

When I first came to St. Mary's nearly 25 years ago it was clear to me that when "the parson" was earning his keep, the sermons were preached, the prayers prayed, the young baptized and married, the old buried, the sick and lonely visited, the poor remembered; what few children were there were caught, taught, cajoled, and confirmed, the wine was poured out and the bread broken at the reredos and in the rectory. Holt Souder and Isabel could almost enfold all of us in their open arms. They were devoted, and we were delivered from doing much; the parson was the principal person of God. Currently, of course, some 600 children and 1600 communicants can't be communed that way anymore. Thank God for all of you, the teachers and toters, vestry and volunteers, servers and sowers and singers, cartoon conveyors, cookers and clean-uppers, funners and fellowshippers, acolytes and ushers and enthusiasts, weeders, and workers and anyone else I have inadvertently omitted, even the contributions of clergy on occasion.

Historically speaking, the first Christian communities founded in faith, learning in love to serve themselves and nurture the needy, were called the *ekklesia*, a Greek word which meant "those called out," a term used to translate the Hebrew equivalent, *qahal*, the people of God, who were "called out of darkness into God's marvelous light," to repeat Peter's phrase. The movers and shakers were by and large not the clergy but loving laymen. No doubt that is part of what Peter meant when he said "Once you were not a people, but now you are God's own people," called to be a "chosen people." Now there's a phrase. Chosen for what? A key question. The problem, the ancient prophets perceived, was when the Hebrews heard it as a call to a place of sacred privilege, rather than a people chosen for special service as God's own. A "servant ministry" was not a title given to indentured unfortunates, but to the presence of God — who gives us minimum protection, maximum support.

Now where do we come in? Exactly where we are, I'd say. Sue Thompson, in her Senior Warden's Report at the end of her term of service this January, expressed her gratitude for the spirit at St. Mary's that had inspired and supported her. She spoke of others, of course, omitting her own infectious enthusiasm and example. She began by speaking of everyone else who made a difference here last year and of the ministry of Margie Miller who even as her cancer increased throughout last summer and into the fall, Sue said, "refused to stop planning and working for our future — for the music we share here, for the nurturing of our children, for fellowship, for the countless efforts she made to make our lives more inspirited... a legacy for us at St. Mary's ... unending and enduring." The symbol which summarized for Sue that indomitable spirit was a silhouette of the church visible and invisible, both the building and the being of those in it who have become the hands and hearts of God's giving to us.

One very cold night in December, she wrote, when she had come to meet her husband after choir practice, they wound up walking unwittingly in back of "the great window behind the altar [which] shone [as a] blazing light from within. It filled the church and appeared poised to burst through the glass, so bright was its shimmering strength streaming through the clear expanse. I was overwhelmed," she continued, "by the contrast of incredible light and black night. For me that light could never have been contained or dimmed despite sorrow and loss. In it was reflected the love, energy, and compassion that exist here today in the people of St. Mary's."

To paraphrase Peter's portrait of God's people, "We have been called out of loneliness into love, out of guilt into grace, out of despair into delight, out of fear into faith, out of terror into trust, out of darkness into light."[2] Without each of you and the light only you can bring, pockets of darkness and despair would persevere and prevail. But your prayers and presence, compassion and commitment, spirit of community and service, gifts and grace go to make up the material the Master Builder mixes to construct the church we cherish. You cannot imagine how important you are!

––––––

1. Frederick Buechner, *Whispering in the Dark*, pp.30-31
2. *Lectionary Homiletics* X, 6, p.2

I DESIRE MERCY, NOT SACRIFICE

2nd Sunday after Pentecost
Hosea 5:15-6:6; Matthew 9:9-13
Year A – June 6, 1999

"What shall I do with you, O Ephraim? What shall I do with you, O Judah? Your love is like a morning cloud, like the dew that goes away early. Therefore I have hewn them by the prophets, I have killed them by the words of my mouth, and my judgment goes forth as the light. For I desire steadfast love and not sacrifice, the knowledge of God rather than burnt offerings."

Hosea 6:4-6

As Jesus was walking along, he saw a man called Matthew sitting at the tax booth; and he said to him, "Follow me." And he got up and followed him. And as he sat at dinner in the house, many tax collectors and sinners came and were sitting with him and his disciples. When the Pharisees saw this, they said to his disciples, "Why does your teacher eat with tax collectors and sinners?" But when he heard this, he said, "Those who are well have no need of a physician, but those who are sick. Go and learn what this means, 'I desire mercy, not sacrifice.' For I have come to call not the righteous but sinners."

Matthew 9:9-13

Three verses left out of our gospel lectionary this morning are important to the meaning of Matthew's text:

Suddenly a woman who had been suffering from hemorrhages for twelve years came up behind Jesus and touched the fringe of his garment, for she said to herself, "If I only touch his garment, I will be made well." Jesus turned, and seeing her he said, "Take heart daughter; your faith has made you well." And instantly the woman was made well.

Matthew 9:20-22

At age seven, I was not exactly the Dale Carnegie of Grace Street in Rye, N.Y., where we lived. After school and on weekends I used to like to be by myself upstairs in my room with the door closed, drawing pictures of World War II battleships and dive bombers, along with Bugs Bunny – and I definitely did not like to go outside and play with the "other nice little boys and girls" on our street. My mother, fearing I was insufficiently socialized and that I might become a misfit, morose and misguided, contrived to have me ensconced in the Christ Church choir, which was in its infancy and looking for bodies.

Oddly enough, before long, we unsung cherubs began to be praised for our performances and we did so well that we got invited to sing elsewhere. We even got to present what we knew as the Mozart Alleluia on the Arthur Godfrey show, where I discovered that despite his comfy, reassuring, easy-going, kindly voice on the radio, he was in fact an irascible tyrant in the recording studio.

Anyway, we got upgraded to wearing red wool cassocks (cossacks, as we called them) and frilly white cottas. And in the bargain, some benefactor bestowed upon us the burden of big highly starched white collars which required two collar buttons and an enormous red satin floppy bow tie underneath, none of which we could control or put on by ourselves. So "they" acquired for us a cadre of overly conscientious choir mothers to encase us in our costumes each service. Whatever attitude attended our anticipation of singing, it was always eroded by the vesting ordeal. The mothers were hell-bent to have us look perfect for our performance, indifferent so it seemed to our several sufferings. We were lined up like sheep to be dressed, shouted at, jerked around, ordered not to move once the iron collars were in place under our faces and the satin bows bound tightly beneath. By the time we showed up for the service we were sullen, surly, cranky and cross – an oppressed, uncooperative, chafing cherubic chorus. If we somehow sang well, it was entirely accidental.

Had Jesus been there to judge, surely he would have made those mothers mad – I can hear him now in the words from Matthew this morning which he preached to the Pharisees: "Go and learn what this means, 'I desire mercy, and not sacrifice'," just what Hosea had said some 750 years earlier. The context for Jesus' judgment came in the middle of a meal. He had just called Matthew to be one of his twelve disciples and had gone with him to his house for a banquet with a fairly large gathering of "tax collectors and sinners," so scripture says.

You may remember that tax collectors, also Jews, were outcasts among other Jews. Because in order to have an income to live on and perhaps get reimbursed for purchasing their positions, tax collectors added to what they collected for the government, an "overage" for themselves – and undoubtedly, they were thought of as traitors for working for the Romans. They were viewed much as we might an aggressive and intimidating IRS agent in our time – with illicit overtones added. Who the "sinners" were at the banquet is not explained. They may have been Jews whose lifestyle or vocation kept them from leading their lives according to the Torah – a dangerous and disreputable influence on others who intended to keep orthodox.

In any case, Jesus agreed to eat with them. Talking with them would have been bad enough, but to be so intimate as to eat with them (eating is an intimate act, after all) was outrageous as well as an indignity to a holy man. (Even back then you were judged by the company you kept.) They were said to be "reclining" with one another at table, Jesus and his disciples among them – which earned for Jesus the title "friend of sinners" – frowned upon by the Pharisees, who wanted to know why Jesus would act so unworthily, defiling himself and debasing the Law which forbade such association.

What Jesus replies to the Pharisees seems almost intentionally insulting: "Go and learn..." he says to them, those whose livelihood was earned by learning, whose learning made legitimate their legislation about how to keep the laws of God. Jesus goes on to denounce them for shortcomings they don't even know they have. And, adding injury to insult, he insists that when it comes to the kingdom of heaven, tax collectors and sinners are in far better shape than the Pharisees, because they at least acknowledge their need for healing. Further, the Pharisees preference for righteous ritual is ridiculous when their hearts are hardened and unrepentant. "Go and learn what this means", Jesus enjoins them, "'I desire mercy and not sacrifice.' For I came to call not the righteous, but sinners."

The Pharisees knew all there was to know about how to worship properly, conscientiously, and correctly, but they had forgotten something essential. Liturgy and oblation, offerings and sacrifices to God are not performances judged for precision and perfection but responses of the whole heart and self, reflections of the soul, offered out of the fumblings as well as the fullness of faith. Or, as Hosea had expressed it earlier as God's expectation of Israel: I desire steadfast love and mercy, not solemn assemblies and sacrifice. I delight in your knowledge of God rather than burnt offerings. How you love to offer sacrifices to the Lord, O Israel, but what I desire is a pure heart.

What was missing in their religious zeal toward God was what he had given to them: steadfast love, compassion and mercy, justice and faithfulness – which they did not witness to in their worship, nor recall in their prayers, or remember in their sacrifices. Love and mercy are what make worship and sacrifice beautiful in God's sight.

Matthew's text this morning reflects one of three narrative sections that contain parallel miracle stories of bodily healing. Symbols, I suppose of the spiritual healing the Pharisees need, Jesus' disciples need – maybe you and I need. Which is why I read the verses earlier which were omitted in our reading. A woman suffering from menstrual hemorrhaging for twelve years silently came up behind Jesus until she could just reach out and touch his *tzitzit*, the fringes of his *tallith* or prayer shawl. Because of her affliction, this woman was considered "unclean"; and if she touched Jesus, he would have to go through purifying ceremonies before he could be accepted as undefiled and ritually clean. For her to intentionally approach a man who was not a member of her family was improper, and to touch him was forbidden. Yet this is exactly what she reaches out for as she seeks to be healed.

This version of her healing differs from the same account told in the gospels of Mark and Luke. Here, in Matthew, the woman is not healed as she touches Jesus' garment – only after he turns to her and says, "Take heart, daughter, your faith has made you well"; then, instantly the woman was healed. In other words, she is healed only when Jesus recognizes the motive behind her reaching out – her faith. And although Jesus is the one with the healing power, he names the woman's faith as the cause of her being healed.

My guess is Matthew chose this story to illustrate his narrative as a means of encouraging those who express their faith by being faithful to their fellow beings as God has been faithful to them. So that love and mercy come first before any rules of ritual righteousness. Where Jesus finds justification for this idea is in the word which governs Hosea's understanding of God, which term is mostly untranslatable in our language: *hesed*, which we sometimes express as "steadfast love" and/or "mercy", depending on the English translation. Even Hosea takes seven verses to explain it in Hebrew (Chapter 2:14-20, if you are curious). For him, *hesed* is the single most important characteristic of God's covenant relationship with his people. Faith and forgiveness, compassion and mercy are more important than proper worship and cultic ritual, a conviction that tends to upset certain life-long assumptions and habits for some of us.

For instance, I found I had to unlearn some of the implications of what I had been taught as a young chorister. Namely, if you had perfect attendance at church services and rehearsals, the grand prize was a new Schwinn bicycle. If you sang well, you got a silver cross; if you sang beautifully, you got a bigger one (on a red lariat). For us sacrifice and burnt offerings were the name of the game; we didn't know much about steadfast love and mercy. I was a Pharisee through and through, probably even more so than the testy choir mothers who preened us for church and presented us perfect before the Lord.

It was many years later, even after college, before I came to consider seriously one of Jesus' earlier sayings in Matthew (5:23-24), which I shall leave you with because it captures the spirit of this morning's scripture readings. "If you have come to make an offering of your gift at the altar, and there remember your brother or sister has something against you, leave your gift and go; first be reconciled to your brother and sister, then come and offer your gift."

WHAT DO YOU WANT FROM GOD?

10th Sunday after Pentecost
Genesis 15:1-6; Hebrews 11:1-3, 8-16
Proper 14 – Year C – August 12, 2001

The word of the LORD came to Abram in a vision, "Do not be afraid, Abram, I am your shield; your reward shall be very great. "But Abram said, "O Lord GOD, what will you give me, for I continue childless, and the heir of my house is Eliezer of Damascus?" And Abram said, "You have given me no offspring, and so a slave born in my house is to be my heir." But the word of the LORD came to him, "This man shall not be your heir; no one but your very own issue shall be your heir." He brought him outside and said, "Look toward heaven and count the stars, if you are able to count them." Then he said to him, "So shall your descendants be." And he believed the LORD; and the LORD reckoned it to him as righteousness.

Genesis 15:1-6

Now faith is the assurance of things hoped for, the conviction of things not seen. Indeed, by faith our ancestors received approval. By faith we understand that the worlds were prepared by the word of God, so that what is seen was made from things that are not visible.

By faith Abraham obeyed when he was called to set out for a place that he was to receive as an inheritance; and he set out, not knowing where he was going. By faith he stayed for a time in the land he had been promised, as in a foreign land, living in tents, as did Isaac and Jacob, who were heirs with him of the same promise. For he looked forward to the city that has foundations, whose architect and builder is God. By faith he received power of procreation, even though he was too old – and Sarah herself was barren – because he considered him faithful who had promised.

Hebrews 11:1-3, 8-11

What do you want from God? ... is a question I used to ask (albeit under my breath and with extended silences) during the days of school and college when I wanted nothing to do with God – let alone wanted God to have anything to do with me. I realize now it was a ridiculous question since, if I didn't believe in God, what sense would it make to ask (either with a naïve question mark or a sarcastic exclamation point) what I wanted from God?

I had been a choirboy since age seven and then had sung sacred music in boarding school and later Palestrina and Liszt and so on in my college chapel choir, but that had nothing to do with God from my point of view; it was just beautiful music. It made my soul (if that was an appropriate use of the word then) soar far beyond the grasp or abandonment of a God who, as far as I could see, wasn't with me when my parents got divorced, or when I was kicked out of school, or when I lost my fiancé and my first job.

But the question kept coming back like an unasked-for refrain; it had a disquieting echo that was audible beneath my angry interrogation, a kind of unwelcome aftertaste from a diet Tab – which was: What does God want from me? Whatever the answer, I was sure it was no concern of mine; I didn't want to hear it. I had already protected myself from those kinds of questions by taking a graduate degree in philosophy, which proved that such inquires made no sense, since in the sentence the subject had no substance and the solution was unverifiable; the asking itself was unreasonable and the answer contained a wish projection rather than an objective conclusion. So much for God; but amazingly and annoyingly, that didn't seem to get rid of the question for me.

I remember the provocative parable philosophy posed for us dutiful doubters. In a country plot a believer and an unbeliever argued over the existence of the great gardener who had produced this profusion of undergrowth. The unbeliever said, surely here is evidence that there is no gardener who tends this plot. Ah, but his order is unlike ours, argued the believer. But no one ever comes and goes here, insisted the unbeliever. To settle it then let's set up our tents and wait to see if he comes. Days and night came and went, but they never saw a sign of any gardener.

Well this gardener is one we cannot see; he is invisible to us, argued the believer. So, they strung the area with a wire fence and tied tin cans with rocks in them to it, but day after day they heard no noise to announce anyone's invisible arrival. Finally, in his exasperation, the unbeliever said: "Look, this great gardener of yours cannot be seen, cannot be heard, makes no sound nor does he speak to us, and the evidence of order in this overgrown ground eludes even our common sense. What, then, is the difference between your imaginary gardener and no gardener at all?"

The answer to the conundrum is contained in this morning's lectionary. Or rather I should say, the answer is assumed in our selections from scripture that talk about the importance of faith. I'm sure that will finish it for some of you because you will say faith isn't the answer, it's the problem! Give us faith, Lord, and we will love you with all our hearts. With the power of faith, we can move mountains, and without it we can't create it. That's clear, isn't it? *What we want from God* is the faith that makes sense for us to ask *What is it God wants from us?* (Or, more meaningfully *from me?*)

But like the elusive logic of an imaginary gardener, the argument in scripture is also inscrutable. The Apostle Paul defines faith, with a straight face, in unfathomable terms: "Faith is the assurance of things hoped for, the conviction of things not seen," he says. How's that for another impossible argument for us to accept, along with implausible evidence for us to assume? And even if we could understand it, who needs it? We have more faith in technology, whether we will admit it or not.

One commentator makes the case: "Would you fly in a plane that was run by a computer which was programmed beyond the intellectual control and comprehension of any human being?" If you replied "No" to that question, then consider this. Remember the old saying that a computer is only as competent as the person who programs it? Well that "hasn't been true since 1987 when a computer scientist John Holland discovered that if [he let] computer programs evolve, such programs turned out to be better than those of human programmers, but they were also beyond a human's mental grasp. Already we are flying on airplanes that run on software no human mind or pilot can understand, much less control." How much faith we place in technology!

Is it then easy to put our faith in God? Ironically, "the easier it becomes to have faith in the technology ... we have created, the more difficult it is for us to have faith in the promises of God." Because as others have expressed it, "'Having faith' is not nearly as comforting as 'having proof.' Living 'by faith' is far more frightening to us than' living on credit' ... [Referring to this morning's lessons] to live 'by faith' may have been okay for some old wandering Aramaean [like Abraham] with no mortgage, no car payments, no deadlines, even no children . . . But faith [for us] is far too shaky a basis for our complex, convoluted lives."[2]

To say "Faith is the assurance of things hoped for, the conviction of things not seen," may be a helpful definition for someone who already has faith, but to everyone else, it's an oxymoron, an incongruous concept. What sense can we possibly make of Paul's explanation? When he talks about how Abraham showed his faith, what he affirms is Abraham's unreasonable assurance, his conviction apart from any evidence, that the future would be as God had promised him, and without that assurance he couldn't count on having a future. How did he demonstrate that dedication to God? In Hebrew, the word "faith" is not an understanding of or intellectual assent to theological propositions, it is always an active, living response to the word of God. Abraham obeyed God even though the land he had been promised was unknown, in a far off foreign country, and already occupied by others (ask the Arabs in the Near East today). And "'by faith,' Abraham, Isaac, and Jacob all dwelt in this land only as wandering strangers, 'living in tents,' never establishing themselves ...."[3] Abraham's obedience was what God asked for, not some internal or intellectual assent to the Ten Commandments or our doctrine of the Trinity.

Faith is not to be confused with what we believe or don't believe in. If you, like my father, cannot stand up in church and faithfully say the Apostle's creed, that doesn't mean you cannot serve God faithfully in your life. The "conviction of things not seen" has nothing to do with your assent to the Nicene Creed or the Virgin Birth or even Original Sin. Plenty of paid theologians cannot always profess their approval of such propositions. "When Protestants spoke of salvation 'by faith,' they meant something different [from] mere belief. To have faith means to trust, to rest one's confidence in God.... to [be willing to] have a relationship with God which changes the texture of [your] life' and the way you live it.'"[4]

The "conviction" of a community of faith is that God does not abandon us in trouble or sorrow or sickness, that he promises to be with us in our pain, in the cross-shaped places of our lives. That is for us neither blind faith nor wishful thinking, but our assurance of God's love along the way even though we are not given an exact itinerary or detailed instructions to our destination. The assurance of the ancient Jews' profession of faith seems somehow simpler than our Christian counterpart. It simply says we trust that God will keep his promises and at the last he will bring us to himself. Anything more, you don't need to know; you just have to trust. In the language of faith: Trust is our truest companion and faith will lead us home.

*   *   *

That's the end of the sermon, you'll be glad to hear, but I am inclined to add an epilogue extracted from my own experience, inexpert as it is. What I've discovered is that the most unintelligible aspect of faith for me is expressed in this inexplicable paradox: We cannot ask for faith to find us first so that we will then be empowered to respond to God. It's the other way 'round. *Only after I have given up trying to find faith, and am willing to try to live faithfully toward God, does the power of faith find me and enable me to be faithful.* Maybe that's my assurance of things hoped for, conviction of things not seen – and the answer to the question I began with.

―――――

1. *Homiletics.* 7, 3 – p.28
2. *Op. cit.* pp.28-29
3. *Op. cit.* p.27
4. *Biblical Preaching Journal* 11, 3-p.16

JOY OR JUDGMENT?

Letting Go the Rotten Fish

10th Sunday after Pentecost
Matthew 13:31-33, 44-49a
Proper 12 – YearA – July 28, 2002

Jesus put before the crowds another parable: "The kingdom of heaven is like a mustard seed that someone took and sowed in his field; it is the smallest of all the seeds, but when it has grown it is the greatest of shrubs and becomes a tree, so that the birds of the air come and make nests in its branches."

He told them another parable: "The kingdom of heaven is like yeast that a woman took and mixed in with three measures of flour until all of it was leavened."

"The kingdom of heaven is like treasure hidden in a field, which someone found and hid; then in his joy he goes and sells all that he has and buys that field."

"Again, the kingdom of heaven is like a merchant in search of fine pearls; on finding one pearl of great value, he went and sold all that he had and bought it."

"Again, the kingdom of heaven is like a net that was thrown into the sea and caught fish of every kind; when it was full, they drew it ashore, sat

*down, and put the good into baskets but threw out
the bad. So it will be at the end of the age."*

Matthew 13:31-33, 44-49a

I enjoy anecdotes about education – not what I call
"schooling," which often passes for education in many of our high
school and college programs where teachers "teach to the test"
and students repeat on exams the information that the teacher
has (so to speak) "taught" them in class. That's probably why I was
drawn to the teaching of philosophy and English, which are not so
much bodies of knowledge that you can memorize, but a process
that is learned through the experience of thinking and writing;
the learning of them comes through the living of them. To take a
somewhat antic example, Steve Winger writes about a last test
in a college course in logic that was known for the difficulty of its
final examination:

"To help us on our test, the professor told us we could
bring as much information to the exam as we could fit on a piece
of notebook paper. Most students crammed as many facts as possible on their 8½ by 11-inch sheet of paper.

"But one student walked into class, put a piece of notebook paper on the floor, and [brought] an advanced logic student
[to] stand on the paper, [who then] told him everything he needed
to know [to answer the questions]. He was the only student to
receive an 'A'."[1]

Winger goes on to add: "The ultimate final exam will come
when we stand before God and he asks, 'Why should I let you in?'
On our own we cannot pass that exam. Our creative attempts to
memorize the formula, to earn eternal life, fall far short. But we
have someone who will stand in for us.... Jesus not only judges us,
but stands in for us."[2]

This week's gospel texts (five parables, count them! And
a sixth one which is for some mysterious reason excised from our

lectionary passage) comprise a story that speaks of a sorting and separation process, what amounts to a final exam, an ultimate judgment in which the "bad fish" are culled and thrown out.

The Greek word translated "bad" in English, really means "rotten," which reflects Matthew's biased theological take on Jesus' parables. Matthew's perspective is not directed at evangelizing or "fishing for people," but at the outcome of the final judgment when the evil are separated from the righteous.

It seems to me that Matthew's personal interpretation of that parable actually violates the spirit of the four other parables he has gathered to lead up to it – except in one respect: The one who judges is also the one who loves us. That means, in odd legal terms, the one who prosecutes us turns out to be our greatest defender. God's love for the sinner and his hatred of sin are part of the same judicial sentence. But before we decide to judge Matthew's Jesus as a theological version of Judge Judy on TV, who "dispenses her decisions with a swiftness not seen since Robespierre,"[3] let's back up a bit.

First of all, some of us ought to own up to our own inclination to smack our lips at someone who "gets what's coming to him.... and [who] feel a thrill when justice is done." Didn't you love it a little "when your mom stuck it to your brother, when your teacher yelled at the class bully, when your camp counselor tore into troublemakers behind the latrine, and ... when a cop pulls over the car that just shot past you at a recklessly high rate of speed"? [4]

Well, one positive way of looking at that reaction is to say deep-seated within us is what you might call a moral inclination that craves justice – maybe an inclination which is no accident, maybe more like the mark of our maker who embodies justice, and which is intended to help us, not hurt us; not to condemn us but to save us from, our errant selves. And it may be helpful to remember that Jesus as judge "is not interested in rolling his eyes and yelling at us, or tossing us like rotten fish into everlasting fire ... His desire is to open our eyes to the nature of sin and ... the path to ... the fullness of life."[5]

How do I know that? In this lesson, all I have to go on are the so-called parables that lead up to the "pop quiz" Jesus gives to test his disciples' comprehension of the kingdom, those in vss. 44-48-which as *I* read them are *not* lessons about what we ought to be doing to receive the kingdom of God, but what *happens* to us when the kingdom comes upon us in the midst of our everyday lives.

What I am referring to are the terse one-liner sayings that are so short they are nearly un-parables: "the yeast that a woman took and mixed with three measures of flour" or the "treasure hidden in a field, which someone found and hid" or "a merchant in search of fine pearls... finding one of great value." If we hear what is said there only as a lesson to be learned rather than a life to be lived, then we see ourselves as the merchant who goes in search of fine pearls, the one who finds the treasure; and the treasure is, of course, Christ or salvation or goodness or the kingdom of heaven – and if we don't find it, we are lost.

But what if we switch our view, so that God is the merchant, we are the pearl of great price; and the parable is about the King of Heaven's quest for us, not the other way around?[6] In that way of seeing it, "the Kingdom is not like the treasure, the Kingdom is like the story of someone finding a treasure." What Jesus is doing then is not moralizing about his disciples' dismal track record in their faith and understanding, not directing them as to what they ought to do to shape up, but telling them a story about a farmer who discovers a treasure "so fabulous that [he] gives ups everything – even a sense of right and wrong – to claim it as [his own]."[7]

That's unlikely, we say; it doesn't sound like what we expect to hear in church and in scripture. When we come to church we "think everything is about 'ought' and 'must' and 'should.'"[8]

My own experience validates that "no matter what preachers say or how they say it [and even if they deliberately avoid saying those words], what people [invariably] hear is 'ought' and 'must' and 'should'" – which is why this unexpected explanation of the parable is so difficult for us to hear. This story, this parable in telling, is more about our joy in finding the treasure, than about what we must do to be sure we find it; not about what we "should" do, not the traditional interpretation that says to find the Kingdom we ought to give up everything.

Listen again to the story: "The kingdom of heaven is like a treasure hidden in a field, which someone found and hid; then in his joy he goes and sells all that he has to buy that field." He gives up all he has joyfully. Not: he will have no joy unless he gives up everything. To me, there's a life of difference between the two interpretations.

As [Presbyterian pastor] Patrick Willson put it, "It's not so much giving up anything as it is about finding what you are really looking for, it is about finding what you're looking for even if you don't know you're looking for it; it's about finding what you're looking for even if you gave up looking and hoping a long time ago."[9] That's the good news – that "when you find it, everything else pales in comparison."

Maybe what Jesus was trying to tell his disciples (and us) was not that he had offered them the kingdom of heaven and they'd passed it up, or that they were so self-seeking they couldn't make room in their lives for anything else, or that they were so blind to the truth they couldn't see it when it was right in front of them. Is it just possible that he was trying to say to them: "One of these days you'll see something that will turn your life upside down. Things that [now] seem so important won't seem so important anymore. You'll discover yourself giving your life away because you have so much to give. People, even your best friends and family will wonder if you've lost it, but of course, its just the opposite: you've found it."[10]

Such a parable of course makes sense only to someone who is searching, searching not because he ought to seek for the kingdom of heaven, and not with the certainty of what he will find, but with the surety that we will surely be found if we will only allow the kingdom to interrupt our lives and give them back to us in new ways we couldn't have imagined before.

My friend Fred Buechner reminds me that, all our lip-smacking moralism to the contrary, Jesus never saw the world only in terms of its brokenness and separation from God, but in terms of the ultimate mystery of God's presence buried in it like a treasure buried in a field. To be whole is to see the world like that; and, I believe, to see the world like that, as Jesus saw it, is to be whole – where we catch glimpses of that holiness and wholeness which is not ours by a long shot and yet is a part of who and why we are. That is why, if we would be whole, we are a part of the kingdom of God, whether we like it or not, even whether we know it or not. Maybe that's why we have a problem with the parable, it's too much for us: we simply cannot let go the story of the rotten fish.

-----

1. *Homiletics* 11,4-p.41
2. *Ibid.*
3. *Op. cit.,* p.38
4. *Op. cit.,* p.36
5. *Op. cit.,* p.38.
6. *Biblical Preaching Journal 15*, 3-p.9.
7. *Op. cit.,* p.l0.
8. *Op. cit.,* p.11.
9. *Op. cit.,* p.11.
10. *Op. cit., p.12.*

RICH TOWARD GOD

10th Sunday after Pentecost
Luke 12:13-21 – Year C August 5, 2007

> *Someone in the crowd said to Jesus, "Teacher, tell my brother to divide the family inheritance with me." But he said to him, "Friend, who set me to be a judge or arbitrator over you?" And he said to them, "Take care! Be on your guard against all kinds of greed; for one's life does not consist in the abundance of possessions." Then he told them a parable: "The land of a rich man produced abundantly. And he thought to himself, 'What should I do, for I have no place to store my crops?' Then he said, 'I will do this: I will pull down my barns and build larger ones, and there I will store all my grain and my goods. And I will say to my soul, 'Soul, you have ample goods laid up for many years; relax, eat, drink, be merry.' But God said to him, 'You fool! This very night your life is being demanded of you. And the things you have prepared, whose will they be?' So it is with those who store up treasures for themselves but are not rich toward God."*

> *Luke 12:13-21*

Part of what I claim to do at St. Mary's is to help people learn how to read the Bible. My grandmother used to read the Bible regularly. I was told that every year she would start on the first page and read it all the way through to the last, as a part of her religious commitment. A grim duty I would think, as well as a fiendishly difficult task. I would never suggest anyone attempt to read the Bible straight through from beginning to end, partly because it was not written that way, either historically or chronologically. But that's a story for another day.

The opposite kind of problem in trying to read the Bible is the temptation to take shortcuts and read only the parts of it we know and like, because reading isolated passages taken out of the context and time they were written in can be misleading or dangerous for the meaning and for our understanding. I bring this up because I am embarrassed by the reading in Luke assigned for us this morning and am tempted to make my task in preaching on it easier by speaking only about the story Jesus tells in it, which commentators commonly call the Parable of the Rich Fool.

...the parable is not really about greed but about what it is to be rich...

That would make it easy for me to explain and for us to dispense with because the story itself seems to be about greed, which most of us are opposed to and few of us feel afflicted with. But Jesus' parable is set in a larger context; it is offered in response to an attempt by someone in the crowd to get him to settle a family inheritance dispute between himself and his brother. The parable Jesus tells is a reply to the question of inheritance; and that reply, as you might expect, is not an answer but a question – to us as well as to the onlookers. So, starting with the brother's inquiry rather than the story itself, the parable is not really about greed but about what it is to be rich, which for most of us in our day comes down to a matter of money.

One of the reasons I am embarrassed by the parable understood in that sense, is that I am, literally speaking, a collector of money. I don't mean amassing stocks and other equities but collecting coins, old obsolete U.S. silver dollars, halves, quarters, dimes, half-dimes, large cents, and half cents. I save them and put them in albums. And although I don't deem myself a money monger, there's no question that my heart goes pit-a-pat when I see a 1796 silver half dollar unexpectedly for sale. That I've not been able to find one I can afford is irrelevant because in truth I covet the coin for my collection and am clearly not exempt from the judgment of Jesus' parable which asks us to consider not just what it is to be rich in life but what it might mean to be "rich toward God."

There, the embarrassment of the bigger-barn-building brother's riches is not the bottom line but his inability to understand what it would mean to be rich toward God. One way to cut through the language, setting, and expectation of that time would be to reconstruct the parable in the currency of our time to see where we register on our own religion meter. [Yale Divinity School Professor] Thomas Troeger says that in the parlance of our day, "Religion is out. Spirituality is in." He confesses that conflicting concepts and confusing claims in the media make it difficult to define spirituality, but that does not mean it is merely muddled or the term meaningless. "Clearly it represents some great hunger that neither our materialistic culture nor our established religious traditions is satisfying" – a quest for what we might call hunger for a "spirituality of the heart."[1]

And a spirituality of the heart is "not inimical to the gospel." So "I would not in the name of Christ attack anyone's search for a deeper sense of spiritual integration. There are, however, passages in the gospels that suggest any authentic spirituality will [ask us to] attend to how we spend our money: 'For where your treasure is, there your heart will be also' (Luke 12:34)." Troeger goes on to suggest that we seriously consider the subversive concept of a "credit card spirituality," saying that "If we want to deal with a spirituality of the heart, our credit card statement...clearly discloses where our heart in fact resides."

"What would happen if we prayed our credit card statement, 'O Source of Every Good and Perfect Gift, I lift before you the following expenses.' And then we read aloud to God our last month's expenditures."[2] What would that reveal about what we value? Surely printed there would be essential expenses we would admire, for food, worthy causes, thoughtful gifts for others. But how much else would we have expended on extras and extravagances that we would sincerely explain are not a sure measure of where our heart is? Except that there they are, printed in black and white for us to ponder and tally up.

I don't desire to set up a straw man here, comparing credit card charges to building bigger barns, but maybe the conflicting concepts will arrest our unawareness, if not nourish our spirituality – and focus our attention on the uncomfortable question: What does it mean to be "rich toward God?" to assuage our hunger for those things that will nourish our deepest emptiness which seems never to be satisfied by our filling it with status and possessions, however precious and costly.

Fred Buechner, in speaking about the agony of listening to the insufferable news of the day on TV, which confronts us with our callousness in the face of unspeakable human need and cruelty, hunger and want, reminds us:

> Hunger in the literal sense is unknown to you and me. In a world where thousands starve to death every day, we live surrounded by plenty. On full stomachs we watch the TV footage of Third World children with ancient faces, and may God have mercy on us if we do not find some way to wipe their hunger from the face of the earth. [And yet] even in the midst of plenty, we have our own terrible hungers.
>
> We hunger to be known and understood. We hunger to be loved. We hunger to be at peace inside our own skins. We hunger not just to be fed these things but, often without realizing it, we hunger to feed others these things because they too are starving for them. We hunger not just to

be loved but to love, not just to be forgiven but to forgive, not just to be known and understood for all the good times and bad times that for better or worse have made us who we are, but to know and understand each other...

When Jesus commanded us to love our neighbors as ourselves, it was not just for our neighbor's sakes that he commanded it, but for our own sakes as well. Not to help find some way to feed the children who are starving to death is to have some precious part of who we are starve to death with them. Not to give of ourselves to the human beings we know who may be starving not for food but for what we have in our hearts to nourish them with is to be, ourselves, diminished and crippled as human beings.

We lie [safely] in our beds in the dark.... We live surrounded by the comfort of familiar things. When the weather is bad, we have shelter. When things are bad in our lives, we have a place where we can retreat to lick our wounds...while tens of thousands of people, thousands of them children, wander the streets looking for some doorway to lie down in out of the wind. "Woe to you that are rich," Jesus said, "for you have received your con-solation. Woe to you that are full now, for you shall hunger. Woe to you that laugh now, for you shall mourn and weep." That is a text not often preached on to people like us because it cuts too close to the bone, but woe to us indeed if we forget the home-less ones who...might as well have no faces even, the way we try to avoid the troubling sight of them in the streets of our cities...and as we listen each night to the news of what happened in our lives that day, woe to us too if we forget our own home-lessness.

To be homeless the way people like you and me are apt to be homeless is to have homes all over the place but not be really at home in any of them. To be really at home is to be really at peace, and our lives are so intricately interwoven that there can be no real peace for any of us until there is real peace for all of us. That is the truth that underlies not just the news of the world, but the news of our own days." [3]

What do we do with these thoughts? That may not be the kind of news we hunger for; ultimately it may be more unendurable than the news of the day we find unbearable on TV or in the newspaper. But the truth it reveals to us gives us a glimpse of what it might cost to be rich toward God. It is an extravagant truth of course, one which is too costly for us only if we think we can afford to ignore it.

———

1. *Lectionary Homiletics* XVIII, No.5-p.i
2. *Ibid.*
3. Frederick Buechner, *Secrets in the Dark*, pp.249-50

TO TELL THE TRUTH

On Talking Back to Your Preacher

13th Sunday After Pentecost
Isaiah 35:4-7a, 8a, 9b, 10; Mark 7:33-34, 37b
Year B – September 10, 2000

> *Jesus took the deaf man aside, and putting his fingers into his ears, he spat, and touched his tongue. Then looking up to heaven, he sighed and said to him, "Ephratha," that is, "Be opened."... So that the deaf hear and the dead have life in them.*
>
> Mark 7:33-34, 37b

How hard it is even for us who are not literally deaf to hear the Word of God, especially when we are encumbered by the efforts of preachers like me, who attempt to transmit that treasure in our earthen vessel which is incorrigibly cracked and has holes in it, so that the truth is not so much locked in as leaked out.

On the other hand, when the prophet Isaiah preaches, who can miss hearing the message? He fairly sings the scripture when he wrestles with the Word of God. Hear this from this morning's reading:

> *Say to those who are of fearful heart, "Be strong fear not! Behold your God who comes with vengeance for your enemies and with recompense to save you. "Then shall the eyes of the blind be opened and the ears of the deaf hear. The lame will leap and dance, and the tongue of the speechless*

*shout for joy. For water in the wilderness will flow
though the desert, and streams spring forth like
lakes in the sand. The parched ground shall become
pools and the thirsty land be springs in the barren
waste.... A Highway shall be there, "The Way of
Holiness,"... and the redeemed shall walk upon it;
those whom the Lord has rescued will return home
by it ... with singing and shouting and everlasting
joy ... They will be happy forever, and sorrow and
sighing will be no more.*

Isaiah 35:4-7a, 8a, 9b, 10

Wow! They never taught me to preach like that in semi-nary. If I had any sense, I'd say to you, "That's it. Sit back. I'll spare you the rest of my sermon." Would that our sermons could spring forth like that from the sanctuary and sing to the soul in your seat and shiver the soles of your feet. Alas, our situation is expressed in the words of Ann Landers quoting a church bulletin in her Gem of the Day: "Barbara C. remains in the hospital and needs blood donors. She is also having trouble sleeping and has requested tapes of Pastor Jack's sermons." Alas poor Jack – I know him, Horatio – speaking the truth in love is not always kind.

In the broken jaw of our lost kingdom, where with the preacher we grope together and avoid speech at the door in the back of the church at the end of the service, one pastor reports that as he stood by to greet the departing congregation, a little boy, on shaking hands with his minister, solemnly placed a quarter in his palm. Which he did again the following Sunday, and the week after that. Finally, the minister said to the little boy, "To what do I owe your generosity?" Whereupon the boy replied, "I'm just trying to help. My father says you're the poorest preacher around."

This Sunday celebrates our return to a schedule of at least three services a week and the routine of regular sermons stretch-ing into the unseen recesses of the year ahead. I have compas-

311

sion for the parishioner who endures the prospect of persistent preaching informed by Dante's advice, "Abandon hope all ye who enter here." So my intent today is to try to make that task less troublesome by telling you how to survive the sermon during the service. Just because the preacher survived seminary doesn't ensure that every Holt, John, and Christopher has successfully scaled the homiletics hurdle. (Homiletics is a required seminary course on the art and act of preaching.) Sometimes, as they say, you can't make a silk purse out of a sow's ear. Homiletics teachers know what it is like to cast their pearls before swine. Not that sermon instructors don't struggle to save us: "One day in homiletics class a student preached an interminable sermon. When he finally sat down, the homiletics professor's initial observation was not about the sermon but about a small Band-Aid affixed to the student's chin. 'How did you cut your chin?' he inquired. The student replied, 'Well when I was shaving this morning I was thinking so hard about my sermon that I cut my chin.' The professor then advised, 'Next time think about your chin and cut the sermon.'" [1]

The best advice he offered to aspiring preachers was the admonition, "Whenever you get up to preach remember this. Every time I enter the pulpit I feel like I am on trial for my life and that I may very well not be acquitted." Such sanguine sentiment aside, an outdated admission is in order. An unwritten assumption, which must be eliminated, is the expectation that all listeners are supposed to be grateful for the efforts of their minister to proclaim the Word of God, even when the preacher has thoroughly obscured that Word by butchering his own words atrociously assembled the evening before. Convoluted congregational courtesy concludes that nevertheless the listener is expected to articulate his appreciation with something like "I enjoyed your sermon" (or "your message"); otherwise, there must be something off kilter about the poor parishioner: sin perhaps, or sheer cussedness. Quite the contrary, courtesy aside, we preachers will never improve unless you give us the straight "poop" (if you'll pardon the impropriety).

Sometimes patience and compassion can inspire preachers to persevere in self-improvement. But more often than not we need to know the truth even if we'd rather not.

Beyond breast-beating, I have for you five simple suggestions to start with, which will help you survive a sermon.[2] Clem Welsh (formerly Warden of the College of Preachers at the National Cathedral) opines that while "a preacher can stand in the way of God's speaking for a long time ... inadvertently [he may] say something true and memorable. So strategy number one is, even if you think the preacher has nothing to say, *Wait for at least one idea [to appear] in the sermon before [you] give up.*"

Second, the strongest strategy for survival is for you to "Fight back" ... [probably it is propitious] to do this silently [at first] ... For every sermon thesis there is an antithesis [an anti-thesis]. Preachers are skilled at presenting half-truths. Discover the truth that has been ignored, articulate it (to yourself), and you and the preacher [together] may have [managed to proclaim] ... a fragment of Christian truth.

Strategy three is subtle: *"Let your mind wander."* The Art of mindwandering is neglected these days. If the minister speaks platitudes, let your imagination create the sermon that is eluding him or her... (Did it ever occur to you that [possibly] the preacher is as bored with the sermon as you are?) [I have a friend, Judd Blaine, who once actually fell asleep while he was giving his own sermon.] So go see the preacher later in the week and talk about it. Preachers need to be stimulated to produce stimulating sermons."

And don't forget the troublesome truth that "a sermon which is boring isn't necessarily untrue. Even a dull sermon can sometimes stab a listener with unexpected relevance." So strategy four is *"Analyze your own disappointment with the sermon."* If the preacher fails to link the tradition of Christian experience with your own, "make the connection for yourself.... The preacher need not know, when you say 'I enjoyed the sermon [or your message],' that the sermon you enjoyed was your own" and your message was the one that mattered.

———◦◦———

...let the preacher know that out there in the pew there is at least one listener expectantly waiting for a sermon that will interest, move and inspire...

———◦◦———

The last strategy, number five, is *"Don't sit there, Do something".* Balance your checkbook (as one of my friends does). That can be both productive and satisfying. Or read a novel, nestled unnoticeably in the pages of your Prayer Book so as not to put the preacher off. But "the best things to do are done between sermons. Take the preacher to lunch and ask a Great Question, such as, 'If pride is a sin, why should I try to do my best?' Or, 'If God the creator is all-powerful; can't he make a stone so heavy he can't lift it?' But do your part as one engaged in the sermon enterprise, to let the preacher know that out there in the pew there is at least one listener expectantly waiting for a sermon that will interest, move and inspire, and who is anxious to help – one listener determined to survive."

All this is said not so much with tongue in cheek as heart in hand. It is not easy to talk about the strange act of preaching in which, unlikely as it sounds, the preacher is at the same time spokesman of God's Word and the one committed to being transformed by it. Preaching is a precarious practice: "Watching a preacher climb into the pulpit is a lot like watching a tightrope walker climb onto the platform as the drum roll begins, [carefully] clearing his throat and [slowly] spreading out his notes ... he must [eventually] step out into the air, trusting everything he has done to prepare for this moment as he surrenders himself to it, counting now on something beyond himself to help him do what he loves and fears and most wants to do. If he reaches the end of his rope safely, it [may be] skill, but more [than likely] grace – God's decision to let daredevils tread the high places where [other] mortals have the good sense not to go." ³

314

I know I have said before to some of you, a preacher preaches first of all to himself as the one most in need of hearing the Word of God. If that is true, then when the holy vision somehow speaks through him, *his* heart will be the first to be pierced. We know what it cost Jesus to announce to us unbelievers and nay-sayers alike the "*victory* over all the gripping evil things" (and even the evil in us), exhorting us to get up from the grave of ourselves where we sometimes prefer to lie, and trust the truth that God has given us the gift of life in himself which not even death can take from us!

But who else could preach that message with power and persuasion so that not only the deaf hear but the dead have life in them? And are *you* sure you really want to risk receiving the Word of God into your otherwise ordered life? "The word that goes forth from my mouth shall not return to me empty," says the Lord, but it shall accomplish what I purpose.... Behold, I make all things new" (Isaiah). If you are not curious about what it will cost you to become a "new creation", frankly it might be more frugal to forget the five strategies for surviving a sermon, and simply cover your ears, endure the inconvenient interlude, and escape any temptation you might have to tell your preacher truthfully, "I wish I hadn't heard your message."

-----

1. From an old issue of *Context* a few years back
2. Quotations following taken from Fall 1979 *College of Preachers Newsletter*
3. *Context* January 1, 1994. pp.1-2

COMING OUT

13th Sunday after Pentecost
Mark 7:24-30
Year B – September 7, 2003

From there he set out and went away to the region of Tyre. He entered a house and did not want anyone to know he was there. Yet he could not escape notice, but a woman whose little daughter had an unclean spirit immediately heard about him, and she came and bowed down at his feet. Now the woman was a Gentile, of Syrophoenician origin. She begged him to cast the demon out of her daughter. He said to her, "Let the children be fed first for it is not fair to take the children's food and throw it to the dogs." But she answered him, "Sir, even the dogs under the table eat the children's crumbs." Then he said to her, "For saying that, you may go – the demon has left your daughter." So she went home, found the child lying on the bed, and the demon gone.

Mark 7:24-30

When I was a teenager, "coming out" meant dancing at a debutante ball, but since then, life has become more complicated. This morning's gospel lesson is about coming out. Obviously, it meant something different for Jesus and his disciples – but to me it seems no less important for us today.

One of the dangers of trying to read the Bible responsibly rather than simply literally, is that in asking, "What does this story mean?" (beyond what the words say), we may overlook (or avoid) asking, "What does the story tell us about what is going on in our own lives?" Asking the first question is safe: "What did the story mean in the lives of those to whom it was told?" That leaves us out of the picture, untouched. "Great story," we say. "Glad Jesus didn't say that to me." But if we risk asking, "How is a Bible story, symbolically or metaphorically, an event that happens in my own life?" then it may possibly pose a life-giving – or life-threatening – question about the alien or shadow parts of my own life and yours.

In the biblical text, when the experience of the speaker and the hearer are miraculously able to meet for a moment, that is where the truth of an ancient story becomes the reality of our story. "So [in the Bible] the mystery of the text's meaning abides, waiting to be born anew within and between us."[1] The preacher's task then is not to deliver a message about the biblical text, but to enable the person in the pew to propose his or her own sermon. As a friend put it: "At the church door, when someone tells the preacher that the sermon has changed his life and then describes a sermon the preacher knows he or she never preached, what may have been heard was what the pew needed to hear more that what the pulpit needs to proclaim."[2]

So it is with the story of Jesus and the Syrophoenician woman. I never much cared for this narrative – probably because it is just a story, not a parable, a smart-aleck story at that, and one which presents Jesus in a peculiar light (or should I say portrays him as an impatient, impolite, and pugnacious person – not the prophet of peace and compassion we expect). This story is about crossing boundaries, his and hers; about stepping out where it's unsafe, away from the familiar and known. I never appreciated the story in that sense until a friend, Bill Dols, wrote about it in a piece called "Finding Life in a Foreign Land." I like my Bible stories to be safe, at least for me, so I can appreciate the storytelling without the trauma of stubbing my toe on what is troublesome to me about my own life. This story doesn't let me escape unscathed.

In it, Jesus comes out of his homeland of Galilee into a foreign country called Phoenicia, where he has to leave the familiarity of his friends and venture beyond the framework of his faith community. The woman he meets there comes out from that region and cries to him to cast out the demon in her daughter. The word "region" in Greek implies "border" or "boundary." Both Jesus and the woman cross boundaries and enter the unfamiliar and the unknown in their meeting one another. As Dols adds, sometimes people "talk about those who are gay and lesbian [as] 'coming out of the closet.' Coming out from boundaries is a risk for any of us; a risk of saying who and what we are about, claiming our lives, being seen and known, unprotected, vulnerable."[3] This story is about Jesus and the woman coming out to meet each other, inviting both the risk and revelation of any real meeting.

The woman steps out beyond her familiar faith and place as a Canaanite pagan, protected by Baal, to call upon an upstart prophet for protection against the impending death of her daughter. She falls at Jesus' feet, begging him to cast out the demon. This was out of his territory (so to speak) because, as he had said, he was called only to the lost sheep of the house of Israel, his gospel not for non-Jews or Gentiles. Nevertheless, this woman comes out of her traditional proprietary role assigned to her in a patriarchal society, shouting at him, the holy man, in public. She is not only pagan and "unclean," she's pushy, and she presumes to talk back to him.

The text shows that Jesus was taken aback; he was unprepared for her: the story tells us he had withdrawn from Galilee, where he had been grilled by the Pharisees and scribes who wanted to know why he did not live according to the tradition of the elders and allowed his disciples to eat with "defiled hands" – that is, without ritually washing them before eating. They wearied him with precepts of the Purity Code, applying the word of God rigidly and mercilessly, unmindful of what the Law intended behind the plethora of prescriptions. So he withdrew to the region of Tyre and Sidon where he would not be recognized and entered a house where he thought he could escape notice. (The Revised

Standard Version of the Bible reads he "wanted no one to know. But he could not be hid" – meaning, I take it, there was nowhere he could hide.)

Any harried young mother knows what that means. Overwhelmed by the demands of her children constantly pestering her for attention, she seeks the safety and solitude of the bathroom, but she has just sat down when there is a beating on the bathroom door and the persistent "Mommy, he hit me." The insistence of unfinished business, the cruelty of continual communication, not only no time for yourself, but nowhere to hide. The Syrophoenician woman was like the knock on the bathroom door for Jesus. No wonder he emerged disgruntled and grumpy. I wonder if there was a silence between her speaking and his responses, perhaps time enough for the woman to hear herself speaking and how she said it, but the text doesn't tell us.

What Jesus replies to her calls us up short. What he says is strong and cruel; moreover, he appears to ignore her cry for help because of her ethnic background and what he presumes are her improper practices. Various biblical commentaries try to make excuses for what he said, to silk purse a sow's speech. For example, when he calls her a "dog," they say he uses a diminutive form of the word in Greek, which refers to small dogs as pets (as if that helps) rather than speaking an insult intended to degrade the one for whom it was used. But clearly his is a hostile response, a sharp rebuke of her. She wasn't one of the lost sheep of the house of Israel, which was his mission, as he put it; she was a misguided mongrel seeking someone else's food.

She was an audacious and intrusive outsider Jesus says it to her face: "Leave me alone, you Syrophoenician dog. Can't you see I have my hands full just taking care of my own people? I can't be bothered with you and your problems."[4] No more mister nice guy, not the one we are told about so often in Sunday school. That may be difficult enough for us to accept, but in addition the story also has what seems to me a miraculous ending. I'm not referring to his healing her tormented daughter, but to the miracle of his changed mind. That may not sound so stupendous to you, but when my mind is made up it takes heaven and earth to move me off the dime. The text makes the woman's rejoinder to Jesus sound deceptively simple. She says to him, [But] "Sir, even the dogs under the table [get to] eat the children's crumbs." Meaning, while she did not expect Jesus to give her what was intended for his own people, even so, she had a right to receive "the crumbs" of what Jesus had offered to others. So saying, she had bested him with the quick wit and repartee he had often used to defeat his adversaries. Astoundingly, he then replies, "for saying that, you may go – the demon has left your daughter." On the spot, he has changed his mind – and with it the entire scope of his mission and ministry thereafter. Why? Maybe he recognized a bond of faith with that woman, which was more powerful than the cultural, religious and ethnic prejudices and hostilities that had separated him from her. Whereas, for some of us, it might "be easier to raise the dead than to change our minds."[5]

Now, as to how we might be a part of that miracle, maybe we could begin by considering that the story is addressed to us also. If so then we might ask, What do we know of the struggle of Jesus and the outcast woman in ourselves? How do you deal with the pugnacious person life puts in your way, "who persists; pre-serves, endures despite your silence or uncertainty [or uncharity], who braves your fierce determination to not yield or bend or sell out or give in, to be pulled beyond your safe boundaries?"[6] Do you know anyone like that in your life? Dols asks us to ask, How can we find it in us to embrace the Syrophoenician woman in ourselves? Or to put the question more positively, "What do you know of a life beyond your boundaries where healing happens because … a persistent, impudent, and outrageous outsider pushes you to discover that … your God is bigger [than you thought], that what is impossible in relationships can yet happen, … that the convic-tions with which you are determined to define yourself" [are not cast in stone]? Think of it – your world and your life are even now "awaiting the moment when you too can come out of hiding, let go of truths that are killing you,"[7] and live the life you never knew you had in you! Will we embrace that unexpected life or let it go to the dogs? Will we turn our backs on the shouting and miss the miracle?

———

1. William L. Dols, *Just Because It Didn't Happen*, p. XIII
2. *Op. cit.* p.XII
3. *Op. cit.* p.122
4. *Lectionary Homiletics* XIV, p.46
5. *Biblical Preaching Journal* 16, 3-pp.27-8
6. Dols, *Op. cit.* p.123-4
7. Dols, *Op. cit.* p.124

TWO ROADS

14th Sunday after Pentecost
Jeremiah 15:15-21; Romans 12:1-8; Matthew 16:21-27
Year A –August 29, 1999

> *From that time Jesus began to show his disciples that he must go to Jerusalem and suffer many things from the elders and chief priests and scribes, and be killed, and on the third day be raised. And Peter took him and began to rebuke him, saying, "God forbid, Lord! This shall never happen to you." But he turned and said to Peter, "Get behind me, Satan! You are a hindrance to me, for you are not on the side of God, but of men."*
>
> *Then Jesus told his disciples, "If any man would come after me, let him deny himself and take up his cross and follow me. For whoever would save his life will lose it, and whoever loses his life for my sake will find it. For what will it profit a man, if he gains the whole world and forfeits his life? Or what shall a man give in return for his life? For the Son of man is to come with his angels in the glory of his Father, and then he will repay every man for what he has done."*
>
> *Matthew 16:21-27 (RSV)*

Following a Sunday morning service, one man said to his friend, "I'll bet you can't recite the Lord's Prayer."

"Oh, yes I can," said the second, "'Now I lay me down to sleep, I pray the Lord my soul to keep...'"

"Wow," said the first man, stunned, "I was sure you wouldn't know it!" (Brian Williams).

So much for familiar formulas we are forever fomenting and forgetting. But what about those frightful phrases we are hoping to forget. Like: "If any of you want to become my followers, let them deny themselves and take up their cross and follow me. For those who want to save their life will lose it, and those who lose their life for my sake will find it." (NRSV)

There it is, that in-your-face text from Matthew's Gospel, which no one wants to listen to, let alone (Lord knows) would want to preach on. Quite a contrast to portions of the other two readings presented to us today. From the prophecy of Jeremiah: "Your words became to me a joy and the delight of my heart; for I am called by your name, ... 'They will fight against you, but they shall not prevail over you, for I am with you to save you and deliver you,' says the Lord."

Or from Paul's appealing Epistle to the Romans: "For as in one body we have many members, and not all the members have the same function, so we who are many, are one body in Christ, and individually we are members of one another. We have gifts that differ according to the grace given to us..."

Each of those three texts in its own way is trying to tell us what it means to have faith, and how to live out our faith; but we are left to choose which one is most important for us. Which one do you want me to preach on this morning? Which one, if I have a choice, do I want to leave out – or leave to someone else to explain? The answer seems obvious to me. Those profoundly disturbing words in Matthew's Gospel, if we are willing to listen to them seriously, are the ones we don't really want to hear: "If any of you want to become my followers, let them deny themselves and take up their cross and follow me." (They should have warned me in seminary that there'd be Sundays like this, when you wish the lectionary would just drop dead. But there it is, and here we are.)

—◦◦◦—

"Oh, you mean one with a little man on it?"

—◦◦◦—

What do you suppose Jesus meant? for himself? for us? And why? and how shall we explain it to aspiring young Christians who want to understand the Gospel but don't want to end up like Jesus? Surely that can't be the Good News for us – however heroic and honorable it might have been for him. Curiously enough, in our time crosses have become designer chic, and there are so many styles to choose among. Have you ever asked for one in a store where the sales person says, "Oh, you mean one with a little man on it?" Did Jesus mean "the cross" for each of us literally? If we were to take that seriously, in reality, pretty soon he wouldn't have any followers left, or anyone interested in being his follower.

How can we explain what Jesus must have meant in our terms today – when we live in a different kind of world; where (incidentally) we have exchanged the cross for the electric chair, but how many people do you see with a gold electric chair hanging from a chain around their neck? Surely that's not the point, but the text still represents a problem nonetheless, one that I would gladly have gotten rid of were it not the gospel reading for today. So let me "take a whack at it" (as they say) while you can choose to sit at a comfortable distance from the suggestions of my sermon.

First, I'd like to read you a poem that indirectly, intuitively, speaks to my understanding of Matthew's text. You have heard this poem before, probably many times, but I'd like you to close your eyes while I read it, thinking on it as a kind of unintentional commentary on Jesus' words, which is profoundly human if not especially theological. "The Road Not Taken," by Robert Frost, talks about facing the choice between two ways in life and the consequences of that choosing:

Two roads diverged in a yellow wood,
And sorry I could not travel both
And be one traveler, long I stood
And looked down one as far as I could
To where it bent in the undergrowth;

Then took the other, as just as fair,
And having perhaps the better claim,
Because it was grassy and wanted wear;
Though as for that the passing there
Had worn them really about the same,

And both that morning equally lay
In leaves no step had trodden black.
Oh, I kept the first for another day!
Yet knowing how way leads on to way,
I doubted if I should ever come back.

I shall be telling this with a sigh
Somewhere ages and ages hence:
Two roads diverged in a wood, and I –
I took the one less traveled by,
And that has made all the difference.

Unless I misread the poem, clearly it is a call to life – but life at a cost. And not without loss and a dying along the way, perhaps many deaths which bring us not only new understandings but a new way of living, cherishing, and offering the life we have to give. A metaphor for living and giving away, holding dear and letting go. If we stop to think about it, we will realize that we have our lives only at the expense of others – whether it is in what we eat or in what our forebears gave up to bring us to where we are. What may take us longer to understand is that the expense is what life is for.

In a sense, Jesus was "called" to crucifixion; he understood that as a necessary sacrifice for him – something his own disciples could not imagine; even Peter "the rock" was blockheaded about it. He took Jesus aside "and began to rebuke him, saying 'God forbid, Lord! This shall never happen to you.'" Which was rudely rejected by Jesus' jarring Satan sentence. But then Jesus turned to his disciples, and his challenge to them (and to us) was not a call to literal crucifixion, but to self-denial and the suffering which they may sustain in his name.

"Whew!" we say, "only self-denial, what a snap." I suspect that somewhere in our subconscious we are seduced by a scenario something like the giving up of chocolate for Lent. But I doubt that was the sort of self-denial or sacrifice Jesus was speaking of. His words, it seems to me, seek to challenge our status quo (then and now). However else we would care to characterize our culture, we live in a self-serving society, which seeks out stimulation and self-gratification. And so it is increasingly difficult for us to understand that self-*denial* is a pathway to life; it simply is not a part of our image or picture of the good life.

In some ways it is simpler to see self-privation as a symptom of psychological maladjustment. As more of us than the baby boomers struggle with growing old, the cultural sirens call us to "find ourselves," not "lose" ourselves, before – it is too late. So we embark on our own individual introspective adventures to embrace our authentic selves, which often excludes an appeal to Jesus' words altogether. We become hard of hearing them long before we become hard hearted.

If we could hear them, one thing Jesus' words would do for us, even if they won't give us the answers we are looking for, is to give us a choice, just as Robert Frost's poem does. I used to wonder why Frost spoke about only two roads; there seem to be a thousand roadways or paths to travel. But I finally understood that there are only two. If we say someone has been kind or loving, we imply that he could have been cruel or unloving. To have a choice about the way, there must be a fork in the road where two paths diverge, so that we cannot be one traveler and travel both. So the crossroad stands as the sign and occasion of our freedom. If there were no choice, we would not be free. If we are not faced with what it is to lose our life, we will never know what it is to find it.

If we are going to accept that God's ways in the world are worthy of our highest hopes or aspiration, then inevitably we will have to abandon our understanding that our life is the ultimate arbiter of what is important. And there's no way that's not going to be an experience of loss and sadness for some of us. If choices direct us to the possibility of a fuller life, at the same time they determine what kind of crosses we are willing to carry. If that sounds to you like bad news, the good news is that no one can decide for us or coerce our commitment. We are free to choose which way to go, who and what will fill our days, and how we are going to give our life away – for it is certain that we will give it up one way or another.

SINGERS OF LIFE

(9/11)

15th Sunday after Pentecost
Romans 8:26-39; Psalm 23
Proper 19 – Year C – September 16, 2001

... though I walk through the valley of the shadow of death,

I will fear no evil; for thou art with me ...

Thou preparest a table before me

in the presence of mine enemies ...

From Psalm 23

Familiar words in an unfamiliar time.

Since that fateful morning of "9/11," as the media are wont to call it, I have read hundreds of newspaper articles and viewed countless hours of television commentary and replays until my head ached along with my heart. And I would be the first to say if there is anything more that needs to be said, let the liturgy speak it: in scripture, psalms, music, hymns – and maybe most of all, our prayers. Indeed, that is where I still stand even as I stand here before you in the pulpit.

But it may be "meet and right" for us also to say something about the power of our faith and hope and courage to give life, rather than to reiterate the refrain of reprisal and retaliation and revenge – which in truth I am no stranger to myself since I served a small stint as an Airborne instructor in the Artillery, and too

many times told myself and others that this was our business –
and even our glory: to dispense death.

If you have come here this morning to hear a stirring sermon that will explain the horror of the Trade Center Towers, the
Pentagon, and the Pittsburgh tragedies, you and I will both come
up woefully short. I have no words of wisdom with which to wrap
the wounds and wailings that will be with us for a wrenching time
to come. My first thought when I finally focused on the TV screen
Tuesday morning at St. Mary's was that we are all in this together,
the terrorists and the terrorized, whether we know it or not and
whether we've lost loved ones in the holocausts or were spared.
And I remember one member of our EfM group saying, I hope that
those people who knew they were going to die had some kind
of faith to help them face their fear and terror. How horrible to
endure the eternity of waiting awake for their oncoming end. One
news report said terrorists told their captives to call their loved
ones on their cell phones to tell them that they were going to die.

It won't do for us simply to say, "My heart is broken," for in
the face of such unspeakable suffering, God's heart was the first of
all to break. We have a mandate from our faith to say more than
that. Fortunately, there are some shining moments mentioned in
the news, which can take some of the sting out of the devastation.
"As United Airlines Flight 93 (the Pennsylvania site) entered its last
desperate moments in the sky, 31-year-old passenger Jeremy Glick
used a cell phone to tell his wife, Lyzbeth, of his impending death
– and pledged to go down fighting." Who knows what the plane's
intended target had been. At the Pentagon, "About 2:30 a.m.
(Wednesday morning), a U.S. flag was hoisted above (the building) by workers, planted just to the left of the crash site. When it
unfurled, the (rescue) workers applauded." These sad times hold
out to us unexpected opportunities for gratitude and kindness and
the help of others.

These are but symbols of the stream of stories that are
surely yet to come. I'm sure you all know of other uplifting incidents that help us focus not just on the precariousness of human

life but on the nobility of spirit that survives the worst we can wreak upon one another. But they will not suffice to salve the suffering all around us, which is self-evident and not simply symbolic. We want explanations – to seek solace in answers. Many of us strive to attach some sort of meaning – spiritual, political, or economic to the terrorist attacks, hoping that by connecting the tragedy to a larger purpose or truth, that will make it easier for us to comprehend the unconscionable and inconceivable.

One Rabbi said, "I still feel shock, and shock is prior to any search for meaning. We're still before the funeral. Our dead are still before us. Literally. The bodies have not all been recovered. We don't know who died (or how many). We don't even know who to blame." One of our most deadly temptations is to fix blame fast, as the media have aired almost from the start. We are enraged at reports of Palestinians celebrating on the West Bank – cheering, congratulating one another, and handing out candy. And we cannot escape the countless choruses that declare, "Of course, we must come up with a devastating military retaliation."

— ❦ —

"Men never do evil so completely and cheerfully as when they do it from religious conviction.

— ❦ —

A friend recalled for me the words of Blaise Pascal: "Men never do evil so completely and cheerfully as when they do it from religious conviction." Some of us forget that foremost this applies to "us" as well as "them." I would argue that this attack is not as much religious as it is about the price of freedom, God-given or otherwise, others' as well as ours. From the earliest ages, we have always known that humankind is capable not only of self-fulfillment but of self-destruction, reserving the right to rebel against the very source of life itself. Sometimes we call that sin, which may have become too small a word for our modern world. We have a hard time hearing it.

330

A day after the attack, one New York commentator noted, "The cloud still hangs over our city – it's still there!" The smoke and the ash. And it's not just a cloud of debris; it is a symbol of the darkness, sadness, anger, ambiguity, and God knows what else that surrounds us. Who could argue? But I see it not just as a cloud of doleful witness, rather as an opportunity to face our future. What will we do? We can always take revenge, for that is the way of the world, but what are we going to do to reawaken our responsibility for redemption? How shall we witness to that? In a courtroom, we can witness either for or against: justice, courage, compassion, and life. In this case we know how to witness *against*, but are we as certain how to witness *for* our faith and what we believe in?

I learned a little about that choice this summer when I conducted my father's funeral, and came to realize that although he had died last May, his service was still a great trial for me. Initially, I had refused to take part in it because I wanted so much to be a mourner with the rest of my family. Father had asked me to sing *Ave Maria* in his service – which I simply couldn't do. But at 93, there were no Episcopal clergy alive and available who had known him, except retired Bishop Porteus of Connecticut, who was not well. So there was nothing for me to do but take the service myself, which I was doubtful I could get through without giving way to my grief for the father I longed to know but who left our household when I was five or six. He lost his second wife to his best friend and his third wife to cancer. It occurred to me that he had spent nearly nine times the number of years with his stepchildren as he had with his own. First married scarcely three months before the Great Depression, he had not had an easy life until he finally remarried for the fourth time in his later years. I was sure he wanted to be remembered for the significant things he did and led during his life, such as the Colonel who served under George Patton and with distinction on Omar Bradley's General Staff in World War II; as vital volunteer, mover and shaper of a dozen communities in which he lived; as Senior Warden of several churches – and so on.

But I wanted somehow to get beneath the earlier life he had led as "old blood-and-guts" or "grim death," as my mother used to call him, to the time when he had been my father and he had sung camp songs to his two young sons each night when we were put to bed. During my preparations for his burial service I finally came to accept him as one of "the singers of life," who teach us to say "yes" to life in the tough of it, rather than to turn away from it; to say "yes" to life as it is, rather than cling to the safety of our sufferings because life is not what we want it to be. Saying "yes" affirms, begins, builds, risks, redeems even the unredeemable. Saying "no" closes off, protects, shuts down, shuts out. Saying "yes" often takes more courage than saying "no."

Which prompts me to read a passage from a real life narrative in the diary of an observant anthropologist, which seems to me appropriate for us to ponder in our time.

One day Loren Eiseley leaned against a stump at the edge of a small glade and fell asleep. He wrote:

> *When I awoke, dimly aware of some commotion and outcry in the clearing, the light was slanting down through the pines in such a way that the glade was lit like some vast cathedral. I could see the dust motes of wood pollen in the long shaft flight, and there on the extended branch sat an enormous raven with a red and squirming nestling in his beak. The sound that awoke me was the outraged cries of the nestling's parents, who flew helplessly in circles about the clearing. The sleek black monster was indifferent to them. He gulped, whetted his beak on the dead branch a moment and sat still. Up to that point the little tragedy had followed the usual pattern. But suddenly, out of all that area of woodland, a soft sound of complaint began to rise. Into the glade fluttered small birds of half a dozen varieties drawn by the anguished outcries of the tiny parents.*

No one dared to attack the raven. But they cried there in some instinctive common misery. The bereaved and the unbereaved. The glade filled with their soft rustling and their cries. They fluttered as though to point their wings at the murderer. There was a dim intangible ethic he had violated, that they knew. He was a bird of death. And he, the murderer, the black bird at the heart of life, sat on there, glistening in the common light, formidable, unmoving, unperturbed, untouchable.

The sighing died. It was then I saw the judgment. It was the judgment of life against death. I will never see it again so forcefully presented. I will never hear it again in notes so tragically prolonged. For in the midst of protest, they forgot the violence. There, in that clearing, the crystal note of a song sparrow lifted hesitantly in the hush. And finally, after painful fluttering, another took the song, and then another, the song passing from one bird to another, ... Till suddenly they took heart and sang from many throats joyously together as birds are known to sing. They sang because life is sweet and sunlight beautiful. They sang under the brooding shadow of the raven. In simple truth they had forgotten the raven, for they were the singers of life, and not of death.

(Robert Raines, Creative Brooding, pp. 36-7)

But let the liturgy lend us the last lines I want to leave you with – a reading from *Romans (8:31,32, 35, 37-39):*

What then shall we say to this? If God be for us, who can be against us? He who spared not his own Son, but gave him up for us all, will he not also give us all things with him? ... Who shall separate us from the love of Christ? Shall tribulation, or distress, or persecution, or famine, or nakedness, or peril, or sword?

... No, in all these things we are more than conquerors through him who loved us. For I am sure that neither death, nor life, nor angels, nor principalities, nor powers, nor things present, nor things to come, nor height nor depth, nor anything else in all creation, will be able to separate us from the love of God which is in Christ Jesus our Lord.

Amen

LOOKING BACK OVER HIS SHOULDER

15th Sunday after Pentecost
Luke 15:1-10
Proper 15 – Year C – September 13, 1998

Now all the tax collectors and sinners were coming near to listen to him. And the Pharisees and the scribes were grumbling and saying, "This fellow welcomes sinners and eats with them." So he told them this parable: "Which one of you, having a hundred sheep and losing one of them, does not leave the ninety-nine in the wilderness and go after the one that is lost until he finds it? When he has found it, he lays it on his shoulders and rejoices. And when he comes home, he calls together his friends and neighbors, saying to them, 'Rejoice with me, for I have found my sheep that was lost.' Just so, I tell you there will be more joy in heaven over one sinner who repents than over ninety-nine righteous persons who need no repentance. "Or what woman having ten silver coins, if she loses one of them, does not light a lamp, sweep the house, and search carefully until she finds it? When she has found it, she calls together her friends and neighbors, saying, 'Rejoice with me, for I have found the coin that I had lost.' Just so, I tell you, there is joy in the presence of the angels of God over one sinner who repents."

Luke 15:1-10

335

This is a new year for old St. Mary's ("Little" St. Mary's as we say in the British euphemism) – restored St. Mary's is now restored to worship. You may remember, Thomas Wolfe is famous for the phrase "You can't go home again" – but you know I think he's wrong, at least when it comes to the church. I can't tell you how good it feels to be back here again this morning in the early bosom of St. Mary's. Some things are missing, like the heavy buzz of lazy hornets and the wicker fans we used to pass out at services to keep the air conditioning away. But so much is the same. While you may not recognize it in the new finish, the special patina of our old pews, which was lovingly applied over the years by the rubbing of restive bottoms on the bare wood, has been pre-served. And John Miller, bless him, has not succumbed to brassy modernity; he has not thrown out the missal stand made of old cigar boxes, which I created many years ago when I discovered I couldn't read the Prayer Book if it was lying flat on the altar.

It is good, "meet and right" we say, to be gathered here once again; I am sure the flock have not forgotten what it is like to be called to worship in this place, to be gathered with familiar fac-es in the familiar places each of us cherishes under this roof. We have raised up big St. Mary's, which is a wonderful dwelling, new with life and promise – but this little sanctuary is still the infusion of its life's blood. I have said to John on many occasions how much difference saying the words here makes – whether in preaching or in celebrating Holy Communion or Baptism or in saying the Burial Office. Some people say they reach out to us more clearly, the spirit seems to speak more dearly, and we find home more nearly when we worship here with those who have gone before us and who are palpably present from the past. (Perhaps it is because we are literally closer to one another here.) I can still hear the voice of Holt Souder, stopping the service at the late arrival of some hap-less soul, saying "Come on in and sit down so we can get on with our worship, we'll wait."

And what a text leads us this morning to start the new year (it is clear to me that when school starts again, that's when the real year begins). The parable of the lost sheep is a familiar passage and deeply loved, and it sounds like home – maybe not the home we remember but the home we always long for and hope to find once again and is, we suspect, at the heart of the mystery of all things. The place that allows any one of us having a hundred sheep and losing one to leave our ninety-nine to go and search for the one that is lost, until it is found. And when it is, the shepherd lays it on broad shoulders and brings it home rejoicing, calling together friends and neighbors, saying "Rejoice with me, for I have found my sheep that was lost. There is more joy in heaven," Jesus says, "over one sinner who has strayed and is found than over ninety-nine righteous persons who were never lost."

Is that romantic? Naive? Surely it is – but it is also profoundly pastoral and theological. God is the Good Shepherd who never gives up searching for those of us who have lost our way from the fold. We do not have to find our way back alone, or fear that we will not be welcomed. It is as though my child had been dead and is now alive again; he was lost, but now he's come home – the prodigal God-father says. God is the "Prodigal," because that word means extravagant, holding nothing back – the parent who races to hug the child who would come home but does not know how, the father who squanders his grace in riotous forgiving.

Jesus tells us an outrageous parable and troubles us to believe it. He has a rich sense of humor, if not of the ridiculous: "Which one of you," he says, "having a hundred sheep and losing one of them, does not leave the ninety-nine in the wilderness and go after the one that is lost until he finds it?" That's a question of course, not just a naive assertion – which implies an answer. We may at first be flattered that Jesus thinks of us in such terms (or does he?) – until we realize that the real-life answer is NO ONE. No one in his right mind, no would-be shepherd worth his salt in his compassionate or lawful duty would think of leaving the ninety-nine defenseless, who might wander off, to bring back the one who has strayed.

Shepherds in ancient times, who literally lived with their sheep, were considered outlaws and untrustworthy, as well as guardians of the flock, and needed to account to the owner for every sheep in their care. If a mountain lion preyed upon one of them, the only way a shepherd could absolve himself of the loss was to bring whatever was left from the mouth of the lion – two ears or a leg and a piece of the tail - back to the owner, as proof that the sheep had not been sold for personal gain. Saving one lone sheep was not worth risking the loss of many. So the parable means the opposite of what it seems to say. God is not a proper or prudent shepherd, he couldn't make a living at it. He is the reckless shepherd, unlawful – even unjust – who does not ensure that others get what they deserve but gives them precisely what they do not deserve. He prefers love over justice (in Hebrew, *hesed* over *mishpat*) – which was a scandal to Jewish law from Moses to the prophets.

If that was not scandal enough for them, his love is not for the righteous, Jesus says, or even for the lovable. The Greeks had a special word for that: love of the lovable, the comely, the admirable is eros, which we have misnomered as "erotic." Jesus is not erotically involved with us; his love is for the unlovable," "the lost," as he put it. We are used to the word "sinner," but "lost" would be more compatible with the way God's love is portrayed in this parable – and maybe thereby we can more readily find ourselves in it. We may not have chosen our brand of sinfulness deliberately, through vicious or willful choice but simply through weakness or neglect. (I think that describes my situation.) Sheep do not stray or become lost out of guilt or malevolence or self-will but from misguided experiences or the mischances of life. The term "lost" suggests sorrow more than condemnation; it speaks of God's loneliness – and "lost" implies that home, not hell, is what we need in order to be "found."

So in the wisdom of the world, the Good Shepherd is too good to be true and too foolish to be effective, reckless in risking everything to recover the one lost soul who may not even ask to be found! Luke tells us how the good people, the thoughtful persons, the righteous leaders of his time assessed Jesus, this so-called "friend of tax collectors and sinners," "this glutton and wine bibber" (read drunkard), who surrounds himself with unsavory sorts. He is known by the company he keeps-disreputable and undiscriminating. Never mind that "friend of sinners" doesn't say Jesus approved of their sin, only that he didn't separate himself from them in their sinfulness. One commentary explains that in the vernacular of the righteous in those days, the term "friend of ..." could be compared to the contemptuous call of "nigger lover" used during the civil rights struggle of the 60's.

It seems to me more sad than sinful that some of us would be dishonest if we didn't admit we can experience deep satisfaction in seeing that people do get the bad things they deserve and don't get the good things they don't deserve. It becomes a vicious circle we can have a hard time breaking out of. The good news is that God offers to free us from that remorseless justice by breaking into our uncharitable insistence on "an eye-for-an-eye" and dealing lovingly with us beyond our disobedient deserving. Maybe that acceptance will enable us to overturn a dark and graceless world by beginning to break out of our bondage and give to others, no more deserving than us, more than they deserve. Do you remember the words of the poet Edwin Markham which, somewhat skewed, were set to music in (I think) the 60's?

> *He drew a circle that shut me out-*
> *Heretic, rebel, a thing to flout.*
> *But love and I had the wit to win.*
> *We drew a circle that took him in.*

We have before us – in spirit and in truth – a new year, a new church, and appropriately enough in our baptism this morning a new life in our newest member of this community, Lydia Jane Aveson – symbols that summon us to a new beginning. And what we can look forward to in the parlance of our parable is the profligate joy of the Shepherd who celebrates our homecoming, who says that sin and suffering do not have the last word because God himself is seeking our lost selves – all the broken and bleating and alone – and when we are found all heaven will rejoice. In our

Easter language: sorrow is answered by joy, crucifixion is answered by resurrection.

The last word is that if we can keep the promise of God's relentless searching before us in our longings and loves, maybe some day the language of this loving God will show in our words, and one day the face of God will show forth in our face when we too are willing to embrace the lost in others and in ourselves. We need not to forget what it feels like to be lost because, as someone else has said "Jesus came to save the lost – lost sheep, lost coins, lost brothers, lost prostitutes, lost loan sharks, lost jackasses, lost weaklings. Jesus came all this way looking for them. And those we have given up on or forgotten about or dismissed because of their unworthiness are the very ones Jesus has headed out to look for. He looks back over his shoulder to see if we are following him..." [1]

---

1. *Christian Century*, August 26-September 2, 1998, p.781)

OUR LOVE OF THE UNMERCIFUL SERVANT

16th Sunday after Pentecost
Matthew 18:21-35
Proper 19 – Year A – September 15, 1996

Then Peter came up and said to him, "Lord, how often shall my brother sin against me, and I forgive him? As many as seven times?" Jesus said to him, "I do not say to you seven times, but seventy times seven. "

"Therefore the kingdom of heaven may be compared to a king who wished to settle accounts with his servants. When he began the reckoning, one was brought to him who owed him ten thousand talents; and as he could not pay, his lord ordered him to be sold, with his wife and children and all that he had, and payment to be made.

So the servant fell on his knees, imploring him, 'Lord, have patience with me, and I will pay you everything.' And out of pity for him the lord of that servant released him and forgave him the debt.

But that same servant, as he went out, came upon one of his fellow servants who owed him a hundred denarii; and seizing him by the throat he said, 'Pay what you owe. 'So his fellow servant fell down and besought him, 'Have patience with me, and I will pay you.' He refused and went and put him in prison till he should pay the debt. When his fellow servants saw what had taken place, they were greatly distressed, and they went and reported to their lord all that had taken place.

Then his lord summoned him and said to him, 'You wicked servant! I forgave you all that debt because you besought me; and should not you have had mercy on your fellow servant, as I had mercy on you?' And in anger his lord delivered him to the jailers, till he should pay all his debt.

So also my heavenly Father will do to every one of you, if you do not forgive your brother from your heart."

Matthew 18:21-35

The Parable of the Unmerciful Servant, we call it. It might have been called The Parable of the Gracious King – or even The Just King, but it isn't. And that's just the point. If we listen to it while it is being read and reflect upon it even briefly, my guess is that most of us will side with the king – who wouldn't? But I suspect that the point of the parable is we are intended to identify ourselves with the unmerciful servant; because the brutal truth is, more often than not, we are more like the servant than the king, our good intentions notwithstanding.

The parable evokes strong emotions in me. I side with Gray Charles who said, "I hear that story and I want the unmerciful servant to rot in jail. How dare he act the way he does? How dare he not have mercy when he was shown such mercy. What a lousy excuse for a human being." The commentary is not finished. "Whatever happened to the Unmerciful Servant whom the king had thrown into jail? Part of me rejoices that justice was done and hopes he rotted in prison. But if that is my hope for him, it must also be a hope for myself, because I have failed to show mercy more times than I dare to remember, and more often than I even know."

Still, the story is not done with – at least for me – because the darker truth of the parable, which may not be a true-to-life tale but a true to what we do in life story is that we do not need a king to throw us into jail, to deliver us to the torturers (as the original text literally says). "The unmerciful servant was in prison long before the king put him there ... because when we fail to forgive, we *are* handed over to the torturers" by our own choice. The parable is not proclaiming impending judgment upon us here as much as describing the unmerciful reality of our own choosing.

I may be wrong, but I think this morning's reading is not about the relationship of mercy and justice; rather, it is about the connection between forgiveness and grace. Maybe it would be helpful to take a look at the meaning of forgiveness – what it is and what it isn't. Last week John Miller brought up the famous passage in Matthew, which begins the Gospel for today, where Peter asks Jesus how many times, is it necessary to forgive someone who has sinned against you – "seven times?" (which in Hebrew is not only a holy number, but twice the number of completeness – plus one). And Jesus says, to the amazement of Peter, "No, not seven times, but seventy times seven" – in effect unendingly. But how can he really mean that and why are we along with Peter put off by Jesus' reply?

Perhaps to find some answers we first have to think about what forgiveness is not – and here I am indebted to Brad Binau, who points out what may not always be obvious: "forgiveness is not forgetting." Think about the impossibility of trying not to remember what it is we cannot forget. "If we were today to ask Jesus if he remembered a fellow by the name of Judas Iscariot, it is unlikely Jesus would say, 'No, never heard of him!'"

"Forgiveness is not toleration." In fact, it is almost the opposite, because what "we forgive is precisely what we cannot tolerate. If it was something we could tolerate, we would not need to forgive it."

In the same way "forgiveness is not excusing." Because in order "to excuse something we would have to understand it, and if we could really understand we would not have to forgive."

Lastly, but perhaps first in importance, "forgiveness is not an act of the will." We cannot will to forgive any more than we can will ourselves to be happy. Forgiveness "is not a power we can invoke or withhold" at will. Forgiveness is more a gift to us than something we ourselves have given to others. If we are able to offer it at all, it is more often the result of what has happened within us rather than what we have caused to happen to us or others. So often forgiveness comes about when we are in the midst of our own healing process – when we finally realize that we no longer have to hold onto our wrongs and resentments and hatreds and self-pity in order to remember who we are. Forgiving becomes possible for us when "we come to define ourselves by the grace that makes us whole, rather than the hurts which break us apart." In a way it is already a gift when we can recognize what it is about us that needs to be forgiven rather than always pointing out what needs to be forgiven in others, when "we discover that we are more like those who have hurt us than we are different from them."

Speaking personally, during the past ten years or so I can recall a couple of grievous wrongs (or so I thought then) enacted against me, and the hardest part has been to let go of the hurt that I felt justified my anger and self-righteousness which were at least satisfying if I could not have justice. But equally hard for me was realizing that if justice was what I wanted, then I would also have to accept all those times I wasn't judged when I fell short. A sobering thought. And what about those people that I judged unfairly, unknowingly or uncaringly? I am able to forgive says John Patton, only "when I discover that I am in no position to forgive others."

...unfairness is a characteristic of grace.

On the other side of forgiveness is that awful word "grace." I say awful because it asks us to accept something more difficult even than forgiveness. In a reading group I have shepherded for nearly a dozen years, I have been astounded to discover that what many of the group really dislike about a number of the novels we have discussed is having to deal with the presence of unconditional grace. (That's a tautology, of course, because grace is unconditional – like it or not.) I have been at a loss to explain why, unless it is that no one wants to believe in a free lunch. Not only do we not believe in it, we cannot abide it – and we don't want others to have it – it's not fair.

Interesting problem: because grace is grace only when it is undeserved. It is outrageous; unfairness is a characteristic of grace. When Peter says "how many times shall we forgive, Lord, seven times?" he is aware that according to sacred law all that could possibly be required would be to forgive three times, the absolute limit to which justice could be pushed. So when he says "seven times," Peter expects a big pat on the back from Jesus – who says to him instead (in effect), "You don't get it! Not seven times, but seventy times seven, a boundless number." No wonder Peter cannot understand, he understands only fairness and justice – surely God is just. The point is, God is unjust precisely when he is full of grace.

In this morning's parable, the king not only has pity on the servant, he goes further. He does not simply reduce the debt or extend the time it is due – what would be reasonable. Instead, he forgives it, cancels it, wipes the slate clean. Since the servant could not possibly repay what was owed, his very life was dependent upon grace. Yet he, like Peter and some of us – found it impossible to accept love which was undeserved, gifts we haven't earned, graciousness we didn't ask for, blessings we are not entitled to.

We don't want to be in anyone's debt. We want what we deserve, what is ours by rights. Like the servant, it seems we would rather face a life in prison than the "imprisonment" of love.

In my experience with pre-marital counseling, I have discovered that what is hardest for people to accept these days about marriage is the idea that in love two persons become one (not just one flesh). So many people find it difficult to understand that love does not ask one another what is mine and what is yours by right – instead it gives to the other precisely that to which he or she has no right. That idea is a real stumbling block for couples today. They can handle the stress of struggling to maintain their independence, but not the strain of striving for interdependence. We cannot bear the cost of loving injustice, we want what is ours and what we deserve; we cannot live with grace at any price. That is the sad message of the unmerciful servant. Sometimes we would rather serve out our sentence of lovelessness.

So often we do not hear the most memorable line of the parable. We pass over it, either because we are satisfied that justice was done in the end or appalled by the end of the servant: "And out of pity for him, the lord of that slave released him and forgave him his debt." Which will we have, grace or justice? Help us to pray: "Lord, spare us from a life of justice; forgive us our fancy that it is better to live in a world of absolute fairness rather than under the unlawfulness of grace. A fair world, a just world, might make life nice for us – but only as nice as we are. There we would indeed get what we deserve. Grace does not give us what we deserve; it offers us the chance for life even in the midst of our unmerciful suffering. Grace us, gracious God." Amen.

―――――

Footnote: Most of the passages quoted above come from Lectionary Homeletics VII, 10 pp. 21, 24, 25. The "ending" prayer is audaciously adapted from a commentary in *The Christian Century*.

OUR NEED TO REMEMBER

17th Sunday after Pentecost
2 Timothy 1:1-14
Proper 22 – Year C – October 8, 1995

I confess that I have rarely given much time or thought to Paul's Pastoral Epistles (2nd Timothy being one of those), not because many biblical scholars have questioned their authenticity as genuine letters of Paul, but simply because their language and focus did not pique my interest.

Recently however, I came across a poetic translation of 2nd Timothy which drew me in because it begins by speaking about the importance of remembering:

> *I remember you in my prayers*
> *I remember your tears*
> *I remember your heritage of faith*

It reminds us of a powerful part of our lives that can help preserve and sustain us in dark times: remembering.

Some of you, like me, may have moved from one house to another – moves which may only have been a couple of blocks away or from one region of this nation to another, or even to a different country – leaving pieces of you that couldn't quite be packed up in boxes and taken along with you. When finally the rooms lie empty, the windows bare, the boxes piled up like so many cartons of Army provisions, as you walk through the spaces that echo, which have been your home, you may hear the sounds of your former footsteps or see a room still filled with familiar furniture, or family and friends ringing the table at Thanksgiving or gathered to put ornaments on the Christmas tree.

⟡

> *You cannot really see or taste or touch*
> *your memories, but they are palpably real,*
> *and you need to take them with you...*

⟡

You may even hear far away conversations that speak of a life once lived there in the house where children were conceived, where your wife or husband lay gravely ill, where secrets were whispered and indiscretions were sworn to keep silent, or forgivenesses offered. You cannot really see or taste or touch your memories, but they are palpably real, and you need to take them with you when you leave so that the life you lived will not be left behind and that part of you die or become lost in an empty house. You need to bring all of you, wherever you go; a part of a person will not do.

In today's epistle, Paul is saying he not only remembers but he gives thanks for the memories. It is important to give thanks, to say "thank you" when we have received some kindness, whenever we receive something that is a gift. As others have said, it is at heart a religious act to give, or to receive, a "thank you." It is, of course, good manners to say "thank you," but it is also important to acknowledge that when we are given to, the gift giver recognizes us in a way that is itself a gift.

As we remember, so we are enabled to give. When we say "thank you" in receiving the gift, we also remember the life and importance of the one who has given it – whether we recognize a wedding present or the part a child played in the Christmas pageant or the friend who kept our children so we could have time alone. That may not seem "religious" because the offerings are ordinary, but 2nd Timothy speaks of such gifts as more than our giving of them:

I remember you in my prayers
I remember your tears
I remember your heritage of faith
And I rekindle the gift of God

that is within you
The gift of God is as a flame
Flame is fire
Fire is light
Light is power
The gift of God is the spirit of power and love

Paul speaks of God as a God of memory and remembrance. He says at the communion table before us: "Do this in remembrance of me." As we take into our lives the bread and the wine, we remember with thanksgiving the one who gave us the gift of his life and spirit, who said he would prepare a place for us: "In my father's house are many mansions – room for us to be, rooms waiting for us – made with memories we are making right here and now, today, when we come together and when we leave this place. Memory has power "to have, to hold, to keep, to cherish," to transform and transfigure us. To take away our memory is to take away our life.

We remember Jesus came that we "may have life." Another way to say that in the language of faith is to say that God "calls" us and "saves" us for his own purpose, that in Christ sin is abolished and death is overcome so we may live our life to the fullest. In the language of the world, that sounds unbelievable, even sappy. We know that none of us will escape death. How can we believe in new life?

My good friend Tim I first met when I was seeking to hire someone to teach in the Religion department at Exeter Academy. He was lively, handsome, with a quick tongue and a disarming smile, a young person with a presence that nevertheless captured our attention. He was joyful, exuberant, well-coordinated, athletic, and sometimes embarrassingly honest – about his feelings, his faith, and his struggles with it; about his competitive relationship with his wife in which he did not feel secure; his doubts about his abilities and gifts – even though they were manifold and manifest to the rest of us. He was grateful and thankful for little favors, even my wife's attempt to introduce him to artichokes.

One summer he and his wife led a group of young people to South Africa, where he contracted malaria, became dehydrated, was released from a meager hospital into the bush with only his wife to attend him along with their group. He became delirious, paranoid, felt that he had let the others down and failed to live up to his wife's expectations. One morning, he slit his throat. The promise his life held was broken. He was broken – and parts of us with him. Death took him, but not the gift of his memories which we hold dear. He reminds me even in his absence never to say more than I mean; to remember when all else fails not to pass up the opportunity to be honest, not to fear wrestling with the dark things; to hold on to faith as a gift too deep to express in reason or even words. I remember his gift of cheerfulness which was for him, appearances to the contrary, not so much natural as an act of courage. I remember also that he would want me to forgive his wife – who is not in need of forgiveness – to forgive myself who needs it instead.

His death cannot be denied, but it is also overcome. How ridiculous, how absurd to say so. "O death, where is thy victory! O death, where is thy sting?" – Holt Souder asked that I read those words here at his funeral service. In the face of death, we have the audacity to say that death does not have the last word – for Holt or for Tim. That there is a power greater than death which sustains them and us – which we remember here at this table.

> *I remember Tim and Holt*
> *and the echo of empty houses and times that were*
> *We remember to say thank you*
> *for them and for their memories*

We remember the words of our Lord Jesus, how he said it is more blessed to give than to receive, who gave his life a ransom for many, who said "Come unto me all ye that travail and are heavy laden and I will give you rest."

Let us also remember this life which has given to us a gift to share:

> *Remember one another in our prayers*
> *Remember our tears*
> *Remember the faith we had and have*
> *And rekindle the gift of God within us.*
>
> *Amen*

———

Footnote: I am in part indebted for insights, examples, and expressions extracted from the offerings of *Lectionary Homiletics* VI, II and Joel L. Alvis, Jr.)

"A NEW HEART AND A NEW SPIRIT"

17th Sunday after Pentecost
Ezekiel 18:1-4, 25-32
Proper 21 – Year A – September 22, 1996

What a great beginning for us today – not to mention for the rest of Page's life. This service of baptism reassures us that she and we are unconditionally accepted by God without our knowing or deserving. And we have here publicly promised to support Page in her life in Christ in whatever way is possible for us, which can be a gift to us as well as to her. In renewing our own baptismal covenant we are also reminded that we are all called to ministry – one that may neither be ordained nor in the organized church, but which is ours to inquire about and to explore. That brings me to a subject unusual to preach upon, but encouraged by our rector. My text is taken from Ezekiel 18 read earlier in the service.

> *Cast away from you all the transgressions which*
> *you have committed against me, and get yourselves*
> *a new heart and a new spirit! Why will you die, O*
> *house of Israel? For I have no pleasure in the death*
> *of anyone, says the Lord God; so turn, and live.*
> *(vss. 31-32)*

Prophets are supposed to surprise us, so we'll stay awake, listen to something we hadn't expected to – like a sermon we are sure we have heard before or could care less about hearing ever. So I shouldn't have been taken unawares when I discovered that Ezekiel's words unexpectedly described for me my experience in a program I went through this summer. I'd like to tell you a little about it because the Rector and Vestry and I are committed to making that program available to anyone interested here at St. Mary's, beginning in January.

First off, I have to confess that what I thought was going to be just another course in Christian education, however broadly conceived, did not hold out much hope of being an adventure that was exciting or even unexpected for me. After all, I have been involved in education in and outside the church for thirty-eight years as teacher and twenty as student. And I didn't think that one more training session would be either life threatening or life giving – but I was wrong.

...the title EfM Mentor Training is not exactly an MTV come on.

I doubt the name of the seminar I signed up for will bring you to the edge of your pew – the title EfM Mentor Training is not exactly an MTV come on. A few of you will know that the initials EfM stand for a nationally known program sponsored by the University of the South (Sewanee), called Education for Ministry. All I really knew about it initially was its intent, which I had heard was to make available what some might call a layman's experience of seminary education. That turned out to be somewhat misleading because in addition to its academic program one of its goals is to offer an educational experience that will help us to discover and develop whatever kind of ministry we may be suited for and choose to offer one another as lay persons.

A lot of people think the word's "minister" and "ministry" mean being ordained in holy orders, but EfM begins by reminding us that in our baptism all of us are called to participate in the whole of Christian ministry, and not just within the formal church. In baptism we were empowered to carry with us and to live out the word of God, which gives us life in many forms. EfM is practical in its understanding of ministry, even in its task of developing our skills in what is termed theological reflection. More about that in a moment but let me return to Ezekiel, who says to those of us who long to become faithful:

Cast away from you all the transgressions which you have committed against me (says the Lord). Those words are certainly addressed to me – because for the longest time, beginning in graduate school in the 60's, I had given up on the course of Christian education and even bad-mouthed the idea of it because it seemed an impossible task. It didn't ask much of us and we gave it little in return. People didn't prepare for classes, they didn't want homework, they felt free to drop out when it was inconvenient, and worst of all it didn't seem important – it didn't matter. EfM seeks to change that by motivating busy people to explore what is of meaning and significance to them in their search for God – surely something we can benefit from at every level of education in the church.

If we can let go the baggage some of us have brought with us, unlearn old habits and reactions we're used to, we have a chance as Ezekiel commends to *get ourselves a new heart and new spirit! Why will you die, O house of Israel?* he asks. EfM believes we can come to see old things with new eyes. A case in point would be the program's emphasis on theological reflection – which at first sounds uninteresting and irrelevant to many people: a dry academic discipline pursued by scholars, monks, and graduate students. (I can well understand that perspective since theology was a fiendish major of mine.)

To turn common wisdom around and suggest that theological education can be exciting and life giving for the laity and non-professional may sound foolhardy at least or just plain foolish at worst. But EfM's conviction is that theological reflection helps us pursue questions of meaning, purpose, and value – and therefore is important for and at the heart of anyone who asks seriously what it means to be human. In addition, as one mentor expressed it, this kind of reflection helps us balance our theology with our behavior. How do we go about this venture? Turn and live, says Ezekiel.

354

Happily compatible with my own understanding and style of teaching, I discovered, the teacher functions as a guide and mentor, not as an authority who has the answers and passes on knowledge.

Not through traditional teaching methods and classroom structure. EfM starts with the idea that a "community of learning" learns best when the group helps shape the way it can best function for everyone involved. It establishes its own norms and expectation for how the class will operate. Happily compatible with my own understanding and style of teaching, I discovered, the teacher functions as a guide and mentor, not as an authority who has the answers and passes on knowledge. The EfM program presents to us traditional disciplines such as biblical interpretation of Hebrew and New Testament scripture, church history, ethics, systematic theology, great religious thinkers, and the development of worship, but the content has more than an academic focus.

In a small group of six, to a maximum of eleven students, the events of each person's life may be looked at in the light of what is being studied at the time. The syllabus provides academic content, but equal emphasis is given to how that material related to our experience and can help us understand our life as ministry.

Logistics are simple. A group meets once a week for a little over two hours (including food time) except during the summer months. The full EfM program covers four years – but asks commitment for only one year at a time. Other years can be taken at other times (even non-sequentially) and in other places across the country. At the end of each year in EfM, Sewanee confers on each participant eighteen hours of continuing education credit, which can be applied to other programs and degrees, but most people who take EfM say that is the least of the reasons they have chosen to continue.

Let me tell you briefly about several "ah-ha!" experiences I had in my EfM group this summer. I cannot relate exactly what was done and said in our sessions since we adopted a rule of confidentiality. Individuals may reveal what they wish about themselves as long as the integrity of others in the group is protected. My luck of the draw placed me in a group with eight women, which began with a remark like, "You seem remarkably open for a man." As it turned out, I was the only ordained person to be trained, the only one with a theological degree, and the only one who had never been through the full EfM before. A precarious beginning for me, but the group was gracious. They encouraged me to add theological insights to the material we choose to examine and unselfconsciously thanked me for my contributions. The stuff of our lives that the group brought to the seminar opened new understandings of the texts to me which my seminary education had not even touched upon.

I began to think that my everyday life was as marvelous a gift and means of revelation as theology tells us.

Early on, when I offered to present an incident from my past for theological reflection, several persons commented that I certainly was brave to volunteer myself when I hadn't been through the program (not that I really had a choice), but they would walk me through it. I was quite undone when they actually applauded my offering, however tentative and simplistic. I began to think that my everyday life was as marvelous a gift and means of revelation as theology tells us. EfM encourages a thoughtful consideration of our lives, not simply of the material presented for study.

One woman told us what she thought was a mundane story about beaten biscuits, which on theological reflection shook her foundations. She had agreed to cook up that part of the meal for a church program, but when a man in the parish presented her with a package of the biscuit mix, she found herself saying she simply had too much to do to make them. When he replied, "You said you would," she went off home with the package, in a snit, and baked the biscuits full of resentment (misplaced modifier intended). In the process she could not avoid asking herself if she was prepared to perpetuate the passive aggressive behavior upon others, and was that the kind of life she wanted to live? Painful questions, but ones which led her to exchange her old life for one which was more life giving. The beaten biscuits battered her into triumph over temper tantrums, you might say.

I may be overly enthusiastic about this opportunity. There's always a fly in the ontological ointment, of course. This offering is not entirely a free lunch, even with St. Mary's support and discount. Still, it costs nowhere near what a course at any of our nine universities in Richmond would charge. A year's program (which doesn't meet during June, July, and August) is $295, not counting what it costs to have a life changing experience along with a thoughtful theological theophany. The lure is learning to do this together in a way that is different from anything most of us have encountered. In a nutshell, (if not in the ointment), what EfM holds out to us is the promise of academic integrity, thoughtful reflection, and spiritual vitality. This mornings baptism is a good beginning, it calls us (if I may say so) to turn a new Page in our spiritual direction, to renew our covenant with what is most important to us, and to rejoice in the interrelation of tradition and life.

THE UNMERCIFUL SERVANT

A Parable About Someone Else

17th Sunday after Pentecost
Matthew 18:21-35
Proper 19 – Year A – September 15, 2002

In the aftermath of all that has been offered about 9/11 among the media, I have nothing to add on this occasion that would be either instructive or uplifting. Except to note my own awareness that so often my life has also been significantly challenged and changed by paying attention to little events which can pass by almost unnoticed in the immense scheme of things.

That awareness was again awakened for me by a chance remembrance this week of an occurrence occasioned by our dog nearly fifteen years ago. I realize that pet stories pale in comparison to shattering incidents surrounding September 11th, but this one is related to the central theme of the scripture appointed for this Sunday: forgiveness. And it posed again this question for me, which I am willing to pass on to you.

Do you know what it is like to need to forgive? Almost everyone knows what it is like to need forgiving – for something we have done and are sorry for. But can you recall a time when you needed to forgive someone and you couldn't quite do it?

Last week I recalled such a time, not over anything earth-shattering, but a small matter – of love – which clearly I cared about more than I knew. Fifteen years ago, when we moved from what we called our minifarm in Manakin-Sabot (which P.O. address, Fred Buechner said sounded like a front for a phony psychiatrist). When we moved from there into the teeming city of Richmond, we brought along with us a pair of pure-bred white German shepherds. One was my wife's dog – Norka, which was Polish for the name of our daughter, Nora – and the other was mine, called Nicko, St. Nick-o-las, a kind of Christmas present. They had had the run of the wild in Goochland and adjustment to suburban living was hard. Nicko was large and loving and faithful – and fierce when it came to other dogs. He would lick me tenderly, a person protector – but put behind a barred yard, whenever he got out of it, he'd act as though he'd like to have every dog for dinner. And he was too huge for my wife to handle by herself.

So the unbearable decision was to put him down. And I have never quite forgiven myself for that. It is a sadness which lingers with me, my only dog, a regret that cannot be undone, a tender spot that hurts when you rub it. But my story has to do with shortly after that when our survivor dog, Norka, was trying to get used to the trauma of starting school (not that she had to go, but my wife and I were both teachers then) – which meant Norka had to stay in the yard alone all day long – after a summer of riding with us most everywhere we went, swimming in the lake, unlimited balls to retrieve every afternoon, and unending biscuits for the begging.

Early in the morning the first day of school, the people who came to paint our house, by mistake left the fence door to the back yard a little ajar – and she was out. At first, she lay down near the house, and the painters tried to grab her. The more they chased her to catch her, the farther away she went – until she didn't dare come anywhere near the house. Finally, she was nowhere around, and by night she had not returned, nor the next morning and on through the day, and by night again we were very sad. Sad because no one intended harm and everyone did the best he could. But all our searching did not bring the sound of her tinkling collar home, or her scratch at the door.

Looking at the readings for this service, I was struck by something in Matthew's gospel that seemed so odd: Despite the blessings and kindness that had been shown to the servant who was forgiven an incalculable debt, he in turn could not forgive others for a very little that was owed him. How could that be, I wondered – before I was rudely reminded of how hard it is sometimes for me to forgive. I wanted to say to the painters: anyone could have done the same thing; don't be distressed over an unforeseeable situation; everyone makes mistakes. But I could not bring myself to say it.

"Lord, how often ought I forgive my brother or sister?" asks Peter, "As many as seven times?" And Jesus said to him, "Not seven times, but seventy times seven." How hard a saying that is. (It is harder still when you realize that in Jesus' tradition the number of completeness is three; and therefore seven times is two times the number of completeness and yet one more! And what about seventy-times seven?)

We all have things we need to forgive others for. Maybe you need to forgive your parents for sending you away to school, and for dumping you off there and leaving. I can remember as a young child being torn, pleading and sobbing, from an iron railing by the pool and dragged into the water because my parents were determined I should learn to swim like the other children my age. Maybe your sister took your favorite dress and ruined it and lied about it to your parents. Or a roommate made fun of you and egged on others to pick on you when you could not defend yourself. Maybe your child could not bear the life he or she knew and took it into his/her hands to end it. Perhaps someone cheated on a boyfriend – or someone on his wife. Perhaps you failed a test or contest which was clearly unfair. Can you think of the wrongs of life and people that you need to forgive – in order to have your own life back again?

I can, and that's why this parable in the Gospel of Matthew does not seem as strange to me as it does to some of the commentaries I have read about it. Lord knows the times I have needed to forgive, and wanted to forgive, trying to remember what a blessed thing it is to be forgiven – and yet I could not, to save myself.

Have you ever thought about the meaning of the words in the Lord's Prayer? Here I give you a more literal translation from the familiar in Matthew: "Forgive us our sins (or trespasses), as we have forgiven those who have sinned (or trespassed) against us." In that same passage Jesus adds, "For if you forgive others their trespasses, your heavenly Father will also forgive you, but if you do not forgive others their trespasses, neither will your Father forgive you your trespasses."

I began to realize that the Lord's Prayer asks God to "forgive us our wrongs as we have [already] forgiven those who have wronged us." An unwelcome understanding for me. It also says we must forgive if we would be heard by God -which explains the not-sowell known saying from Matthew: "If you are offering your gift at the altar (meaning for most of us, putting money in the collection plate) and remember that your brother or sister has something against you, leave your offering there before the altar and go and be reconciled with him; then come and offer your gift." It means that being reconciled to our brothers and sisters is a precondition for asking God's forgiveness for ourselves.

Forgiveness enables forgiveness; showing mercy brings love to the heart of the one who is forgiving. What an astounding idea. When we choose to remain angry, determined to get what we feel we are owed, we discover we are no longer able to experience the forgiveness of others. As the saying goes: "We are not so much punished for our sins as by our sins."

Back to the parable: If we cannot find a crumb of mercy for the hard-hearted servant, we then end up no better than the unmerciful servant himself, who has failed to forgive. If we forget to return the mercy we have been shown by others, we will bring down upon us the very judgment we have pronounced on someone else.

The wonderful and terrible secret I discovered about this parable is that it is a mirror. As I point the accusing finger at the unmerciful servant who cannot forgive what he is owed (from his friends, his family, his life) – as I point the finger at him in the mirror, what I see is my finger pointing back at me. I am the unforgiving one! That's the bad news.

The good news is that when the unmerciful servant asks forgiveness, it is given. *That* is what I want to leave with you.

The end of the story I started with did not come until the third day when Norka, dirt stained and depleted, under the cover of night leapt unseen into the back of the Jeep I had left open. In the light of the sun we rejoiced to find her there, but by then I still had not made my peace with the forgiveness I needed to give. A little like the annual lesson of the school year, which I had struggled with ever since I could remember: Even though it comes to an end, the light and life, the darkness and disappointments are not done yet. They live on in us the following year, awaiting our forgiveness – not so much for others as for ourselves.

If only we could remember to seize this moment, this time, this day while we have it. Forgiveness gives life. If God could forgive even the unmerciful servant (whom I know firsthand and not as a stranger because I know myself), why would I, you, we not know that we have already been forgiven. Let us accept that forgiveness, that we may live and give life not just this day but in the days to come.

LIVING OR DYING TO THE LORD

17th Sunday after Pentecost
Matthew 18:21-35
Proper 19 – Year A – September 11, 2005

Four years ago on the 11th of September we woke up to a beautiful day, and it nearly killed us. How well we remember the beauty of the day and the horror of the events that followed. Some say it was the worst attack on America in history; in any case, it burned into our brains a series of heart-breaking images that we'll never forget. And what does the church lectionary appointed for this day have to offer us in this time of remembrance? A parable about forgiveness – and an outrageous one at that. Give us a break. No wonder people accuse the church of being other-worldly.

To be fair to the scripture, Jesus' words have a sense of urgency to them – for him not just a matter of liberty, but of life. But at the start of what is to me a new year, I'm almost too overcome to give them the time of day. For me, today is the beginning of the church year; for most of my life the academic calendar has always supplanted the official church year calendar, which as we know begins with Advent, somewhere around the beginning of December. Just last week a lot of people were in the Labor Day barbecue mode, and suddenly the Fall has fallen upon us and some of us may now feel more like the pig on the spit roasting over the fires of life, most recently in New Orleans and in our remembrance of 9/11.

Every year I say to myself, I'll spend more time preparing for the Fall, but summer seduces me into forgetting that, and the

363

first Sunday after Labor Day pounces upon us with list of Fall tasks, lists of school supplies, new demands starting up, committees, and classes beginning again after a summer of benign neglect – and now in addition the memory of 9/11 which smacks us in the face along with the offal of New Orleans. And in the midst of all that, the church in its belligerent blessedness asks us to ponder seriously Peter's petulant petition: "Lord, how often shall my brother sin against me and I forgive him? As many as seven times? (which represented twice the Hebrew number of completeness, plus one).

You all know Jesus' answer, and it's certainly not what I want to hear right now: "Seventy times seven," he says. What kind of help is that? Peter was not asking the question philosophically or theoretically, but personally. He wanted help, not homilies. Be realistic, I hear him say. When have I finally done my duty and have the right to send those S.O.B.s packing? To which, Jesus replies with a story of the servant who received mercy from the king who forgave him a debt he could never possibly have repaid; whereupon, the servant then fell upon someone poorer than himself, seized him by the throat, and refused to forgive him a minor debt, demanding full payment or being imprisoned. A debtor himself, he is unable to forgive the debts of others. I know something about that – I've been there.

The problem with forgiveness, as the parable points out if we have the patience to pay attention to it, is that while we can point to numerous times when others have not been forgiving to us, that doesn't address the dilemma. Because, just as God has been willing to forgive us time and time again, well beyond what we deserve, so I can also always find more that is in need of forgiveness in others. We can always assume there is more room for forgiveness then we think we owe. Furthermore, in the face of 9/11, the problem becomes more prickly; we may be persuaded by the words of one rabbi who said, "I have no right to forgive the suffering and death others caused someone else – that's God's business."

And some people still wonder about the place of God in such an awful event. The Bible, of course, has no direct answer to our particular problem, but it speaks to the place of God in the midst of suffering and in the need of forgiveness. I'm sure some of you remember in the Old Testament the fate of Joseph in his personal 9/11 when his own brothers, overwhelmed with jealousy, conspire to kill him; they strip him, throw him into a pit and sell him into slavery in Egypt (the equivalent of death) telling his father that his son is dead. There, Joseph manages to survive and eventually to become governor of the land, second only to Pharaoh himself, and is put in charge of food during a merciless famine.

When his brothers come to Egypt from Israel, begging to buy grain, he reveals to them his true identity, and they fear for their lives. But he says to them, "Do not be afraid. Am I in the place of God? Even though you intended to do harm to me, God intended it for good.... So I myself will provide for you and your little ones." We expect that he would have been bitter and angry and sought to avenge the wrongs done him, but his willingness to forgive empowers him to seek reconciliation rather than revenge. Maybe we have to remind ourselves that this story is about grace and forgiveness, not about justice.

So where is God in all of this? The answer is simpler to say than to see: "God is in God's people [those who are willing to be God's people]. And if the world can see this, it provides a powerful lesson in our post 9/11 world,"[1] which may just begin to transform evil into good. Does that sound to you simply like a weak and sniveling sort of strength? Well, only the strong are willing to try themselves in that strength. And because we cannot be God, that does not mean we do nothing. Sometimes we have to carry on in the face of hurt in strength that is not our own.

Some will ask cynically then, where is the church in all of this? Where is the church when it hurts? Author Philip Yancey says, "If the church is doing its job – binding up wounds, comforting the grieving, [sheltering the homeless], offering food to the hungry – I don't think people will wonder so much where God is, when it hurts. They'll know where God is, in the presence of his people....[2] We in our own strength cannot transform the reality of evil into the promise of good; that's God's doing, and a mystery few of us can fathom except in faith; but we can join in the process and marvel at what can happen if we are willing to become the people God has called us to be.

Sometimes, it seems, we can do nothing to change things, only pray that we ourselves may be changed. We know that prayer changes the people who pray, but what does it do to change the lives of those for whom we pray, those in whom death and despair and anger and violence have a foothold? Henri Nouwen, in his book The *Wounded Healer*, recommends prayer, "not as a 'decoration of life,' but as the breath of human existence. A Christian community is a healing community," he says, "not because wounds are cured and pains alleviated, but because wounds and pains become openings or occasions for a new vision."[3]

Speaking for myself, to have a new vision, I need the fuel of forgiveness to help get me started moving beyond the set ways I'm comfortable with and am usually unwilling to give up. It may be that I have not the right to forgive the suffering and death someone else has caused in the lives of others – that that's God's work, so to speak – but I can forgive the person himself who has wronged them or me, and thereby free myself from the roadblock which keeps me from acting to change myself first and then be available to help the kind of change that brings life to others.

The most powerful symbol of that process is in a story we are all familiar with, in Jesus' own 9/11 on the cross, when God takes the evil of the crucifixion and transforms it into forgiveness, new life, and what we call the day of salvation. If we can remember on this September day the power of that day, which did indeed irrevocably change the world, perhaps we could go forth in hope rather than bitterness, in faith rather than un-forgiveness – and in the power of God who changes the world one day at a time, beginning with me. Who knows what we could do together?

———

1. *Homiletics* 17, 3-p.17
2. *Homiletics* - p.1
3. *Homiletics* - p.20

HEARING CHRIST'S REVOLUTIONARY WORDS ABOUT BELONGING TO THE COMMUNITY OF FAITH

18th Sunday after Pentecost
Mark 9:38-48
Proper 21 – Year B – September 29, 1991

I doubt you're as deaf as I am. I am clearly capable of hearing a revolutionary statement and not understanding that it is revolutionary. May be that is because, as the saying goes, "If you're not part of the solution (the revolution), then you're part of the problem" (the part that's deaf to the call for revolution.) Nevertheless, even I am able to hear something revolutionary in what Jesus says in the gospel reading today.

"Revolutionary," if I may define it, is something like a fundamental and radical change in a position, perspective, or point of view. What Jesus says to his disciples is upsetting, off-putting, and uplifting. I wonder if you, too, caught it. "John said to Jesus, 'Teacher, we saw a man casting out a demon in your name, and we forbade him, because he was not one of our followers.' But Jesus said, 'Do not forbid him; for no one who does a good work in my name will be able soon after to speak ill of me. FOR WHOEVER IS NOT AGAINST US IS FOR US.'" What is so *revolutionary* about that? Only everything.

His disciples were scandalized that someone who stood outside their Christian community dared to perform a work of healing in Jesus' name. What right had he to invoke Jesus, when he wasn't even one of his followers. The disciples were clear about who was "in" and who was "out" and why. They wanted to establish themselves collectively as better than those who were not part of their group and therefore had no right to call upon the name of Jesus. That reminds me of the time when, as a child, I wasn't allowed in the Black Skull Club – which I had helped found – because I didn't weigh enough. After all, you couldn't call yourself a terrorist if you weighed only 80 pounds.

Jesus' disciples wanted the boundaries of Christian community to be clearly drawn. A school I taught at in New Hampshire was visited by a group called FOCUS (which stood for Fellowship of Christians in Colleges and Schools.) These young people thought themselves so correctly Christian that they caused a split among the students at our school who called themselves Christian, by implying "You're not really Christian because you don't understand the faith the way we do. Their evangelism became so divisive that I actually had to forbid that Christian group from coming on campus; they set one part of our fellowship against another, making some "in" and others "out."

In his response to John, Jesus reacts sharply to the smugness and certainty of the disciples who were so sure that they were his true followers. Instead of demanding some orthodox statement of belief or behavior, which would qualify them to call upon his name, thereby throwing up a barrier to the so-called "outsiders," Jesus throws open the doors to his community: "Do not forbid him ... he that is not against us is for us." Jesus' point is clear as one commentator puts it: anyone who performs a service in Christ's name becomes a member of his fellowship and community.

Dangerous thinking! Imagine a club, or even membership among a close group of friends without at least some "unwritten" rules to determine who can be a part of it. That's as subversive as saying "The last shall be first and the first last" ... which our educational systems and our own expectations of success often refuse to acknowledge when push comes to shove. One of the reasons that kind of thinking is so subversive is that it not only threatens our security, it asks us to get beyond our comfortable certainties and expand our established ideas of what belonging to a community of faith is all about.

———⊸◦⊶———

"I listened carefully to the liturgy and I felt I was invited."

———⊸◦⊶———

One Sunday at St. Mary's a familiar visitor, who happened to be Asian, came forward to take the sacrament at Communion. After the service, the rector, who had said all Baptized Christians were welcome to receive the body and blood of Christ, spoke to the man, expressing how pleased he was that this fellow had come forward. The rector then asked him where he had been baptized. The man said he hadn't; in fact, he was a Buddhist. "But," he explained, "I listened carefully to the liturgy and I felt I was invited." Sometimes in spite of ourselves we catch the spirit of the occasion which is bigger than all of us and which frees us in spite of the barriers we carefully put up to protect us.

My father, who was a pillar and Senior Warden of a small church in Connecticut, would sit in the front pew every Sunday and very visibly refuse to say the Creed when it came time – because, he said, in being honest about his faith, who could ever believe that? In contrast, I remember a former Mathematics teacher of mine (who declared himself an atheist, but who also had to go to church along with the rest of us students who were required to be there eight times a week at that school) would very deliberately stand say the Creed aloud. I asked him how he could do that when he wasn't a Christian. He said, "I say the Creed not because I believe it is true, but because I hope that it will become true."

I have thought often about the question who was more faithful, my father or my Math teacher? My guess is that Jesus wouldn't be offended either way, and would rejoice in the quality of the lives both of them lived.

I sometimes think it is *less* true that *God* works in strange ways than that *we* do. We can get so bogged down in the *formulas* and language of the Church that we fail to listen to the stories the church tells of how God speaks and works his way with us in spite of our invincible certainty about how God ought to work and speak with us. Beginning with the stories of our lives.

Frederick Buechner reminds us that if we want to know where God is in the world we have to begin by looking at ourselves. Wherever we have received courage or kindness or forgiveness or mercy, there God is at work, even if we do not recognize it or call it by the proper name. Wherever we have somehow managed to show kindness and caring, generosity and love, there God is at work in us, though we deny it to his face.

I once taught a course in Christian theology with Buechner who, when he was asked in a faculty meeting which theological terms he required the students to learn, scandalized our colleagues by saying, "None. What I want them to know is how to recognize the experience behind those terms in their own lives; but I could care less whether they know the proper words." Martin Copenhauer, in an eBook called *Living Faith While Having Doubts*, says it is time we outgrew our "truth fairies" and tried to prevent "truth decay." He says we need to face up to our fairy-tale faith in "Heaven and Oz, God and Santa Claus, life after death and the enchanted forests" – which we held as children and find new ways to express the reality of them as adults. Otherwise we will love the life out of them the way they *were*. We need to recover the blessing they once had for us in a different disguise:

> One needs to be able to say "Bless you, Truth Fairy" just as one says "Bless you" to a sneeze. Ever wonder why sneezes evoke a "Bless you" from total strangers, while coughs, hiccups, burping or breaking wind do not receive the same reverential treatment? In early Roman times the proper response to a sneeze was *Absit omen!* ("Evil

Spirit, begone!") The contemporary "Bless You" was made official by an early pope, because, during the seventh century, Italy was infested by an unidentified plague which was characterized by several sneezes followed by sudden death. The pope told his flock to ward off the sneezes with a blessing.

(If you never thought of *Gesundheit!* as a theological word, here's your chance to rethink it.)

In that same vein; and unknowingly, I'm sure, Theodor Seuss Geisel, celebrated author of children's books, left us a freewheeling commentary on today's gospel reading, which I will leave you with. In a commencement address at a college in Illinois, he said:

"It seems behooven upon me to bring forth great words of wisdom to this graduating class as it leaves these cloistered halls to enter the outside world ... My wisdom is in rather short supply, and I have managed to condense everything I know into this epic poem consisting of fourteen lines, entitled 'My Uncle Terwilliger on the Art of Eating Popovers'"

> *My uncle ordered popovers*
> *From the restaurant's bill of fare*
> *And when they were served, he regarded them*
> *With a penetrating stare...*
> *Then he spoke great words of wisdom*
> *And he sat them on the chair.*
> *"To eat these things," said my uncle,*
> *"You must exercise great care.*
> *You may swallow down what's solid...*
> *But... you must spit out the air!"*
> *And, as you partake*
> *of the world's bill of fare,*
> *That's darned good advice to follow*
> *Do a lot of spitting out of the hot air,*
> *And be careful what you swallow.*[1]

———

1. Theodor Seuss Geisel, Lake Forest College Lake Forest, Illinois, June 4, 1977

ON BEING USED

18th Sunday after Pentecost
Hebrews 13:1-2; Luke 14:34-35
Year C – September 30, 2007

Let mutual love continue. Do not neglect to show hospitality to strangers, for by doing that some have entertained angels without knowing it.

Hebrews 13:1-2

Salt is good; but if salt has lost its taste, how can its saltiness be restored? It is fit neither for the soil nor for the manure heap; they throw it away. Let anyone with ears to hear listen!

Luke 14:34-35

On this 130th year of the building of St. Mary's Church, this morning's testament to Tuckahoe is a theological treatise of sorts on the blessings of being used – offered with gratitude, with great affection and, for the sake of this sermon, with a proposal for us to ponder or put off. As texts, I have taken two verses from Paul's Letter to the Hebrews on the ministry of hospitality and entertaining angels unawares and added two other verses from the Gospel of Luke reflecting on the cost of discipleship and the price of salt. So, cutting short the commentary let me now come back to our context.

Tuckahoe, as some of you know is inextricably a part of St. Mary's parish. It embodies our roots. Because little Mary Mitchell

Allen, who lived here, became the soul and source of St. Mary's Church when, after she died in August of 1865, scarcely 8 months old, her parents sought some fitting and lasting way to remember her life. They managed to raise some $1,500, a significant sum to garner at that time in the South, enough to begin building a small white Carpenter's Gothic church on River Road in 1877. (The Wickhams of nearby Woodside donated the land.) So the beloved daughter's name became inseparable from the selection of our patron saint and lives on in the enduring life of historic "Little St. Mary's."

And in our day, the Thompsons who were probably here at Tuckahoe about the time that I and my family came to St. Mary's in 1975, have continued to carry on the mission work of our church with and among all sorts and conditions of us. I, as many of you, have been wined and dined here on numerous occasions, even when Sue and Tad Thompson knew not me or you from Adam. Whether or not they had read our first text from the Letter to the Hebrews, they have continued to act on Paul's pronouncement: "Let mutual love continue. Do not neglect to show hospitality to strangers, for by doing that some have entertained angels without knowing it."

From way back, I knew I was no angel, but that never dampened Tuckahoe's welcome to me and countless miscreants who have made their way to these traditional halls. Members of St. Mary's may have had special treatment over the years, but I can attest that I was welcomed royally under other auspices, in organizations that never knew St. Mary's Church. I rejoice in the thought that God knows how many angels are in the making for having partaken of Tuckahoe's unselfish welcome. In church we would call that outreach, here it goes unaccounted for – it's just what Tuckahoe does best.

My gospel text is also a trademark of Tuckahoe and could be an inspiration to us all. It has to do with salt. You've heard Jesus' expression of admiration: "You are the salt of the earth," with which he addressed his disciples. And elsewhere when he said, "Have salt in yourselves, and be at peace with one another." This, as academics say, may need some unpacking since we do not usually use the metaphor that way anymore. We still say "Pass the salt," but doctors warn us against even that, pressuring us to pass it by to avoid high blood pressure among the French fry faithful or the frozen food fanciers.

Some of you may be surprised to learn from *Salt: A World History* by Mark Kurlansky, that in ancient times salt was "often more valuable to humans than gold.... In the first century world of Jesus, salt was used as cash currency. The Roman soldiers... were often paid in salt." You may not know that "the Latin word for salt (sal) became the basis for the word 'salary' and the origin of the expression 'He's worth his salt'.... The ancients knew that salt was an essential element ... as a food preservative, a seal for wooden shipping containers, and even as an aphrodisiac." (I suddenly see more interest evidenced on the faces of the faithful here.) Plato went so far as to say it was "especially near to the gods."[1]

Biblically speaking, "The Israelites took it a step further... [covering] their sacrifices in salt as a sign of the eternal nature and preservation of the covenant between God and God's people." Leviticus refers to Israel's connection to God as a "covenant of salt" (2:13). And they rubbed salt on newborn infants to protect them from evil.[2]

On the shadow side of the shaker, so to speak, "salt could also be used as a sign of judgment and destruction, as in Judges (9:45) where Abimelech destroyed the city of Shechem and 'scattered salt over it' ..." This is more in line with our lectionary reading where Jesus comments with a curious slant on salt. "Salt is good," he says (it makes things taste better and last longer). "But if salt has lost its taste, how can [its] saltiness be restored?" He didn't want his disciples "to lose their flavor and usefulness." A peculiar usage because we assume that the salt on our table never loses its saltiness.

The explanation behind his saying is that salt in Jesus' day, coming from evaporation of sea water or salt lakes such as the Dead Sea, contained contaminates such as calcium salts which when standing for a long time would absorb water and leach away, leaving mostly chalk, "something that's great for the blackboard and ball fields but useless in your salad."[3]

Applying the metaphor this morning, true to the Tuckahoe testament, Jesus implies that if disciples lose their saltiness, give up their "flavor," their usefulness, then they become of no use to God or anyone else – even for the manure pile (which comment probably needs some more unpacking). In ancient Israel, where wood was scarce, they used camel and donkey dung for fuel, which they gathered and patted into patties to dry in the sun. They learned that "dung patties burn better when they are salted and placed on a block of salt in an earth oven," but when the salt had been leached it lost its ability to make the dung burn and so it was no longer good for anything, neither fit for the table nor the oven, and was simply discarded.[4]

By now, the metaphor Jesus commended to his disciples may have become somewhat distasteful to some of you. He implies that unsalted disciples are not of much use, not even "fit for the manure pile" or "to preserve animal droppings for field fertilization."[5]

Imagine being deemed a disciple of Jesus so useless that you don't even qualify as endearing for the dung heap, which pungently makes the point that followers can be useful ("worth their salt," so to speak) only if they are used. Of course, these days we have convinced ourselves that being "used" is a bad thing. We are fearful of being taken advantage of, becoming servile to or dumped on by someone else. So Jesus' words are not all that compatible for us when he says "whoever would become great among you must be servant of all." What, then do we do with that? Well, whatever else, it raises a question many of us don't often consider, namely: where does God want to use me? Who among those around me that are hurting, in need, desperate, cast down could use some of me right now? (That's intended as food for thought, not salt in our wounds.)

Remember Paul' s pleading: "Do not neglect to show hospitality to strangers, for by doing that some have entertained angels without knowing it." And pay attention to Jesus' proposal to us that when we are willing to be used, we too become" the salt of the earth" – common, but companions of the kingdom.

So it is that St. Mary's has been handed the heritage of Tuckahoe. We are becoming receivers and givers of this savory blessing: "You are the salt of the earth. Go forth with a taste of God's goodness on your tongues and tell the world of his love."[6] Amen.

———

1. *Homiletics* 16, 5-p.17)
2. *Ibid.*
3. *Op. cit.*, p.18
4. *Op. cit.* p.17
5. *Ibid.*
6. *Op. cit.*, p.20

ON BEING NOT PREPARED FOR LIFE

19th Sunday After Pentecost
Mark 10:35-45
Proper 24 – Year B – October 22, 2000

James and John, the sons of Zebedee, came forward to Jesus and said to him, "Teacher, we want you to do for us whatever we ask of you." And he said to them, "What is it you want me to do for you?" And they said to him, "Grant us to sit, one at your right hand and one at your left, in your glory." But Jesus said to them, "You do not know what you are asking. Are you able to drink the cup that I drink, or be baptized with the baptism that I am baptized with?" They replied, "We are able." Then Jesus said to them, "The cup that I drink you will drink; and with the baptism with which I am baptized, you will be baptized; but to sit at my right hand or at my left is not mine to grant, but it is for those for whom it has been prepared. "

When the ten heard this, they began to be angry with James and John. So Jesus called them and said to them, "You know that among the Gentiles those whom they recognize as their rulers lord it over them, and their great ones are tyrants over them. But it is not so among you; but whoever wishes to become great among you must be your servant, and whoever wishes to be first among you must be slave

*of all. For the Son of Man came not to be served but
to serve, and to give his life as a ransom for many."*

Mark 10:35-45

"*Sky and Telescope* magazine's website tells the Hale-Bopp comet watcher's story of the anonymous four-year-old who exclaimed, 'Mommy, Mommy, I saw the vomit.' We all see what we are prepared to see, and we all hear what we are prepared to hear. ... [So saying] What are we prepared to see and hear about Jesus, and what is the gospel we are not prepared for?"[1]

Depending on who you are, the reading from the Gospel of Mark may happily serve to satisfy your dislike for James and John, the "opportunists" among the disciples. But if you hear the story slightly differently, it may strike you as singularly offensive. The offense would not be the result of our dashed image of two "saints" among Jesus' disciples, who were inelegantly if not inexcusably attempting to wrangle an unworthy personal promotion. Rather, what may really rankle us is the image Jesus uses to inform his followers how they are to see themselves and to understand their potential for greatness – as "slaves" or "servants" (depending on your translation of the Bible), the words intend the same meaning. We can't soften the stigma by insisting that "things were different" in the first century, where the step between slave and free was "relatively small" in the Greco-Roman world. It is said that sometimes people sold themselves into slavery in order to climb the social ladder. Slavery offered status to the servant if the master had status in that society. But in the Jewish world at the time of Jesus, slavery was looked down upon because it was an enactment of oppression and servility upon God's people. That kind of humility was indeed humiliation.

The importance of humility could prove to be a problem for them *and* for us. The pericope pictures James and John seeking to procure for themselves positions of prominence and honor – to sit at Jesus' right and left hand "in his glory." Not so unthinkable – surely it was only a matter of time before someone else among the disciples would ask for the same thing. James and John simply had the chutzpah to speak first. Jesus tries to tell them that they do not understand what they are asking. He offers them his cup of suffering instead, but he cannot promise them the prestige they presume comes with suffering for the greatness of God's kingdom, even if they were willing. They won't hear that: "We're ready for anything," they say, "we just want the seats of honor that come with the Kingdom." Ready for anything except Jesus' understanding that the greatest of them is the one willing to be the servant of others. "Whoever wishes to be first among you, must be willing to be slave of all," Jesus says patiently and with a certain sadness.

The other ten, it turns out, turn on James and John not because their inflated egos are insufferable but because the brothers were willing to sacrifice their friends' opportunity to be first and to ensure their own comfortable futures. Peter echoed not only the outrage of the others over the arrogance of James and John, but their anger at the apparent loss of that appointment for them all. And yet, amazingly to me, Jesus does not judge them, nor does he berate them for their unwillingness to understand. He asks only "Are you willing to put yourself on the line so that the lives of others may be better?" Maybe we, like they, are offended not because he seeks to impose upon others the idea of slavery as a way of life for "poor unfortunates," but because he invites us to accept it as our intentional way of everyday living. That's what we find unacceptably offensive.

I can readily relate why that idea is obnoxious by explaining my own experiences and my unwillingness to accept the outcome of that wisdom when it overturned many of my unspoken expectations and entitlements, which I assumed in my education. The forge of my formative years took the form of a Northeastern boarding school, which in my case inadvertently encouraged a sort of spiritual aristocracy. For instance, I remember learning the French for one of the beatitudes, best known as "Blessed are the gentle ("the meek," as the King James says it), for they shall inherit the earth." The French says "Blessed are the *debonnaire*." Secretly, we assumed we were destined to speak as the debonnaires. The school motto was "Teach us those things on earth, the knowledge of which endures in heaven." I knew I must be on the right path: only embrace these lofty and virtuous precepts and you too will inherit a world in which you can afford to send your son to a school such as that, whose facilities would put the finest of our Southern schools (and, many colleges) to shame.

---

*"Ah, Christophe! What will become
of you when you go out to conquer the real
world and you tell them, 'All I can do is row'"*

As I remember it, the exalted expectations of the honor system there made the ones at UVA seem almost adolescent. (How I survived, I can't say.) The school symbol pictured the pelican tearing open its own breast for its babies to feast on when it had found no food to feed its young – which I recall finding inspiring if not impossible. I must have learned my lessons well since graduation bestowed on me The School Medal. (When the engraving on it misspelled "virtue" [in Latin], I should have suspected something.) The only hint I had at my lack of humility came from my favorite French teacher who told me, "Ah, Christophe! What will become of you when you go out to conquer the real world and you tell them, 'All I can do is row'" – the sport of kings. Would that I could have given him the memorable rejoinder from *Ben Hur*: "Row well and live."

Many years later a friend of mine said it best for me when he spoke about his own experiences at that school: "It didn't prepare me for life," he said sorrowfully; it assumed the impossible and the impractical, the world doesn't work like that. He was serving in the government in Washington at the time as a civil servant, who gave his idealism and his all for an amorphous position related to arms appropriations (or some such), attempting to limit the extent of nuclear armament. He didn't bother to dress like all the others who were ascending the ladder, bucking for a higher rung on the civil service stairway; and if he didn't always punch the time clock promptly he would stay late into the evening after everyone else had gone home. As one co-worker expressed it, "He was too good to be true." It was true; they fired him because he did not fit the mold – his career flushed, his dedication download-ed. What he stood for wasn't rewarded in that work place, where vision and virtue were not viewed as virtues.

After I had finished flinging myself out of airplanes in my military service, I walked the streets of New York City looking for work, college diploma in hand. Having nobly rejected my father's business contacts to get a job – that would have been cheating others who had no entrée – I finally managed to get an assign-ment to work in the mail room in a small family-run religious publishing house – that is, religiously right, almost Birch Society, along with an allegiance to health foods and Irish poetry. Because the firm was poor, larger, "name" firms stole our authors and bought their manuscripts out from under us. My mistake was that I wanted to be in publishing because I believed, naively, that it was the last noble business. What I discovered was neither it nor I could survive nobly that way against the cut-throat competi-tion who had learned those things on earth that would yield an economic increase of thirty to a hundred-fold well before heaven. (Granted, I was young in mind as well as heart.)

I still didn't grasp the logic until I turned to teaching in an-other boarding school where (also as crew coach) on my first day at the boathouse I spied a sign on the wall which said "Winning isn't everything, it' s the *only* thing." I recalled years earlier, on my school debating team, visiting that highly competitive institu-tion to challenge what we called the unruly intellectual barbar-ians on their team who had no respect for the rules of rhetoric or fair argument and who stamped their feet, impatient for us to begin, and who were implacably certain we had no chance of winning. (They were right – *despite* our impeccable declamation.) On their impressive academic building, chiseled into the massive granite stones over the entrance, the forbidding Latin inscription said, "Come hither boys, that you may be made men." (That was inscribed in the days before the school invited co-education, but

I am told it still stands as an enduring acerbic if inappropriate epithet.)[1] In those days their Senior class had more National Merit Scholarship finalists than any other high school in the country. They did not suffer fools lightly, and they prospered in the knowledge that you didn't get ahead unless you stepped in front of someone; selfdenial was sentimental suicide. Being servant of all would surely end in slavery.

So why do we keep struggling with Jesus' words about finding greatness in serving others when the way of the world warns us that humility doesn't pay off in the honor or the high places we expect? Let me offer some suggestions. Maybe it begins with our unexpected awareness that the world we live in is better for us when it is characterized by random acts of kindness and people practicing tolerance, tenderness, and self-restraint. Or with the realization that we all need a helping hand now and then. Maybe it's our reticent recognition that James and John aren't the only social climbers, name-droppers, and brown-nosers we have known who maneuver for personal gain – beginning with ourselves, who probably pestered our teachers for higher grades or pushed for personal promotion at work or have been less charitable to our cherished institutions in the service of creating a larger nest egg for our retirement. Maybe it's my reluctant recognition that the highest service my school could have done me was *not* to "prepare me for life," so that I might come to understand (even if I didn't like it) that worrying about why the world isn't the way it ought to be may be more transforming for us all in the end than our trying to figure out how we can adapt ourselves to the world the way it is.

Jesus' words remain for us more a challenge than a condemnation, a "come hither" invitation that is oddly affirming. He doesn't cast off James and John; neither will he cast us off. He only asks us to consider seriously what we are called to do with our talents in the time we have left to live and work and play and pray. Servanthood is not a requirement God lays upon us. Rather, a recognition that our service, saintly or self-serving, is used by God and others to reveal to us the kind of life we believe God intends for us. Let us therefore, with gratitude and glad hearts "Go in peace to love and serve the Lord."

———

1. *Biblical Preaching Journal* 10, 4 p. 7

2. When the Phillips Exeter Academy Building was dedicated in 1914, a Latin inscription over the main doorway read: "HUC VENITE PUERI UT VIRI SITIS" ("Come hither, boys, that ye may become men"). In 1996, honoring the first quarter century of coeducation, a new inscription was added: "HIC QUAERITE PUERI PUELLAEQUE VIRTUTEM ET SCIENTIAM" ("Here, boys and girls, seek goodness and knowledge"). https://libguides.exeter.edu/c.php?g=441877&p=3056132

3. I am indebted at various points for insights and observations purloined from the *Biblical Preaching Journal*, Vol. 13, 4 pp. 9-10 and *Lectionary Homiletics* XI, II p. 30.

A CASE OF THE EXPLODING TURKEY

A Sermon for the 19th Sunday after Pentecost
Luke 17:11-19
Proper 23 – Year C – October 14, 2001

> *On the way to Jerusalem Jesus was going through the region between Samaria and Galilee. As he entered a village, ten lepers approached him. Keeping their distance, they called out, saying, "Jesus, Master, have mercy on us!" When he saw them, he said to them, "Go and show yourselves to the priests." And as they went, they were made clean. Then one of them, when he saw that he was healed, turned back, praising God with a loud voice. He prostrated himself at Jesus' feet and thanked him. And he was a Samaritan. Then Jesus asked, "Were not ten made clean? But the other nine, where are they? Was none of them found to return and give praise to God except this foreigner?" Then he said to him, "Get up and go on your way; your faith has made you well."*

> *Luke 17:11-19*

The teaching story or parable about the Ten Lepers who were cured and the one leper who alone among them returned to say "Thank you" may not be of great interest to many of us. That's not just because we heard it read in church and that few of us would admit much experience with leprosy, but also what we may take to be the moral of the story can seem banal, chiding, even childish. Something like: We ought to remember our manners, we ought to be more thankful for the gifts we are given, and we ought to be grateful to those who do good things for us.

Still, to me the story is disturbing, not just because I think of my many unconscious lapses in gratitude but for the spiritual leprosy of one sort or another which many of us have and yet have a hard time recognizing. And the real moral (if that word is appropriate here) is not one I can easily dismiss. It has to do with the profound difference between being cured and being made well, which is uncomfortable enough to apply to your own life; and further, the accompanying judgment that so often (here I'll speak for myself) I "just don't get it"; and worse, the appropriate joy at the heart of the story which I rarely open my eyes to see.

In trying to figure out what to say about all this, I was arrested by two stories this week, which I thought I would pass along to you to think about while I struggle to expound the scripture. The first one comes from Maxie Dunnam[1] who relates an incident told by the famous plastic surgeon Dr. Maxwell Maltz. A woman came to see him about her husband who had been burned and disfigured while attempting to save his parents in a house on fire. He didn't get to them and they both died in the flames. Deeply scarred, he had given up on life and had gone into hiding, refusing to let anyone see him, not even his wife. Dr. Maltz told the woman not to worry. 'With the great advances we've made in plastic surgery in recent years,' I can restore his face.' She explained that he wouldn't let anyone help him because he believed God disfigured his face to punish him for not saving his parents.

Then she made a shocking request: "I want you to disfigure my face so I can be like him! If I can share in his pain, then maybe he will let me back into his life. I love him so much; ... and if that is what it takes; then that is what I want to do."

Of course, Dr. Maltz would not agree, but he was moved deeply by that wife's determined and total love. He got her permission to try to talk to her husband. He went to the man's room and knocked, but there was no answer. He called loudly through the door, "I know you are in there, and I know you can hear me, so I've come to tell you that my name is Dr. Maxwell Maltz. I'm a plastic surgeon, and I want you to know that I can restore your face."

There was no response. Again, he called loudly, "Please come out and let me help restore your face." But again, there was no answer. Still speaking through the door, Dr. Maltz told the man what his wife was asking him to do. "She wants me to disfigure her face, to make her face like yours in the hope that you will let her back into your life. That's how much she loves you ...."

There was a brief moment of silence, and then ever so slowly, the doorknob began to turn. The disfigured man came out to make a new beginning and to find a new life.

The second story is told by Patricia Houck Sprinkle. It first appeared in 1978[2] and tells of a plain, old shoemaker's awl that is on prominent display in the French Academy of Science.

"What makes this awl so special? It was the awl that fell one day from the shoemaker's table and put out the eye of his nine-year-old son. Soon, the child became blind in both eyes and was forced to attend school for the blind. At this school, the child learned to read by handling large, carved, wooden blocks." When the shoemaker's son grew up, he thought of a new way for the blind to read. It involved punching dots on paper, and Louis Braille devised this new method by using the same awl that had blinded him to create a whole new reading system for the blind. "There will be a falling awl in each one of our lives. The choice is ours how it will affect us. In Sprinkle's words, 'When it strikes, some of us ask, "Why did God allow this to happen?" Others ask, 'How will God use it?'"

Back to the story about the lepers. Luke tells us that as Jesus was on his way to Jerusalem, ten lepers approached him. According to the law, any person with a leprous disease was not permitted to live within the city but was required to make his home outside the walls, where people flung their garbage and the dung heaps were also. And whenever anyone else approached, the unfortunates, with their eyes cast down, had, from afar, to cry out "Unclean, unclean." Should the disease somehow be cured, before he (or she) could return to the community, a priest was required to certify that the person was "clean."

To make their lot less pitiable, we could argue that in those days the term "leprosy" could describe any number of skin ailments and that the Ten may not have been fatally infected, only that their skin exhibited a state of decay which was considered "unclean," but that is not the point of the parable or the moral of the story. Neither is it to show that Jesus was a miraculous healer. These verses are only a part of what Jesus said in a series of sayings responding to his disciples who (six verses earlier) had implored him "Increase our faith!" So we miss the purpose of the story by focusing on the dire disease, the miraculous healing, or the bad manners of the other nine outcasts. In fact, Jesus doesn't even take credit himself for the cure. The text tells us that they were made clean "as they went" on their way to show themselves to the priests. And to the one who returned, Jesus said, "Your faith has made you well."

Moreover, the ten lepers, who had stood "at a distance" from Jesus, did not ask to be healed; but "raised a voice" (the Greek says), in unison, crying out "Master, have mercy on us!" when he "saw" them, as Luke puts it. You may think me nitpicking when I say that saying he "saw" them is significant. But a few verses further on Luke returns to his use of that word, saying "One of them, when he saw that he was healed, turned back." In both instances, of course, the "seeing" referred to is not just physical sight, but perceiving the importance of mercy, recognizing that God's mercy has transformed his life.[3]

This story makes a distinction between the physical making clean of the ten lepers and the being made well of the one who turned back to thank Jesus. There is a difference between being healed and being made whole, between being cured and made well, even though we often use the words interchangeably. Some doctors will tell you that when they sew up a wound, or set a bone, or cut out a cancer, they do not do the healing, God does, or you do – with the power of God or life in you. Most of us very much want to be healed or cured. But the real question is, are we also willing to be made well and whole?

Our physical being and our spiritual being are not healed in the same way. In fact, one might argue that healing in the "whole" sense requires an integration of our heart, soul and mind that may be independent of the extent to which our physical body is cured. "Go on your way, your faith has made you well," Jesus tells the one who recognizes that God's grace has touched his life. All ten were healed, but only one "saw" the healing for what it was, being touched by God's love and mercy. That's when his eyes were opened and he became whole, not when his leprosy had left him. You may know that the words health, whole, and holy all come from the same word root, a knowledge that in this case could save your life. The faith of the one who returned to give thanks was not expressed by his cry for help, but by his gratitude to God. Faith enables God to work in our lives in ways that defy our ordinary experience.

I want to leave you with a story and a question. The story comes from Sue Bender, in her book *Everyday Sacred*[4] that describes how she began to develop an attitude of gratitude. She said it had something to do with an exploding turkey:

Last month my husband Richard and I decided, at age 60 and 63, it was finally time to be grown-up and responsible. Neither of us is practical about business or financial matters. We went to a lawyer and started the process of making a will and a living trust for our sons.

"What would you like to do in case there's an 'exploding turkey?'" the lawyer asked.

"Exploding turkey?" I asked.

"What if the whole family was together at Thanksgiving and the turkey exploded?" he asked. "If the four of you were killed at that moment, who would you want to have your worldly goods?" [Who would you want to have thanked?]

That turned out to be a terrific assignment. A chance to think about the people in our lives, a chance to be grateful and express our gratitude. I decided to create a new ritual. I would stop at the end of the day, even a particularly difficult day, and make a list: a gratitude list. Who or what do I have to be grateful for today?

My question to you, of course, is: "What are you grateful for, and how do you show it?"

———

1. Maxie Dunnam, *This is Christianity*, pp.60-61, 1994
2. in *Guideposts*
3. I am much indebted throughout to ideas and phrases taken from *The New Interpreter's Bible*, Vol. IX, pp.325-7
4. Sue Bender, *Everyday Sacred,* p.110, 1995

REPAIR FOR DESPAIR

19th Sunday after Pentecost
Psalm 22:1-11; Mark 10:17-27
Proper 23 – Year B – October 15, 2006

As Jesus was setting out on a journey, a man ran up and knelt before him, and asked him, "Good Teacher, what must I do to inherit eternal life?" Jesus said to him, "Why do you call me good? No one is good but God alone. You know the commandments: 'You shall not murder; You shall not commit adultery; You shall not steal; You shall not bear false witness; You shall not defraud; Honor your father and mother.'" He said to him, "Teacher, I have kept all these since my youth." Jesus, looking at him, loved him and said, "You lack one thing; go, sell what you own, and give the money to the poor, and you will have treasure in heaven; then come, follow me." When he heard this, he was shocked and went away grieving, for he had many possessions.

Then Jesus looked around and said to his disciples, "How hard it will be for those who have wealth to enter the kingdom of God!" And the disciples were perplexed at these words. But Jesus said to them again, "Children, how hard it is to enter the kingdom of God! It is easier for a camel to go through the eye of a needle than for someone who is rich to enter the kingdom of God." They were greatly astounded and said to one another, "Then who can be saved?" Jesus looked at them and said, "For mortals it is impossible, but not for God; for God all things are possible."

Mark 10:17-27

My God, my God, why have you forsaken me? and are so far from my cry and from the words of my distress?

O my God, I cry in the daytime, but you do not answer; by night as well, but I find no rest.

Yet you are the Holy One, enthroned upon the praises of Israel.

Our forefathers put their trust in you; they trusted, and you delivered them.

They cried out to you and were delivered; they trusted in you and were not put to shame.

But as for me, I am a worm and no man, scorned by all and despised by the people.

All who see me laugh me to scorn; they curl their lips and wag their heads, saying,

"He trusted in the LORD; let him deliver him; let him rescue him, if he delights in him."

Yet you are he who took me out of the womb, and kept me safe upon my mother's breast.

I have been entrusted to you ever since I was born; you were my God when I was still in my mother's womb.

Be not far from me, for trouble is near, and there is none to help

Psalm 22:1-11.

Money is not a popular topic of conversation in churches. And for many parishioners the annual fall financial stewardship campaign is their least favorite time of year. Attendance at worship often drops, preachers sometimes make excuses to visitors for their overt appeals for money, and no one looks forward to calling upon the laggard pledgers or those who don't want to pledge to the budget at all. Whatever happened to the idea that giving to enable the work of the church is an act of faith, a thankful gift for all that we have been given in our lives, and a means of spiritual discipline? Where did that kind of giving get a bad name?

Maybe part of the problem is that we don't think of ourselves as wealthy, what with bills to pay and mouths to feed. So let the people with extra money give theirs. Or perhaps our natural inclination is to keep, to hold, to hoard for a rainy day. Or maybe just being asked to give makes us uncomfortably aware of an emptiness deep inside us that we'd rather not face, and which all our personal successes can't seem to fill.

Whatever it is, the liturgical committee has given us what some people think is the perfect gospel text for the annual every member canvass: the story of a rich man who asks Jesus what he must do to inherit eternal life. He's a pillar of the church and of the community, he obeys all the commandments, he has kept the faith – what more can he do? Jesus tells him he lacks something, and that if he gives away what he has to the needy, he will learn what he lacks in becoming a follower of Jesus. But the man cannot quite bring himself to do that, and so he walks away sorrowful, distressed over his dilemma.

I would argue that the use of that passage to prod parishioners to open their wallets is not appropriate to the point of the parable – which is not about keeping wealth, or making good use of our money, or the goodness of giving it up. What the rich man lacks is trust in God and an understanding that no one can earn eternal life, no matter how many good works he does. He despairs over his inability to get what he wants by doing all the right things, even what he thinks are the godly things.

Barbara Brown Taylor comments aptly on the poor rich man's plight: "We can keep the commandments until we are blue in the face; we can sign our paychecks over to Mother Teresa and rattle tin cups for our supper without earning a place at God's banquet table. The kingdom of God is not for sale. The poor cannot buy it with their poverty any more than the rich can buy it with their riches. The kingdom ... is God's consummate gift....

"The catch is, you have to be free to receive God's gift. You cannot be otherwise engaged.... You cannot accept God's gift if you have no spare hands to take it with. You can't make room for it if all your rooms are already full. You can't follow if you're not free to go."[1]

So I'm not going to talk about money this morning. I'm going to address an equally upsetting idea: despair. And if I'm right, many of us do the same thing with the biblical text most associated with that subject, Psalm 22, as we do with the one about the rich man: we miss the point that the passage intended. But first of all, some comments about the relevance of the topic for our time. "We've got over the yellow smiley faces that the '70s bequeathed to us along with 'Have a nice day.'" We're into the harder stuff now in the 2000s: what with "terrorism, bunker busters, [some years of] a shock and awe stock market and massive layoffs," our motivation has moved toward the darker side of things and what we might call "pragmatic pessimism."[2] We may not be exactly despondent, but we're no more nice-guy-smiley. We feel the pain, ours and others!

Enter a company with accoutrements for our time, calling itself Despair, Inc., which offers what it calls "demotivational" products to "feel the collective angst of a depressed populace." The biblical passage that seems to capture our collective concern is the first verse of Psalm XXII: "My God! My God! Why have you forsaken me?" The cry of Christ on the cross. We want to know the reason for our suffering. But Despair, Inc. does not claim to be religious, only realistic. They sell the Pessimist's Mug – which has a line marked at the middle of it, with the inscription, "This cup is half empty."[3] They sell Frowny faces, to put on T-shirts, hats, and backpacks – along with Bitter Sweet candy hearts that have messages on them like Call a shrink, Up yer dosage, or C that door? The centerpiece of Despair, Inc. is a lithograph collection: beautiful photos on which are printed depressing texts, such as the one titled ADVERSITY with the subscription, "That which does not kill me postpones the inevitable"; or the one named DESPAIR with the saying, "It's always darkest just before it goes pitch-black." The company claims its take on life will inspire you to new lows. Despair Inc. trumpets the truth that suffering is a grim reality of the human condition; that "good or bad, rich or poor, conflict and calamity are just a word, ... an accident or an illness away."[4] The song of the Psalmist captures that cry of calamity. We hear it called out on Good Friday, Jesus from the cross, crying to God: "My God! My God! Why have you forsaken me?" For years I was told in church that this was Jesus' cry of dereliction and despair – "Why is God so far from helping?" – a view preachers have used to illustrate a venerable theological theory.

But I came to discover this is a misunderstanding of the intent as well as the text of the Psalm. The truth is deeper than that – and curiously more triumphant. The mistake is multiplied every time the liturgical committee assigns us to read only the first eleven verses of Psalm XXII. It is as though they had never read past the 11th verse. There is a lot in the other verses that would surprise them, and us. And it is not just some of the Hebrew words, but Hebrew custom we need to understand.

First of all, for the Hebrews, to quote the first line of a sacred text invokes the saying of the entire passage. The intent conveys the action. As a devout Jew, Jesus would have known well (perhaps by heart) the 22nd Psalm, which embodies "Israel's traditional understandings of God, of the world, of life, and of death."[5] Yes, the psalm begins with an unforgettable lament, but part way through it changes from lament to praise – because it reflects the conviction that wherever people suffer, God is there.

As the psalm progresses, the sufferer says to God, "I will tell of your name to my brothers and sisters. In the congregation I will praise you. For [you] have not despised or distained the suffering of the afflicted; [you] did not hide your face from me, but heard when I cried to you ... They who seek the Lord shall praise him.... All the ends of the earth will remember and return to the Lord." "My God! My God! Why have you forsaken me?" is the start of the sufferer's cry, but not the end of it. The first line calls into being all the words of the psalm that follow, including the ending, which says of God, "I shall live for him ... and proclaim his deliverance to a people yet unborn." Even from the cross then, those words are "not a cry of abandonment but an affirmation of faith." Jesus puts "his trust in a God ... who hears the cry of the afflicted and draws near."[6]

"Assured of God's presence in the midst of his suffering, Jesus is able to see his own suffering and death as a source of life for all who suffer and despair."[7] Despite what you may have been told, Psalm 22 is an Easter Sunday hymn, which knows we do not get there apart from Good Friday.

It may be difficult for us at first "to see our suffering as a means of grace whereby we receive the assurance of God [with us] and offer God's presence to others in distress."[8] But for those who can, fear gives way to hope and helps us understand the gift of those difficult and comforting words of the Apostle Paul, which we hear in the burial service:[9]

"If we live, we live unto the Lord; and if we die, we die unto the Lord. Whether we live, therefore, or die, we are the Lord's."

As someone else has put it, "The repair for despair isn't gallows humor or wallowing in the whys and wherefores of suffering. It is in drawing closer to God and to others who suffer." The blessing of Psalm 22 is that it gives us "a way to howl as well as to praise, permission to bewail the darkness and permission to hold on to a vision of light."[10] Read it over to yourself sometime when the service here seems to drag.

------

1. *Biblical Preaching Journal* 16, 4-p.6
2. *Homiletics* 15. 5-p.42
3. *Ibid*
4. *Op. cit.* p.43
5. *New Interpreters Bible IV* – p.762
6. *Op. cit.* p.44
7. *Ibid.*
8. *Ibid.*
9. *Book of Common Prayer*, p.469
10. *Op. cit.* pp.44-45

THE GOOD NEWS:
YOU DON'T HAVE TO GIVE IT AWAY

20th Sunday after Pentecost,
Mark 10:17-31
Year B – October 9, 1994

A cheerful thought to begin this meditation with is this: One day we all must give it away; we have no choice. The question of life is, then, when and to whom? The rejoinder is, one day God will hold us responsible for when and to whom we gave it all away.

I'm sure everyone shudders when the Gospel selection for today comes 'round in the lectionary – preacher as well as people – because whatever else it says to us, it speaks of money. And it always seems to come up about the time the Every Member Canvass of the church has just begun.

I have no idea how much money you have or what you do with it – and it's none of my business. (And I swear this sermon is not a follow-up on the recent newsletter about St. Mary's financial needs.) What disturbs me about the biblical text is not that Jesus says to the rich man, "You lack only one thing to enter the kingdom of God, go sell all you have and give to the poor." What is disturbing to me about the passage is that Jesus said this to him *because he loved him* – imagine that!

Tell me it's my duty, tell me I cling too tightly to life or that I value money more than people; tell me I hold on to the old life I know close-fistedly instead of opening my hands to receive a new one – all these I can find defenses for. But don't tell me to give it all up because you *love* me. That's bad fiscal policy, and annoying as the devil.

One footnote before getting to the biblical text. Most people assume that Jesus spent most of his time in parables and sermons teaching about God and love and forgiveness and salvation, but a computer analysis of the text says that the two subjects Jesus focused on most often were (1) the kingdom of God, and (2) – a close second – money.

When Jesus told the rich man to give away all he had, he was simply speeding up the process each of us has to go through in our lives. Even if we recognize that we can't take it with us and that we plan on leaving it "to the kids," we are still going to give it away. Even so, few of us would identify ourselves as "the rich" – especially where taxes are concerned. But the truth is, for many of us the real division today is not between being "rich" and "poor," but between those who are "making it," and those who are not.

The familiar biblical story known as the Rich Young Ruler presents us with one of the hardest sayings in the Bible – one that strikes fear in the hearts of would-be Christians everywhere: "Go, sell what you own, give the money to the poor, and you will have treasure in heaven..."

As one commentator notes, Mark does not say at the start that the man is rich, but you can tell – because of the question he asks: "What must I do to inherit eternal life?" That is a question posed by someone whose bills are paid, whose income is secure, who is not preoccupied by lesser questions such as "Where can I find a job?" or "How can I feed my family?" He doesn't have to figure out how to make ends meet in life – he is free to pursue the question of *eternal* life. He is secure in the knowledge that he is one of God's chosen – because that is what wealth meant in his day – it was understood as a sign of God's blessing.

So this man is not ashamed to come before Jesus with his great possessions. If anything, they are his credentials, why he has the temerity to ask his question in the first place. He is prepared to do whatever is required of him to add eternal life to what is already his. "Perhaps he imagined he would be asked to buy shoes for every man, woman, and child in Palestine; or, better yet, to put on hold the life he is leading in order to accompany Jesus on his travels and learn the great truths this man has to teach." He wants something he can do and do well, as he had done at keeping the Ten Commandments, which he said he had kept "since my youth."

As someone else has pointed out, he did not say that pompously, more as a confession: I have been able to keep the Law all my life – which is why I know it is not enough to give me the enduring life I want (which is why Mark says that Jesus loves him). He loves him because the rich man has come to the end of what he can do for himself and he is ready for God, ready to do whatever is required. So when Jesus looks upon him, really looks at him, he loves what he sees – a true seeker, who has kept his word and God's, who translated his beliefs into a faithful life, who now knows there is more to be done.

Others have suggested that Jesus must have looked upon him with compassion – as much as he would have had for anyone who was blind or deaf or paralyzed – for here was someone who knew he was not yet whole – and desired to become whole. Jesus also looked into him, deeply, to see what the matter was – and what it would take to heal the problem. And then he chose carefully the words that would lessen the man's burden. "Go, sell what you own and give it to the poor." Terrible words for *me* to hear, let alone for the one whose worth in God's eyes was measured by the wealth God had bestowed upon him.

I have heard a number of sermons on this passage that do us a great disservice in two ways: Either in saying that this is not really about money – the money is only symbolic of what we need to give up; or the opposite, that it is *only* about money – money is the root of all evil: "It is easier for a camel to pass through the eye of a needle than for a rich man to get into heaven."

I have to be honest. Clearly the story *is* about money. Money can do a lot of good, but many of us do not know how to handle it wisely. I know from experience how easy it is to want it badly or use it manipulatively, to be seduced by its power or wield it carelessly.

But in fairness, this is not a story only about money. If it were, we could infer from it that we could buy our ways into heaven by cashing in our chips now – which the gospel says is not so; no one can *earn* eternal life. Put another way, "We can keep the commandments till we are blue in the face, we can sign over our paychecks to Mother Teresa – and still that will not earn us a place at God's banquet table. For that matter, the poor cannot buy it with their poverty any more than the wealthy can buy it with their riches." It is, as Jesus says, purely a gift of God, no matter how outrageous that may seem to us.

I cannot receive a gift if I have no spare hand to reach out for it. I can't make room for it if all my rooms are already full. I cannot follow if I am not free to go.

A Gift – but there is a catch: we have to be free to receive it. I cannot receive a gift if I have no spare hand to reach out for it. I can't make room for it if all my rooms are already full. I cannot follow if I am not free to go. That's why the rich young ruler "went away sorrowful." He discovered he was not free. The wealth, which was supposed to give him freedom, had not made him free; he dragged his possessions behind him "like a ball and chain," (I understand this well because I cannot bear to throw anything away.) It has been pointed out that he is the only person in the Gospel of Mark who walked away from the offer to be healed!

What caused him to walk away? Probably, in our terms, the usual things: the mortgage to pay, the children to look after, aging parents to care for, doctors bills to deal with, the economy to wrestle with, the future which is unknown and uncertain. In contrast, those who chose to be Jesus' disciples didn't do it in order to be disciples – nor because they *had* to – but because they wanted to. When they decided, "stuff just got left behind; it wasn't bad, it was just in the way."

The rich young ruler's plight is not so very different from my own. I cling to what I have and what I know – everything else seems scary. That's the bad news. But the good news is that Jesus did not require the disciples who would follow him to be heroic. Faith in God set them free to risk, that's all. It was not their achievement; it was his gift – to them and to us.

————

Footnote: For some of the quotations and ideas above I owe much to the following services: *Help in Homiletics* and *Lectionary Homiletics* which quotes Barbara Taylor from *The Preaching Life*.

THE STEWARDSHIP OF OURSELVES

20th Sunday after Pentecost
Isaiah 5:1-7; Matthew 21:33-43
Proper 22 – Year A
October 6, 2002

Let me sing for my beloved my love-song concerning his vineyard:

My beloved had a vineyard on a very fertile hill.

He dug it and cleared it of stones, and planted it with choice vines;

he built a watchtower in the midst of it, and hewed out a wine vat in it;

he expected it to yield grapes, but it yielded wild grapes.

And now, inhabitants of Jerusalem and people of Judah, judge between me and my vineyard.

What more was there to do for my vineyard that I have not done in it?

When I expected it to yield grapes, why did it yield wild grapes?

And now I will tell you what I will do to my vineyard.

I will remove its hedge, and it shall be devoured;

I will break down its wall, and it shall be trampled down. I will make it a waste; it shall not be pruned or hoed,

and it shall be overgrown with briers and thorns;

I will also command the clouds that they rain no rain upon it.

For the vineyard of the LORD of hosts is the house of Israel,

and the people of Judah are his pleasant planting;

he expected justice, but saw bloodshed;

righteousness, but heard a cry!

Isaiah 5:1-7

Jesus said, "Listen to another parable. There was a landowner who planted a vineyard, put a fence around it, dug a wine press in it, and built a watchtower. Then he leased it to tenants and went to another country. When the harvest time had come, he sent his slaves to the tenants to collect his produce. But the tenants seized his slaves and beat one, killed another, and stoned another. Again he sent other slaves, more than the first; and they treated them in the same way. Finally he sent his son to them, saying, 'They will respect my son.' But when the tenants saw the son, they said to themselves, 'This is the heir; come, let us kill him and get his inheritance.' So they seized him, threw him out of the vineyard, and killed him. Now when the owner of the vineyard comes, what will he do to those tenants?" They said to him, "He will put those wretches to a miserable death, and lease the vineyard to other tenants who will give him the produce at the harvest time. "

Jesus said to them, "Have you never read in the scriptures:

'The stone that the builders rejected has become the cornerstone;

this was the Lord's doing, and it is amazing in our eyes'?

Therefore I tell you, the kingdom of God will be taken away from you and given to a people that produces the fruits of the kingdom."

Matthew 21:33-43

When I used to teach comparative religion, I would often begin a course with some version of this ponderable: An eager searcher seeks an audience with a great sage, who agrees to meet with him briefly. "O Great One," begins the young inquirer, "I have come to you to ask the nature of truth and how I can find it. Please speak to me out of your wisdom." After a few moments of silence, the old monk picks up a stout stick and hits the man a hard blow on the head with it.

Hurt and confused, the man withdraws from the presence of the great one, with apologies, to think about what has happened. Having convinced himself that the monk must have misunderstood his question, the seeker requests a second audience with him. Bowing before the old man, the seeker says humbly, "Master, pardon my ignorance in asking, I have come seeking the truth — pray tell me where I can find it." After some minutes of silence, the monk again picks up the stout stick and inflicts several severe blows upon the man, this time drawing blood.

Deeply distressed, dumbfounded, and downcast the young man backs away from the guru and withdraws to salve his wounds and ponder where he might have offended. After several days, somewhat recovered and still eager to speak with the incomprehensible master, the sincere seeker again requests access to him and a third time asks to be told of truth and how to find it. After many minutes of silence, the old man seizes the stick and gives the young man a beating, this time near to death.

The truth is, words cannot speak it, only talk about it, and that only at second hand. Words cannot tell us what we want to hear; they merely point the way to it. Only silence can speak the truth, and often anticly and comically through eccentric images that point us where we hadn't thought to go or consider – sometimes a kind of ineffable joke: "The man with no legs who sells shoelaces at the corner. The old woman in the [elegant] fur coat who makes her daily rounds at the garbage cans ... the pusher, the whore, the village idiot who stands at the blinker light waving his hand as the cars go by."[1] The joke we cannot tell, the truth we can perceive but have no words to explain, a way of seeing something too rich for us to speak about. What all these have in common is the saying, "If you have to explain it, don't bother."

That's a little bit the way I feel about the story of the wicked tenants retold in the Gospel of Matthew this morning. The early Christian church must have had the same problem with the original parable, which probably ended with the killing of the heir and did not provide an explanation or conclusion but left the sad story open to us and to our decision about what to do with it. But Christian storytellers were not satisfied with the situation left unsettled or open ended, the way Jesus might have told it. So, the version passed on to us is handed down as an allegory, a form Jesus seldom used, explaining to us that the owner of the vineyard is God, the tenant farmers are the Jewish people, the slaves sent to collect the harvest are the prophets and Jesus is the heir.

But try reading the text in chapter 21 yourself, the parable proper, without the addition of the interpreted ending – that is, verses 33-39 only. It is very powerful, disturbing, confounding that way. For me, the wordless truth of it can only be captured in something like the cry of anguish we heard read from the prophet Isaiah who, in our Old Testament lesson, sang to his beloved a love song concerning his vineyard: "What more was there to do for my vineyard that I have not done in it? When I expected it to yield grapes, why did it yield wild grapes?"

My guess is, either intuitively you understand what he is talking about or you do not. And no amount of biblical interpretation will more fully name, explain, or reveal the pain in God's heart that Isaiah speaks for him in his love song. Another example, which we see immediately or are blind to, is Barbara Brown Taylor's way of speaking about what happens at the Eucharist. She says: "The breaking of bread at holy communion can break you right open. Sometimes you can be right in the middle of it when suddenly the tears start rolling down. It is like the gates to your heart have opened and everything you have ever loved comes tumbling out to be missed and praised and mourned and loved some more. It is like being known all the way down...."[2] If that has not been your experience, explaining it will not make it so or even make it more understandable to you. If you have to explain it, forget it.

But Barbara Brown Taylor also has pity on us less lyrical souls who need more spoon-feeding so we won't starve to death in our spiritual speechlessness. She suggests that maybe in order for us to hear the story of the wicked tenants we need a more mundane parable to probe than Jesus' version of it. How about "Once upon a time there was a rich businessman from Orlando who bought a derelict apple orchard in Clarkesville, Georgia. He pruned the trees, fertilized them, fixed up the sales shed and put a brand-new hand painted sign on the highway. Then he leased the place to a local family for less than market value, with the understanding they would give him ten percent of the apples.... The tenants agreed...loved the place [as if] it was their own.

"Come October, ... the trees were so heavy with fruit they looked like emerald ladies with too much jewelry on. It was time to harvest, ... so the tenants worked in shifts, half of them sleeping while the others picked ... and mountains of apples rose from the wooden bins in the sales shed ... Happily exhausted, the tenants ... heard gravel crunching . . . a sixteen-wheeler with Florida plates backing into the shed. Two big guys with bulging biceps got out and started loading apples ... and when one of the tenants went up to negotiate the ten percent business, one of the big guys just picked him up and set him out of the way.... So the rest of the tenants held a quick huddle and decided to introduce the trucker to the mountain version of People's Court.... and before long they had persuaded the landowners to return to Florida empty-hand-ed. 'Get lost,'" ...[3]

Now what can we make of that? Yes the tenants were wrong, because the orchard wasn't theirs, and they had made a deal with the owner before they were aware of the riches of the harvest – and no one likes an absentee landlord. It's not our way, the American way – tending someone else's land. We want our own harvest and the profit we think is due us from our love and labor. That's the American value system: individual ownership, self-reliance, self-government.

The problem is, as Matthew sees it, these are not the val-ues of the kingdom of God, which upsets us as much as the ten-ants of the vineyard. And the reason the parable makes us so de-fensive is that, as Barbara Brown Taylor points out, the real issue is not justice (God's or ours) but stewardship (I am quick to say this is not a warm up for Every Member Canvass) – which challenges our notion of ownership, what we have a right to and what we have earned. As we see it, we have worked hard for what we have and hanging on to it requires courage, cleverness, and conviction when it comes to our contractual rights – even coercion if need be.

What we have forgotten about the vineyard in which we work is that it has been lent to us to love, labor, and luxuriate in. We neither created, nor bought or earned it – and to consume it is not to conserve it. But the covenant our spiritual ancestors con-sented to was conceived so long ago that we have forgotten and forsaken it, the image of it long lost to us, alive only in ritual and remembrance (church services and perhaps prayer). There, we re-call if we can, the relationship between the owner and the tenant was reciprocal. What we received was not ours to own but, to use and enjoy; and in return we were to proffer a portion of what we produce – whether in the coin of compassion, commerce, love or labor – to the lord who has lent us life and livelihood. Not because he needs what we give him (in fact he returns what we give him with interest), but because we need to give it, to grant what we have been given to others, to remind ourselves we are grateful guests.

I am reluctant to remind us: that conception is only the context for the parable. The conclusion of it is ours to conceive for ourselves and to carry out. But again Barbara Brown Taylor takes pity on our propensity to procrastinate, offering this perspective on the truth, which we are free to adopt or exclude:

The son whom the tenants killed "would not stay dead and to this day he is still haunting in the vineyard, reminding us that we are God's guests – welcome on this earth... so long as we remember whose it is and how it is to be used.... All we may not do is spurn the owner and persecute his messengers, because to do that is ... to forget who we are and where we came from. We are God's sharecroppers. We tend the earth and its riches on someone else's behalf. [The truth is] we are expected to represent God's interest [by] being as generous with each other as God is with us."[4]

1. Frederick Buechner, *Telling the Truth*, p.66
2. Barbara Brown Taylor, *Gospel Medicine*, p.23
3. *Ibid*, pp.96-97
4. *Ibid*, p.100

A PEST IN PRAYER

20th Sunday after Pentecost
Luke 18:1-8a
Proper 24 – Year C – October 17, 2004

> *Jesus told his disciples a parable about their need to pray always and not to lose heart. He said·, "In a certain city there was a judge who neither feared God nor had respect for people. In that city there was a widow who kept coming to him and saying, 'Grant me justice against my opponent.' For a while he refused; but later he said to himself, 'Though I have no fear of God and no respect for anyone, yet because this widow keeps bothering me, I will grant her justice, so that she may not wear me out by continually coming.'" And the Lord said, "Listen to what the unjust judge says. And will not God grant justice to his chosen ones who cry to him day and night? Will he delay long in helping them? I tell you, he will quickly grant justice to them."*

> *Luke 18:1-8a*

No point in preaching about parables that appeal to us – that takes all the pugnaciousness out of them! Last month, some of you may remember, we were bedeviled by the blessing of the dishonest steward. This week we are confronted with the case of the corrupt judge and, what I call, the whining woman – sometimes spoken of as the parable of persistent prayer, maybe the motto of which would be that people, not prayer, are the problem, as proclaimed on bumper stickers, like: "How can I miss you if you

411

won't go away" and "Be nice to your kids, some day they'll choose your nursing home."

A little exposition here might be in order in case your mind was wandering while the gospel was being read. Luke's parable exemplifies the unexpected and unconventional characteristics of the way Jesus enjoyed teaching. The judge, clearly not always just, and hardly genial, grants the unrelenting widow's request, not because her case has merit, nor because he aspires to be impartial but simply to be rid of her. His motives remind us of Luke's illustration in an earlier parable about the person who was awakened at midnight by an insistent friend asking for three loaves of bread, and who, finally, grudgingly gives in to the request purely because of the friend's persistent pestering. And Luke's assessment of the unjust judge is as puzzling and unconventional as his commendation of the dishonest steward.' What are we to do with this disturbing story?

Well, one way into the wiles of the whining widow and the unjust judge is to take Jesus at his word when Luke tells us that the parable is in part a metaphor about prayer and the disciples' need to pray always and without losing heart. Let's see what we can come up with on that account. Try this approach – I find it instructive because my feet have often been an affliction for me, especially my big toe, one in particular: unsightly, ingrown, and always an anguish of mine. Anyway, on to the account:

She was an elderly woman. About 50 years old. Moderately well-preserved, although a bit dried out. Not likely to attract much attention.

Granted 50 is not so old – unless you're living 3,000 years ago in ancient Egypt. This 50-year old woman was recently found in burial chamber TT-95 in the Egyptian necropolis at Thebes-West. For someone who'd been buried for three millennia, she looked remarkably well-preserved. Yet even to archaeologists, she was not likely to attract attention because she appeared to be an average, everyday, garden-variety mummy ... until someone noticed the odd-looking big toe on her right foot. It was totally artificial.

It consisted of three pieces of carved wood fitted onto her foot with leather straps, making it the world's oldest known prosthesis. The wooden toe still looked ready for use, still lashed to the patient's mummified toe by a textile lace.

For paleo-pathologists around the world, this big toe was *big news*. X-rays revealed that the Egyptian woman's actual toe had been surgically removed ... Soft tissue and skin had overgrown the site where the toe had been taken off, and then the prosthetic toe had been added.

She must've been a persistent woman to go to all the trouble!

Evidence shows that the device must've worked. Scuff-marks on the toe's underside indicate that the artificial toe had assisted the woman for some time while she was alive. Without it, she would have had a very difficult time walking like an Egyptian.

Two millennia ago, there was another persistent woman of record, who evidently didn't have trouble getting around like Mummy did. Say what you want, but she was persistent. A pain. A pest. And Jesus uses her for an instructive lesson. Like a terrier at your cuff, she sunk in her teeth, snarling to the judge handling her case: "Grant me justice against my opponent" (18:3).

Finally, the judge couldn't stand it anymore. "I have no fear of God," he admitted to himself. He even confessed that he didn't care for people. "Yet because this widow keeps bothering me, I will grant her justice" (vv. 4-5). He simply wanted to get her out of his hair, because she was wearing him out with her continual griping. The widow's pleas were like a big wooden toe, one that kept jabbing and jabbing and jabbing away.

"Enough!" shouted the judge. "I get the point!"[1]

But do *we*? It's not just that the *woman* was unrelenting as well as un-toe-ard, the metaphor tells us *God* is, and he will grant justice or give grace to those who "cry to him day and night," as Jesus says. The analogy is instructive: If a corrupt and uncaring judge can respond to pestering and persistent pleas, will not a merciful and loving Lord do as much? But God does not have to be browbeaten before he will hear our prayers; God is insistent before we are persistent. As Jesus put it: "Ask and it shall be given. Seek and you shall find. Knock and the door will be opened unto you." Making a metaphor of the mummy, prayer is no prosthesis. It's not an add-on, there's nothing artificial about it. It's not a crutch to keep our faith from falling over, it's the expression of our faith. It's not a toe-hold into God, and we don't need to keep kicking God in the shins just to get his attention.

But praying for most of us is probably a part-time practice, which will be perfected only with persistent practice. Only with an ongoing determination will we be willing to enter into an ongoing conversation with God. We need to free up the feisty woman in us – day after day, not only at the midnight hour or at the last minute.

When I was being trained to jump out of airplanes, one of the life-giving truths they taught us was not to wait until the parachute failed to open to decide what to do. Practicing a procedure persistently, until it becomes automatic, is the only alternative that will prevent a way to the ground which is only straight down. You can't think about pulling a reserve parachute unless you've practiced the process until it is second nature; persistent practice is not just practical, it is life preserving.

Barbara Brown Taylor offers this anecdote about her efforts to educate her 7-year-old granddaughter, Madeline:

What I want Madeline to know is that the best thing about prayer is the relationship itself. Whether or not she gets what she asks for, I want her to keep asking. I want her to pester God the same way she pesters her mother, thinking of twelve different ways to plead her case. I want her to long for God the same way she longs for her father, holding fast to him even when his chair is empty.

When she complains that none of this does any good, I am going to ask her to tell me the difference between how she feels while she is praying versus how she feels when she thinks about giving up. If I am lucky, she is going to tell me that she feels more alive when she is praying, and that is when I will tell her the story about the persistent widow...[2]

Prayer need not be something peculiar, set apart from what you practice the rest of the day. Fred Buechner speaks of it as primarily a response to what we experience: Everybody prays whether he thinks of it as praying or not. The odd silence you fall into when something very beautiful is happening or something very good or very bad. The Ah-h-h! that sometimes floats up out of you as out of a Fourth of July crowd when the skyrocket bursts over the water. The stammer of pain at somebody else's pain. The stammer of joy at somebody else's joy. Whatever words or sounds you use for sighing with over your own life. These are all prayers in their way. These are all spoken not just to yourself but also to something even more familiar than yourself and even more strange than the world.

According to Jesus, by far the most important thing about praying is to keep at it. The images He uses to explain this are all rather comic, as though He thought it was rather comic to have to explain it at all. He says God is like a friend you go to to borrow bread from at midnight. The friend tells you in effect to drop dead, but you go on knocking anyway until finally he gives you what you want so he can go back to bed again (Luke 11:5-8). Even a stinker, Jesus says, won't give his own child a black eye when he asks for peanut butter and jelly, so how all the more will God when his children [ask] ... (Matthew 7:9-11).

Be [persistent], Jesus says – not, one assumes, because you have to beat a path to God's door before he'll open it, but because

415

until you beat the path maybe there's no way of getting to your door.[3]

Luke's lesson for us might be that being a pest per se may not be what "pays off" (if we can put it that way), but God's compassionate response for the person who prays persistently may be what prevails. The God you call upon will finally come, promises Buechner, "and even if he does not bring you the answer you want, he will bring you himself. And maybe at the secret heart of all our prayers, that is what we are really praying for."[4]

------

1. *Homiletics* 13, 5 – p.62
2. Barbara Brown Taylor, "Bothering God" *Christian Century*, March 24 -31, 1999, 356
3. Frederick Buechner, *Listening to Your Life*, pp.211-212
4. Frederick Buechner, *Wishful Thinking,* p.87

"MANY ARE CALLED BUT FEW ARE CHOSEN"

A Theology of Ducks for All Saints

21st Sunday After Pentecost
Matthew 22:1-14
Proper 26 – Year B – November 5, 2000

Jesus spoke to them again in parables, saying:

"The kingdom of heaven is like a king who prepared a wedding banquet for his son. He sent his servants to those who had been invited to the banquet to tell them to come, but they refused to come.

"Then he sent some more servants and said, 'Tell those who have been invited that I have prepared my dinner: My oxen and fattened cattle have been butchered, and everything is ready. Come to the wedding banquet.'

"But they paid no attention and went off – one to his field, another to his business. The rest seized his servants, mistreated them and killed them. The king was enraged. He sent his army and destroyed those murderers and burned their city.

"Then he said to his servants, 'The wedding banquet is ready, but those I invited did not deserve to come. Go to the street corners and invite to the

banquet anyone you find.' So the servants went out into the streets and gathered all the people they could find, both good and bad, and the wedding was filled with guests.

"But when the king came in to see the guests, he noticed a man there who was not wearing wedding clothes. 'Friend,' he asked, 'how did you get in here without wedding clothes?' The man was speechless.

"Then the king told the attendants, 'Tie him hand and foot, and throw him outside, into the darkness, where there will be weeping and wailing and gnashing of teeth.'

"For many are called, but few are chosen."

Matthew 22:1-14 (The Narrated Bible)

About this time of year, when Lynne and I make a trip to our little house in the mountains among the myriad leaves turned magnificent colors: magenta, martyr red, yolk orange, squashed-bug yellow, and you name it, we eagerly anticipate the fall flight of regal birds. There, for some reason we have come to expect on a certain day the exodus en masse of majestic birds like eagles, hawks, ravens – glorious winged creatures in flight soaring above us at one section of mountain and ravine.

That image stands in contrast to a time when we lived in Goochland and my wife raised mallards from an incubator. Because they had no other experience, they adopted Lynne as their mother duck or alpha elder and would follow her faithfully in predictable procession as she (and they) perambulated about our property. A poor substitute for the vision of being borne up on eagles' wings into the towering emptiness of light and the very eye of the sun. So also on All Saints' Day when we are gathered with: "Greetings to you all who are called to be saints at St.

Mary's," some people may think that the salutation must be for the more exalted among us instead of the more plodding. Not so – even from the earliest times in the church – but still, some of us may see ourselves, spiritually speaking, more like ducks than eagles. Which is the more appropriate metaphor, the more salient symbol, for All Saints' Sunday? I suspect, given the choice, most of us would opt for the image of an eagle as apt, as opposed to the designation "duck." After all, who would want to be thought of as an odd duck, lame duck, dumb duck-or even "ducky" when we recall God's inspiring words to Israel in *Exodus*: "Remember how I bore you on eagles' wings and brought you to myself" (Ex. 19:4). And in Isaiah: "They who wait for the Lord shall renew their strength, they shall mount up with wings like eagles, they shall run and not be weary, they shall walk and not be faint" (Isa. 40:31).

Whereas, if you consult a biblical concordance, you will come across "dug" and "dull" and "dumb" and "dung," but no "duck" – in all of scripture. References to pigeon and partridge, fowl and even vulture abound – but it is absolutely bereft of duck, not even an instance of a phrase like "duck your head." Who wouldn't want to be an eagle? It's a logical de-ducktion.

So I want to speak this morning on our celebration of All Saints' Day to the eagles among you (even the closet eagles) about a theology of ducks. I first thought of it out on our Goochland farm where I was awakened each day at dawn to the quackery of a dozen demanding ducks directly beneath their mistress's bedroom window – strange survivors there in a savage world of raven-ous raccoons, owls, 'possums, snakes, foxes, and our two white German Shepherds. Impossible as it was to escape the insistent "quackers" (which label we purchased for the personal license plate on my wife's car) somehow, putting up with them strangely empowered me to speak about the good news (or should I say the good noise).

You may well ask what on earth ducks have to do, symboli-cally or sacramentally with sainthood, or All Saints', or St. Mary's or St. Peter's Wort, or whatever. Scripture doesn't say. What it says of those saints who are called to the kingdom of heaven is simple enough. I'm sure you've heard it said before: "Many are called, but few are chosen." Of ducks, it says nothing; of demons plenty – 73 references to none. "Saints" is used 99 times in the Bible, but not in the sense of 99 and 44 one hundredths percent pure, which is important for all of us to acknowledge before we're done.

Not only do most of us not think of ourselves as saints, we probably don't want to be one? Who wants to be holy, let alone holier than thou? Saints are not usually described as The Grateful Dead. (My wife, who was taught in a convent school, says we ought to be grateful that the saints are dead because they were always being roasted alive over a fire or rolled through the streets bound to a spiked wheel. Let All Saints' be for someone, else you might say; I don't really want to be among the many who are called, let alone fuss with the few who are chosen. I'd rather be an eagle, any day.

You may know that in the early church the word "saint" was never used in the exclusive way we now use it. (It wasn't until 12 centuries later that you had to be canonized with 2 "n"s – or even with 3 – to be declared a saint.) When the apostle Paul traveled among his churches during the first century, he often addressed the people there as saints. He wrote his famous epistles "To the saints in Ephesus" or "To all in Rome... called to be saints." It is in that sense I bring greetings to you all who are called to be saints at St. Mary's.

Maybe the reason most of us would rather not be saints is because that means, first of all, we would need to accept ourselves as we are for what we are, and all of us don't always find ourselves all that likable. Second, and maybe even worse, we would need to accept that we are no different from the other saints we sit among, gossip about, party with – even sometimes betray.

If we have difficulty believing that many are called to be saints, we have less difficulty believing that few are chosen. Looking at it that way, if I'm not among the few that are chosen, I don't have to worry about whatever it means to be a saint. Or, if indeed I am called, surely "George" (as they say) isn't – God has better taste than that, by George! The troublesome truth is that God is (so-tospeak) tasteless, in that He calls us all – all of us, that is, who are willing to be chosen. (That doesn't sound eagle-itarian.)

***Call me a lame duck if you like, Lord,
but don't call me to be a saint.***

Now a bit about ducks, surely an awkward simile for saints. You know the derisive ditty, "Be kind to your web-footed friends, for a duck may be somebody's mother." And, in addition to lame duck and odd duck, there is duck-out-of-water, ugly duckling, and so on. Not especially compatible with the way we speak about saints. Unless, with all the outlandish translations of the Bible available today, we might imagine rephrasing those famous words of Jesus, "I come not to call the righteous but lame ducks to repentance" If that's what the gospel means, even I can understand it, as long as I don't have to be a saint. Call me a lame duck if you like, Lord, but don't call me to be a saint. The problem is, that is what the good news is all about: "Grace unto you and peace in the Lord, to all that are at St. Mary's, beloved of God, called to be saints."

Which raises the theological question, what does it take to love a lame duck? Not God alone, Lord knows, but also the self-same saint sitting in the seat next to you and the saint sitting in your seat, who can look into the eyes of the one next to you and see yourself reflected there. Perhaps the most difficult truth to accept is that, by God, "George" and I are called to the same destiny, we are called to be saints – not as holy persons, but just as we are, as lame ducks.

Not long ago I came upon the following poem called "I Am *Not* a Duck," by John Foster. (If you'd rather be an eagle, just ignore the quackery):

I am not a Duck

*I may look like a duck and walk like a duck and
quack like a duck and drink like a duck-
But I am NOT a duck. I'm an eagle in disguise.
If you could prove to me that it's respectable to be a
duck, I might consider being one.
But don't waste your time – my mind is made up.
I think it's shameful to be a duck. I won't be a duck.
It's so lonely here among all these ducks. I'm so
out of place here. But for some reason, none of the
other eagles will have anything to do with me.
Why are eagles so cruel?
Some of the ducks are quite nice. It' s too bad I'm
an eagle.*

*No, it isn't! I'm glad I'm an eagle.
Even if I WERE a duck, I wouldn't stay a duck. I'd
become an eagle.
I can be anything I want to be and I owe it to myself
to be an eagle.
Ducks are terrible. I HATE ducks.*

*I keep trying to swoop down and grab a rabbit in
my claws. But, I can't do it.
I have webbed feet.
It's all GOD'S fault. Why would he make an eagle
with webbed feet?
If I starve to death, God will have only himself to
blame.
I do my part – why doesn't he do his?*

*The ducks all want to help me. But how can they?
What does a duck know about an eagle's problems?
Why can't they mind their own business?*

*Why don't the eagles offer to help? Someday I'll get
even with those eagles. I HATE them!*
I'm beginning to like ducks better than I do eagles.

Being an eagle is killing me.
> *Not being a duck is killing me.*
I don't know what's killing me.
I just know I'm dying.
> *Help me, God.*
>> *God, help me.*

Guess what, God!
> *I am a duck... whether I like it or not... I'm a
> duck.*
(Why didn't you tell me?)
I've forgotten how to act.
> *Show me God, how to be a duck.*
Help me.

Help me be a good duck.
Ducks are the best people in the world
> *I love ducks.*
>> *I'm grateful to be a duck.*

When is a duck not an eagle? When he understands that
God calls him as a duck. When is an eagle not a saint? When he is
unwilling to be the duck he is called to be.

Grace unto you and peace in the Lord to all that are at St.
Mary's, beloved of God, called to be saints – both the saints we
are and the saints we aren't, the saints we would be and even the
saints we don't want to be called to be.

OF MINISTRY AND MARTINIS

Stewardship or Ownership?

22nd Sunday after Pentecost
Mark 10:35-45
Proper 24 – Year B – October 19, 1997

I came across a story in my commentary reading this week which I believe is worth repeating for the sake of the gospel:

"A boy whose mother was sick searched all over the city to find a gift for her, but he found nothing he could afford. He walked past a beautiful rose garden and sought out the gardener, saying to him, 'I don't have much money, but I would like to buy some roses for my sick mother.' He was told that this was the king's garden, and the roses were not for sale.

"The boy went away dejected, but the prince had overheard the conversation and ran after him to say, 'The gardener was right. The king does not sell his roses. *But he does give them away.'*

Whereupon, the prince cut a bundle of roses and gave them to the boy for his mother."[1]

You may be wondering what that has to do with the lesson about James and John in Mark this morning. And I think I'll leave you dangling there, until I hang myself with an attempted explanation or you get the hang of it yourself. (I haven't forgotten the saying, "If you have to explain what the story is about, forget it – your hearers already have.")

Seeing as this is Stewardship kick-off Sunday, to mix the metaphor, I'll run with the ball far enough to say that the commentary I was reading tackles the issue of what it means to be a steward in the story about James and John. It calls us to consider the contrast between being a caretaker and an owner – or, as the author expresses it, the difference between ownership and stewardship. But before I contest your concern that this is just a commercial for the Every Member Canvass, let us legitimately have a look at the text itself to determine what it is trying to tell us.

This week's reading, to borrow a pugnacious phrase, describes the disciples' third and most blatantly wrong-headed response to Jesus' third and most graphic prediction of his upcoming passion, when he will be delivered up and put to death. And while none of the disciples is absolved from his decisive misunderstanding, surely James and John drop the ball before it is put into play. The only sign of Jesus' signals they find significant – the only part they hear – is Jesus' pronouncement that when he is killed, "after three days he will rise up." (It's time to pass off the football analogy – it's beating me to death.)

Returning to James' and John's response, "Right on!" they reason. "So how about doing something significant for us: Grant us to sit, one at your right hand and one at your left, when you come in your glory." One commentary quips, "As disciples of the Son of Man, it went without saying that perks, priority, privilege and position would be part of the [package]."[2] All the same, can you believe the belligerence of James and John – the gall and greed of the godly?

However, before we get too satisfyingly self-righteous over their boorish behavior, I believe one point of the passage is to propose that before we pass judgment upon the inappropriateness of their petition, we are invited to examine our own expectations and intentions. True, James and John didn't start out small, circumspectly, simply requesting a raise in rank to deacon or to be promoted to chairperson of the property committee or even to be invited on to the vestry – expecting to up the ante at the first sign of approval. While they had the floor, why not hold out for something really big?

If we are inclined to be indignant at their intemperateness, we ought also to be expected to explain how it is possible to offer an effective witness in our world without the power and [prestige] to promote it. Our culture is commonly uncoerced by the concerns of the church, one which does not normally value the views and advice of the clergy and ecclesiastical counsel. We need power, position, prosperity to implement unpopular programs and promote the prominence of a gospel that in the minds of many appears irrelevant and outdated. "Could it be that James and John were aware that they too needed power to fulfill the expectations placed upon them and thought this might be one way of wangling it?"[3]

In any case. Jesus was not quick to condemn them; in fact, he declines to denounce them. Instead he draws them and the other disciples into a discussion about the meaning of his mission and the ministry of anyone who would be his follower – hoping patiently, I suspect, that one more time might at last unlock their understanding of what he was trying to tell them. Mind you, they were not the only ones not to get it. When the other ten "began to be indignant at James and John," as Mark notes, it wasn't their inordinate ambition that the ten objected to, but that they had been outmaneuvered. They responded jealously and angrily because they too wanted to be first in line as much as James and John did, only they were not quick enough to speak up first.

Jesus must have sensed this because he does not single out and cast-off James and John (which is an unexpected bonus for us because that may mean that neither will we be cast out when our questions and requests are outrageous). Instead, Jesus says," Whoever would be great among you must be your servant, and whoever would be first among you must first be slave of all, For the Son of man also came not to be served but to serve...."

You can imagine at that point how his disciples must have squirmed, stared at the ground, shuffled their feet in embarrassment at what he was saying. And what are we doing as we eavesdrop on their conversation, if we take seriously what was said? Is theirs not our story too? Would we willingly spend our self-serving in serving others? Not easily, I suspect. A competitive capitalistic culture teaches us, "God helps those who help themselves." And how many times have I caught myself jibing jealously at the favor and good things that came to my brother instead of me?

Is there any application of that to the life of the church? One commentator concludes that even there it is easy to become a receiver rather than a giver, to accept the position of one who is served rather than helping to serve: "The irony is that when you begin to think primarily about what you are 'getting out of' church, you soon begin to feel that you are not getting as much as you want. [Whereas], when you concentrate mainly on what you can 'put into' your church in the way of personal work and prayer and participation and money, you feel that you are getting a lot."[4]

Let me return to consider the story I started with. Robert Miles, Jr. wants to be sure we don't miss the meaning in Jesus' use of "servanthood," which implies not only service but stewardship. When someone starts to speak about stewardship, we assume he or she is going to put the bite on us for money. Not surprising that we misunderstand the use of the word. "A steward is a caretaker, not an owner ... one who [looks after] another person's property, a trustee of another's riches. There is a profound difference between ownership and stewardship, and the distinction is illustrated in today's gospel lesson."[4]

James and John did not understand what Jesus was saying to them because they assumed that being followers of his was a means of being first in the kingdom of God. So they asked for positions of power and authority as signs of their discipleship. But Christ confounds them by saying that to seek the kingdom is more about gathering gifts of giving than getting; "more about being concerned about caring than keeping, more about [being called upon] for sharing than possessing."[4] It is to see that what we do with what we have is a measure of our response to what God has given us.

You may recall that when the boy asked to buy roses for his ailing mother, the gardener (or the steward of the king's garden) said the roses were not for sale. The boy was heartbroken until the prince ran after him and said, "You cannot buy the king's roses, but he does give them away" – and gave him a bundle. Maybe that means that when God offers us the kingdom and our place in it, he asks that we receive his gifts as stewards rather than owners. Because, as Ellen Williams reminded us in her Forum talk here last week: What we are hell-bent to keep, we shall surely lose; only what we offer to give away becomes ours.

The joy of giving is a little like drinking martinis - both are learned tastes.

Bishop Hall once said to me that those words are probably too highfalutin' for most of us to understand. A more down-to-earth way of saying it will strike home quicker: The joy of giving is a little like drinking martinis – both are learned tastes. And, as Bishop Hall would have been the first to admit, drinking in the holy spirit costs a lot less in the end.

---

1. *Lectionary Homiletics*
2. *Homiletics, 9,4 - p.24*
3. *Ibid., p.24*
4. *Biblical Preaching Journal* 10, 4 – p.10
5. *Lectionary Homiletics* VIII, 11 - p.24

SPIRITUAL GRAFFITI

22nd Sunday after Pentecost
Matthew 25:14-15, 19-29
November 15, 1987

"For it will be like a man going on a journey, who called his servants and entrusted to them his property. To one he gave five talents, to another two, to another one, to each according to his ability. Then he went away. Now after a long time the master of those servants came and settled accounts with them. And he who had received the five talents came forward, bringing five talents more, saying, 'Master, you delivered to me five talents; here, I have made five talents more.' His master said to him, 'Well done, good and faithful servant. You have been faithful over a little; I will set you over much. Enter into the joy of your master.' And he also who had the two talents came forward, saying, 'Master, you delivered to me two talents; here, I have made two talents more.' His master said to him, 'Well done, good and faithful servant. You have been faithful over a little; I will set you over much. Enter into the joy of your master.' He also who had received the one talent came forward, saying, 'Master, I knew you to be a hard man, reaping where you did not sow, and gathering where you scattered no seed, so I was afraid, and I went and hid your talent in the ground. Here, you have what is yours.' But his master answered him, 'You wicked and slothful servant! You knew that I reap where

I have not sown and gather where I scattered no seed? Then you ought to have invested my money with the bankers, and at my coming I should have received what was my own with interest. So take the talent from him and give it to him who has the ten talents. For to everyone who has will more be given, and he will have an abundance. But from the one who has not, even what he has will be taken away."

Matthew 25:14-15, 19-29

The parable of the talents in Matthew 25 which was read this morning is probably as well known as the parable of the laborers in the vineyard in Chapter 20 – and just as obnoxious. You may remember in that parable the homeowner goes out early in the morning to hire laborers for his vineyard and he hires some on the spot for a denarius a day, and others at the "third hour," the "sixth hour," the "ninth hour," and the "eleventh hour" – saying to them "Go ye also into the vineyard, and whatever is right I will pay you." When evening was come, the lord of the vineyard sent for the laborers and asked the steward give them their hire, beginning with those who had signed on last. And damned if he didn't give each one the same wage, a denarius, even those who had borne the burden and heat of the day, saying "Is it not lawful for me to do what I will with my own?" and, adding insult to injury, "So the last shall be first, and the first last; for many are called, but few are chosen."

I can't imagine how the faithful in the AFL-CIO read that passage, not to mention the ACLU. The labor relations lawyers of that time must have had a field day. And less than five chapters later (not counting the parable of the two sons, the marriage feast, and the wise and foolish virgins) he again lays on with the parable of the talents, equally pugnacious and unfair, ending with the verse that our lectionary for today excludes. It is not enough that he proclaims "To him that hath it shall be given, and to him that hath not, even that shall be taken away." He adds, "Cast the unprofitable servant into outer darkness where there shall be weeping and wailing and gnashing of teeth." Amos and Jeremiah were pussycats in comparison to Jesus here.

<hr>

"...the Lord can also find it in his heart to loveth the grudging giver."

<hr>

My Sunday School teacher never wasted much time on these stories, saying that was what the grown-ups heard about in church – meaning that's big stuff, or big people's stuff. I imagined that parable must be the one the senior warden used when it comes to the annual canvass: If you give no more than the minimum required, you are (soteriologically speaking) cast into outer darkness, if not placed on the list of those to be called – meaning phoned. That passage could, of course, be alternated on alternate years with the one about how God loveth the cheerful giver. However, I remember indelibly the time a senior warden said in his curmudgeonly way, "I'm sorry to tell you that the Lord can also find it in his heart to loveth the grudging giver."

Back to the next to the last line of the parable of the talents, which seems patently unfair, if not unintelligible. I remember saying the very same thing to one of my eleven college roommates, pertaining to his marriage arrangements in comparison to the rest of us, he the son of a California shipping magnate, planning to marry a Long Island Hitchcock who commanded a stretch limo herself. Namely, "To him that hath, it shall be given; and to him that hath not, even that shall be taken away." (I think I knew even then that marriage itself bestows gifts which have no price, but it was difficult not to take notice of a corporate merger in our midst.)

One way to get around the parable of the talents is to say first that the parable is offered in the context of the coming of the Kingdom of God, when those who hold back their faith and commitment in a wait-and-see posture will be treated to the consequences of withholding themselves 'til they know what's in it for them. On the "Day of the Lord," when the vineyard is pruned and the sheep are separated from the goats, if you're out on a limb when the dead wood is cut off, your fate will be no surprise.

Second, another means to get around the parable is to say that Jesus is really talking about the psychology of faith. Some of us are free to venture more than others. There are the type T personalities whose addiction is to "living on the edge," whether in racing sports cars or lying down in front of bulldozers to protest social injustice or buying on the margin. And then there are those who play it close to the chest, who have difficulty declaring themselves, who know how to "carry out orders" or to buttress the status quo or to hoard gold in their mattresses. Spiritually speaking, nothing ventured is, indeed, nothing gained; and if the kingdom of God is within, the Lord needs ESFPs to bring it out.[1]

But if one were ruthlessly honest in assessing one's vision of God's world and were more oriented to scatology than eschatology, to getting one's due rather than giving it away, to the law rather than to justices, then the parable of the talents not only becomes a problem, it is probably an indictment. Surely even before October 13th I would have been sure that the Master was repaid what he was owed, rather than venture my spiritual capital, especially when I wasn't sure how much I had to draw upon. One step at a time. You remember St. Augustine's famous one-liner in dealing with his mistress, "O Lord, make me chaste, but not yet." (No Chuck Robb,[2] he.)

In the same vein, I have always been outraged with the treatment of the older brother in the parable of the prodigal son. The reward for his plodding faithfulness was no banquet. Whoever killed the fatted calf for him? Nice guys finish last (or some such). It is hard to accept a gift with no strings attached. It is hard to let go and let God. It is hard to accept that you are cherished in the midst of the you you have a hard time accepting as lovable. At least, I have a hard time with it.

It may be even more difficult if you look upon the parable of the talents as referring to the words at face value, to the talents one has been given. I have always had a gnawing suspicion that I was at heart an overachiever, which surely gets in the way of achieving the stature of the person I would like to be (I need to emphasize the phrase, what I would like to *be*, not what I would like to *do*.) That is where the parable of the talents is a reproach to me. The third servant (and I keep wondering whether that was not the youngest son, the one who should have had the least to lose) was condemned not because he saved his talent, but because he didn't venture it or risk it – for his own sake. How many times have you not offered yourself where help was needed, out of fear that what you had to offer was not adequate? (I can only begin counting on my fingers for me.)

A talent is like a primary muscle group. Some of us are able to get through life without exercising much, but the muscle's capacity is enlarged through testing its limits. I spent the equivalent of 13 seasons rowing in an eight-oared shell. One summer we traveled to England to compete in the Henley Royal Regatta, the premier international event of rowing, where we learned about the quaint English training formula for racing: you have to row the last half on desire. (That is a high price for an overachiever to pay.)

There is also a quaint saying in spiritual matters, that the Lord himself helps you fulfill what he requires of you. And that is where *faith* is necessary along with courage. Few of us are called upon to wager our faith in momentous events; all of us are called to be faithful over little things – over what we sometimes mistakenly refer to as the "small change" of love in our common life. "Celebration Rock," on the radio Sunday mornings, ends by saying, "In the week ahead, remember to be gentle with others, and be gentle with yourself" – no small task for the week. The week ahead, God love us, is never the week that is past but always to the week to come – where we will, like Fred Buechner, have the opportunity and the obligation individually, with words and deeds, to "scratch up in a public place ... longings and loves, ... grievances and indecencies," like graffiti..."[3] With our talents, great and small,

433

we will make our mark upon the walls of the week. We are called upon to scribble up our talents, not to squirrel them away. That will be sufficient, and that is the reminder that renders the parable of the talents palatable.

Graffiti, by Robert Fulghum, writings on the walls.

Did you ever write something on a wall?
Come on, now, didn't you ever do a little graffiti somewhere?
Or at least think about it – something a little dirty or cute or cynical or clever?
On a school desk, a fence, a telephone booth or a bathroom somewhere?
Even God is supposed to have done it at least once.
In the Bible – in the Book of Daniel – handwriting on the wall.
"Mene Mene Tekel Upharsin" he wrote – and scared old Belshazzar out of his wits.
"Your days are Numbered – you and yours shall be destroyed."

And they were and they were and he was.
Heavy-duty graffiti, that.
Anyhow.
I've never actually seen anyone writing on a wall, come to think of it.
And nobody I know will actually admit doing it.
But there it is – all over the walls, all over the world.
Political, sexual, literary, humorous, bitter, angry, racial, religious.
There it is.
A record of the passing of the human race.
Archaeologists have uncovered graffiti that's over 15,000 years old.
And on the walls of every civilization uncovered to date, it's there.
In some private, secret moment, the human hand and mind contrive to leave a mark.

*Some investigators have discovered that janitors
who are supposed to wash it off, in fact do much of
the writing.*
*Paint and maintenance men and parents and po-
licemen notwithstanding, it goes on.*
*There's something a little strange, a little sad and
lonely about graffiti.*
*But something kind of invincible about the universal
urge to write on the walls of existence.*
*All the billions of ordinary people who will never
write books or songs or history or poetry,*
*put their loves and hates and fears and hopes and
dreams and laughter on the walls of this earth as a
gesture toward oblivion and eternal mystery.*
*Sometimes I think, upon contemplating a restroom
wall, that I'd like to write something so fine, so en-
nobling, so elegant,*
*so succinctly meaningful and perfect that it would
have the power*
*to change lives while people were washing their
hands.*
*Something that would be picked up and passed
on to walls everywhere – something to add to the
inevitable, "Kilroy was here" ...*
I think about that a lot....

In the midst of your graffiti of the week ahead

Remember to be gentle with others, and be gentle with
yourself.

That is a talent that will multiply itself.

––––––

1. "Type A" and "ESFP" are among the abbreviations used in
   the publications of the Myers-Briggs Type Indicator and
   other personality assessment tools to refer to various per-

sonality types. The MBTI assessment was developed from the work of Carl G. Jung in his book Psychological Types. (Wikipedia)

2. Chuck Robb was the 64th Governor of Virginia from 1982 to 1986, and a United States senator from 1989 until 2001.

3. Frederick Buechner, *The Alphabet of Grace, 1970*

LOVE, SWEET LOVE

23rd Sunday after Pentecost
Matthew 22:34-40
Proper 25 – Year A – 27 October 2002

> *When the Pharisees heard that Jesus had si-*
> *lenced the Sadducees, they gathered together, and*
> *one of them, a lawyer, asked him a question to test*
> *him. "Teacher, which commandment in the law is*
> *the greatest?" He said to him, "'You shall love the*
> *Lord your God with all your heart, and with all your*
> *soul, and with all your mind.' This is the greatest and*
> *first commandment. And a second is like it: 'You shall*
> *love your neighbor as yourself.' On these two com-*
> *mandments hang all the law and the prophets. "*

> *Matthew 22:34-40*

Published in the magazine *Christianity Today* was this pithy little piece: "Next time you hear, 'All you need is luv,' think of the captain of the Titanic singing it to his passengers. As for me, I'd rather have a lifeboat," says Peter Kreeft.[1]

That caught me up short because it took me back to a time more than thirty years ago at Exeter Academy when I was Chairman of the Religion Department, sitting naked in the faculty sauna of the then opulent new $5 million gym, along with some of the Athletic Department coaches, sweating and swapping jokes. The "Muzak," selected by them was piped in along with the steam; and the song that was hot at that time, which they would play over and over, was the one that kept repeating (I can hear it now):

"What the world needs now is love, sweet love; it's the only thing that there's just too little of" – only they made up for it by playing the record again and again. It was their theme song, but it made me cringe.

When I politely said something about too much of a good thing, one of the young turks with a buzz cut slapped me on my wet thigh, saying "Relax Reverend (although I was not the slightest bit ordained at that point), you can take that as your text for your Sunday sermon and you won't even have to crack a Bible," followed by great guffaws from all the fellows.

I suppose the song has at least one redeeming verse, the last half line of the refrain: What the world needs now is love, sweet love ... *not just for some, but for everyone.*" But I can't forgive the rest of it because I can't stop the tune from playing over and over in my head. The good news is it's a lead in for the famous formula familiar to us, found in Matthew this morning, where Jesus is confronted by a bunch of the Pharisees asking "Teacher, which commandment in the Law is the greatest?"

...there were in the Torah 613 commandments — 248 positive ones, corresponding to the number of the parts of the body and 365 negative ones for a year's worth of days...

It's a trick question of course; it was not sincere or collegial, only designed to trip him up (the Greek says to "test" or tempt" him) because there were in the Torah 613 commandments – 248 positive ones, corresponding to the number of the parts of the body and 365 negative ones for a year's worth of days, a "'Thou shalt not' for every day of the year."[2] But the point for the Pharisees was all God's laws were equally binding, and any attempt to rank them was seen as sheer human duplicity in discriminating against the divine law. Besides, "If Ten Commandments were good, twenty commandments were better."[3] If Jesus, drawn into debate, should choose one of them, that would show him disparaging some part of God's law. Instead, Jesus chose two commandments: the first taken from Deuteronomy, "You shall love the Lord your God with all your heart and with all your soul and with all your might" (6:5) and a second, from Leviticus, "(You Shall) love your neighbor as yourself..." (19:18).

A "two-fer," we might say: Jesus' answer to the dilemma of an unanswerable theological question and the undoable practical problem that applying all 613 commandments at once was impossible (even if you could manage to remember them) – damned if you didn't and outdone if you did. How to get Jesus off the hook? Well if you had to hang all the laws on one nail, which one would hold the weight? You could say that the love of God and love of neighbor is really two nails, but the point is, he treats them as one. Why? Not just because he needed something simple for simple-moraled people, and its simplicity is appealing – framing the familiar formula we have heard so often we hardly know what it is saying, even though Jesus adds, "Upon these commandments hang all the Law and the Prophets."

But they become one because of his astute use of the word "like." After the first and great commandment ("greatest" by definition because it was the *first* given by God to Moses on Mt. Sinai) comes a second one *like* the first – which does not simply mean it is similar, but of equal importance and inseparable from the first. So that the great command precludes our loving God first and then finding the heart to love our neighbor. Rather, as he said it, to love God is to love one's neighbor, and of course that's what causes the problem for us.

Moreover, Matthew does not explain the theological issues that may interest us most precisely at this point, namely what did he mean when he used the words "love" and "neighbor"? One commentator explains that Matthew's omission was because he focused on Jesus' polemic, his attack, on the Pharisees' understanding of love and neighbor, making a kind of pun on the word "Torah" or "Law" which comes from the verb "*yarah*," meaning "to throw something." So "God's words are torah and we are the target," not the interpreters.[4]

In any case, in the Old Testament context familiar to the Pharisees, "neighbor" was applied to one's fellow Israelite: family, friends, tribe. Whereas, in Matthew's meaning, Jesus' disciples had been enjoined to extend their love to embrace even an enemy, which was clearly contrary to the core of earlier biblical injunction. But the key is his concept of love. That's where the canker festers for us. Loving humankind and loving a bed partner are not the same thing. And some of us simply couldn't care less about the people across the street or around the world. Then there's our fear that offering love opens us to rejection – or that in our efforts at love we will impose on others or offend them.

───◦◦───

I don't know what the Aramaic term for "hogwash" is...

───◦◦───

Distrust is also a deterrent. We fear that if we show ourselves vulnerable we will be violated. Our self-interest can keep us from loving others because encouraging someone else's advantage allows them to take advantage of us. And of course you hear a lot these days about how unless I can love myself first I cannot learn to love someone else. I don't know what the Aramaic term for "hogwash" is, but it would have been characteristic of Jesus to use it in response to such a suggestion.

"Love your neighbor as yourself" is not a treatise on learning how to love yourself. In fact, our self-preoccupation is in large measure what Jesus was trying to free us from. Our primary problem is that we are so often inherently selfish: "Our inclination is to love ourselves first, putting our personal needs [and interests] before the needs of others."[5] In that, we are not "sick," but simply self-centered. In that sense we already know very well how to love ourselves. And because we are inclined to put ourselves first, placing ourselves at the center of our universe, we also have a problem putting God before our own needs – or, in terms of today's text, loving God first.

That's why the command to love, as we call it, is first of all a commandment. It has nothing to do with whether we feel like loving; it only asks us to act lovingly in God's name. Yes, it is dangerous to love and be loved, yet ironically for many of us, to be loved unconditionally is our greatest desire. As children, we learn from our parents life's great lessons of love long before we know how to name them or have learned to say what love is or to understand Oscar Hammerstein's lyric "... love in your heart is not put there to stay. Love is not love until you give it away."[6]

What does it mean to love your neighbor? Russell Seabright says it simply and, if you will, right out of the Old Testament. Practice love as what the Hebrews called justice and mercy: Protect the rights of others as you would want your own to be protected, not as charity but as a just response to the rights of fellow human beings. Offer forgiveness and mercy when and where you would desire them for yourself. In order to claim justice for ourselves we must have practiced justice for others. The measure of my love is what I do, not only with what I have been given, but with what I have given of what I have to others.

Whether you agree with how Jesus put it is not as important as how you decide for yourself what is most important for your life and living. That means setting priorities and making choices, and nowhere I know of did Jesus make simple those decisions for us. When someone asks him which of God's commandments is the most important, in his answer he forces us to confront what is most important to us. Something like in the story Fred Craddock tells about two missionaries in China. They were a married couple with two small children. When the communists came to power, somebody told them, "You will have to leave the country. You can only take one hundred fifty pounds between you." They surveyed the beautiful treasures they had accumulated: the hand-carved breakfront, the ivory carvings, the priceless ink sketches on rice paper. It was an agonizing process to choose only a few special items that they wished to keep.

When they arrived at the dock with their carefully packed bundle, a man with a clipboard said, "Did you weigh your children?"[7]

"The measure of my love is what I do with what I have been given...."

------

1. *Homiletics,* 11, 5 p.65
2. *Ibid.*
3. *Lectionary Homiletics* XIII, 11 p.31
4. *Biblical Preaching Journal* 15, 4 p.10
5. *Lectionary Homiletics* XIII, 11 p.30
6. *Op. cit.,* p.28
7. *Op. cit.,* p.31

THE LAST LAUGH

23rd Sunday after Pentecost
Luke 10:1-10
Proper 26 – Year C – November 4, 2007

Jesus entered Jericho and was passing through it. A man was there named Zacchaeus; he was a chief tax collector and was rich. He was trying to see who Jesus was, but on account of the crowd he could not, because he was short in stature. So he ran ahead and climbed a sycamore tree to see him, because he was going to pass that way. When Jesus came to the place, he looked up and said to him, "Zacchaeus, hurry and come down; for I must stay at your house today." So he hurried down and was happy to welcome him. All who saw it began to grumble and said, "He has gone to be the guest of one who is a sinner." Zacchaeus stood there and said to the Lord, "Look, half of my possessions, Lord, I will give to the poor; and if I have defrauded anyone of anything, I will pay back four times as much." Then Jesus said to him, "Today salvation has come to this house, because he too is a son of Abraham. For the Son of Man came to seek out and to save the lost."

Luke 10:1-10

I'm sure if our old friend Phebe Hoff were able to be with us this morning, she would be the first to ask "Why is the gospel reading about Zacchaeus being used on All Saint's Sunday?" My defensive response would be "I was not on the liturgical commit-

tee that assigned the reading for the 23rd Sunday after Pentecost."
But I would then add that Zacchaeus is the perfect person to remember on this day because he was anything but the kind of saint
we are likely to think about on All Saint's Day, those who were
martyred upside down or slowly roasted over the fire for their
faith. Zacchaeus was more like the motley ones St. Paul addresses
as "saints" in his letters: flawed, sometimes faint of heart, fully
aware of their unfaithfulness. Furthermore, whatever sort of saint
we might first think of, Jesus chose to lift up Zacchaeus, however
unlikely we or the world might judge him to be.

And what further commends the story to me is that the
text itself, in keeping with the comic figure Zacchaeus cuts, is a
kind of cosmic joke, where the laugh is on us and our often small
view of sainthood. Fittingly, Zacchaeus is small, short on so many
things. I'm sure I'm not the only one to call Zacchaeus the Danny
DiVito of First century Palestine. He's a hoot, not a hero; but at the
heart of this story is laughter that lets us rejoice when God's love
unexpectedly bursts exuberantly into the life of the one we might
think of as least deserving among us. Maybe we should weep,
for him or for us; but it's hard not to be overjoyed when we hear
Jesus' judgment: "Salvation has come to this house (your house,
my house) today."

What an odd thing to say considering the circumstances
and Zacchaeus himself, the hated tax collector, flunky for Rome,
a sawed-off, cocky, crooked, pompous little jerk whose first encounter with Jesus is up a tree, Zacchaeus hanging on to a limb
for dear life with one hand while waving wildly with the other as
Jesus passes by beneath him. Furthermore, he is rich, and not
even taking into account how he amassed his wealth. That means,
as someone else has said, much of the good news in Luke's gospel
is bad news for him.

There are a number of curious things in the text itself that
sets one to speculating if not snickering. Like: Why is this chief tax
collector, one who dishonestly makes himself rich at the expense

of his own people, called by a name like Zaccai which means "pure" or "righteous?" Is Luke purposely perpetrating upon us a poor pun? (I suppose it's no less believable than my being called Christopher, Christ bearer, when sometimes the way I live out my faith can't be called Christian in any sense that I can believe matters much to Christ or anybody else.)

Then there's the phrase "small of stature," which according to the unfortunate Greek syntax of the sentence somehow refers to Jesus, not to Zacchaeus, but which is inseparably central to the reason why Zacchaeus had to climb the tree in the first place. Speaking of the tree, one commentary calls it "a detail with a light sense of humor." But I cannot find anything inherently funny about a sycamore tree – unless it is that this type of wild fig tree would not likely be growing in downtown Jericho – so that in that setting the tree is a fig-ment of Luke's imagination.

Lastly, among the oddities in the text, in the last verse, Jesus is said to have said what he said to Zacchaeus, but by the end of that same verse Zacchaeus is spoken of in the third person. Somewhat disconcerting for a sometime English teacher expected to explain the simple meaning of the narrative.

But if those peculiarities don't help us to decipher, they also don't allow us to dismiss, the story of Zacchaeus. Nor do they enable us to explain why Luke thought this vignette was important enough to include in his Gospel (it is not in the others'). Or why you should be interested in it if you don't have to preach a sermon about it. So I'm going to venture an answer out of my gut, not out of a biblical commentary.

The first glimpse we get in the narrative is not of Zacchaeus but of Jesus, and the first question that comes to my mind is why did Jesus so often run off among queer people, into unfamiliar places, to do what needed doing? Why didn't he try to nourish the upright and proper people (like you and me) who were trying to uphold traditional values and conventional religious practices?

That same question was put to Jesus earlier in Luke's text by the Pharisees and the Scribes, the learned men and religious leaders of the community, in this form: "Why do you eat and drink with tax collectors and sinners?" – implying that a person is known by the company he keeps. And, fortunately, for once, Jesus gives a clear and direct, unambiguous answer. He says "Those who are well have no need of a physician, but those who are sick. I have come not to call the righteous, but sinners to repentance." (Luke 5:31-32)

His answer is so simple, so succinct, and so thoroughly unacceptable to us – because when we read the story, we suppose ourselves to be the good and decent people, protectors of venerable values and virtues. But Jesus tells us straight out that he prefers the company of cutthroats and crooks, adulterers and extortionists, prostitutes and petty thieves – because they at least are honest about who they are, and they know that they are in need of help.

Where the gospel turns out to be good news, not good riddance, where the gospel is most effective and we are caught up in it, is when we are caught off guard and don't expect to hear it, when we are taken by surprise and are least able to defend ourselves against it.

The Zacchaeus zero-sum (a word, I lately learned, referring to a situation in which a gain for one must result in a loss for others) is that Jesus prefers the company of shyster Zacchaeus to the upstanding citizens of Jericho and the proper priests of the temple, those whose lives are invariably in order and whose vision leaves little room to be surprised by joy and less inclination to contemplate a change in values, financial goals, or friends. It seems to me we are *meant* to be offended by that.

But that would at least be a beginning for us, a foot in the spiritual door of our invincible uncharity toward those who "haven't got it" or haven't "made it." Annoying as it is, that little man, Zacchaeus, has something to teach us, not only about saints but about ourselves. He shakes the tree of our conventional certainties. In Jesus' meeting with him we meet the gospel "on the road," as Luke tells it – not in the temple or in the church where we have all our religious defenses in place – and it is there that we meet the unexpected.

Clearly, outcast Zacchaeus is "out of his tree" when he receives Jesus joyfully. Just imagine, right there, Zacchaeus changes his mind, changes his ways, changes his life – all in one verse! While we're rummaging about in the text, seeking for clues about how God works, God is seeking *us* out in Zacchaeus (or seeking out the Zacchaeus in us, out on a limb, hanging on for dear life). That little nobody is so dumbfounded by that unlikely gift that he says; "I'm going to get my priorities straight. I'm going to give half of everything I have to the poor, and if I've cheated anyone I'll restore to them their loss fourfold."

That one chance moment made all the difference: in it his shadowy past is redeemed, his uncertain present is transformed, his predictable future is redirected. The Zacchaeus' logic becomes something like this: If we are either upset or grateful that Jesus prefers the company of sinners, why not invite him to our table? After all, did God not bless Abraham the liar and Jacob the thief and Rahab the prostitute and David the adulterer before us? What do we have to fear?

Maybe what is more upsetting than anything else to some of us is that, secretly, we wish we could believe in God without anything having to come out of it. If only something didn't have to happen in faith, or if we didn't have to do anything different from what we've always done. If only we could climb a tree for a better view – and not find Jesus inviting himself right into our lives.

Can we imagine what Jesus might have said to Zacchaeus? If all Jesus asked him was, "Zacchaeus, what did you see that made you want this peace?" And if all Zacchaeus said was, "I saw mirrored in your eyes the face of the Zacchaeus I was meant to be," that would be enough.

But the kicker is Jesus' unexpected reply: "Today salvation has come to this house," which may not sound much like salvation that concerns *us* – more like a laughing matter. It's much easier to take seriously the hopelessness we see in the world around us, which we learn to laugh at so we won't continually weep over it. But our laughter at the heart of the Zacchaeus story is of a different kind. It is about God's love that comes barging into the life of the least deserving dude in town and draws out of him an unlikely response of openness and charity – not the laughter of escape for us, but the last and best laugh that we can hardly keep inside us: the laughter of joy, which we can spread around – if we are willing.

A RIDICULOUS RESURRECTION

23rd Sunday after Pentecost
Luke 20:27-35
Proper 27 – Year C – November 11, 2001

> *Some Sadducees, those who say there is no resurrection, came to Jesus and asked him a question, "Teacher, Moses wrote for us that if a man's brother dies, leaving a wife but no children, the man shall marry the widow and raise up children for his brother. Now there were seven brothers; the first married, and died childless; then the second and the third married her, and so in the same way all seven died childless. Finally the woman also died. In the resurrection, therefore, whose wife will the woman be? For the seven had married her."*
>
> *Jesus said to them, "Those who belong to this age marry and are given in marriage; but those who are considered worthy of a place in that age and in the resurrection from the dead neither marry nor are given in marriage.*
>
> Luke 20:27-35

This week, all unawares, I came face to face with the resurrection (the word, that is)- which I hadn't planned on raising until Easter, if you'll pardon the pun. In our scripture readings, the Sadducees, who raised the question about resurrection in the first place, obviously didn't give a fig about whatever Jesus might have answered them because they didn't believe in resurrection anyway. So we are left in our gospel text with a ridiculous riddle about the woman with seven husbands – whose wife will she be in the resurrection? But that's the kind of thing that ministers are often asked to explain.

A couple of weeks ago I was at Burger King early one morning for breakfast when a man at the table next to me leaned over my eggand-sausage biscuit and asked, "Doesn't the Bible tell us when the world will end?" Not my Bible," I answered and he looked as though I had struck him. He assumed I should know about those kinds of things. Which is why I suppose I took note when I read recently what one pastor wrote:

"I heard a child's voice asking the secretary, 'Could I talk with Pastor Willson?'... She had a question, she said. Week before last her puppy dog had been run over.... She wondered ... and decided to ask me: ... Was her puppy with God in heaven? She loved her puppy, but... she was not certain that puppies counted for enough to be included in the Kingdom, ... It is the kind of question lovers ask." She asked me because pastors are supposed to know about such things.[1]

"On another occasion, a second question came, this time from an 80s-year-old elegant southern lady as I sat with her in a hospital corridor.

"Her husband was dying .... Both in their mid-eighties, they had been married almost three years. He had been a widower, she a widow. Each had come to a nearby retirement village to die. Instead, they fell in love-tender, giggling love. They held hands in church and smooched under the pecan trees. The three years had been as happy as any they had known. Now he was dying .... He didn't know what year it was or with which congregation [I] was affiliated, ... but he knew ... I was his pastor.

"The problem was, his mind slipped back and forth as to which name his beloved wife should be called ... He spoke to his wife sometimes addressing her by his first wife's name, sometimes

450

using her own name. While that distressed this gentle woman, she understood ... [but] a question was nevertheless raised.... Whose wife would she be in the hereafter, whose husband would he be? It is a question love asks, and with eyes full of tears and trust, she asked me. Pastors are supposed to know about such things."[2]

I hate to interrupt this poignant human drama to talk about the acerbic Sadducees and their scheme to discredit Jesus, let alone about the law of levirate marriage, which Luke assumes in his antagonistic anecdote. And the question the Sadducees advanced was not asked in love. The problem posed proceed from the legal provision (in the book of Deuteronomy 25:5-10), not widely practiced any longer in first century Judaism, that "if brothers live together and one of them dies leaving no son, the other brother shall marry the widow. The first son of this union shall take the name of the brother who dies."[3]

Thereafter, his house was to be called, "The house of him whose sandal was pulled off." So you see this was serious stuff!

The Israelite community, it is said, as a whole accepted endogamy. If the brother-in-law refused to perform the marriage (that is, to have sexual relations) with his brother's wife, she was to bring him before the village elders. And if he again refused to do his duty, she was to tear off one of his sandals, denounce him and spit in his face. Thereafter, his house was to be called, "The house of him whose sandal was pulled off." So you see this was serious stuff! Not strictly the subject of the Sadducees' scenario on which they ridiculed the reality of resurrection life. The situation they set forth was ridiculous, but they regarded the resurrection as ridiculous. The only help they held out beyond the grave was that by marrying and carrying on the family name through their children, they thus lived on after death and achieved an immortality of sorts.

Jesus was judicious enough to join the argument on their own grounds, invoking the authority of Moses. "You want to talk about Mosaic Law, well then what did Moses say?" First and foremost he testified that God is the God of Abraham, Isaac, and Jacob. What was it he must have meant? Jesus asks. Does logic lead us to the conclusion that God is essentially absent; only present in the experience of non-existent individuals – to put it bluntly, "the dead god of dead men"? Or does it mean God abides in our understanding of enduring life – "a living God," whose people live in him and live on in his love? Jesus summarizes it more strikingly by saying, "Now God is not God of the dead, but of the living; for to God all of them are alive."

You may not be convinced by what he said, but the Sadducees were struck speechless. For us, the question might be expressed more expansively: What experience endures between this life and the life to come? If the dead live on in God, what kind of life do they enjoy? What is the outcome of the experiences that have made us who we are – do they continue on? And what about the future of our families, friends, spouses and special relationships we have cherished, children, and kitty cats we have cared for, puppies we have loved? As someone else has asked, "Scripture invites us to love one another, but is the end of all our loving simply the end?"[4] Or put more personally, "If I die, shall I live again?"

Appropriately, Jesus does not offer us an easy answer and we resume our wrestling with the resurrection. In such situations I seek out the observations of Fred Buechner. If anyone can come up with the right words, often he will. He explains the affirmations of faith contained in the creeds that speak of resurrection, this way: "... The belief that what God in spite of everything prizes enough to bring back to life is not some disembodied echo of a human being, but a new ... version of all the things which made him the particular human being he was and which he needs something like a body to express: his personality, the way he looked, the sound of his voice, his peculiar capacity of creating and loving ... "[5]

452

If that doesn't finally satisfy us, maybe we have to appeal to our own experience of life to approach an understanding. "For those who have lived through violent, abusive marriages, the [idea] that in the resurrection we will neither [need to] marry nor be given in marriage [as Jesus put it] may come as liberating good news. On the other hand, those who have enjoyed lifelong intimacy and companionship ... may well [insist] that God has invested so much in establishing faithful, loving, and fulfilling relationships in this life that it is unthinkable that such relationships would be terminated in the resurrection." [6]

Maybe that is what resurrection is really about: the realization that love never ends, that the God who gave us life and the longing for loving relationships in marriage and elsewhere has proffered us life after death "for those who have cultivated the capacity to respond to God's love" living in us and in others.

When it comes to words, one thing at least is clear to me, I cannot answer the impertinent parishioner who (as Patrick Willson puts it) protests she will not be satisfied until she hears the subject addressed in the sermon "Will There Be Sex in Heaven?" And Other Quaint Questions, like: "If it's the body to be raised, will it be this overweight one? Can I apply for a new set of knees? Will I have hair?"[7] I have no answers to the problems we want replies for about resurrection, not even in the prayers of the pastor who is supposed to know about such things, and who professes that above all, love never ends. Maybe our task is just to trust and see, and "in the meantime try to love one another as best we can ... asking the questions lovers ask, and knowing all the while that they can only be answered fully in God's love for us."[8]

---

1. *Biblical Preaching Journal* 14, 4-p.17

2. *Ibid.*

3. *IDB* 4, p.116

4. *Biblical Preaching Journal*, p.17

5. Frederick Buechner, *Wishful Thinking*, pp. 42·3
6. *New Interpreters Bible* IX, pp.389-90
7. *Biblical Preaching Journal*, p.18
8. *Ibid.* I owe much of my ideas and enthusiasm for this pre-posterous passage to the thoughtful and perceptive piece by Patrick J. Willson, "Love Asks the Question."

READY OR NOT

24th Sunday after Pentecost
Matthew 25:1-13
Proper 27 – Year A – November 10, 1996

Jesus said, "Then the kingdom of heaven will be like this. Ten bridesmaids took their lamps and went to meet the bridegroom. Five of them were foolish, and five were wise. When the foolish took their lamps, they took no oil with them; but the wise took flasks of oil with their lamps. As the bridegroom was delayed, all of them became drowsy and slept. But at midnight there was a shout, 'Look! Here is the bridegroom! Come out to meet him.' Then all those bridesmaids got up and trimmed their lamps. The foolish said to the wise, 'Give us some of your oil, for our lamps are going out.' But the wise replied, 'No! there will not be enough for you and for us; you had better go to the dealers and buy some for yourselves.' And while they went to buy it, the bridegroom came, and those who were ready went with him into the wedding banquet; and the door was shut. Later the other bridesmaids came also, saying,' Lord, lord, open to us.' But he replied, 'Truly I tell you, I do not know you.' Keep awake therefore, for you know neither the day nor the hour."

Matthew 25:1-13

This morning's gospel parable is wonderfully unfair – as long as I am not seen as one of the five foolish bridesmaids, of

455

course. (You may remember them as the wise and foolish "virgins" in your translation of the Bible, because that's what the Greek word says, but it may not be politically correct to call virgins foolish these days.) Anyway, the parable is wonderfully unfair because if you were at all present while it was being read, you must have been set wondering either about what would be fair or what on earth Matthew must have meant by it.

A traditional interpretation would begin by saying the bridesmaids represent the people of God, and in the parable, they await the return of the bridegroom (who is Jesus) who has promised to be there but has not yet come. The task of the bridesmaids, foolish or wise, is not just to wait for his coming so as to enjoy the wedding feast, but in the interim faithfully to prepare for living the full Christian life. Their oil lamps are symbolic not only of preparation but of the willingness to carry out what they are preparing for. At that time oil was used for food (they weren't worried about cholesterol back then), fuel, medicine, for anointing people for sacred purposes and for sacrificing in the temple. Oil was also a symbol of trustworthiness; it represented deeds of mercy and love.

That kind of tidy explanation may let us off the hook too easily; nothing much sounds unfair in such an interpretation. Whereas, in the parable, ten bridesmaids show up and wait but five are shut out entirely when they go to get more oil to keep their lamps burning. Furthermore, the bridegroom says to them, through the closed door, "Truly I tell you, I do not know you."

Do you remember Woody Allen's assertion that 90% of success is just showing up? Surely the worst thing we can do is fail to show up for the moment God has given us – to show mercy, meet a need, tell the truth, give a hand, heal a hurt; to hope, to pray, even to wait if that is what's necessary. The bridesmaids showed up. So what's the problem? Why were they shut out?

It may be that "90% of success is just showing up;" the problem is, "Just showing up doesn't get the job done." It takes more than good intentions to be a faithful member of the community. It may well be that this is not the world we would have chosen to "show up" in. Sometimes it may be more than we can handle. Maybe it asks too much of us. If you read the Richmond paper at all, maybe morally and materially if not metaphorically, you'd "rather be in Philadelphia."

⸻∘⸻

"Showing up" may be courageous, cowardly, cranky, or cool on our part - but it is not enough.

⸻∘⸻

Jesus doesn't ask us to like the world we are called to. He doesn't say we have to accept it the way it is, only to show up and struggle to do what we can do to make it and us whole. In Joseph Heller's preface to his novel Catch 22, he writes: "All events in this book were based on reality, but have been changed to make them more believable." How about the airline survey which found that "one in three pet owners talks to his or her animal over the telephone while away from home." Heaven knows what we may find unacceptable about the world we live in. The world may not be made in our image, and what we are called to show up for may be the lonely, confused, self-absorbed, and heartsick – if we by chance are none of those. "Showing up" may be courageous, cowardly, cranky, or cool on our part – but it is not enough. Being present may or may not be pleasant – but what is needed from us is more presence.

The five foolish bridesmaids had no presence of mind for the moment God presented them with; they ran out of oil (or gas or gumption) to get them where they wanted to go. They needed not just to show up but to be "present." I'm not sure whether that's the right word for it – to be part of all that is, with all of yourself. Not having it all together as much as being there in altogetherness. You can say better than I what it means for you to give life all of yourself, to be fully (in the moment).

To "be present" may mean to see things as they really are, but not to settle for what we see. An Urban League billboard says, "Life is unfair. Get over it. Get a job." In keeping with the watch-words of this morning's parable, is the motto of Atlanta 's version of Starbuck's coffee, Caribou Cafes: "Life is short. Stay awake." When you're driving you don't want to fall asleep at the wheel of life. Remember, to give as much as ninety percent to the moment still means we are ten percent dead to it. Total focus is what we're after, even if it is unattainable for most of us.

Have you heard this story about Albert Einstein? He was "famous for his 'altogetherness,' his heightened powers of concentration legendary. At one dinner party in Princeton, the after dinner discussion kept on into the small hours of the morning until finally Einstein got up and said apologetically, 'I hate to do this, but I must put you out now because I have to be on campus in the morning.' 'Albert,' his host said, 'you are in my house.'" Do you remember the nervous remark of the newly trained psychiatrist whose beginning assignment was the psychiatric ward in a hospital? Not sure just what to say to his first patients gathered before lunch, he said, "Now why do you suppose we are all here?" Whereupon, one person spoke up enthusiastically, "Doctor, it is clear why we're all here, it's because we're not all there."

Being fully present means being passionate for where you are and what you are doing. I have been told that "Immigrant students ridicule American kids on college campuses, who are seen as lazy, loose, unappreciative, not 'all there' for the gift of an education. A slur these immigrants apply to one another when they see themselves becoming less enthusiastic about their college responsibilities is 'You're becoming American.'" Matthew does not reflect on the metaphorical nationality of the five foolish bridesmaids. What he slams them for is not being fully present for the moment in which God calls them to go in with him to the great feast. They were an hour late and oil short; eager, but ill equipped for the unexpected.

William Holmes Border, the late pastor of Atlanta's Wheat Street Baptist Church, liked to pray before church services: "Lord, let something happen here today that's not in the bulletin."

The five bridesmaids were not fully focused on what they were called to do. A little like the executive who, while traveling, was writing ingratiating postcards to the people back home. "He wrote the usual, 'The scenery is beautiful, wish you were here,' except that he inadvertently sent to his secretary, 'The scenery is here, wish you were beautiful.'" Some gaffs cannot be got over gracefully. (Quotation from Homiletics, 8, 4 pp. 26-28)

As one commentary concluded: "The futile attempt to buy oil after the arrival of the bridegroom, though historically unrealistic, shows the futility of trying to prepare when it is too late. For Matthew, there are finally only two groups: those who are ready and those who are not ... Having the right confession [of faith] without the corresponding [quality of] life is, ultimately [insufficient).

"At the beginning of the parable ... Jesus tells us that five of the ten bridesmaids were foolish. He has to tell us this because at the outset we cannot tell by looking at them. All ten have come to the wedding; all ten have their lamps aglow with expectations; all ten presumably have on their bridesmaid gowns. How could we guess from appearances that half are wise and half foolish?

"It is not their looks or lamps or fine garments that sets the wise apart from the foolish – it is their readiness ... The wise have enough oil for the wedding to start whenever the groom arrives; the foolish have only enough oil for their own timetable."

Readiness for Matthew is being prepared to live all of life as an act of faith, willing to have our life shaped by what we believe – and not the other way around. "At the beginning of the life of faith you cannot really tell the followers of Jesus apart. They all have lamps; they all know how to say 'Lord, Lord.' Only deep into the night when we are surrounded by darkness, some of us trying frantically to fan a dying flame to light, do we begin to understand the difference between wisdom and foolishness." (NIB VII pp. 450)

Pardon this parting benediction I purloined – too tempting to try to suppress:

Just walk it. Just talk it. Just preach it. Just pray it. Just teach it. Just tell it. Just live it. Just give it. Just wear it. Just share it. Just shout it. Just sing it. Proclaim it. Just claim it for Jesus. Just do it.

———

Footnote: Putting together this sermon, I am indebted to a variety of sources for insights and quotations. The concluding commentary is largely taken from the *New Interpreter's Bible* VII, "Reflections," p. 451. Some of the other material quoted comes from *Homiletics* 8,4, pp. 26-7 – and I also borrowed familiar anecdotes, gratefully.

HIGH FIVE

24th Sunday after Pentecost
Matthew 25:1-13
Proper 27 – Year A – November 7, 1999

Last Sunday we celebrated All Saints Day; this Sunday is After Saints day- we're not done with them yet. So often it seems, our saints are someone else somewhere else; seldom do we see them in our midst. But today we salute one of us, not the only saint to be sure, but saint enough to speak of this day as Sam Day, Sam Bruce booster day. You may wonder what Sam has to do with the famous Five Wise and Five Foolish Virgins (or, as our text translates, "bridesmaids")? At first blush, not much, but then I didn't choose this text for the gospel this Sunday. Not to worry, in preaching on the purpose of the parable, I'm going to propose that it is not as inappropriate as you might first perceive for the point of the party we have planned after the service.

In case you missed the first sentence of our scripture this morning, it says, "The kingdom of heaven will be like this." And the story that follows has always been spoken of as The Parable of the Wise and Foolish Virgins – suppose because the Greek text says, literally, "ten virgins." Some of our older English translations use the less restrictive "maidens," justified on the older assumption that a young woman would of course be a virgin. Not so in the translations of our times; it's probably not P.C. to impose that burden upon anyone, let alone invite a lawsuit over whichever way you don't want to be referred to, virgin or otherwise.

Why does the NRSV use the word "bridesmaids"? My guess is that it makes the parable about a wedding feast more appropriate and less complicated. So for the sake of the sermon I'll play along with the current translation, but I want to state at the start that if we get rid of our virgins, we will have lost more than the literal Greek. Because the symbol for "virgin" in the story stands for the presence of the unpretentiously enthusiastic, the unfailingly faithful, the unadorned trustworthy and good willed – even if that perspective prevents us from accepting a simple interpretation of the parable. Whether we are "wise" or "foolish" doesn't depend on losing our virginity, so to speak, but such insight is lost when we use the word "bridesmaids" in the story, it seems to me.

So saying, what are we to make of Matthew's meaning in the tale of the five wise and five foolish bridesmaids? What's the point of the parable? I could quote a caption from the Caribou Cafes in Atlanta, whose slogan selling their coffee is, "Life is short. Stay awake." But that doesn't quite compute in this case because while waiting for the bridegroom, all ten bridesmaids became drowsy... and fell asleep. Why then does Jesus call five of them foolish and five wise? It wasn't their presence that made the difference, or their eagerness, or even their watchfulness.

"Ten bridesmaids took their lamps and went to meet the bridegroom," Jesus says. Outwardly, they were identical. Apparently, nothing in their appearance set them apart; their dresses were gorgeous, their lamps aglow as they awaited the arrival of the bridegroom together, and when he was delayed until midnight they all dosed off – the wise and the foolish. You couldn't tell one from the other. Their difference depended on their readiness, not their I.Q. What determined whether they were wise, writes one commentator, was their S.I., their spiritual intelligence, not their I.Q. If five were foolish and five were wise, it was because "half had high S.I. and half had low S.I."[1] Since all ten did the same things, it goes to show that "spiritual intelligence cannot be assessed from outward appearances." That might be of some small comfort to those of us who don't know, spiritually speaking, whether we're wise or foolish. But back to the text.

At midnight came the cry: "Look! Here is the bridegroom! Come out to meet him." The bridesmaids all awoke and trimmed their lamps, but the foolish maidens who forgot to bring with them any reserve of oil, asked the wise ones for theirs. The high S.I.'s refused, knowing that if everyone shared the reserves, all the lamps would be burned out before the feast was finished. So the low S.I.'s made a run for it to the all-night oiler; but by the time they returned, the groom had received all who were ready and the door to the feast was shut. When the Susie-come-latelies beat upon the door and begged to be admitted, the bridegroom answered, "Truly, ... I do not know you."

I can't remember whether it was Woody Allen who said "Showing up is 90% of the job," but Jesus would have wanted the wisdom of John Wayne in "Rio Bravo," when he said to his side kick, "Just showing up doesn't get the job done." Matthew's parable seems to say something of the same: it takes more than good intentions to be a faithful member of the community. What, then, matters most in the message of the five wise and five foolish bridesmaids? Let me suggest three possible insights from the story for starters, and you can add your own.

Maybe the first requirement of receiving the kingdom is to be personally present. Anyone who has faithfully "shown up" and then slept through eight o'clock Monday morning college course lectures, Friday afternoon faculty meetings, or Sunday services of worship (all of which my repertoire has been replete with), will know that sometimes simply showing up isn't enough. If you're here but not all there, that may not mean you are in a psychiatric ward; it just means you may have missed the one significant moment you didn't even know you were waiting for-to be enlightened, to be of service, to save a life (yours or someone else's). What the Quakers call "all thereness," means being fully present in order to know the need or opportunity.

An old cowboy saying says "You can put a boot in the oven, but it won't come out a biscuit."

The second insight I can't cite without cringing because it sounds like a 60's saying I have repressed, which went something like "I am me and you are you and if we should chance to meet one another that would be groovy, but we don't want to lose ourselves." A bad paraphrase I fear, and almost the opposite of what I mean when I say, be yourself. Maybe the feast of the kingdom is where we serve up ourselves, the unique gifts and strengths we have, to one another – just as we are and who we are. An old cowboy saying says "You can put a boot in the oven, but it won't come out a biscuit." Spiritually speaking, we have to make either the hard tack or croissant of ourselves from scratch each morning. The third thought for the lesson is for me the simplest and still the hardest: to let go. The tragedy of the unmindful maidens, the vacant virgins, and the bereft bridesmaids is that they miss out on the party, on the joy and exuberance of what they had been waiting for. Because they were not prepared, not ready for the call, they were not able to be present, could not share the selves they brought, and at the last could not let go and let the spirit fill them with the joy of his presence. They could not pray with the impatient pastor, "Lord, let something happen in the service today that's not printed in the bulletin."

Fortunately, we are delivered from dependence on bulletins at St. Mary's, and today is Sam Bruce day, when we salute the servant who didn't simply show up, he served up himself for our musical feast; he was faithfully prepared and fully present week after week until we didn't know we depended upon him. And when he went aloft, ensconced on his bench, he really let go, let God work through his fingers and finesse and fugues. For sixty weeks (that's, the number of the apostles times five), he never lost his sense of humor nor the metaphorical virginity of Matthew's maidens: that unpretentious enthusiasm, that unfailing faithfulness, that unadorned trust and good will I spoke about at the start.

Since Sam plays down his gifts and often enlivens us with a light touch, I'm going to memorialize his magnificence with a bit of bad doggerel, which I pray will not minimize those gifts or our thorough thanksgiving for them and for him. I call it:

High Five!

Sam Bruce is the man who plays when he can,
with bagpipes and Beethoven, Widor and ham,
bestowed with good humor and blessed with élan.

He practiced and polished until he was blue
accomplished and finished before he was through.
No pretense, not perfect, but faithful and festive and
      fabulous Sam,
a surfeit of service and no also-ran.

So cheerfully, joyfully, playfully, Sam
will pull all the stops out whenever he can:
the organ that roared, the music that soared, alive
      to the Lord!
(pianissimo too,
to give him his due)
and no one was bored.

The gift of himself,
great hearted and free,
with gusto and gladness,
good graces and glee
occasionally saving
some wretches like me.

The sound of his playing still sings in our ears,
 gift to us always and over the years.
With praises unending

and thanks in arrears:
our love, admiration,
confessed acclamation,
thanksgiving and cheers.

---

1. *Homiletics* II. 6-p.12.

A SECOND (LANGUAGE) COMING

24th Sunday After Pentecost
II Thessalonians 3:6-13
December 1998

Now we command you, brethren, in the name of our Lord, Jesus Christ, that you keep away from any brother who is living in idleness and not in accord with the tradition that you received from us. For you yourselves know how you ought to imitate us; we were not idle when we were with you, we did not eat any one's bread without paying, but with toil and labor we worked night and day, that we might not burden any of you. It was not because we have not that right, but to give you in our conduct an example to imitate. For even when we were with you, we gave you this command: If any one will not work, let him not eat. For we hear that some of you are living in idleness, mere busybodies, not doing any work. Now such persons we command and exhort in the Lord Jesus Christ to do their work in quietness and to earn their own living. Brethren, do not be weary in well-doing.

II Thessalonians 3:6-13

Jim Arends tells of an old cartoon that pictures a preacher at the pulpit and a deacon sitting behind him with a grumpy expression on his face. The preacher says, "So until next Sunday, remember that God loves you, I love you, and Brother Al here is working on it."

467

In "Dennis the Menace" cartoons, as you know, Dennis is indeed a menace to his next-door neighbors, Mr. and Mrs. Wilson, and yet Mrs. Wilson continues to be kind and gracious to him. One cartoon shows Dennis and his little friend, Joey, leaving Mrs. Wilson's house, their hands full of cookies.

Joey says, "I wonder what we did to deserve this?"

Dennis answers, "Look Joey, Mrs. Wilson gives us cookies not because we're nice, but because she's nice."

Anyone who has been around St. Mary's much during the last six months or so will probably have noticed a subtle but significant change in the way we have been functioning as a parish family. For many years, this church operated with a rector-of-all-trades and (at one time) with only a volunteer part-time secretary. St. Mary's prided itself on keeping things spartanly simple. Essentially, a few generous souls supported a slim budget, and the church programs consisted mostly of parishioners going out from here and contributing their time and talent to projects in their own communities. It was cozy; by and large the church didn't ask people for money, and they didn't have to join or run any programs either – and that's the way they liked it. A sort of worship-and-run affair.

My memory may have turned to mush, but it seems to me that before 1975 there couldn't have been many more than 125 members of this parish, although there were a lot of drop-ins and satellite stalwarts that circled around the rector. But there were stirrings, murmurings of educational programs and formal outreach inroads, and there was talk even then about forming a mission church so that St. Mary's wouldn't get over crowded. Metaphorically speaking, getting rid of the pot-bellied stove in the church would only provide seats for a handful of additional parishioners, so something had to be done.

Some of you will remember fondly Ebbe Hoff, who got up before the congregation – it may have been on an annual meeting

Sunday – and said: "The future of this church is with the children but at the moment our parish has very few children. Therefore gentlemen go home and do your duty."

...we are moving toward functioning as a contagious church rather than a quiescent congregation.

As you can see, all that old time religion has changed. We now have 650 children in Sunday School. Our parish budget is nearing nine times the budget of St. Mary's back then. We have created multiple in-reach and out-reach programs. And, fortunately, we don't have enough professional staff to do all the work – which brings me back to my initial point of what has begun to be manifest over the last six months. There is a growing "What can I do?" "How can I help?" and best of all "I'll do this" movement that is subtly insinuating itself in our midst, which is significant beyond the good that is getting done because of it – because it means we are moving toward functioning as a contagious church rather than a quiescent congregation. As a parish, we are learning a second language: to take the lead, not waiting to be led.

It seems clear to me that the really great churches are widely known more for the quality of their lay leaders than the strength of stellar clergy. From my point of view, shared leadership is not a luxury; it is essential. A church is not defined by the building or the liturgy or the clergy but by how the people of it function. A church is the people – you (even me). In reality, if the church isn't here when we come, it's because we haven't brought it with us.

Which brings me to Paul's point in the Epistle this morning. Not his well-known "Those who won't work, don't eat," but rather, *"Brothers and sisters, do not grow weary in well-doing."* I focus on those words not to suppress Samaritan burnout among you but to avoid enthusiasts' entropy. It is easy to grow weary of well-doing. To let George do it. Or, in this context, to let Jesus do it.

What Paul was addressing in the Thessalonian church were those believers who had ceased working altogether while they waited for the promised coming of Jesus. Paul, not in the slightest suave or tactful, starts out by saying, "Anyone unwilling to work, should not eat." What I take it he means is they cannot sit back and rely on others to shoulder the burden, to do the work. So he adds, Don't grow weary with well-doing – because that's what the health of the community and the Christian life of it depend on.

An old proverb may be instructive:

Fear less, hope more
Eat less, chew more
Whine less, breathe more
Talk less, say more
Hate less, love more
And all good things will be yours.

These are the words of a second language, the language of the kingdom coming – which we are willing to help bring about. In the early church, as you may know, ordained persons were those set apart only for special functions, such as celebrating the Eucharist; while the "ordinary" people were the lifeblood of the church. They did the work of the church – and there wasn't much they didn't do. They arranged the meetings, provided the hospitality, brought the bread and wine, said the prayers, read the scripture, visited the sick and dying, even preached the Word – not to mention raising money for missions and instructing the youth. The priests were a small part of that spiritual undertaking. The language of the church was the language of lay men and women who spoke for its work and health. And remember Jesus' warning against priests: "Beware those who like to walk about in long robes."

Somewhere, further along the way, the word "church" became associated with the work of the clergy, the authority of vestments, and the mystery of liturgy – and the heart and soul of it, the lay people somehow willingly left it to them. It is time to

470

take back the church, to speak again what has become a second language, of love and lay leadership. And I hear the sounds of it in the parish hall and the programs of this church, and I rejoice – fearful only that it is easy to grow weary with well-doing after the initial enthusiasm has become ongoing work. The language of the laity is our lifeblood and we need to relearn it and reclaim it.

"In reality, if the church isn't here when we come, it's because we haven't brought it with us."

Daniel Matthews tells a story of a mother cat out for a stroll with her three small kittens, when suddenly she sees a huge ferocious dog approaching. After carrying her kittens to safety under a nearby porch, she turns to face the dog. Finally, they are nearly nose to nose and she stares straight into the dog's eyes and says "Ruff, Ruff, Ruff." Whereupon, the dog turns and runs the other way. The mother cat returns to the kittens' hideout, looks them in the eyes and says, "Now do I have to explain to you why I want you to learn a second language?"

The problem with a second language, of course, is that if you don't use it, you lose it. And that's as true in the church as in our formal education. It is also true of what Jesus tried to teach us. You may not think of that as a second language, but the language of his kingdom, even of the church, is different from the language of the world we're familiar with, because the reality it speaks of is the kingdom of God in our midst. We do not find it easy to speak such things as "Forgive seventy times seven" "Go the second mile" "Love your enemies" "Do good to those who persecute you." To do so, we may have to unlearn some of what has always been successful for us in the world in the past; and in the church, as in "What we've always done is..." The signs of the times at St. Mary's say to me that we are on our way toward unlearning some of our old ways and being willing to risk new ways of living out our faith.

I want to leave you with a story that speaks another language. Richard Selzer, a former surgeon, writes in his book *Mortal Lessons*:

I stand by the bed where a young woman lies, her face postoperative, her mouth twisted in palsy, clownish. A tiny twig of the facial nerve, the one to the muscles of her mouth had been severed. She will be thus from now on. The surgeon had followed with religious fervor the curve of her flesh; I promise you that. Nevertheless, to remove the tumor in her cheek, I had cut the little nerve. Her young husband is in the room. He stands on the opposite side of the bed, and together they seem to dwell in the evening lamplight, isolated from me, private. Who are they, I ask myself, he and this wrymouth I have made, who gaze at and touch each other so generously? The young woman speaks. "Will my mouth always be like this?" she asks. "Yes," I say, "it will. It is because the nerve was cut." She nods, and is silent. But the young man smiles. "I like it," he says, "it is kind of cute." All at once I know who he is. I understand, and I lower my gaze. Unmindful, he bends to kiss her crooked mouth, and is so close to me, I can see how he twists his own lips to accommodate hers, to show her that their kiss still works.

The young man knew the language. He was so fluent in that second language that it came to him effortlessly. The more we speak it the less effort it takes; and God willing, someday the language of the Kingdom could also become the language of our lives.

-from Daniel P. Matthews (The Protestant Hour)

BEWARE THOSE WHO LIKE TO WALK IN LONG ROBES

25th Sunday after Pentecost
Mark 12:38-44
Proper 27 – Year B – November 9, 1997

I want to assure you at the start that the story often re-ferred to as "the widow's mite," found in Mark's gospel reading for this morning, is purely coincidental – not part of the plan of our Every Member Canvass. A good thing too, because a fund-raising campaign that appeals to guilt instead of gratitude, shame instead of self-giving, surely bankrupts the basis of congregational support that St. Mary's has been built on. However, one blessing of the text we might benefit from is the message that giving out of her poverty, the widow outshines all others who give only out of their abundance. Equal giving is not equal sacrifice.

But let me not detour us from addressing the deeper adul-teration Jesus denounces in this deceptive story. I say deceptive because the way the lectionary presents it cuts us off from the full meaning propounded in the text. The flow of Mark' s pericope (a fancy theological word for a discrete literary unit) continues on in the text to include two verses we were not given to read, where Jesus says of the great Temple in Jerusalem, "There will not be left here one stone upon another, that will not be thrown down." Then does the pericope celebrate selfless giving, or does it condemn a corrupt and oppressive institutional religion? – one problem of trying to explain the story out of context.

If the destruction of the Temple is intentionally linked to Jesus' observations about the widow's selfless gift, then the message is not simply that the widow gave sacrificially out of obedience that the scribes and the religious establishment taught her, but that she has given excessively to a system which abuses and exploits her – one which is a lost cause and will ultimately be destroyed. That interpretation may give you a lot less to worry about, but for me it focuses on the false piety of those who, as Jesus puts it, "like to walk around in long robes" – the clergy of course, who have constructed this abusive and morally bankrupt system.

Some of you may have noted the fuss created earlier this year when the national media carried the story of an unexpected winner in the American Family Publishers' Sweepstakes. "The Bushnell Assembly of God Church in Sumter County, Florida... was a finalist in the $11 million top prize. [The announcement said:] 'God, we've been looking for you.' It went on to suggest how surprised God's neighbors would be to hear God had won! Many surprised to discover God's mailing address was in Florida. Others wondered [whether] his neighbors would be impressed with God's good luck. Some [would think] that since God is now so rich, [he would] no longer need the few dollars and cents, not to speak of the time and talent that we have to offer..."[1] In effect, hang the church and the Every Member Canvass!

Although we may avoid admitting it, the truth that is hard to escape today is "We are a society that judges everything and everybody according to monetary value .... If something costs a lot, it must be good – if another version costs even more it must be better. That is why when some colleges have raised their tuitions, their enrollments swelled," as one commentator says.[2] For us to take seriously the story of the widow's mite, we have to entirely upend the prevailing expectation.

Looked at from the perspective of the extended pericope, the "widow's act of sacrificial giving brands her as an unwitting dupe of unscrupulous religious [rogues]" who have bought into the system and perpetuate her poverty under the pretext of piety. What is saddest about this story is that although the poor widow's mite (worth, I am told, one eighth of a cent, one 400th of a shekel, one 128th of a denarius) may represent the might of love, we are almost immune to its meaning who no longer look up to "the poor in spirit." Perhaps the reason I have sacrificed so little in my life is that somewhere along the line I came to believe I was entitled to a lot.

A story which is still able to assault my defenses can do so only because I was once trained as a paratrooper – a situation I volunteered for because it was the only way I could escape the unendurable eight-hour days in a cement building with no windows, where I was condemned to continually calculate the artillery mathematics of high-angle fire. (Besides, I thought it might be a cure for my fear of heights.) Anyway, as John Maxwell relates this story about the making of parachutes during the Second World War: "These parachutes were packed by hand in a tedious, repetitive, boring process. The workers crouched over-sewing machines [stitching] eight hours a day. The endless line of fabric was the same color. They folded, packed and stacked the [unending] parade of parachutes. All that was left was for someone to pull the rip cord.

"How did they stand it? They stood it because every morning before they began their work, they gathered as a group. One of the managers reminded them that each parachute would save someone's life. They were asked to think as they sewed and packed, how would they feel if the parachute was strapped to the back of their son, their father, their brother? Those laborers labored sacrificially, unerringly, uncomplainingly, because someone connected what they were doing to a larger picture, to a larger mission that involved the saving of lives." [3]

—◦◦—

*Could I find the compassion within
me to ... put my whole life in to the collection
plate?*

—◦◦—

Our Every Member Canvass aside, what would happen if we were to reassess ourselves and begin to measure our life by the acts of love and giving that we use to fill it? Would we find ourselves "rich" or "poor"? Could I find the compassion within me to stop dribbling out my stores of love and selflessness and sacrifice and offer my heart, risk my being, put my whole life in to the collection plate for the spirit -starved of the world? (Don' t ask me after the service: I haven't yet come up with a clever answer.)

In today's text Jesus condemns the clergy first of all. As one commentary explains: "A successful first-century scribe wore a long robe with a long white mantle decorated with beautiful long fringes. White robes identified the wearer as someone of importance... Tradition dictated that common people 'in the market place' should respectfully rise to their feet when a scribe walked past. The scribe's synagogue seat of honor placed him up front with the Torah, facing the congregation.... The problem Jesus pinpoints... is that they like it.... They have confused the respect intended for the position they hold with their [spiritual] advancement."[2]

They allowed, even encouraged the poor to impoverish themselves, supporting the needs and wants of the scribes who said "Do this" or "Do that" while they themselves were exempt from giving sacrificially. It is a scathing story if we take it to heart. In contrast, the widow who had only two small coins did not give one and hold back the other for herself; she gave both, provoking Jesus to judge the self-serving scribes as those who "devour widows' houses." Her giving was sacrifice, not surplus generosity. We, properly, praise her example although most of us would not dare to follow it, even though we know that giving – not saving – is at the heart of the gospel. We say that "stewardship proceeds not from what we give to God but from what God has given to us," but we are at the same time embarrassed and wary about the wisdom that says what we "have" is not ours to "keep" but only to give.

Where does that leave us? Speaking only for myself, plenty uncomfortable. Something like a situation when I was a struggling seminary student some 37 years ago when my bishop came to an early morning Communion service, the collection at which was designated to go to his fund for world relief. When it came time to put my contribution in the plate I discovered that I had only a $20 bill in my wallet, which was to go toward my meal budget for the rest of the week (in those days $20 could almost do that). I reasoned manfully with myself: this will not go to benefit my parish or my postulancy, and the bishop will never know that I was the one who allowed his offering to come up twenty dollars short.

So what did I do – pass the plate on to the next person or put in my pecuniary prize? I was sorry I had shown up for church that morning. My pride aside, what do you think I gave? The answer is, nothing. And the outcome is I've never forgotten it.

Of course I can take refuge in the words many of us are familiar with: "God sent his son into the world not to condemn the world, but that the world might be saved through him." But I also remember the cost of that, said in some other familiar words: "God so loved the world that he gave his only begotten son..." And I am reminded of the story of the widow's mite that seemed so simple when I first read it and said to myself she was foolish to offer up all she had.

I ask you to pray with me:

O Lord, our God, you who are always more ready
to hear than we are to pray, and are wont to give
more than either we desire or deserve, only speak
to us that we may hear you.

Then speak to us again and yet again so that when in our hearts we answer you by saying No, we may at least know well to whom we say it, and what it costs us to say it, and what it costs our brothers and sisters, and what it costs you.

And when at those moments that we can never foretell we say Yes to you, forgive our half-heartedness, accept us as we are, work your redeeming grace in us and give us strength to follow wherever love may lead. *Amen.*[4]

––––––

1. *Homiletics* 9, 4 – p.42
2. *Op. cit.*, p.39
3. *Op. cit.*, p.41
4. Adapted from Frederick Buechner, *The Hungering Dark*

ADULT FORUM

I confess I cannot represent responsibly the reflections of such as Shirley MacLaine, Ram Dass, Henri Nouwen, or Matthew Fox, to name some who have expanded the meaning of the term in our time. My reading has been in some of the spiritual classics such as *The Cloud of Unknowing*, Julian of Norwich, the writings of Meister Eckhardt, *The Little Flowers of St. Francis*, *Waiting for God* by Simone Weil, the Journal of John Woolman, Francis de Sales' *Introduction to the Devout Life*, the Letters of von Hugel, and some study of eastern religions. My more modern readings include Kierkegaard's *Purity of Heart*, *The Diary of a Country Priest* by Bernanos, Silone's *Bread and Wine*, selections from Jung's writings, Joseph Campbell's "Power of Myth," and more recently some of Annie Dillard, Thomas Keating, and Thomas Moore (which my wife lent me).

Christopher Brookfield

"GOD'S SPIES"

Unexpected Images of Faith in Modern Poetry

February 10, 1986, St. Mary's

I was intrigued by – indeed grateful for – Temple Martin's presentation to us last month on images of grace in the novels of Frederick Buechner. I was grateful because traditional theology has a lot to say about the vision of the saints, the role of creeds and the sacraments (not to mention the Church) in our search for God – all of which is overwhelming to one who is not quite certain about what he believes or not sure about how much he believes with any certainty. In mattes of faith and grace, forgiveness and salvation, the average churchgoer or pew sitter is often overwhelmed by the authority of doctrine and scripture, much of which seems out of reach except to the heroes of faith like Abraham, St. Augustine, Albert Schweitzer, and George Burns – all of whom seem already to have a pretty *direct* relationship with God, all of which is not overwhelmingly helpful for lesser luminaries *seeking* a relationship.

Mostly, what we have not been overwhelmed with in much of the theology or modern literature we are familiar with are the visions of grace that we are granted in the everyday, safe in the assurance that there is plenty for everyone. That Temple was willing to share with us what she herself believed and articulate what she referred to as those brief glimmering glimpses of the broken image of Christ within us, which Fred Buechner artfully portrays, was a great gift to us all. What intrigued me further was the question of whether we receive grace "vertically" or "horizontally," and what those terms might mean. Let me take a swipe at what I hope may be useful, if somewhat overly simplified, definitions.

The "vertical" relationship, presupposed in the more traditional theological, biblical, and creedal formulations is an encounter directly with the divine, with God, in faith. God, though he is referred to as transcendent, eternal, absolute, "wholly other, omnipotent, omniscient, immortal, immutable (all the im's and om's you can construct), nevertheless is perceived to break into history, into time; to intervene directly in human affairs – even, occasionally, face to face with his servants. (It is perhaps ironic that in the same texts where we encounter such promethean figures as Abraham, Moses, and Job, we also confront the strong biblical injunction that no man can see God and live.)

However it is described, the "vertical" relationship – whether awesome, awe-full, or just plain awful, is a direct experience of faith. Sometimes the distance between God and man seems so great that an intermediary is necessary to bridge the "yawning qualitative abyss" between the two. So that angelic beings, or the Church, or the sacraments, or even Christ himself functions as mediator, go-between, buffer, shield, messenger, interpreter, intercessor, referee, in what would otherwise be an intolerable personal encounter between God and the solitary individual.

What Temple was drawn to are the "horizontal" channels of faith and grace between God and us, experienced in human relationships, in the ordinary (even insignificant) events of our life, in the moments of our everyday lives that give substance and meaning to our human struggles or baptize our struggles to be human. Here God is portrayed in different, sometimes mundane forms that we may have difficulty recognizing as special or extraordinary: the blessing of the ordinary, if I may so call it – which takes a special eye to perceive and to redeem the time being from insignificance (as T.S. Eliot put it).

> ### *What we need is a different way of seeing, freeing, being with God that invites images of grace rather than avoids them.*

Here God is shown in unlikely faces and in unlikely places, doing unlikely things in the obscure if not obscene ways in which he has chanced to expose himself to us. It may not take a *saint's* eye to see him strange guises, but it probably takes more imagination than most of us operate within the everyday to truly meet him there. What we need is a different way of seeing, freeing, being with God that invites images of grace rather than avoids them. We have to "take upon us the mystery of things as if we were God's spies," as King Lear puts it in Shakespeare's tragedy by the same name.[1] We must learn to see through the eye of God, to understand that the only hands and feet God has to work his will with in this world are ours – however inadequate, inappropriate, or impure we may think them to be.

You must know that at the moment the ancient Lear comes to this revelation, he has lost his earthly sense, he is mad in his divine vision, he has literally stripped away all his finery and authority and, like the "poor naked wretches" exposed to the fury of the storm on the heath, all he has left to hold onto is the faithful love of the very daughter he had banished from his sight. In his blindness, at last he truly sees. The nagging question is, Is it too late? He says, as he and his beloved Cordelia are being led away to prison, in what seems to be an inappropriate euphoria:

> *Come, let's away to prison.*
> *We two alone will sing like birds i' th' cage.*
> *When thou dost ask me blessing, I'll kneel down*
> *And ask of thee forgiveness. So we'll live,*
> *And pray, and sing, and tell old tales and laugh*
> *At gilded butterflies,...*
> *As if we were God's spies: and we'll wear out,*

In a walled prison, packs and sects of great ones
That ebb and flow by th' moon.

———

1. William Shakespeare, *King Lear*, Act 5, Scene 3

"OUR SPIRITUAL JOURNEY"

A Presentation to the Adult Forum
September 17, 1995

Two provocative propositions arrested my attention recently: "What it means to be spiritual," Bill Moyers has said, "is the biggest story of the century." and, Mark Dyer has observed, "I am delighted that many today distinguish spirituality from religion... religion as commonly practiced, can be a devastating bore. God never is. And spirituality usually isn't." (*Episcopal Life*, Jan. 93, p.22).

My interest in those ideas notwithstanding – it occurred to me (rather too late, I'm afraid) that I may be the wrong person to talk on this topic. Because the more I pondered the subject of spirituality, the more I became aware that my association with and understanding of it are incorrigibly traditional. By that I do not also imply stodgy or staid – just slightly out of step with current conceptions and use of the word spirituality.

I confess I cannot represent responsibly the reflections of such as Shirley MacLaine, Ram Dass, Henri Nouwen, or Matthew Fox, to name some who have expanded the meaning of the term in our time. My reading has been in some of the spiritual classics such as *The Cloud of Unknowing*, Julian of Norwich, the writings of Meister Eckhardt, *The Little Flowers of St. Francis*, *Waiting for God* by Simone Weil, the Journal of John Woolman, Francis de Sales' *Introduction to the Devout Life*, the Letters of von Hugel, and some study of eastern religions. My more modern readings include Kierkegaard's *Purity of Heart*, *The Diary of a Country Priest* by Bernanos, Silone's *Bread and Wine*, selections from Jung's writings, Joseph Campbell's "Power of Myth," and more recently some of Annie Dillard, Thomas Keating, and Thomas Moore (which my wife lent me). I tell you all that so you will know "where I'm coming from" (as they say) and so that I cannot claim to represent more than I do. Having said so, that will not keep me from taking on the topic, speaking out about what I think I know about the subject, and saying something about my own spiritual journey. I am not courting consensus here, nor do I presume to speak with special authority but only for myself – and I invite your energetic disagreement.

I shall begin with four personal pugnacious propositions, which you may wish to take issue with:

1. There is no such thing as a separate "life of the spirit." That expression is a tautology, because life is spirit.

2. To speak of "setting out" on a spiritual journey is misleading because we are already on one by virtue of being given life. Like it or not, know it or not, as you live and breathe, living is a spiritual journey.

3. Contrary to what your dictionary may tell you, "spirituality" has nothing to do with the clergy or the church. In fact, as Paul Tillich has said, the ultimate escape from God and the demands of the spirit is to seek safety in institutional religion. Meister Eckhart said it another way, "I pray God to rid me of God."

4. Spirituality is not a condition or activity set apart from everyday life because it must be evident in the midst of the everyday if it is to have life and give life.

Now forgive me a few explanations I have found helpful:

The word spirit, Fred Buechner says, has come to mean something pale and shapeless, like an unmade bed. School spirit, the American spirit, the Christmas spirit, the spirit of '76, the Holy

Spirit – each of these points to something you know is supposed to get you to your feet cheering but which you somehow can't rise to. The adjective *spiritual* has become downright offensive. If somebody recommends a person as spiritual you tend to avoid him, and usually with good reason (*Wishful Thinking*. p.90). *Inspirational* is worse still. Inspirational books are invariably for the birds.

For the word lovers among you, the Hebrew word *rua(c) h* meaning breath, wind, or spirit is used in the Old Testament to explain why we have life. In the second chapter of Genesis, the Lord God scoops up the earth or ground, the *adamah* (literally – dirt, dust, clay, clod, mud, manure) and breathes into it the *rua(c) h YHWH*, the breath of God – and *Adam*, the man (the name taken out of Adam-ah) becomes a living being. The breath or spirit of God is what inspires or inspirits us, gives us life. We are by nature then spiritual beings. When we are inspired, we are full of life; when we expire, the breath of God leaves us – dead.

The corresponding New Testament Greek word (breath or spirit) is *pneuma*, which you may recognize in the word "pneumatic" – as in tires. When they are inflated, you can ride on them easily; they carry us like the wind. When they are deflated, we as well as the tires are flat out, can go no longer. When a woman is referred to as "pneumatic," it does not usually mean she is simply pumped up with hot air (or other additives); in any case, what it ought to mean is that she has a kind of life in her that is breathtaking; we take in our breath at the sight of her.

Our word "soul," sometimes spoken of as "self," is connected to "spirit" in that the Hebrew word for "self," *nepesh*, referred to the indissoluble unity of body and spirit. For the Hebrew, there was no such thing as a disinspirited body or a disembodied spirit. You couldn't have one without the other – else how would you recognize it. The Greek word *psyche* meant life or soul, so that psychology was not understood merely as a study of the mind. Unfortunately, we have (literally) disemboweled it in our use of the term today.

Bear with me for one more definition. What do I mean by *spirituality*? Surely not simply "a term made up by middle-aged people to express their disaffection with religion (Koenig)"; rather, it is the yearning, the longing, "the deep-seated striving and struggling for a higher and ultimate meaning to existence" (as Victor Frankl puts it). So our *passion* for meaning, which drives us to explore, to seek, the highest expression of what it means to have light and life is the expression of our spirituality – which significantly makes no clear division between the realm of the sacred and the secular. Spiritual values are enacted in everyday life, because life without spirit is life-less – dead. Interesting that our word "sacred" comes from *sacer* in Latin, which means both "holy" and "taboo," so close is the relationship between the holy and the forbidden, the sacred and the profane – sometimes spoken of as the extraordinary and the expected, the otherworldly and the everyday. Which is another way of saying that spirituality cannot live apart from life in sacred isolation from it because it is the "stuff" of life. As Thomas Moore says, "spirituality is seeded, germinates, sprouts and blossoms in [the midst of] the mundane. It is to be found and nurtured in the smallest of daily activities." (*Care of the Soul*, p.219). Thich Nhat Hanh says washing the dishes is a spiritual exercise (which will delight some of you and dismay others), but if you are washing the dishes in order to get through with them, then you are neither engaged in a spiritual expression nor in washing the dishes.

Unless Moore and Hahn are right about the intertwining of the sacred and the secular, my own spiritual journey would seem a sorry and sordid affair isolated from the well-spring of wellness – which I don't believe. I'm not certain I should tell you about my own peculiar pilgrimage, but I'm not sure how I can avoid it entirely in agreeing to talk about our spiritual journey.

———⊙———

...it has seemed to me I had more influence, have been more effective with individuals, outside my collar than I have under the protection or "authority" in it.

———⊙———

First thing I have to acknowledge is that in looking back over my life, it has seemed to me I had more influence, have been more effective with individuals, outside my collar than I have under the protection or "authority" in it. That is to say, I have been more persuasive as an ordinary person than as an ordained emissary. (Parenthetically, I would do well to remember that the familiar English term for clergy, "parson," is really a transmutation of the word "person.")

While I couldn't have named it then, my spiritual journey began when I realized that my world was not "safe" – not within my home, where there was anger and alienation – and certainly not outside it. At seven, the world seemed a dangerous and pre-carious place – which threatened torment and trauma, especially for an introverted, introspective, isolationist like me. The first experience of peace, unqualified acceptance, and security I could count on came when I was invited to join the choir of the local church. There it felt the way I thought "home" should feel. The spiritual journey for me is in large part the search for a place to be, for peace – for inner peace at least.

I suppose that early imprint eventually led me to seek boarding life at a church school, where I somehow became very successful in the ways of that world – but at the cost of my cozi-ness with the church. By the time I graduated, I hated the church – its "stupid" repetitive ritual, its irrelevant language and hypocrit-ical institutions and values. The clergy at that school were emo-tional and moral cripples and objects of pity and derision as far as we students were concerned. That influence was enduring, so that by the time I was ready to leave college, I felt impelled to make three vows. I even pronounced them publicly, as I remember it:

1. I would never undertake graduate study.
2. I would not consider going into teaching. and
3. I swore I would have nothing whatsoever to do with the church again. (I never thought of "Never say never.")

I forgot to mention that although I abhorred the study of Religion when I entered college, I ended by majoring in it – my excuse being that the most exciting and demanding professors taught it, and it was the only subject that spoke honestly and persuasively about the human condition, questions of meaning, and the things that mattered in life. I have a quotation in my notebook which says, "The mind wants a simple and self-evident meaning, but the soul (psyche) craves depth of reflection – a many layered meaning, not simplistic moral lessons or statements of belief. That's why the spiritual journey is so difficult – because the media, the world, common sense, and even the church are bent on applying palliatives and platitudes to the pain of asking crucial questions such as "Is it true?" and "Does it really matter?"

Back in the early 70's an unexpected irony again intruded on my life when the local minister of our church in Exeter, NH started to lose his grip on himself, found he had doubts about his own faith and ministry, and began the tortuous path toward a nervous breakdown and a change of vocation to becoming a Jungian analyst. I was assisting him in the process (not the process of losing his parish), helping out as a volunteer, when Bishop Phil Smith (former Suffragan of Virginia) began assigning me more extensive duties at the church in an effort to relieve the rector of some of his burdens. When the Senior Warden expressed concern about "some English teacher and crew coach meddling in the ministry" (I was not a priest in the least in those days), Bishop Smith said to him, "Upon my soul, do you mean to tell me Brookfield is not ordained?" Then it was I decided that I had either to stop playing priest or to confirm and conform to what for good or for ill my life had been pushing upon me.

———◦○◦———

Bishop Hall turned to me and said, "Christopher, how have you managed to escape ordination?"

———◦○◦———

The coda to that unfinished symphony came when I first showed up at the Annual Council of the Diocese of Virginia in 1975 as Dean of Church Schools. Council had to take a special vote so as to grant me seat and voice (but no vote) in order for me to make the report to council I was supposed to give. No one forethought the dilemma of the Dean not being ordained. Bishop Hall turned to me and said, "Christopher, how have you managed to escape ordination?" – which process he promptly shepherded me through.

It is important to inject here that the spiritual part of my journey was not the ordination bit, but the difficult task of recognizing and wrestling with what we collared types refer to as "the call." That "call," while opening some doors for me, did not make my life any easier, more saintly, more stable, or less sinful. It brought home to me that Jesus was either a mad poet or a solemn joker when he said," Take my yoke upon you ... and I will give you rest. For my service is easy and my burden is light." The spiritual part comes in the travail of trying to make sense out of that oxymoron of the spirit. That my name happened to be Christopher (meaning Christ-bearer) must have provoked God to a peal of great laughter or a wail of despair.

I want to make it clear that when I use the term "God" in this context, I do not mean the God of systematic theology or of the Christian church or of St. Paul's School Chapel – or the "religious right," or the Schwenckfelders, or of the West End or even St. Mary's – the particular God of our own making, with whom we can live quite easily, whom we call upon when we are in need. The God I am talking about is the one who calls us out of ourselves, into the depth of our lives where we know no sure footing, into the dark where in faith we must journey blind; the word "God" that every culture has to name even when they don't believe in him (her, It); the name we give to that reality life cannot do without – regardless what you call it.

In my experience, God is frequently found not where I think he is supposed to be but where I least expect him, often when I am unawares, sometimes when it is the last thing I want; not in the delight of getting what we think we deserve but in the pain of not having what we need, not as the one who keeps us from suffering but who helps us bear what we are called upon to suffer; who cannot be expressed but only experienced – if not in the absence of his presence, then in the presence of his absence.

But alas, we bore God, if not ourselves, to death with such theological theories, which pontificate rather than point to a reality beyond our bumbling wordiness. As a friend of mine says, "It is as impossible for us to demonstrate the existence of God as it would be for Sherlock Holmes to demonstrate the existence of Arthur Conan Doyle." A Christian is so-called because he "points at Christ and says, 'I can't prove a thing, but there's something ... about the way he carried his head, his hands, the way he carries his cross – the way he carries me!'" (*Wishful Thinking*, pp.31-32)

When the author Graham Greene was asked why he did not write about his theology of God, Greene replied that he had done so in his novels, that the God enfleshed in fiction was the most profound expression of faith and spirit Greene could speak about.

I often refer to fiction to explain theology that is otherwise inaccessible, which is one reason why the reading group I have guided for the past ten years has been a gracious gift to me on my spiritual journey. Such reading may help us regain the religious insight we relinquished when we rebelled against the vision that we thought no longer spoke to our reality.

Thomas Moore writes: "Another aspect of modern life is a loss of religious practice in many people's lives, which ... deprives the soul of valuable symbolic and reflective experience (211) ... Some people are fortunate in that their childhood [religious] tradition is still relevant and lively to them, but others have to search (212) ... There are two ways of thinking about church and religion. One is that we go to church in order to be in the presence of the holy, to learn and to have our lives influenced by that presence. The other is that church teaches us directly and symbolically to see the sacred dimension of everyday life ...[that] religion ... is inherent in everything we do (214) ... For some, religion is a Sunday affair, and they risk dividing life into the holy Sabbath and the secular week. For others, religion is a week-long observance that is inspired and sustained on the Sabbath ... Church-going can become a mere aesthetic experience or ... even a defense against the power of the holy (215)..."

What about the role of ritual? In and through the diverse traditions in which we were brought up, ritual "maintains the world's holiness." It is an "action that speaks to the mind and heart but doesn't necessarily make sense in a literal context. [For example] in church people do not eat bread in order to feed their bodies but to nourish their souls (215)."

Where eastern and western thought both collide and collude on the spiritual journey is that whereas meditation as a spiritual discipline in the west traditionally has meant *thinking* about God, the scriptures, and the reflections of the mystics so as to be able to pray and speak out of that experience, in the east meditation has meant *not* thinking – because God cannot be grasped by the intellect. Prayer then is not our effort to speak to God but our willingness to stand silent and undefended before God so that we may hear his speaking to us, and we are where he can get his hands on us. There is no separation between us and God except what we make with our own minds. What we need for our spiritual journey is not a store of appropriate prayers and theological thoughts but only the spirit of willingness to make ourselves available to God.

Strangely enough, one of our greatest spiritual resources is the empty places in us, which can put us in touch with the transcendent or the eternal but which we are likely to ignore or to flee. The way we avoid them is to keep busy – which leaves in us no vacuum or emptiness for the deep waters of God to fill. We cannot stand the silence; we fill it with noise and the sound of our own speaking – anything to keep us from our alone time with God.

We do not take seriously the saying of the Psalmist "Be still, and know that I am God." That stillness may come to us only after we have exhausted all our efforts and can think of nothing else to do. Or it may sneak upon us unawares when we have let go for a moment the seriousness of life we seek to control, and we are deeply touched by a phrase of poetry or of music, the glimpse of a painting that takes our breath away, an unexpected and moving act of kindness, a joke that lets us laugh at a truth we've defended ourselves against; Lord knows, even an uplifting insight in a sermon we were determined not to hear.

Fellow seekers throughout the ages have seen all this and spoken of it more eloquently than I could hope to: St. Augustine spoke of the inevitability of our spiritual journey when he said, "O Lord, thou hast made us for thyself, and our hearts are restless until they find their rest in thee." Or, if you prefer the more voluptuous and passionate metaphors of John Donne's intense desire for salvation and for the full knowledge of God:

> Batter my heart, three person'd God; for you
> As yet but knocke, breathe, shine, and seeke to mend;
> That I may rise, and stand, o'erthrow mee, and bend
> Your force, to breake, blowe, burn and make me new...
> Yet dearly I love you, and would be loved faine,
> Take mee to you, imprison mee, for I
> But am betrothe'd unto your enemie:
> Divorce mee, untie, or breake that knot againe,
> Except you enthrall mee, never shall be free,
> Nor ever chaste, except you ravish mee.
>
> *Holy Sonnet XIV

T.S. Eliot tells us in familiar words about the task and transformation that lie ahead for each one of us on our spiritual journey:

> We shall not cease from exploration
> And the end of all our exploring
> Will be to arrive where we started
> And know the place for the first time.
>
> "Little Gidding," Four Quartet)

WHY DO I PRAY?
WHY DO I BREATHE?

The Meaning of Prayer in Everyday Life

Adult Forum Address
December 8, 1996

Forgive me if at the last minute I change the title of what I am going to speak about. I have to change it because I want to express in a sentence some of the enthusiasm and imperative that characterize the prayer of everyday (or any day). My title is taken from a novel of the contemporary writer Elie Wiesel, who survived the holocaust and who now describes himself with the words "writer as witness." His novel called *Night* is the story of how he endured the horrors of the Nazi death camps in Auschwitz and managed to be the lone survivor of his family. One day his friend and mentor, Moshe the Beadle, asked him, "Why do you pray?" He thought a moment, a strange question, "Why did I pray ... Why did I breathe?" That's the title I want: Why Do I Pray?... Why do I Breathe?

I admit I first thought about choosing a clever title, which would catch your attention, like "How to Be Prayerful Without Praying" or "How <u>Not</u> to Pray to be Prayerful" or simply "Mindless Prayer." But I decided to play it straight because prayer is too important to be put off with presumptuous puns. I warn you at the start, however: I am not an expert in prayer or at praying. You are dealing strictly with an amateur, meaning of course a lover, who is no stranger to the difficulties of daily discipline. Prayer is not the problem, I am.

The second confession I must make is I suspect almost nothing I say today is original with me, except perhaps my attempts to say something in a new way; it's all been said before. So saying, I want to begin with a saying that is not mine but feels as close to me as what I might have written had I the wit to express myself the way my friend Fred Buechner does. It is too long to say all at once, so I'll split it – half here and half to end with:

"Everybody prays whether he thinks of it as praying or not. The odd silence you fall into when something very beautiful is happening or something very good or very bad ... the stammer of pain at someone else's pain. The stammer of joy at somebody else's joy. Whatever words or sounds you use for sighing with over your own life. These are all prayers in their way. These are all spoken not just to yourself but to something even more familiar than yourself and even more strange than the world.

According to Jesus, by far the most important thing about praying is to keep at it. The images he uses to explain this are all rather comic, as though he thought it was rather comic to have to explain at all. He says God is like a friend you go to borrow bread from at midnight. The friend tells you in effect to drop dead, but you go on knocking anyway until finally he gives you what you want so he can go back to bed again ...

Be importunate, Jesus says – not, one assumes, because you have to beat a path to God's door before he'll open it, but because until you beat the path maybe there's no way of getting to your door."

I figure if that is all you hear today or take away with you, it will have been worth your trouble to come. So much to be said, so little time; so there are several areas I am not going to be able to get to: such as, How to pray with The Book of Common Prayer – that's a subject for another day, or Praying the Lord's Prayer – a subject in itself. I am not going to focus on prayer that is exclusively Christian or specifically Episcopal or restricted to the Medieval Mystics; rather, to speak of prayer that is more catholic (meaning universal) and which may be a part of Eastern as well as Western experience, reaching out for the unknown and the familiar at the same time. For instance, have you ever heard something like this prayer, and would you find it prayerful if you were seeking words to say/ pray for/ with a friend before her dangerous surgery? "Like an ant on a stick both ends of which are burning, I go to and fro without knowing what to do and in great danger. Like the inescapable shadow which follows me, the weight of sin haunts me. Graciously look upon me. Thy love is my refuge." It is a prayer from India, foreign but not wholly unfamiliar to us.

Some of you may be relieved to hear that I am also going to say something practical about the prayer we practice (or don't practice) every week, because prayer which is purely theoretical seems to me about as useful as a fishing pole without a hook. In fact, I'll give you three guarantees: Prayer is efficient, Prayer works, Prayer is life giving. Of that I am sure. Whether I can explain it to your satisfaction remains to be heard.

———⊸○⊷———

Our two greatest fears about prayer are: first, that it is true; and, second, that it is not true...

———⊸○⊷———

Prayer is efficient, meaning that it initiates activity and brings about change, even if the only thing that is changed is the one who prays. At its most mystical and solitary, prayer causes things to happen. Our two greatest fears about prayer are: first, that it is true; and, second, that it is not true – and that either way, we may have missed out. We have been told that God hears and answers prayer. I believe that; I also believe that the answers to our prayers may not be the ones we have prayers for – but that no prayer goes unanswered, ultimately; and no prayer can be answered if it hasn't been prayed. I don't believe there is any such thing as "idle prayers." Prayer is not an idle pastime; it is a powerful provider. We have within us a great untapped potential – so much so that we have to be careful what we pray for. There is no worse punishment than getting what we have prayed for when it is unworthy of us.

Prayer works – incredibly well, at least if the newspaper articles I have read report it rightly. In several controlled experiments the results astounded almost everyone except those who pray. In two groups of some 200 hospital patients randomly selected and consistently monitored, the ones in the group who were prayed for daily had a 66% better recovery rate than the ones who weren't prayed for, and had only 2% fatality as compared with 20% among those for whom no prayers were offered.

An interesting side study indicated that those whose healing was prayed for in general terms, rather than specifically, resulted in a markedly higher percentage of healing – as in "Lord, we pray for the healing of your suffering servant Christopher," rather than "Lord, heal the festering sore on Christopher's leg." (Maybe what that means is that God doesn't like to be told how to do it.)

I hesitate to add one further observation from the article which said that in groups of plants, the ones prayed for thrived and markedly outgrew those that were not prayed upon. You'll think I've lost it – or at least that I'm implanting propaganda. I am aware the effectiveness of prayer does not rise or fall on pseudo-scientific data. I know only that the power of positive prayer is profound, impartial, and impossible to prevent.

Prayer is life giving – I have no doubt about it. If it is true that when we pray, in some small way, ultimately not only we but the world is forever changed – maybe that is what the mystics mean when they say "No prayer is lost, no prayer is wasted, no prayer falls on deaf ears." It always results in something; or some thing is the result of it, so that life, our life, is made different from what it was before – and our prayer has made a difference, helped create a different life. Maybe that also means that the act of praying is more important than the words we struggle to use in prayer. The specifics of what we seek through prayer are not as life giving as the repetition of our request. Jesus said, all we have to do is ask

– difficult as that may be for us when we insist on our own will, our own way, our own words, in a world we shape in our image.

* * *

Now to the less practical but perhaps more important part of the program. Let me ask directly the question that goes to the heart of the matter: "Why pray?" The answer is deceptively simple and more difficult to defend than the obvious "It works." Why pray? Because we desperately need quiet time in the presence of God. Praying is the central human act that puts us perceptively and lovingly in touch with the innermost reality of everything. To say that less pedantically, let me turn to a poem by Christian Rainsford:

> I cried to God,
> I beat upon the door
> Until my knuckles bled;
> God made no answer,
> gave no sign.
>
> "There is no God," I said.
> I stopped my clamor
> and lay spent,
> A channel at ebb tide,
> And slowly in the silence,
> The door swung wide.

Or, as Newsweek put it, the life of prayer (or prayer life) is a journey with God as well as toward God, a journey in which prayer becomes for those who pursue it as natural as breathing. The first step is to cease talking to God and start listening for God. And that requires silence. Silence is the language God speaks; everything else is a translation. "As long as you know you are praying, you are not praying properly," says Benedictine monk David Steindl-Rast. When every thing we do is prayer, the fruit is an increase in love, patience, and compassion for others, leaving behind the unmistakable taste of holiness.

So far, what I have been speaking of may sound a little like La La Land. The real world of work and play is hard with us, especially with Christmas coming. Our motto is Go, Go! We are impatient with the preparations of Advent; let's get on with Christmas, and then to the New Year, and so on – and on and on. If we do not picture ourselves as go-go dancers we also do not see ourselves as the little tramp in Beckett's Waiting for Godot, whose favorite line is "Nothing to be done" – sounds like the original sin. We are ill at ease "wasting time" or just "hanging out" with God. We may have a hard time believing God wants to hang out with us.

Abbot Thomas Keating, a Cistercian monk, has written a book which expounds those ideals, called Open Mind, Open Heart, Contemplative Prayer: Taking Time to Hang Out With God, which I want to come back to in a minute. First let me note a curious phenomenon. Starting with the 60's, we have become deeply disturbed about the problem of drugs among young people and throughout our culture, including the accretions that tend to come with it, such as the obsession of the young with games like Dungeons and Dragons and what seems an unnatural interest in satanic cults. It may interest you to learn that those who have been able to work successfully with the survivors of such experiences tell us that there is a deep hunger in adolescents to probe the limits of what is possible to know and to know who they are. What hooks them into fascination with the occult is the promise that this will put them in touch with transcendent power. So one way to look at their involvement, which we might call by other names, is a compulsive search for God or the ultimate, an attempt to meet a need they do not even know how to articulate.

In our own tradition, the 46th Psalm translates that idea as "Be still, and know that I am God" — the opposite of the popular motto carpe diem, sieze the day, fill it full of busy-ness to get things done.

Maybe we can offer a better way, one the whole family could enter into. It has various names: contemplative prayer or meditation, centering or apophatic prayer. Whatever else you want to call it, it is taking time to hang out with God, something we might at first think is "wasting time" because while we are doing it, nothing gets done. A Taoist expression sets that right when it says, The Tao does not *do* anything, but nothing does *not* get done. In our own tradition, the 46th Psalm translates that idea as "Be still, and know that I am god" – the opposite of the popular motto *carpe diem*, seize the day, fill it full of busy-ness to get things done. Rather, we need to take time to "do nothing;" knowing we cannot make significance happen, we can strive instead to let God's will be done in us. We spend time with God because, as Philippians puts it, he is at work within us to will and to work for his good pleasure: "Here I am, do your work in me, Lord." This kind of prayer is about changing us, not changing God; it is about being available to be changed.

This kind of prayer does not replace the prayer of petition, when we pray to God to bring about change, even our own; or prayer of praise, when we give thanks for what God has done for us or for our world. Rather, it underlies both of them and gives us access to the source of prayer itself. It helps us discover that we "are" and were something before we allowed the world to define us and tell us who we are. Have you ever thought that at the time of your or my conception there were not 20 million possible combinations that could have come into being, but 200 million? That this "I" alone was selected, chosen for life from all those possibilities seems to me incredible, beyond random selection. It makes more sense to me to say that I or we were loved into life by whatever name we want to give God or that process of bringing life into being.

In prayer we can put aside, shuck off everything that others tell us we are; we do not have to be anything. Prayer is not our efforts to speak with God as much as our willingness to stand silent and undefended before God so that we may at last hear him speaking to us, and we are where he can get his hands on us.

501

When we in the West use the word meditation, we often mean think about some thing deeply in order to gain knowledge or understanding of God; but in the East, meditation is *not* thinking, because God cannot be apprehended by the intellect. To meditate, to contemplate, is simply to rest in the presence of God. There is no separation between us and God except what we make with our own mind. God is not absent from us; it is we who are out to lunch (so to speak). All we need is the spirit of willingness to make ourselves available. Creation waits.

We say we have no time for that in the midst of a busy day — but I say we have all the time there is. What we choose to do with it is our decision. Prayer is making "alone time with God" in which there is no "have to's," no "right way" to pray or to be; it is quietness that invites God to act in silence. Many of us have no vacuum into which the deep waters of God can flow. We need to make some part of our day open time, open for expectancy, open for change, open and undefended before God — where God may reach us, touch, us, even begin to transform us.

Father Keating, in Open Mind, Open Heart, tells us "Contemplative prayer is an ancient method of praying based on the conviction that God resides within us and not out in the cosmos somewhere. In contemplative prayer we open our minds and hearts to God's presence within us..., the process by which we start to hang out with God, so to speak. We begin to wait on God as one would a friend ... We develop a loving knowledge of God beyond our thoughts, feelings, and concepts ... We discover that God is present in every experience ... that we are really in an abiding state of union with God and that we can be moved by the spirit in both prayer and action."

What we call centering prayer came out of trying to devise an approach to Christian spirituality that would be comparable to methods of the East. Thousands of young people were visiting India every year to be trained in Eastern meditative practice. They were starved for the Spirit but had no idea a rich contemplative tradition existed in their own Western Christian culture. They were not looking for a new religion, but an effective discipline of prayer and action.

"To practice centering prayer you need to take time once or twice a day, even ten to twenty minutes will do, to sit in a comfortable position, keeping silence, with the intent of opening yourself to the interior presence of God and trying to let go all thoughts that keep you separated from God. Of course your mind will wander naturally as you try to empty it of thoughts when they intrude, but you don' t have to hang onto them. Let them go and recenter your attention to the place where there is God. One way that helps many people is to focus on a significant or sacred word – a Christian mantra if you will – to keep from dwelling on stray thoughts and feelings. Such a word might be Lord, Abba, Father, Shalom, Holy – whatever word for you is set apart. When a thought intrudes, recall that word and it will recenter your attention toward God."

If you practice that simple exercise regularly, as a spiritual discipline, as important in your daily schedule as physical exercise or eating right, you will develop the capacity to let go of things in your life that are upsetting, harmful, stressful, and which contribute to a false view of yourself. With repetition, in time you will find yourself moving away from accustomed ways of thinking, reacting, and judging toward a deeper interior silence; you will begin to feel rested and refreshed, as well as spiritually awake. Your life will feel less hurried and hungered. Were there time, I would offer to lead you in several small meditations to begin to show you that this works and to let you discover the truth of it for yourself. This way of meditation is not specifically Christian; it is inclusively human.

But let me finish where I began, picking up on the passage which is directed toward the Christian faith and the experience of prayer that is offered out of our speaking:

"Whatever else it may or may not be, prayer is at least talking to yourself, ... Talk to yourself about your own life, about what you have done and what you have failed to do and about who you are and who you wish you were ... Talk to yourself about what matters most to you, because if you don't, you may forget what matters most to you.

Even if you don't believe anybody's listening, at least you'll be listening.

Believe Somebody is listening. Believe in miracles. That's what Jesus told the father who asked him to heal his epileptic son. Jesus said, "All things are possible to him who believes." And the father spoke for all of us when he answered, "Lord, I believe; help my unbelief!"

What about when the boy is not healed? When listened to or not listened to, the prayer goes unanswered? ...Just keep praying, Jesus says ... Even if the boy dies, keep on beating the path to God's door, because the one thing you can be sure of is that down the path you beat with even your most half-cocked and halting prayer the God you call upon will finally come, and even if he does not bring you the answer you want, he will bring you himself. And maybe at the secret heart of all our prayers that is what we are really praying for." (Wishful Thinking, pp. 70-71)

JOHN AND MARGIE

I give thanks that John in his infinite mercy has encouraged, embraced, emboldened, lifted up my life and ministry here – and I say that for me because I know that many of you might say the same for yourselves. But our appreciation would be artless without mention of Margie: creator, convener, composer, completer – whose many ministrations quietly, caringly, creatively, complement John and enable all that they do together.

Christopher Brookfield

A WORD ABOUT JOHN
AND A NOTE ABOUT MARGIE

In thanksgiving for these ten terrific years
and the remembrance of many more

*On the Occasion of John's 10th
Anniversary as Rector of St. Mary's Church*
February 6, 1994

You have heard it spoken in sonorous Souderian syllables: "'There was a man sent from God whose name was John.'" Or, he adlibbed in the biblical text, "maybe I should say, first, 'There was an organist sent from God to St. Mary's, whose name was Margie.'" I want to add to his adaptation, that is not the equivalent of saying that behind a successful man stands a stalwart woman – rather, that behind the man and the woman sent to us at St. Mary's stands God in his infinite wisdom.

I give thanks that John in his infinite mercy has encouraged, embraced, emboldened, lifted up my life and ministry here – and I say that for me because I know that many of you might say the same for yourselves. But our appreciation would be artless without mention of Margie: creator, convener, composer, completer – whose many ministrations quietly, caringly, creatively, complement John and enable all that they do together. In a sense these two are timeless, because there never was a time when we needed their time that they were not willing to give it, generously and graciously.

You have heard it said that you cannot enter the kingdom of God unless you become like a little child. My wife says that for

507

her the foremost image of John at St. Mary's is the blessing of his holding a baby in his arms at baptism. Apart from their parents, children rarely cry when *he* holds them. Secure in his loving grasp, they are comfortable with him and he with them – spreading warmth, good will, and new life throughout the congregation as he walks among us with the newest wee one.

Neither John nor Margie is a showman, but each is a team builder, enabling us to work together to enliven the Church. Encouraging our offerings of food, fellowship, flowers, and a flourishing Forum, they allow this congregation to work for itself, sing for itself! serving us and others in our involvement and outreach. And it thrives – we are thriven (present perfect) – inclusive of all ages, shapes, sizes, and sexes.

A major mark of John as Rector is his open-mindedness. He gives people space and room, a master of many mansions – whether in the practice of his preaching and teaching, or in permitting the pageant to propagate and persons of different perspectives to appear and the Forum to re-form and flower.

If John commissions us to choose life, Margie orchestrates our spirits and hones the harmony we hymn (and her) here at St. Mary's. They make us members of the whole, not just mindful of the holy. *Thanks be to God.*

WORDS FOR MARGIE

October 12th, 1998

A *few* words to remember her by are simply not enough to speak our hearts with; but, barring a barrage from *Roget's Thesaurus*, let me suggest some of them that friends have offered to describe her: loving and loyal, courageous and compassionate, candid and kind, truthful and thrifty, adventurous and exuberant, genuine and generous, spontaneous and self-effacing, nurture-in-motion, maddeningly modest, a fountain of ideas, stylish without being self-conscious; witty, funny, delightful – where shall I stop? Margie's a mouthful, and more – so much spiritual energy and power rolled into one God mindful grace-given silver- and black-haired beauty!

Fear not, I'm not just warming up for a eulogy, Margie wouldn't permit it; she would protest against such praise. Not so much because she has always been modest, but because so often she simply had no idea of the extent of life she extended to others in the way she lived and moved and gave us being. "Almost perfect teacher, friend" is the way headlines in the *Richmond Times-Dispatch* put it.

One day John asked her, "What do you really teach at St. Catherine's?" and she said, "Anything I want." But the truth is she was teaching young women (and a whole lot more of us crotchety types) how to live – and, as the Bishop added, how to live in dying. It is hard to remember a time when we saw her down; she had contagious courage in the face of intolerable suffering. She put us at ease, no matter how sick she was; she always wanted to know what was happening in our lives. Bill Wells has said on more than one occasion, "Margie is what the face of God looks like on our campus, in her teaching and music and in her dealings with others."

One day when Margie was trying to explain the power of adrenalin to her students, she said to one of them, "Right now I am not strong enough to pick you up, but if my adrenalin got pumping, I would be able to pick you up, put you on my shoulder and carry you." And what her students have written to her again and again over the years is, Thank you for carrying us, and teaching us how to carry each other, and helping us to carry other people.

On John Miller's tenth anniversary as Rector of this church, some special words were said of him and a note added about Margie who as organist "orchestrates our spirits and hones the harmony we hymn (and her) here at St. Mary's," not to mention Margie as "creator, convener, composer, completer – whose many ministrations quietly, caringly, creatively complement John and enable all that they do together. In a sense these two are timeless, because there never was a time when we needed their time that they were not willing to give it." Several months ago, long into her travail and still hoping for healing, Margie said to me "I wouldn't want a miracle for me if it was not also going to be for the next person who comes down the block." She would not ask the extraordinary for herself. And I replied "Why not for you (or me)?" but what I could have added is that for many of us she has been the miracle – empowering us and bringing forth the good which would never have been manifest without her – a lasting miracle

510

that had its way with us for some 49 years already and won't give us up easily.

One day when I went to visit her while she was still well enough to sit out back on the porch of the house, which she loved, I saw in passing what looked like a needle-point pillow on the sofa in the living room. What it said was typical of her even in the midst of what she was going through. "The Best Is Yet to Come," it read, in white letters on a black background. And that smarted, because I wasn't as sure of that message as Margie was. But since she has always been a woman of her word, I cannot help trust with her that that is what God has in store for her; and, who knows, since she has gone on before us, if she puts in a good word, that may be true for you and me too. Down at MCV, the day the doctors told us Margie could come home for hospice care, one of our priestly brothers said, "I know it doesn't feel like it, but this is an Easter moment." I could have cheerfully choked him in that moment. But I've changed my mind since, because whenever I think of Margie I think of light and life and hope and wholeness where ever she is – which she raised up out of us, unintentionally, when we weren't looking: a gift with no strings attached, which she gave us gladly, gracefully, and with great love.

The theme of this service is "Abide with me," after the hymn Margie loved. And of course, it means we want God to abide with us, through cloud and sunshine, when the darkness deepens, when others fail and comfort flees – as it sings so eloquently. But God knows, we want to be assured that Margie abides with us also.

HOW DO WE DEAL WITH OUR GRIEF?

19th Sunday after Pentecost
October 11, 1998

A look at the lectionary and the gospel lesson in Luke left me longing for something else to preach on this morning in the light of Margie's death three days ago. I haven't much appetite for a commentary on the ten lepers who were healed and the lone one who returned to give thanks; nor even on the abiding faith of Ruth, who, otherwise, was deemed an outcast in Israel. I need to say something about death instead of passing over it until Monday afternoon's service: What does it have to do with God's will? And where are we in the wake of it?

Margie never asked me, "Is there Life after death?" because I don't think she needed to. She had something some of us are sometimes short on – trust. Trust that God will be faithful to his word, that we will one day go in together to that house of many mansions he has prepared for them that love him. But in the meantime, many of us have questions about our sadness and Margie's unwarranted suffering. How do we deal with our grief? How do we deal with our anger? How do we deal with our unbelief?

I remembered what I received from a long-ago friend, a former chaplain at Andover Academy and at Yale (where he was something of an enfant terrible and the bane of the college president), who went from there to be Senior Minister of the famous Riverside Church in New York City. He spoke some words in the face of his son's death which were of great help to me then. I have used some of them here at St. Mary's in a different context, but it occurred to me that in some ways they are timely once again and might be worth repeating on this occasion. Some of you will remember William Sloane Coffin, Jr. His son Alex did not die from cancer but from a senseless car accident. However, at least some of the same issues, and certainly many of the same feelings are present for us in Margie's dying as were there in his.

Somehow, Bill Coffin managed to express his own grief and faith in a poignant kind of open letter to his congregation and friends. Less than two weeks after the death of his son, he wrote:

> As almost all of you know, a week ago last Monday night, driving in a terrible storm, my son Alexander – who to his friends was a real day-brightener, and to his family "fair as a star when only one is shining in the sky" – my twenty-four-year-old Alexander, who enjoyed beating his old man at every game and in every race, beat his father to the grave.

> Among the healing flood of letters that followed his death was one carrying this wonderful quotation from the end of Hemingway's A Farewell to Arms: "The world breaks everyone, then some become strong at the broken places." My own broken heart is mending, and largely thanks to so many of you...for if in the last week I have relearned one lesson, it is that love not only begets love, it transmits strength.

> Because so many of you have cared so deeply and because obviously, I've been able to think of little else, I want... to talk of Alex' s death, I hope in a way helpful... When a person dies, there are many things that can be said, and there is at least one thing that should never be said. The night after Alex died I was sitting in the living room of my sis-

ter's house outside of Boston, when the front door opened and in came a nice-looking middleaged woman, carrying about eighteen quiches. When she saw me she shook her head, then headed for the kitchen, saying sadly over her shoulder, "I just don't understand the will of God." Instantly I was up and in hot pursuit, swarming all over her. "I'll say you don't, lady!" I said. (I knew the anger would do me good, and the instruction to her was long overdue.) I continued, "Do you think it was the will of God that Alex never fixed that lousy windshield wiper of his, that he was probably driving too fast in such a storm, that he probably had had a couple of 'frosties' too many? Do you think it is God's will that there are no streetlights along that stretch of road, and no guard rail separating the road and Boston Harbor?"

For some reason, nothing so infuriates me as the incapacity of seemingly intelligent people to get it through their heads that God doesn't go around this world with his finger on triggers, his fist around knives, his hands on steering wheels. God is dead set against all unnatural deaths. And Christ spent an inordinate amount of time delivering people from paralysis, insanity, leprosy, and muteness. Which is not to say that there are no naturecaused deaths... deaths that are untimely and slow and pain-ridden, which for that reason raise unanswerable questions, and even the specter of a Cosmic Sadist – yes, even an Eternal Vivesector.... The one thing that should never be said when someone dies is, "It is the will of God." Never do we know enough to say that. My own consolation lies in knowing that it was not the will of God that Alex die; that when the waves closed over the sinking car, God's heart was the first of all our hearts to break.

I mentioned the healing flood of letters. Some of the very best, and easily the worst, came from fellow reverends, a few of whom proved they knew their Bibles better than the human condition. I know all the "right" Biblical passages, including "Blessed are those who mourn...;" these passages are true, I know. But the point is this: While the words of the Bible are true, grief renders them unreal. The reality of grief is the absence of God – "My God, my God, why hast thou forsaken me?" The reality of grief is the solitude of pain, the feeling that your heart's in pieces, your mind's a blank, that "there is no joy the world can give like that it takes away." (Lord Byron)

That's why immediately after such a tragedy people must come to your rescue, people who only want to hold your hand, not to quote anybody or even say anything, people who may simply bring food and flowers – the basics of beauty and life – and people who sign letters simply, "Your broken-hearted sister." In other words, in my intense grief I felt some of my fellow reverends – not many, thank God – were using comforting words of Scripture for self-protection, to pretty up a situation whose bleakness they simply couldn't face. But like God Herself, Scripture is not around for anyone's protection, just for everyone's unending support.

And that's what hundreds of you understood so beautifully. You gave me what God gives all of us-minimum protection, maximum support....

After the death of his wife, C. S. Lewis wrote, "They say, 'the coward dies many times;' so does the beloved.

Didn't the eagle find a fresh liver to tear in Prometheus every time it dined?"

Still there is much by way of consolation. Because there are no rankling unanswered questions, and because Alex and I simply adored each other, the wound for me is deep, but clean. I know how lucky I am! I also know that this day-brightener of a son wouldn't wish to be held close by grief (nor, for that matter, would any but the meanest of our beloved departed), and that, interestingly enough, when I mourn Alex least, I see him best.

Another consolation, of course, will be the learning- which better be good, given the price. But it's a fact: few of us are naturally profound; we have to be forced down into the depths. So while trite, it's true:

> I walked a mile with Pleasure,
> She chattered all the way;
> But left me none the wiser
> For all she had to say.
> I walked a mile with Sorrow
> And ne'er a word said she;
> But oh, the things I learned from her
> When sorrow walked with me.

> Robert Browning Hamilton

...And of course, I know, even when pain is deep, that God is good. "My God, my God, why hast thou forsaken me?" Yes, but at least, "My God, my God;" and the psalm only begins that way, it doesn't end that way. As the grief that once seemed unbearable begins to turn now to bearable sorrow, the truths in the "right" Biblical passages are beginning, once again, to take hold: "Cast thy burden upon the Lord and He shall Strengthen thee;" "Weeping may endure for a night, but joy cometh in the morning;"

"...for thou hast delivered my soul from death, mine eyes from tears, and my feet from falling." "In this world ye shall have tribulation, but be of good cheer, I have overcome the world." "The light shines in the darkness, and the darkness has not overcome it."

Finally, I know that when Alex beat me to the grave, the finish line was not Boston Harbor in the middle of the night. If a week ago last Monday a lamp went out, it was because, for him at least, the Dawn had come.

So I shall – so let us all – for Margie's sake, seek consolation in that love which never dies, and find peace in the dazzling grace that always is, even when our eyes are too blurred with tears to see it clearly.

AIRING OUR FAITH

*On the Occasion of John's 20th
Anniversary as Rector of St. Mary's Church*

5th Sunday after the Epiphany
Year C – Luke 5:1-11
February 8, 2004

Once while Jesus was standing beside the lake of Gennesaret, and the crowd was pressing in on him to hear the word of God, he saw two boats there at the shore of the lake; the fishermen had gone out of them and were washing their nets. He got into one of the boats, the one belonging to Simon, and asked him to put out a little way from the shore. Then he sat down and taught the crowds from the boat. When he had finished speaking, he said to Simon, "Put out into the deep water and let down your nets for a catch." Simon answered, "Master, we have worked all night long but have caught nothing. Yet if you say so, I will let down the nets." When they had done this, they caught so many fish that their nets were beginning to break. So they signaled their partners in the other boat to come and help them. And they came and filled both boats, so that they began to sink. But when Simon Peter saw it, he fell down at Jesus' knees, saying, "Go away from me, Lord, for I am a sinful man!" For he and all who were with him were amazed at the catch of fish that they had taken; and so also were James and John, sons of

Zebedee, who were partners with Simon. Then Jesus said to Simon, "Do not be afraid; from now on you will be catching people." When they had brought their boats to shore, they left everything and followed him.

Luke 5:1-11

A little later in this offering you will understand why I was unsure just how to start my sermon on this particular 5th Sunday after Epiphany, which is also fittingly, Fellowship Sunday for us at St. Mary's – and much more, which I shall mention momentarily. So to start somewhere and invite your attention, I have opted to present you with an improbable image to picture and an implausible choice to ponder between the advantages of owning an opulent car or a carried-away church. I couldn't resist repeating this report from *The Washington Post*:[1]

"It's hard to believe, but for the price of a well equipped Infinity G35 luxury car, you can now buy yourself a fully loaded, 47-foothigh place of worship. It's got Gothic arches, an organ, a pulpit, an altar, space for 60 and even some stained-glass-style windows. All for 35K, which sounds like a deal, or even a steal," except for the fact that this building is a balloon, so be sure you set aside sharp objects when you come there to worship.

"The world's first inflatable church made its debut last May in England, and its creator hopes that it will 'breathe new life into Christianity.' Featured on CNN and other media outlets, the church is designed to fit into the back of a truck so that it can be hauled to village squares or open fields and set up for impromptu services."[2]

"What shall we say about an inflatable church?" we might ask skeptically. Well perhaps it could address the problem of people who, seeking to refill their spiritual tanks each week, are always complaining that all they ever get from church is gas.

And maybe, so to speak, "to be inflatable [can] be incarnational" – filled with the spirit. But seriously, whatever else we might choose to say about that pumped up sanctuary, it is a church on the move. And one commentary on our gospel reading for today soberly suggests that is exactly what Jesus was about when he launched his ministry beside the lake of Gennesaret by hopping into one of the two fallow fishing boats, persuading Peter to push off a little way from shore, and proceeding to preach to the people from out of the boat. He didn't have "an inflated organ, a pop-up pulpit, or an air-filled altar,"[3] but he spoke a healing word from that impromptu platform to the hopes and needs of all those who crowded round to hear the gospel preached to them.

That story in Bible-speak is often called "the miraculous catch of fish," but it could also be spoken of as a parable for our time; only for us it's not so much about the multitude of fish as a miracle that can change the way we understand ourselves as the church. And, that's where, unlikely as it may at first seem, this scriptural selection and our own story of St. Mary's intersect – symbolically if not specifically in the abundance of fish. The only "catch" in Luke's fish story is that it is not a parable about how to turn a small parish into a successful mega-church but a tale about building up the kingdom of God. When Jesus tells Simon to put out into deep water, the catch he intends for Peter is "the deep things of God." (I Cor. 2:10)[4]

Shortly I'm going to shift from the scriptural story of the miraculous catch for this morning to the miracle of the day in our midst. But I have to note in passing, since this passage is such a familiar one to many, that some of us oldies still talk about how the newer translations are a travesty on the "real" (that is the 1611) words. We all knew what Jesus meant when he said to Peter and Andrew "Follow me, and I will make you fishers of men." Now, the translations seem so flat and awkward in saying with the times: "I'll show you how to catch men and women instead of perch and bass" or even uninclusively, "I will teach you how to catch men" – which sounds almost off-color.

P.C. or not, Jesus was extraordinarily effective at finding ways to bring his message to the heart of where people were living and playing and working. Symbolically speaking, that story represents the result as a great catch of fish, so many that the nets could not hold them and were beginning to break. If you think about it, over the past fifteen years something like that has been happening right here at St. Mary's. The church has hardly had time to recover from one expansion before another was on the way, which brings me to my excuse for shifting the focus from the story of Jesus and the great gathering at Gennesaret to the advent of the apostle John. By apostle, I mean what the Greek word says literally: "messenger, one who is sent" (not to be confused with the bollards and bitts in a sailing ship, which we also call apostles). Anyway, I'm about to do a dirty deed and depart from the lectionary to dedicate this day to the divinity of John, not the Baptist, or the Evangelist, or even the Beloved disciple – but to parts of all three rolled into one, incarnate in the resources of our resilient rector. Not that John Miller is God – only of God, by whom and with whom and in whom we have encountered the holy spirit full of grace and truth, if not always with peace and heavenly benediction. John has become a fisher of persons, old and young – not because they get hooked on what he says or does; he just holds out to us the bait of the traditional gospel compassionately tempered by timely thought, word, and deed; and when it's all done so well it always hauls them in – and St. Mary's has acquired a reputation in Richmond for being a church on the move, without the hot air that sometimes surrounds a hot preacher.

I say a dirty deed because John has already enjoined us not to inflate the fact that to the day, this is the 20th anniversary of his first Sunday as rector of St. Mary's ("snow fall heavy," the service register reported on that 5th Sunday after Epiphany in 1984). John would not want us to make a big deal of it, so we're not, but we want on this occasion to remember and celebrate John's contributions to the new life of St. Mary's – not to blow them up, but to affirm that indeed inflational can be incarnational; in becoming bigger we may have aired but not strayed like lost sheep.

I'm going to read a little known citation, which was composed for the vestry meeting to note the 20th year of John's ordination – which, with a little tweaking, will serve as a salute on this significant Sunday. It was originally entitled: *20 Years of Un-ordinary Ordination – Off beat observations on the ongoing enthusiasm, inspiration, agony, élan, and enduring offerings of our resilient Rector*. But on this occasion, it probably could be called simply *A Score of (In)spirited Service and Inspiration to All Souls at St. Mary's:*

Peering upon John's portrait in the old parish hall, you may perceive him young and innocent, but he's not; he's wily, worldly wise and overworked. Lo these 20 years (and more), he has labored long and lovingly in the vineyard of the Lord at St. Mary's. Holt Souder once began a sermon on the 4th Gospel (and of course there were three of them before John: Giles Palmer, Stan Ashton, and Souder himself), saying, "There was a man sent from God, whose name was John." And he ought to have added, "He was not himself the light, but he lent the light that illumined the life of St. Mary's." No dim bulb, he – but the beacon that beckoned vitality and vision, enlightenment and unceasing expansion among us: from around 200, near Nineteen Seventy-Five, now approaching 2000 in Aught Four.

Think what he has led us through: the demise of the wasps and the handheld fans, the respectful repose of the Rectory, the comings and goings of the undying Adult Forum, the shouting surrounding the start of the Christmas pageant that has become an august institution under another name. The addition of Assistants and Associates – enthusiastic, unformed, even incompetent, but unable to undo the durable and endearing ministry John has masterminded; the advent of planned parishood that planted the enlarged parish hall, the groaning kitchen, and Great St. Mary's topped off with a tower – without losing the life of Little St. Mary's, Lord knows.

Saying goodbye to the Souder era, not burying the past, but lifting up the life of it; invoking the addition of another organ, extending our outreach, and advancing the unusual idea that everyone is entitled to contribute treasure as well as time and talent to balance the budget; missing Margie, mainstay in ministry, remembering her prayers and plans to empower the parish.

The future is not ahead of us, it is even now among us as we bask in the bong of bells, the multiplication of music, and education out the ears – not to mention the marvel and ministry of St. Mary's School, the increase of ordinations among us, even an award for outreach. So St. Mary's thrives and prospers under the thoughtful and prolific presence of Parson John, touched by the spirit, unspoiled by success, servant of all sorts and conditions of us miscreants at St. Mary's.

———

1. *Before faith fills the air, air fills the cathedral* – May 17, 2003, B9.
2. *Homiletics* 16 - 1 p.36
3. *Ibid.*
4. *cf Lectionary Homiletics* XV, 2 p.12

FAREWELL

Eleanor Wellford even presented me with a large stack of fond wishes from the Sunday school classes. One said simply "Dear Christopher" – which seemed to me more than enough. A bright orange card with big smiling blue teeth, said "Mr. Brookfield You Rock!" And then there was one written in green, saying "Peace old Christopher. Hope you have a life." I will – thanks to the life you have bestowed on me.

Christopher Brookfield

SOME SERMON INCITES

4th Sunday after Pentecost
Matthew 9:9-13, 18-26
Proper 5, Year A – June 8, 2008

As Jesus was walking along, he saw a man called Matthew sitting at the tax booth; and he said to him, "Follow me." And he got up and followed him.

And as he sat at dinner in the house, many tax collectors and sinners came and were sitting with him and his disciples. When the Pharisees saw this, they said to his disciples, "Why does your teacher eat with tax collectors and sinners?" But when he heard this, he said, "Those who are well have no need of a physician, but those who are sick. Go and learn what this means, 'I desire mercy, not sacrifice.' For I have come to call not the righteous but sinners."

While he was saying these things to them, suddenly a leader of the synagogue came in and knelt before him, saying, "My daughter has just died; but come and lay your hand on her, and she will live." And Jesus got up and followed him, with his disciples. Then suddenly a woman who had been suffering from hemorrhages for twelve years came up behind him and touched the fringe of his cloak, for she said to herself, "If I only touch his cloak, I will be made well." Jesus turned, and seeing her he said, "Take heart, daughter; your faith has made you well." And instantly the woman was made well. When Jesus came to the leader's house and saw the flute players and the crowd making a commotion, he said, "Go away; for the girl is not dead but sleeping." And they laughed at him. But when the crowd had been put outside, he went in and took her by the hand, and the girl got up. And the report of this spread throughout that district.

Matthew 9:9-13, 18-26

One Sunday after the preacher had preached a vigorous sermon, he was met by a little old lady at the door who said, "You know Pastor, every sermon you preach is better than your next one."

A preacher preached a stirring sermon and a lady in the congregation praised him highly and suggested that he should publish his sermons. The preacher told her he was planning they be published posthumously. To which she replied, "Well good, the sooner the better."

A young man preaching for the first time stood before the people as the moments passed. At last, opening his mouth, slowly he began to speak, "On the way here this morning, only God and I knew what I was to share with you, and now only God knows!

This can hardly be called my last sermon at St. Mary's if, as the saying goes, all preachers have only one sermon (which they continue to preach each time they get into the pulpit). So consider it my first, which I began to preach at St. Mary's some 11,834 days ago on the first Sunday of 1976. For this occasion, I searched my files to find out what exactly I said at that time, to see if there might be anything worth saying again today. But alas (or halleluiah) it is mercifully missing. There may be a message for me in that, which I won't think too long and hard about.

Now, to the gospel reading in Matthew 9, which contains two of my favorite Jesus' sayings. First, "I come not to call the righteous, but sinners..." he said. Which reminds me of what my predecessor as Dean of Church Schools in the Diocese of Virginia said when he opened a chapel service at one of the schools: "A church is simply a gathering of great sinners, and nowhere is that more evident than right here in this place." And here I have felt adopted, nurtured, and lifted up at St. Mary's these past 20 years on staff, not as a righteous leader but as one who has shared with some of you the experiences of disappointment and falling short. Righteousness was never my strong suit.

My memories of St. Mary's today are not mainly about the amazing increase of parishioners or twice building a bigger church. When my family and I first came here there were about 200 in the parish and 13 students enrolled in Sunday school -and St. Mary's gave life and laughter to all who came. That was the era of no air conditioning, handheld straw fans, and the lazy "z-z-z-z" of wasps or hornets cruising during worship. I can still picture one of them perched placidly on the bridge of Holt Souder's glasses as he gestured vigorously at one point in his sermon. Or the one on another occasion, which John Miller had deftly flicked out of the full communion cup and which staggered drunkenly across the fair linen on the altar in search of the chalice again.

Once I start on this track, I remember other marks of St. Mary's that remind us of what this church was and is, being and becoming. I am made glad that amid all the newness and grandeur of a growing St. Mary's, new brassy fittings have not replaced the home-made Communion cigar box missal stand held up by the humble French one-holer underneath, used in Little St. Mary's (it still opens, for the inquisitive). And the spectacle of John or the celebrant calming the distressed individual infant at baptism has remained a part of our liturgy, not the cattle-car format adopted by many other churches.

I remember when the vestry beseeched our rector to pray for rain at one especially dry meeting time and there followed three days of torrential downpour. And the blessing of a bagpipe bracing funerals in our church yard (which you heard again recently at Dick Lower's service), Susie Salsitz blowing her heart out – an amazing grace in itself. Then the glare of the great window here, glazed over to keep the celebrant from being fried in the sun flooding the elements at Communion (and my chagrin when I insisted during the building of New St. Mary's that the window be lowered closer to the ground, as we had requested of the architect – a $10,000 additional bill (not counting his commission) for a few panes of glass and a big pain for the budget.

I think also of the luxury of two windows in my office that look directly out onto the playground and the raucous play of the little ones, the fast-growing future of St. Mary's, squealing joyfully and sometimes painfully. Not far from there, in the old sacristy, the so-called "new" faucet that never worked shortly after it was installed for the altar guild. And in this new sanctuary the black blotches of blood of the bothersome lady bugs bludgeoned by those who thought them bothering, backed into the floor boards behind the altar until the evidence was artfully removed. I still mourn them missing. St. Mary's was not otherwise known for violence. Except there's this stone I hold in my hand, with a big "2" written on it, given to me by an EfM student who explained: "No one wants to be the one to throw the first stone – but everyone wants to throw the second."

There was a time when people joined the church here because they knew they would never be asked for money nor asked to do anything. And people spoke their minds. I recall one parishioner who one day owned up to me and said, "We hated everything you said when you first came here." (He then added, "Of course, now we love anything you say.") All of us no spotless saints, but surrounded in our sinnerdom by the saving grace of St. Mary's and the myth of little Mary Allen that bequeaths us a preposterously pure heritage to carry on.

Now to the second saying I savor from the gospel scripture for this morning: the story of the woman who could not be cured of her hemorrhaging until she dared to reach out and touch Jesus and she was healed. "Your faith has made you well," he said, which word I welcome. Heal, whole, and holy come from the same root word-those things we cannot do on our own, of our own strength, but only in faith, in community, which we sometimes call a church.

Having spent so many years in school work, in the mind, in the classroom, by the time John Miller asked me to join the staff at St. Mary's I was fearful of what I might have – or not have – to offer a parish church. Especially one that was debating whether to be or not to be little St. Mary's, or two St. Mary's, or (heaven forbid) a new St. Mary's. Earlier I had unofficially assisted Holt Souder from time to time, starting in 1976, not many years removed from when this church had only a pay phone and a volunteer part time chain-smoking secretary who would keep the take from the Sunday service collections safe at her house each week.

But in 1988 St. Mary's had become a formidable parish with a problem: it had outgrown itself. The storied "waiting list" to join had been overthrown. I wasn't sure how to preach here; but I'd had some experience asking questions, which seemed a good thing for sermons to do, if not always welcomed. Sometimes people heard what struck some as off-beat or cranky words from me, but they didn't simply condemn it as irritable vowel syndrome, they laughed and encouraged me. Two members of our choir began what I call a comic strip ministry – passing on to me particularly provocative pieces from the funnies (perhaps in hopes of hearing them said in some homily). I could rejoice in that. Remember, laughter is the closest we come to full forgiveness on earth.

Small adult education classes that my wife, Lynne, and I sometimes taught together helped me understand something of the mystery of parish ministry. And to my surprise, St. Mary's gave me a new life also in teaching Education for Ministry courses and in shepherding what I have called the St. Mary's Book Group for some 23 years: enabling in me new styles in mentoring and leading, which I hadn't found in former years in the classroom. The inimitable, loyal and stalwart Bible study gathering, which has put up with me each week for 11 years changed my way of exploring the biblical text for seekers and skeptics. Could it be that all un-knowing and unasking I was slowly becoming more whole in the ministry I had known so little about? In any case it was a whole lot of fun. New life may sound like a cliché, but it was what I was receiving – because your faith was lifting me up.

I have delighted in taking part in weddings and burial services over the years and I shall miss the life of St. Mary's more than I can say, along with my rich association with our fantastic staff members and many on the vestry (past and present), and of course my long-time colleague, friend and guide, John Miller who (with Margie) has been my supreme advocate for 33 years. None of this unexpected and long run here for me would have been possible without their love, loyalty, and sometimes long-suffering support, theirs and yours.

Speaking of which, I don't know how to thank the horde of you who helped create my humongous going-away fund and sumptuous surprise picnic in my honor. My family and I were undone. Eleanor Wellford even presented me with a large stack of fond wishes from the Sunday school classes. One said simply "Dear Christopher" – which seemed to me more than enough. A bright orange card with big smiling blue teeth, said "Mr. Brook-field You Rock!" And then there was one written in green, saying "Peace old Christopher. Hope you have a life." I will – thanks to the life you have bestowed on me.

One last note on memorable things is the marvelous music here many may take for granted – St. Mary's revenge on those who loudly and for so long refused to have a choir. Dwight Graham has graciously prepared one of his special pieces on the organ at the end of the service – don't miss it.

It's hard to say good-bye, but it's easy to say thank you. I am so grateful for all you have given me, God knows. God bless, Godspeed, Shalom and great laughter to you all.

APPENDIX:
NON-ST. MARY'S ARTICLES

"Despair? Why would I despair? In the darkest day of my people, I did not despair." A quarter of a century ago, if I can stand the truth spoken in such stark terms, I sat in a class in McCosh Hall in some course (which one, I cannot now remember) and heard the renowned Martin Buber say those words. I cannot easily forget them because when he spoke, he was sitting precariously on the writing arm of my desk, leaning forward literally shouting, his face so close to mine that I dared not breathe.

Christopher Brookfield

IN MEMORIAM

Princeton, February, 1983

"Despair? Why would I despair? In the darkest day of my people, I did not despair." A quarter of a century ago, if I can stand the truth spoken in such stark terms, I sat in a class in McCosh Hall in some course (which one, I cannot now remember) and heard the renowned Martin Buber say those words. I cannot easily forget them because when he spoke, he was sitting precariously on the writing arm of my desk, leaning forward literally shouting, his face so close to mine that I dared not breathe. Why he addressed me at that moment, I do not know. I had not asked him the question about the Jewish experience of suffering and death in World War II which provoked his passionate outburst.

"Don't you ever despair of God's love?" someone had asked him, this man who was known to us primarily as the author of *I and Thou*, a most difficult and beautiful volume of philosophical poetry which focuses on man's relation to the "eternal Thou," this man whose curious affliction was his inability to pronounce the word "thou." "Vow!" he would say with difficulty, with the sunlight caught up in his flowing white hair that billowed out on the sides so that it appeared almost incandescent. "Why despair?" he answered the question I had not asked, with words of courage and hope which I have remembered to this day.

Although the question that prompted them was not mine at the time, it is one that has come to mean a great deal to me in the intervening 25 years because it does not deny the reality of death that we inevitably meet in life, death that can confront us either as a cross upon our hopes or as an opportunity for faith.

Perhaps in the presence of both realities, we have come today to offer thanks and praise for the lives of loved ones and friends, lives that even now can be the bearers of courage and hope to us who must continue to live with death we cannot control in the course of life that we fancy we control, order, and shape.

That reminds me of what is not simply a sectarian joke, the familiar story about the minister who always had everything under control down to the last detail, who was always on time, and whose assistant was never allowed to do anything without first obtaining the rector's blessing. As the story goes, one day when the appointed hour for a funeral drew near and, uncharacteristically, the rector had not appeared to take charge of the services and to start the procession down the aisle behind the casket, the assistant was beside himself. He sent frenzied signals to the organist to repeat the Prelude, but five minutes later, when that was over for the second time and the rector still had not appeared, clearly the time had run out. So the assistant at last decided to begin the service himself and stepped off down the main aisle, saying the familiar words, "I am the resurrection and the life..." Whereupon he heard behind him rapid footsteps and the unmistakable voice of the rector saying, breathlessly, "No, no, *I* am the resurrection and the life...." Perhaps what we despair of most when it comes to questions of life and death is loss of control. What we fear, as Hugh T. Kerr ('31) has said more than once, is that "Life is what happens when we have made other plans."

When *The Book of Common Prayer* proclaims, "In the midst of life we are in death," it affirms an uncomfortable truth which we want to deny. Unfortunately, all we have to do is to confirm that truth is to turn on the Today Show or pick up the daily newspaper. We are reluctant to accept that before our lives are done we will die many times, but part of the rites of passage from this life to whatever we hope awaits us depends upon that acceptance. To deny that is to deny the reality of life as well as death. Several personal examples, which will be no strangers to your lives, may be appropriate for me to offer:

My 18-year-old son, Christopher Lord, about to go off by himself to his freshman year at Duke while my wife and I were on vacation in New Hampshire, decided to invite a few friends to a late August cookout at our house. They called the occasion The Last Dinner. "Why?" I asked, naively. "Because it was the last time we would be together," said my son, "and, after all," he said ingenuously, "I am the 'Lord.'" "Was it fun?" I asked. "Yea, it was great! But it was so sad. All of us knew we would never be the same again, and there was nothing we could do about it."

My wife, by herself on the last of many exhausting days packing the totality of our belongings and scrubbing the house for its new owners, cried into the echoing emptiness. We were leaving the place where we had spent the first 12 years of our married lives living, loving, laughing, and raising our children. We were moving to a new part of the country, a new job and new ways in an unknown future; breaking the security and rituals of the only life we had formed together, the friendships we had forged in common. I had already left; some friends had asked her out for the evening to wish her good-bye and good morrow. Alone in the wee hours of the morning, she lay on the floor of our house, throwing up. What she was retching out was not the fruits of an evening of overindulgence, but a life that, willing or not, she had to give up before she could accept a new one.

My grandmother died grandly and grotesquely, full of love and cancer, both of which she lived out with dignity and hard-nosed realism. Generous as she was frugal, she expected much from those she loved, yet never laid that burden upon them. At her funeral, when time came for the great Easter hymn, "The strife is o'er, the battle done, / The victory of life is won," I could not for the life of me sing it. I could hear the question asked of Martin Buber, but I did not yet understand his answer. Years later I still remembered that she had been given over to pain and suffering and God-knows-what-else. What I had forgotten was, had it not been for her, I would never have gone to seminary; indeed, I wouldn't have *been* at all. So often we have our lives at the expense and grace of others.

One more incident, as the 25th Anniversary Year Book of 1958 will relate if I do not. Upon graduation from Princeton, I felt called to make public pronouncements to family and friends, such as: "I will under no circumstances consider doing graduate study, I will never go into teaching, and I will have nothing whatsoever to do with religion." (I am not sure if that says more about whether I am to be trusted or God is.) Clearly, I needed the grace to die to each of those promises to life if I would choose life.

What, at last, Martin Buber's words helped me understand was the difficult truth that, even in the depths of suffering, we always have the right to choose for life rather than death. That is part of what he called "the exalted melancholy of our fate." Another way of stating it is to reverse the words I quoted earlier – to say, as Martin Luther is said to have said of the story of Abraham's call to sacrifice Isaac, "In the midst of death, we are in life."

Those whose names are listed in your order of services have, one way or another, confronted the questions that determined the quality of each one's life. Some of us have shared intimately in the answers they have bequeathed us, sometimes even before we had time to form the questions for ourselves. I think of the warmth and wit of my friend William Ernest Gillespie ('33), former Principal of The Phillips Exeter Academy, where I taught for 12 years. In his last commencement address, which he gave knowing that his death was near, he expressed his hopes for the departing Seniors: "It is nearly time for you to be off. You have a lot to do. This is not time for nostalgia…. But I hope, and I expect, that when you find yourselves involved in skirmishes on the frontiers of barbarism, which are not very far away, you'll strike some shrewd blows in favor of civilization. Someday you'll come back to show us your trophies and your scars, and we'll be glad to see you."

Ernie carried with him in his life's work the ideals of "Princeton in the nation's service;" although, being a schoolmaster, he knew that lots of us would fall short of them. He was not so much interested in the trophies that many of his students would undoubtedly win as in the scars that some would assuredly bear. We honor today the trophies and scars embodied here in the names printed before us. We give thanks for the skirmishes that they, and we, have been given to along the way, hopeful that in God's good time we may also be granted the courage to seek answers to the questions we have yet to ask.

We have come here to this Chapel because, as someone else has said, it is always to this kind of place, set apart, that we come to raise questions about the bewildering problems and mysteries we encounter in life and in ourselves – whether joyous or sad. It is the one place in this community, in any community, where in the midst of death we are in life; where we may come to speak against God, to shake our fist at God, to register our doubts and disappointments or to express our faith and our joy. We ask God to fill this place with Himself and to use it and us so that we may begin to live our way into the answers we ultimately seek – in hope and courage and, of course, in love.

***God help us never to confuse easy
answers with success or impossible answers
with failure.***

Remembering especially those who have gone before us, O Lord, the God no less of those who know Thee not, than of those who love Thee well, be present with us also in our times of choosing. God help us never to confuse easy answers with success or impossible answers with failure. Help us to see through our darkness, to believe through our unbelief, that no one in God's love is finally lost to Thee or to us. "Vow," who alone knows what the future holds, help us to understand that there are words of truth and healing that will never be spoken unless we speak them, and deeds of compassion and courage that will never be done unless we do them. Help us through our tears and our laughter to forgiveness of one another and to faith at the last, this day and always, *AMEN.*

SOME NOTES ON SEEING A FRIEND IN THE INTERIM

It was my turn and my privilege to sit with him in the early morning hours when only 7-Eleven was open and the streets were absolutely still.

I found Robert peaceful but with labored breath, almost shaven, among the bags and tubes suspended from racks around him. He might almost have been asleep. On the table by his bed was his medallion with Reinie Niebuhr's gift to A.A.:

*God grant me the serenity to accept the things
I cannot change; courage to change the things I can;
and the wisdom to know the difference.*

A hymnbook lay open to "Just As I Am Without One Plea," which I remember as O Lamb of God, I come, I come. But Robert could not come yet.

Had he been an observer, Robert would have been amused at what he might have called the artifacts of his room, beginning with the large television set leaning drunkenly off the wall at a precarious angle. A can of diet Coke, empty, side by side with a Big Block of Hershey's with Almonds. A box of tapes, News from Lake Woebegone, A Prairie Home Companion, on the ledge by the window, accompanied by Pavarotti's Songs the Whole World Loves" and a bright red book, *Teach Only Love*.

A touch of the practical, a Teddy Bear nurse, faced him on the bureau, overseeing a box of "Medical Wipes" (alias Kleenex), a box of 100 Examination Gloves: Medium; and catheters, "Frosted finish, Whistle tips/ Two Eyes."

The nurse would wipe Robert's brow every now and then. Occasionally he would take a deep breath and exhale with relief. Ben Campbell was just leaving: "I guess what I've decided these past two hours is that he's sleeping. He has not gone with God yet. This is an interim time. He's not struggling."

"Are you a priest of the Church?" the nurse asked me.

"Yes," I answered.

"You don't have to wear a collar?"

"Only when I'm on official business. I'm a friend, part of the vigil."

"There's not a lot to be done right now," she said apologetically.

I read the hymn again.

Just as I am, without one plea,
But that thy blood was shed for me.
And that thou bidst me come to thee,
O Lamb of God, I come, I come.

Just as I am, thou wilt receive,
Wilt welcome, pardon, cleanse, relieve,
Because thy promise I believe
O Lamb of God, I come, I come.
Just as I am, thy love unknown,
Hath broken every barrier down,
Now to be thine, yea thine alone,
O Lamb of God, I come, I come.

Be at peace, Robert.

THE DIVINE IN WOMAN AND WOMAN IN THE DIVINE

What in God's Name is Feminism?
(on being Candide about the issues)
*Presented to the Richmond, Virginia, Torch Club
February 4, 1986.*

In search of a commonplace, rather than an esoteric meaning of the word feminism, I consulted several dictionaries. *Harper's Bible Dictionary* knew not feminism. *The Theological Dictionary of the New Testament* knew it less. Commenting on "Women in the Contemporary New Testament World," it began with "the common male saying ... that it is a matter of thanksgiving not to be an unbeliever or barbarian, a slave, or a woman."

Christopher M. Brookfield

In a more conclusive if no less combative vein, the *Concise Oxford* defined feminism as "extended recognition of the claims of women"; while *Webster's* allowed feminism as a movement, which advocates "the theory, cult, propaganda, or practice of legal and social change to establish the political, economic, and social equality of the sexes; the emancipation of women."

Such deficient definitions may not delight you; they dumbfounded me.

Worse, they pointed out a kind of complicity, more commonplace than culpable, in my task as teacher, whether of world religions or theological thoughts in contemporary literature. For instance, it never occurred to me that in recognizing the devious disguises of Shiva the Destroyer (in Hinduism) or in acknowledging Graham Greene's gaffs in forgoing the gifts of the Holy Mother (in Christianity) I was unwittingly fanning the flames of friends or foes of feminism. Like Candide, I was tempted to try tending my own garden as the greatest gift I had to offer. What has come to flower was tended to blossom neither pulchritudinous nor pugnacious; it is intended to be apolitical and apolemical as well as apologetic in the "archaic" intention of that adjective.

Only lately it occurred to me that, in taking on this topic, I might well end with no friends at all at the finish of my paper. On the other hand, why flatter myself. These are merely the musings of a middle-aged, minister-administrator, school teacher-theologian type touched with the illusion that he is no more mossback than feminists are antifemale and that the issue of feminism is as much theological as political and sociological. Now, beyond the apology; or, should I say, to the apologia:

Laughter or Silence

It used to be said that you can tell the character of a man by what he laughs at. Not so long ago, the great thigh slapper among clergymen and "Good Morning, America" media types was this response of an evangelical social-reformer in the face of an attack upon the authority by which he presumed to speak: "I have seen God, and she is black."

We no longer find that funny, not because laughter in public could bring down the wrath of the ACLU or the NAACP upon us, but because most of us have become more sophisticated about such talk. As some would say, our "consciousness has been raised." We have witnessed the ordination of women to the priesthood, Vanessa Williams' challenge to the ethics of the Miss America pageant, Geraldine Ferraro as a viable vier for the vice presidency of the United States. We have even seen men's underwear become fashionable for women, and househubby tending to the infants and domestic chores, while the woman is out chasing the bacon in her own BMW.

—◦◦◦—

Along with the advent of words like input, parameters, meaningful relationships, consciousness-raising, coredump, interface, futuring, and the like, we have come face-to-face with feminism...

—◦◦◦—

We have had a switch thrust upon us in the way we view reality. Along with the advent of words like input, parameters, meaningful relationships, consciousness-raising, coredump, interface, futuring, and the like, we have come face-to-face with feminism, ready or not. In libraries that have banned Huckleberry Finn because it is coarse, vulgar, and irreverent, you may find Fear of Flying. Even Christian theology, traditionally concerned with reconciliation, redemption, and renewal, has lately found itself hostile not only to the cause of women's liberation but to inclusive (that is, nonsexed) biblical language as well, and on scriptural grounds (some would say). We have compounded the racism and sexism of our time with chauvinism and feminism in religion as well as politics.

I would like to leave you with a perspective on women's liberation and feminism, but I want to get there through theology and anthropology. So if you are here to hear an anatomy of feminism, forget it. "Where the action is" this time is in theological "drag," the godly garb of man's awkward attempts to speak about what once upon a time he was forbidden to name: namely, God, who created man male *and* female.

The Bible tells us that man was told to call things names, which may account for the so-called "patriarchal captivity" of both the scriptures and the Christian theological tradition.

Western Christendom has not profited much from the worldly wisdom of the East and the insight of the Buddha who said, "Whereof one cannot speak, thereof one must remain silent." Western theology is suspicious of silence. We believe that "in the beginning was the word."

Eating What You Are

It has also been said that a man is what he eats.

Nel Noddings has recently written, on the feminine in moral education, "I suspect no *woman* could have written ... Genesis ..." (italics mine).[1] Furthermore, she says on the subject of inclusive biblical language, "I would not agree to 'feminize' the traditional Bible, ... I would not want the feminine pronouns 'she' and 'her' associated with the terrible God of the Old Testament." Noddings has no use, either, for a Christian "church dominated by St. Paul" and his "misogynic doctrines." She has come to hate him "with all my heart," she writes, "and so must all true women hate him...."[2]

What is at issue for her is a dichotomy between what she calls the feminine religious attitude and the traditional masculine attitude; between what she describes as Western religion characterized by the masculine logical approach to ethical problems, with its appeal to "principles, power, and obedience" and the feminine ethic of caring, nurturing and maintaining relationships, committed to "the celebration of earthly life and love."

Noddings is not alone in insisting that there are significant differences between the masculine and feminine experience, and that Western theology as well as religion and ethics, particularly theological doctrines of sin and love, do not provide an adequate interpretation of the human situation of women – or men.[3] You may be familiar with Carol Gilligan's *In a Different Voice*,[4] the research for which was partly prompted by her colleague at Harvard, Lawrence Kohlberg, who observed in his *Six-Stage Schema of Moral Development* that women were, for the most part, "stuck" in Stage Three and couldn't get past conventional morality to appeal to the highest principles in making moral judgments. Gilligan discovered that Kohlberg's research for such findings was done with men only.

Where the Western Christian church finds feminism most threatening is not in its challenges to doctrines or even practices within a particular religious tradition, but in its judgment upon the validity of the tradition itself in speaking of the nature of religious experience for men and women. That aspect of feminist criticism goes well beyond the current demand for "gender-neutral" language in speaking of the divine, particularly in scriptural pronouns and nouns that name the deity in terms like "Father," "Lord," "Son of Man" (overlooking the issue that the excision of such familiar language would be destructive of the liturgical and emotional roots of devout persons). The greatest threat of feminism is calling into question the validity of the tradition as received, on the grounds that its reception as recorded excludes "one-half the human race."

I doubt that any revisionist history or textual reform is going to be able to recapture, reshape, or rewrite the experience of personal religious encounters in any tradition – let alone get around the Judeo-Christian reverence for the power of the spoken word, present or previous (whether pronounced *dabar* or *logos*). What is needed is not an irrelevant apology for the sins of the fathers that have been visited upon the children even unto the tenth generation, but an apt apologia which attempts to make room for some of those who have been shouted out of their religious inheritance – whether by fundamentalists, feminists, or rigid traditionalists. Let us return to the beginning.

God and the Feminine

We do not have to appeal to first century Jewish speculation to advance the notion that Adam was originally male and female. Whether you read in the text of the first chapter of Genesis that God created ad-ham, the man (not simply a man called Adam Evergood) "male and female," or read into the second chapter that Eve, ish-shah (taken out of man), was the human embodiment of the feminine – either way the intention seems clear. Not only was it "not good that the man should be alone," as scripture has it; it was evident that neither the man nor the woman could stand alone among created beings.

It is true if you read on that the Bible does not promote the cause of women's liberation. Notwithstanding Adam's recognition that woman is "flesh of my flesh," Eve is clearly the proximate cause of his fall; and, at least aetiologically, is to be subordinate to him. Moreover, the Old Testament patriarchal influence is nowhere more evident than in the head of the family, the father's, right to determine the fate (including the power of life and death) of the other members, whether figuratively or in reality. However, incredibly enough, in the same scriptures we find Deborah named among the Judges of Israel, Miriam included as a recognized prophetess, even Jael celebrated in song for her single-handed slaying of the great Canaanite chieftain Sisera by driving a tent peg through his head while he slept.

In Pauline portions of the New Testament, women are portrayed as second-class citizens and God is represented in almost exclusively masculine terms such as king, judge, father. But if you are looking for a balanced view, not just a soapbox, Jesus numbered women among his disciples. Women are recorded as the first witnesses to the resurrection of Christ. St. Paul said, "There is neither bond nor free, there is neither male nor female; for all are one in Christ Jesus."[5] Women are shown as leaders in the church, as deacons; and Paul himself chose Phebe to be the bearer of his Epistle to the Romans. That may be a far cry from "women's liberation," but it is an unexpected emancipation of sorts.

Certainly the scriptural evidence is ambiguous, and it is not easy to distinguish neatly between theological intention and the culturalsociological emphasis of the time. And certainly the acceptable ways of serving the Lord are inseparable from the mores of the day. The problem is not as great in the text as in the biblical tradition which is reflective of a seemingly thoroughly masculine deity and an absence of the feminine – at least in today's terms.

If we were able to alter or transform the tradition or the text, we would be naive to overlook, as religious beings, that there are real differences between the sexes which we would not want to give up in human experience – the sexual difference, for one. We are also nourished by the mental and spiritual differences which for better or for worse are reflected in our cultural and sociological histories. The difficulty seems to be in recognizing that they are real differences, rather than in judging them as superior or inferior. As the New Testament affirms, there are many ways of serving, but one service.

———⚬———

The divine wisdom that says it is not good to be alone also understands that loneliness is not life-giving or sustaining.

———⚬———

Applying that perspective to the Genesis accounts of creation, we may read the text with a different eye. It is clear across the spectrum of humanity that Adam is an incomplete being until the creation of Eve. The divine wisdom that says it is not good to be alone also understands that loneliness is not life-giving or sustaining. In Martin Buber's words, there is no "I" without a "thou" to address; the one brings the other into being. In the Bible the separateness of sexuality is sustained, but at the same time its unity is affirmed as the basic form of all human community; each is incomplete without the other; being "one flesh" brings about a new union and new life. If Eve is indeed designated "a helper fit for him," Adam in fact is not fit for much of anything less himself.

In the other creation account of Genesis, God is shown creating man and woman simultaneously. Both are in the image of God, and the divine image needs both male and female to be reflected on the finite level. No one is a person in isolation; both are to be distinct, but one flesh – the masculine and the feminine reflecting the unity of and union in God's love, creation being no less than the overflow of God's love,

What in God's Name?

"What in God's name is feminism?" can be answered succinctly, if not simply: there isn't. In God's name there is neither male nor female; we are created in the image of God, male *and* female. Names, the early scriptures understood, were what brought things into being. To name is to give life to what is named. No wonder we are warned to be careful about giving and taking names, in vain and otherwise. For the ancient Hebrews, God's name was not to be uttered because no representation of the divine, either visual or verbal, was less than a profanity of his being. Harold Oliver points out:

> The problem is not – as the feminists often say – one of the inadequacies of *certain* nouns/names, but of the inadequacy of *any* naming of the deity. It is no accident that the closest analogue to religious language is profanity; for without naming the deity, neither religious nor antireligious sentiment can be expressed.

If I swear to you in the name of God, in God's name I am calling forth a divine guarantee that I will be faithful to my word, whether feminist or otherwise.

In the face of "feminist theology's claim that misogyny (woman hating) infects all traditional expressions of the gospel," Brian Wren's contemporary hymns are witnesses to the contrary. He is "not afraid to explore feminine imagery, but he avoids substituting matriarchal language for patriarchal without changing any basic descriptions of God." The 1983 hymn, "Who Is She?" points to God as the one who "originated yet transcends gender," who "can be glimpsed only through the concrete images of human relationships":

Who is she,
neither male nor female,
maker of all things

only glimpsed or hinted,
source of life and gender?
She is God
mother, sister, lover:
in her love we wake,
move and grow, are daunted,
triumph and surrender. [7]

Here, in metaphor and analogy the power of woman is manifest (as it always has been) not through the aggression and violence of male dominance, but through the relationships, loving-kindness, nurture, and reconciliation that grow out of vulner-ability. This assertion echoes in a different voice Nel Noddings' observation that "an ethic built on caring is, I think, characteristi-cally and essentially feminine – which is not to say, of course, that it cannot be shared by men..."[8] I take it we are in it together, God willing. Would it be antifeminist to say that the exalted melan-choly of our fate is that machismo is doomed to lie down with the lamb regardless who sleeps with the lion?

Woman in the Divine

A great many men, if not most, know instinctively about the divine in woman. Our early childhood experience of that real-ity changes to hot pursuit during the teenage years and often an unending quest into adulthood to attain it. But theologians in the Western tradition seem on uncertain ground when we ask about woman in the divine. The feminine traits of God are one thing; we can accept that caring and compassion, responsiveness and self-giving are indeed godlike, especially raised to the level of identifi-cation in Christ. But Jesus the Christ, you remember, was a man, and despite our assertion that God is neither male nor female, we have had a hard time addressing the biblical God with a pronoun other than "he."

However, recently James A. Sanders, well-known biblical scholar, has stated his preference for "she" as the proper pronoun for the Holy Spirit. He cites a primitive tradition among Jesus' early followers, which asserted that the Holy Spirit was the "mother" of Jesus. The Hebrew word for spirit, *ruach*, is of the feminine gender, and although the Greek word for spirit, *pneuma*, is neuter, the New Testament texts do not use the pronoun "it," since Christian theology regards the Holy Spirit not as an impersonal force, but as a person of the Godhead. [9]

I offer this as incomplete but initial evidence that even patristic theology may not be wholly redeemable from the feminine perspective. Even so, apparently women scholars are not all that enthusiastic about the promise of a revamped Trinity. Even if the Holy Spirit becomes wholly "she," with Father and Son, it's still two against one. (The key to balancing out the genders of the Trinity may be found in the theory that Jesus was, theologically at least, androgynous – reinforced by the first century speculation that Jesus, as the "last Adam," like the first, was originally male and female.)

I Never Promised You a Rose Garden

In the beginning I also promised you a word about women's liberation. If in God's name feminism isn't, what does the feminine have to be liberated from, or for, or to? I assume that the liberation in question is more an affair of the spirit than something to do with a desire for upward mobility, the impressing of women into military service, a ploy for permissiveness, insistence upon sex-neutral insurance life expectancy actuarial tables, or getting even in sexual standards. I also assume that, in fairness, liberation is something that women wish for men as well as themselves. I do not know whether liberation in any gender would run toward or away from the problem viewed in the light of this Jungian understanding of feminine psychology:

> A man depends largely on the woman for the light in the family, as he is often not very good at finding meaning for himself. Life is often dry and barren for him unless someone bestows meaning on life for him. With a few words a woman can give

meaning to a whole day's struggle, and a man will be very grateful. A man knows and wants this; he will edge up to it; he will initiate little occasions so that a woman can shed some light for him. When he comes home and recounts the events of the day, he is asking her to bestow meaning on them. This is part of the light-bearing quality of a woman.

The touch of light, or acknowledgment, is a fiery thing. It often stings a man into awareness, which is partly why he fears the feminine so much. A woman or his anima, often leads a man into new consciousness. It is almost always the woman who says, "Let's sit down and talk about where we are." A man does not often say this. The woman is the carrier of evolution from him in one way or another. She sometimes lights him into a new kind of relationship. The man is terrified of that, but he is equally terrified at the loss of it. Actually, a man greatly appreciates a woman who bears a lamp; he depends on the feminine light more deeply than most men are willing to admit.[10]

If Jung failed to grasp the depth of the problem, wrestling with the issue in biblical terms is not likely to lead to greater freedom in any conventional sense. However, the New Testament is clear about what it values and what constitutes a whole person. The liberation it espouses, for men and women alike – liberating or not - lies in servanthood: "Submit yourselves to one another out of reverence for the Lord."[11]

If such biblical injunction is not compelling; or if, like Candide, you find religious language of no particular use, perhaps the language of gardening will prove more down to earth. In this memorial service blessing, I hope you will find the liberation that "Biggsie's cousin" (the cousin of E. Power Biggs) intended for those left among the living. Fortunately, from my point of view, the feminine images in the following passages are expressed in the midst of masculine pronouns. Here, the unity of male and female, in the flesh and in the spirit, is abundantly clear.

Everyone must leave something behind when he dies, my grandfather said. A child or a book or a painting or a house or a wall built or a pair of shoes made. Or a garden planted. Something your hand touched someway so your soul has somewhere to go when you die, and when people look at that tree or that flower you planted, you're there. It doesn't matter what you do, he said, so long as you change something from the way it was before you touched it into something that's like you after you take your hands away. The difference between the man who just cuts lawns and a real gardener is in the touching, he said. The lawncutter might just as well not have been there at all; the gardener will be there a lifetime.[12]

<hr>

1. Nel Noddings, "The Feminine Experience and Moral Education," *Independent School*, February 1985, p.4

2. *Ibid.*, p.5

3. Valerie Saiving, *The Human Situation: A Feminine View*, University of Chicago Press, 1960, p.27

4. Carol Gilligan, *In a Different Voice: Psychological Theory and Women's Development*, Harvard University Press, 1982.

5. Galatians 3:28

6. Harold Oliver, "Beyond the Feminist Critique: A Shaking of the Foundations," *The Christian Century,* May 1, 1985, p.446

7. Brian Wren, *The Christian Century*, July 17-24, 1985, p.677

8. Noddings, *Op. cit.*, p.2

9. John Dart, "Balancing Out the Trinity: The Genders of the Godhead," *The Christian Century*, February 16-23, 1983, p.147

10. Robert A. Johnson, She: Understanding Feminine Psychology, Harper & Row, 1976, pp.26-27

11. Alfred Krass, an editor of "The Other Side," *Context*, March 1, 1979

12. Context, date unknown.

This paper was presented to the Richmond, Virginia, Torch Club on February 4, 1986.

AN HISTORICAL NOTE: A CELEBRATION OF CHURCH SCHOOLS IN MEMORY OF JOHN PAGE WILLIAMS, DEAN 1951 - 1975

St. Stephen's Church, Richmond
January 25th, 2001
by
The Very Reverend Christopher M. Brookfield
Dean of Church Schools 1975-1988

What many of us remember with great affection is the amazing (and on this occasion unmerciful) modesty of John Page Williams, who asked that in any memorial service for him there be neither eulogy nor homily on his behalf; he never considered himself special. Makes it hard on us preacher types, but honoring his wishes, there will be neither, notwithstanding in the prayers a thanksgiving for the life of John Page. Instead you'll have to settle for a simple historical snip-

Deans with Shared Perspective. *John Page Williams and his friend and successor, Christopher M. Brookfield, served consecutively as Dean of the Church Schools in the Diocese of Virginia from 1951-1988.*

pet about Church Schools in the Diocese of Virginia where he was Dean for almost a quarter century. And in keeping with his genial good humor, he would want me to keep that light, not heavy handed. He knew that the reason angels can fly is because they take themselves lightly. And my hope is that his service itself will serve to celebrate the spirit of his life with our singing and psalming and saying thanks.

At the time John Page became the first exclusively full-time Dean and chief administrative officer of the Church Schools corporation in 1951, even then its educational arms encompassed the Diocese – from St. Anne's in Charlottesville in the west to St. Margaret's and Christchurch in the Tidewater to the east; and from St. Catherine's and St. Christopher's in Richmond, north to St. Agnes and St. Stephen's in Alexandria. You may have heard in New England academia of the Seven Sisters; well, here we have had the Seven Saints – each with its own fiercely individual mission but legally owned, organized, and operated as one, and from its founding as an educational ministry for the Episcopal Diocese of Virginia.

The year 2000 marked the 80th anniversary of the institution of Church Schools (now more than 3,100 students strong) which initially was founded, funded and fondled by the Diocese, and whose unique system was appropriately commemorated by the publication of Dr. Williams' book chronicling its early history. "The Working Out of a Partnership" is what he subtlety subtitled it. When I first asked John Page in his retirement to write that history, he declined, saying there were too many books being published for the public good and too many in need of being thrown out. But when I added that he was himself the living history, which would be lost if he didn't write it down, he demurred – protesting that as a personal penance he would try to pen it, if we didn't pay him for it. By penance, he didn't mean punishment but an endeavor of Christian stewardship that he was willing to undertake not just for the life of the Schools but also for his own.

One of the ways John Page was able to win his way among the many headstrong Heads of Schools and Boards of Governors over the years was with his wily and winsome wit as well as an un-pretentious wisdom. Whenever he was asked to explain what he really did as Dean, he would say it was like being a superintendent of schools without having the authority of a superintendent. (Of course a superintendent would rarely be addressed as The Very Reverend, The Dean – which he would have eschewed). However, it was not smoke and mirrors but consensus and cooperation that were the stuff and strength of Church Schools under his leader-ship. (The collegial concept has changed somewhat since then because beginning in 1988 David Charlton was empowered to preside as President and CEO of the corporation; the designation Dean was done.)

When ... it was suggested to him that some students secretly spoke of him as "Creeping Jesus," he simply shrugged and smiled, saying, "Well the good thing is they know where I'm coming from."

John Page learned to prevail not only by personal persua-sion but also with the power of his generous rejoinders. When as Headmaster of St. Christopher's (before becoming Dean) it was suggested to him that some students secretly spoke of him as "Creeping Jesus," he simply shrugged and smiled, saying, "Well the good thing is they know where I'm coming from." He had had some practice persevering previously at Groton School in Mas-sachusetts when he was teacher and chaplain there for six years, and where he was kindly kidded for his quaint Southern way of speaking in chapel talks, such as when he would say, "The children of Israel struggled with God in the wilderness, for they were nek-kid and afraye-yed."

The Church Schools themselves were struggling even into the early 50's simply because in those days finances were in short supply, facilities and faculty salaries were still Spartan and the curriculum was simple by today's standards. John Page taught trustees as well as teachers that the trick was to make do with what they had and make things go as far as they could, that the more might be shared among many. Faithful frugality was not just a virtue; it was a virtual necessity to ensure their survival.

From the sayings and stories I saved from my educational excursions among the Schools comes this composition, which explored the idea of frugality for the fifth graders in one of our more demanding schools. They were assigned to write a short story that illustrated the meaning of the word "frugal," which they had been told meant, "sparing and saving." This is what one little girl wrote: A beautiful damsel walked in a dark forest and a fierce dragon breathing fire from his nose attacked her and she cried out. And a white knight on a black steed rode up and frugaled her, frugaled her and rode off again.

Dr. Williams would not have approved of the student who got all A's in academics and then flunked life. The aim of education in that era was not primarily to get students into this or that college but from the Latin, *educare* (to lead forth, bring out, bring up) the whole person, to help shape the moral and ethical life of the young. A Church Schools education was supposed to be an experience from which you never entirely recovered.

⎯⎯◦◦⎯⎯

...if a school community cannot come together religiously, it will come apart regularly

⎯⎯◦◦⎯⎯

John Page often said that a church is no more than a gathering of great sinners and that nowhere is this more evident than in a church school; even in those that take sin seriously, expect attendance at chapel services, and insist on regular instruction in religion. Some parents would question from time to time why, among three divisions in a school, students might have as many as 240 chapel services a year when worship was never optional. I would answer what I learned from Dr. Williams: that if a school community cannot come together religiously, it will come apart regularly.

That doesn't mean all students are expected to become expert at expounding biblical truths. For instance, if you'll endure another example taken from a paper written for what used to be called a course in sacred studies (I don't know how old this student was). Across the top of the page was written only: Emily Bible Hing Saul. She must have meant King Saul, but her imprecise penmanship hadn't fully persuaded his "h" to become a "k" (which, if you recall was part of Saul's problem). And she probably had forgotten it was David, not King Saul, who had stolen another man's wife for his harem. Anyway, this is what the paper said (I'm reading-in the "k"s):

> The thing I like about King Saul is his character, ... and he has such an exciting life. When he tried to kill David it was very exciting. And when he threw his javelin at him.
>
> I like people with bad tempers, except when King Saul loses his he really loses it.... King Saul probably didn't like the life of a king because he spent so much time ruling everybody... what he really needed was a vacation...
>
> When you come down to think about it he could have made a really good king if he did some things like go on a vacation, have more time to spend with his real wife, and went to a psychiatrist to tell him what's wrong with him.

There is a moral to this story, even Emily's version of it, which is still worthy of what is worth teaching in a Church School (for faculty as well as students): namely, when the days of the year grow longer and your temper grows shorter and you feel like pinning someone to the wall with a javelin, try to remember that likely as not God has loved that person too.

John Page Williams was able to tell the story of Church Schools and of education effectively across Virginia, in the public school sector, and eventually nationally. I even heard about him up in New England when I first started out as a fledgling English teacher at Exeter Academy, probably before he ever received the first of his several honorary degrees. He could speak of education from the inside; he never accepted the idea that school was only what you did until you got out into "the real world." For him it was a vocation, a calling, a gift of God – for it spoke profoundly about the way life ought to be and what it was created to be. And, as John Page would add, "the gift is great, but the giver is greater still."

A Prayer of Thanksgiving

We thank thee, O God, for all the goodness and graciousness, the courage and encouragement which have flowed from the life of thy servant John Page Williams and have passed into the lives of others, and have left the world richer and wiser for his presence

- for his servant leadership among our schools and his loyal devotion to faculty, friends, family, and the faith of his Church

- for his commitment to Christian ideals which he accepted for his own life, and his unassuming habit of making do with less

- for his contagious excitement about education, his enthusiasm for fresh ideas, and his search for new ways of expressing old and enduring truths

- for his genial good humor, and his generosity in giving praise; his patience and grace as a gardener and grandfather encouraging new growth in the persons and places he touched

- for his quick wit and fine mind with which he never made others feel inferior, and which he put in the service of education locally and nationally

- for his willingness always to listen, his love of spirited conversation and discussion of lively books, and for his eagerness to learn more about what engaged and made vital the young

- for being willing to take unpopular stands and to say what he thought was the right thing to do

- for his integrity and humility, modesty and simplicity, his personal penances undertaken often on other's behalf

- finally, for his being to many of us mentor, guide, teacher, colleague, companion and cheerleader

And so, Lord, for a life's task faithfully and honorably discharged; for sadness and pain faced without surrender, and weakness endured without defeat; we bless thee, for John Page and ask thy blessing upon him. Amen.

HUNGERING FOR HARKNESS HALF-COCKED

Gratitude for What George Bennett Never Said
By Christopher M. Brookfield '72 (Hon.)
Fall 2007 The Exeter Bulletin I 67

Christopher M.
Brookfield '72 (Hon.)

Who was George Bennett '23; P'60? If you weren't one of his students or didn't teach at Exeter around the time it was emerging from the era of the "nego;"*[1] you might not know. For one thing, he was a man of few words; he observed and encouraged, and he listened intently. He edited two slim volumes of unusual and engaging short stories that most people have never heard of, and put together a collection of poems and commentaries. He was a master teacher – cryptic, kind and courageous.

One measure of his courage was in allowing me to teach English – I, a fledgling teacher of religion whose graduate degree was in philosophy and who had coincidentally concentrated on courses in modern European literature in college. The formidable faculty of the English Department, many of whom had doctorates and were authors of numerous books, did not want anyone who was "not qualified" teaching in the classroom. But George had a mind of his own, and he was department chairman. For reasons he never spoke about, he gave me a section of ninth-grade English as my first teaching assignment.

Fresh from graduate school and married barely a week, I went to his house to talk about the course and what books I was to teach. I was overly organized in those days, and carried a pad of paper around with me to be sure I put down on paper what I was supposed to do. I had even written out some pretty good questions to ask. George was on the porch propped up on a chaise longue – thin, brown and agile, with smiling eyes. He was silent for a while, as I asked my organized questions to keep the silence at bay.

Where was the syllabus? He hadn't made it up yet, even though classes started the next day. Finally, he said to me, "I don't care what you teach, but don't teach the students anything you've learned. "

"What do you mean?" I said, incredulous.

'Just don't ruin them. Don't use any 'good books' in class, nothing off a department reading list."

"What do you want me to use?" I fumbled.

"Anything you want to, as long as they never saw it before and you haven't either. Something fresh. It doesn't even have to be good literature."

After some silence, he said, "I've got some old English notes from 30 years ago; you might be interested in using them." Was he serious?

I was bewildered; hurt, insulted and scared. He was going to be of no help. I was getting panicky, and I could already feel the weight of all those eyes of the English Department faculty assessing my efforts in class each day. Best to leave. George had cancer, and I didn't know how to talk to him about that either. Neither did he.

But before I was all the way out the door, he said, "Why don't you sit in on my class tomorrow? That's the best way I can explain."

The kids filed in, subdued, but with new-student energy spilling over into tapping fingers, instant smiles and wriggling in chairs. The bell rang. George returned the smiles, reading out the names of the 12 students. "I'm Mister Bennett," he said, and then fell silent. So did the students and I. And the time dragged on; minutes seemed forever.

Finally, one faculty member's son said something about the football team, and, relieved to be able to talk about something, others joined in. After a while, almost abruptly, someone said, "What are we supposed to be doing here?" My question exactly.

"What do you want to do?" George asked, smiling slightly.

"Learn English, I guess," one ventured.

"Learn how to write?" another offered.

George looked back at them intently, but said nothing.

"C'mon, sir, this is a waste of time," said one serious student.

The bell rang.

"The assignment for tonight is to write a paragraph about something that happened in the Post Office today," said George, over the scraping of chairs.

"What?" came the chorus. Then one brave soul sputtered, "What d'ya mean? Nothing happened in the Post Office.... You mean that place we get our mail, in Jeremiah Smith Hall? You must be joking!"

"See you tomorrow," said George, reassuringly.

Unfortunately, I couldn't make that morrow's class, but I went the day after when the students were reading aloud to each other their elaborate efforts at describing a paper clip (that was the assignment), cracking up at their futile attempts to describe effectively to someone else such a familiar object. At the end of class, the students were told they were to write a few paragraphs every day, and for the first three months they could write only about their experiences on campus – no science fiction stories, no romantic tales, no "creative writing" – nothing but what they observed, in their own words.

Before becoming a teacher at Exeter, I had been educated in the best schools, taken courses in book editing and worked in publishing in New York City. I attended night school at Hunter College and taught recruits in the Army Reserve. I had also taken the Army instructors course and had been assigned to teach in the Jump School at Fort Benning. What we taught the young men were facts vital to their survival. And by God, they learned them, exactly the way we taught them. So I assumed I wasn't starting at square one in teaching.

But how could you teach this stuff?

The answer George was intent on helping me understand is that you can't teach students *anything* – if, by that, you mean trying to teach them didactically how to appreciate good litera-ture, internalize the rules of grammar and syntax – even to know what is essential in a study of Strunk and White's *The Elements of Style*. You may learn more about the teaching of English from your students than they will from you, unless you can enable them to converse with each other in class about what they are trying to do and why – and whether or not they are accomplishing what they have set out to do.

What he never spoke about to me but illustrated by his example was the art of inventing crucial questions. The quality of class time depends upon the kinds of questions raised and re-sponded to. Answers are important only after you have learned to live your way into the questions.

Of course George never would have offered such a clumsy explanation. I learned more from what he didn't say to me than he could ever have told me. His silence was contagious. Eventually I learned how to sit in the silence for 50 minutes, if that's what it took to let the students take the initiative to talk about what they knew (or didn't), what they cared about, and what needed to be done with what they had read and written. George also had a keen sense of humor, and he knew that if you have to try to explain a joke, forget it – and how that related to the art of teaching.

Jack Heath '52, '56, '62, '70 (Hon.); P'67, P'70, P'72, P'75, who has written persuasively about how the Harkness system works (*Exeter Bulletin*, fall 1983), once remarked to me that what I didn't do for his son Jeff '67 in the English class I first taught was just what Jeff needed at the time. Assuming Jack wasn't pulling my leg, I never asked Jeff about what that might have meant for him. So I don't know what it was I "didn't do," in hopes of doing it again.

When I applied to teach at Exeter, the Academy had the largest number of National Merit Scholarship students of any high school in the country. And when teachers from other schools wrote to the English Department asking how they taught grammar, George would reply in his cryptic fashion, "We don't." Then he would add, "All we do is ask them to write something three days a week and talk about it in class."

George Bennett gave me the gift that made my struggles to become a good teacher for the next 45 years rewarding and revealing (sometimes crushingly so) – and I'm still at it, thank God, and thank George.

---

[1] *In his book, *Now and Then*, Reverend Frederick Buechner,'62, '67 (Hon.), former school minister; described "nego" as such: "The late fifties at Exeter were the period of the nego, and a nego, in Exeter parlance, was a student who was negative, against, anti, just about everything."

PRAYERS

Written by Christopher Brookfield on various occasions

O God, we give thanks for the visions of grace we are granted in the everyday, safe in the assurance that there is plenty for everyone. We rejoice in them however they find us, however we may get there, "horizontally" or "vertically." Wink at us this day, Lord; take us by surprise in the ordinary, that we may welcome a moment of grace, that brief glimmering glimpse of the broken image of Christ within us. Help us not to fear the price we may have to pay in exposing ourselves to others, nor the pain it may cost us. Help us to unbolt the doors of our hearts to the home which is each other – and yours – this day and in the days to come. *Amen.*

Prayer after Temple Martin's paper on
images of grace in Frederick Buechner
St. Mary's Church, January 13, 1986

Remembering especially those who have gone before us, O Lord, the God no less of those who know Thee not, than of those who love Thee well, be present with us also in our times of choosing. God help us never to confuse easy answers with success or impossible answers with failure. Help us to see through our darkness, to believe through our unbelief, that no one in God's love is finally lost to Thee or to us. Thou, who alone knows what the future holds, help us to understand that there are words of truth and healing that will never be spoken unless we speak them, and deeds of compassion and courage that will never be done unless we do them. Help us through our tears and our laughter to forgiveness of one another and to faith at the last, this day and always. *Amen.*

In Memoriam, Princeton, February, 1983

Watch over all those who have gone out from this place,
    O Lord,
bless them and guide them
wherever they may be.
Be by their side when the dark hours
shall come upon them;
strengthen them with love and laughter,
comfort and keep them
when they are weak-hearted,
raise them up if they fall.
Help them to know there are words of truth and healing
that will never be spoken
unless they speak them,
and acts of compassion and courage
that will never be done
unless they do them;
give them that understanding which
does not mistake success for fulfillment
nor failure for defeat.
Bestow upon them
on their journey
your joy and forgiveness,
your peace with deep restlessness,
your love – and theirs – to heal
the wounds along the way;
And bring them finally to yourself.

NOTES

NOTES

NOTES

ST. MARY'S EPISCOPAL CHURCH

12291 River Road
Richmond, Virginia 23238
(804) 784-5678
http://www.stmarysgoochland.org/